AF479079

MRS. THATCHER'S CULTURAL POLICIES: 1979–1990

A Comparative Study of the Globalized Cultural System

By

CHRISTOPHER H. J. BRADLEY

SOCIAL SCIENCE MONOGRAPHS, BOULDER

DISTRIBUTED BY COLUMBIA UNIVERSITY PRESS, NEW YORK

1998

CONTENTS

Chapter 1
The New Right, Conservatism and Mrs Thatcher

Two antagonistic views prevail concerning Mrs Thatcher and her cultural policy. The common view is that she did not have one at all. At the other extreme certain left-wing critics argue the case for a carefully structured hegemonic plan in the cultural field. The former assert that Mrs Thatcher did very little to influence the workings of the cultural market-place. Indeed, production and consumption according to this laissez-faire thesis were left alone to evolve in a largely organic way. The latter, on the contrary, view Mrs Thatcher's use of inner cabinets and their secret ways as evidence of private schemes in the oligopolistic cultural industries.

It is clear that both views have their relative strengths and weaknesses, but the truth must logically lie somewhere in-between. There certainly is a case for saying that Mrs Thatcher did not have an explicit cultural policy. But what about the implicit nature of such a policy? One can also make a reasonable case about secret dealings between Mrs Thatcher and various media magnates, but care should be taken of not falling into the trap of plot theories which cannot be proved. If the prime minister had generalised the system of secret agreements, then information would eventually have leaked out and this was not the case. What comes out most clearly in the present study is in fact the implicit nature of Mrs Thatcher's cultural plan which can only be examined in the light of more general policy considerations. Added to this, another caveat is necessary. In particular, it is often claimed that Mrs Thatcher belonged, ideologically, to the New Right camp. The validity of this assertion will be contested.

The New Right

The New Right or new Conservative school of thought is closely associated with the political economist Professor Friedrich von Hayek, whose The Road to Serfdom was written in 1944. A leading figure of the Chicago School of Economics, Milton Friedman, is likewise often placed in the New Right camp. To the right of this group, but at the extreme end, come anarcho-libertarians such as M. Rothbard,[1] who believe in the total privatisation of all social institutions and agencies, the army and the police force included. Some right-wing hard-liners such as R. Nozick,[2] argue that the state should play a minimalist role in regulating society. According to him, only the army, police force and legal profession should be allowed to function as social regulators. Few in the New Right believe in these ultra-liberal ideas. However, economic theorists, such as von Hayek and Milton Friedman, who concentrated their efforts on economic problems in general and inflation in particular, claimed that inflation in the 1970s was caused either indirectly through the subsidising of uncompetitive industries or directly by the payment of social benefits. Thus, because the New Right theorists focus their attention on the problem of inflation and the money supply, they are often termed 'monetarists'. In addition, they stress notions such as freedom of the individual and individual responsibility. The latter notions are certainly present in one of Mrs Thatcher's most famous pronouncements on record:

> I think that we have been through a period where too many people have been given to understand that if they have a problem, it's the government's job to cope with it. 'I have a problem. I'll get a grant.' 'I'm homeless. The government must house me.' They're casting their problem on society. And you know there is no such thing as society. There are individual men and women, and there are families. And no government can do anything except through people, and people must look to themselves first. It's our duty to look after ourselves and then, also, to look after our neighbour. People have got the entitlements too much in mind, without the obligations. There's no such thing as entitlement, unless someone has first met an obligation.[3]

However, right-wing Conservatives who were present in Tory think-tanks such as the Centre for Policy Studies, that was set up in 1974, and the Adam Smith Institute that opened in 1981, used these ideas to put forward many innovative proposals. The British New Right thesis was that the state needed to re-establish its authority over the various pressure groups that existed in civil society, before liberating the economic market-place and asserting a new moral order.

Quite logically, the British version of the New Right argued that Mr Heath had been forced to resign under pressure from the 1974 miners' strike, that in 1976 the Labour government had been given a lesson by the International Monetary Fund (IMF), and that the Winter of Discontent in 1978 had shown that a total breakdown of the state was in fact very close. British industry had declined in relative terms, since the Second World War, when compared with the rest of Western Europe. The New Right further argued that this decline had been caused by the combined effects of greedy unions and overspending by both central and local governments. In order to strengthen the authority of the state, a showdown with the unions was necessary and this had to be carefully prepared and coordinated. Furthermore, the army had to be ready to protect Britain from communism. The police force was to be built up and given a new nation-wide coordination. Civil servants were to be shown that their role was to serve and not lead politicians. Above all, government spending had to be reduced and this is of particular relevance to cultural policy. These were the necessary preconditions for the emergence of a free and liberal state.

Once the authority of the state had been re-established, the New Right hoped that the economy would be freed from the chains of social democracy. However, this was only its second priority. The British New Right, as seen in the ideas of Sir Keith Joseph or Sir Alan Walters, stressed the need to reduce government spending, sell off nationalised industries and reduce inflation, in order to produce 'sound' money. According to certain monetarist theorists, such as von Hayek, inflation had to be brought down very quickly, while other monetarists like Milton Friedman claimed that it could be done more progressively. The state had to impose the new rules of non-intervention, to refuse all forms of subsidy and the market would quite naturally find a new equilibrium. This is of particular significance to the present analysis. The result was to be the elimination of 'lame-ducks' (that is to say subsidised loss-making companies) and the emergence of an efficient economy.

In Britain, the New Right was also particularly worried about another aspect of its socio-economic evaluations: the state of British society. It proposed to wage an ideological war against the caring, permissive, anti-enterprise ethos which riddled the Establishment, the mass media and all the professions. Traditional family values, which it considered to be the foundation of a strong society, were seen to have been eroded by a combination of social factors, such as feminism, single-parent families, permissiveness and homosexuality. This 'enemy from within' was to be combated by all means because it was threatening to destroy the very fabric of society. Traditional paternalism had to be re-established. Many of these values can be detected in the following London Broadcasting Company (LBC) radio discussion, given by Mrs Thatcher on April 15th 1983, with obvious New Right sympathies expressed by the prime minister:

I was brought up by a Victorian grandmother. We were taught to work jolly hard. We were taught to prove yourself; we were taught self-reliance; we were taught to live within our income. You were taught that cleanliness is next to godliness. You were taught self-respect. You were taught always to give a hand to your neighbour. You were taught tremendous pride in your country. All of these things are Victorian values. They are perennial values. You don't hear so much about these things these days but they were good values and they led to tremendous improvements in the standard of living.

This radio interview shows the concern that Mrs Thatcher felt over what she considered to be a decline in British moral values. It is also one of the central ideas of the New Right. A few more points in this most basic statement need to be elucidated. There is a very subtle way of mixing the first and second persons singular and the first person plural. Indeed, Mrs Thatcher implicitly suggests that there is a consensus on the subject matter, that you and we agree with her ideas.

Another point that needs stressing is the selective interpretation of history. Only the positive aspects of Victorian society are singled out, but nothing is said about the prostitution problem that existed in London during the 19th century due possibly to the rigid moral code of the Victorian period. The economic development certainly brought better living conditions with it, but also extremely long working hours for men, women and children, while also polluting the environment. Also, at this stage, the British economic system had an Empire from which it could obtain cheap raw materials. In 1983, this was no longer the case. Mrs Thatcher's reference to pride in her country can be set against the current 'immigration problem' that is said to be undermining the traditional British way of life. It is, therefore, implied that promoting a national culture is the only way of stopping the country from being swamped by alien cultures. Evidently, this declaration demonstrates that Mrs Thatcher selected from the past and presented her case in what can be termed a populist package. One may add that this type of clarity and simplicity served her well in her dealings with cultural problems and in particular with the mass media.

The extent of Mrs Thatcher's theoretical commitment to the New Right can be seen in the following extract from her memoirs:

> There were three points to which I had returned again and again during this period. (The early 1980s) First, everything we wished to do had to fit into an overall strategy of reversing Britain's economic decline, for without an end to that decline there was no hope of success for our other objectives. This led to the second point: all policies had to be carefully costed, and if they could not be accommodated within our public expenditure plans they would not be approved. Geoffrey Howe and his very talented Shadow Treasury team combed through everything in great detail to ensure this was the case. Finally, we had to stress continually that, however difficult the road might be and however long it took us to reach our destination, we intended to achieve a fundamental change of direction. We stood for a new beginning, not more of the same.[4]

In this statement can be seen a clear preference for New Right principles which were in reality only half applied because of political pressures. One should also stress the fact that the prime minister aimed at fundamental change. She wanted a break with the past and did not mind upsetting a significant minority in the process.

Needless to say, such neo-liberal ideas, as expressed by the New Right and sometimes voiced by Mrs Thatcher, had important and sometimes contradictory implications for her cultural policy. Reducing state spending would have a direct impact on cultural activities which were subsidised by the state. Yet at the same time national culture and identity had to be given prominence in order to combat foreign influences. Strengthening the authority of the state might also lead to greater intervention by the state in the mass media, which ran against the tradition of conservative libertarianism. The moral crusade against the permissive anti-capitalist ethos of the 'social democratic consensus' was to replace unproductive artistic and intellectual thought with a new enterprise culture stressing the entrepreneur and the self-made man. Such were the tenets of the New Right and Mrs Thatcher's pronouncements at the time had clearly been influenced by this current of ideas. What must be added is that these statements for a new policy implied not only a political change. They called for a complex cultural debate which was never actually carried out in all its various dimensions and possible consequences. The New Right and the various Thatcher projects which used many of these innovative ideas were, indeed, very ambitious and wide-ranging. What can, however, be said is that the New Right had a very clear agenda for change in Britain in the 1980s.

To what extent did Mrs Thatcher agree with these ideas? On a theoretical level she agreed with almost all the propositions of the New Right. In the case of inflation, Mrs Thatcher argued a clear monetarist case during her first years in power as seen in a speech made on 28th February 1980. For instance when she stressed that: "Experience shows that the only sure way of tackling inflation is to keep the money supply closely related to the output of goods and services."[5] Yet, in her speeches and the Conservative manifestoes pure monetarist principles were rarely stated. Indeed they were applied even less. She also agreed with the New Right idea of modernising the British economy. In the early 1980s the market was allowed to eliminate old inefficient manufacturing companies. This slimmed down the economy but not necessarily the costs, as the state had to pay for between 2 and 3 million unemployed people. One area where Mrs Thatcher fully supported and fully implemented the ideas of the New Right was in the supposedly temporary re-establishment of the state's authority. Mrs Thatcher waited for the miners' strike to teach the unions a lesson. This she did by modifying union legislation on closed shops.

However, the link between Mrs Thatcher and the New Right should not be over-emphasised. She was above all interested in practical politics and political survival and for this purpose was forced to adopt expedient and practicable policies. The prime minister was a pragmatic conservative politician who actually often applied the 'one nation' philosophy of Benjamin Disraeli, another conservative pragmatist of the 19th century, although claiming to be of another tradition. She stressed individual responsibility but also the ideas of family values, community and duty to others. This can clearly be seen in the Woman's Own interview. Therefore, Mrs Thatcher can be said to have been strongly influenced by both the ideas of the New Right and traditional conservatism. Her heart was with the New Right but her practical politics remained very much in the conservative tradition. It is this difference between what she declared and what she in fact did that must be evaluated, the so-called 'implementation gap' between what was proposed and what was actually done.

Mrs Thatcher's attitudes and reactions in three key areas, economics, local government and housing will demonstrate this 'gap' and will help in the understanding of her cultural policy.

A) Economic policy

This was at the centre of all Mrs Thatcher's policies and yet, if closely examined, it is pragmatism and the absence of a grand strategy that come to mind. According to the prime minister, economics would influence attitudes in society: "If you change the approach you really are after the heart and soul of the nation. Economics are the method: the object is to change the heart and soul." (1981). Mrs Thatcher's principal aim was to reduce inflation: "Our prime economic objective - the defeat of inflation. Inflation destroys nations and societies as surely as invading armies do. Inflation is the parent of unemployment. It is the unseen robber of those who have saved."[6]

Along with inflation, the Conservative Party manifestos and her speeches, and those of her chancellors, Sir (subsequently Lord) Geoffrey Howe and later Nigel (subsequently Lord) Lawson, stressed six points:

1. A rejection of Keynesian fine tuning of demand;
2. A rejection of price controls and incomes policies;
3. An emphasis on medium term stability;
4. Supply side economic policy leading to economic growth;
5. Tight control of the money supply;
6. A reduction of public expenditure.

The examination of Mrs Thatcher's economic policies provides us with some startling results. Inflation did go down temporarily but rose significantly at the end of the 1980s. If the 1979-89 period is taken for Great Britain, very ordinary inflation figures are to be observed when compared with other industrialised countries. The economic growth average of 2 per cent per annum for the 1980s period is similar to the figure of the preceding decade. Employment certainly did recover, in the mid and late 1980s, but not as much as the manipulated statistics suggested. Therefore, many monetarist measurement techniques such as Sterling M3 were quite simply dropped after 1983 because they did not deliver the expected results. In fact, the familiar cycle of recession followed by modest economic growth, sometimes termed stagflation because a mixture of stagnation and inflation, continued very much as it had done before 1979. In economic affairs Mrs Thatcher's message was well understood, but the economic results of her policies were certainly closer to traditional conservatism than to the hopes of the New Right. The idea of an 'implementation gap' will, therefore, be useful for this study of her cultural policy, since economic policy crucially influenced all government legislation and action.

B) Local government

This is another area where Mrs Thatcher's policies had, necessarily, great influence on cultural practices. In the United Kingdom, for example, local government spends as much as central government on cultural affairs in real terms. Mrs Thatcher had three main objectives in local government: to reduce expenditure, to strengthen accountability, to weaken the Labour opposition in local authorities. The last of these aims was an implicit, unstated one. However, in all three of these areas Mrs Thatcher merely continued policies which had applied before 1979. This meant, basically, less consultation between central and local authorities. One can even make a case for Mrs Thatcher finishing the centralising process that was set off by Clement Attlee's Labour government in 1945.[7] Block grants were introduced in 1980 and rate-capping began after the 1984 Rates Act had been passed. However, many authorities built up reserves or used what is termed 'creative accounting' to get around the problem of rate-capping. Nevertheless, despite more than forty Acts of Parliament on local government, there was no significant fall in local authority spending.

In addition, it would also appear that the supposedly high spending local authorities were subsequently singled out as scapegoats for the failure of Mrs Thatcher's aim of reducing central government spending. In fact, this failure was due to her refusal to implement the necessary policies. Local authority spending could have been reduced by fixing low levels of support for both Labour and Conservative councils. This, however, would have been politically unacceptable. One encounters here another example of Mrs Thatcher's implementation gap. On the one hand, she claimed that reducing state and local government spending were top priorities. On the other hand, she did not have the political nerve to alienate conservative voters and therefore acted in a traditional conservative manner. One of the few original personal ideas that Mrs Thatcher decided to implement was the Community Charge, and it proved to be a costly political fiasco leading to the prime minister's fall from power.

C) Housing

Another example of traditional conservatism can be seen in the field of housing:

> Thousands of people in council houses and new towns came out in support of us for the first time because they wanted a chance to buy their own homes. We will give every council tenant the right to purchase his own home at a substantial discount on the market price and with 100% mortgages for those who need them. This will be a giant stride towards making a reality of Anthony Eden's dream of a property owning democracy.[8]

Mrs Thatcher placed home ownership at the top of her political agenda. This measure, along with privatisations of nationalised industries, was part of her project for winning votes through popular capitalism. The other main aims were the reduction of public spending on housing and an increase in privately rented accommodation. There can be no doubt that home ownership was one of Mrs Thatcher's great successes. Home ownership increased by 25 per cent, while government spending on housing was reduced by 33 per cent over the 1980s. There were, however, various unforeseen consequences to this policy. People opted for home ownership because of three factors: a buoyant housing market, tax incentives (relief on interest) and a lack of private rented accommodation due to fair rent regimes. Tax relief, of course, was not on the New Right agenda and could be seen as government interference in the housing market. It was of course a vote winner and benefited the middle and upper classes proportionally more than the lower classes. When interest rates climbed up at the end of the 1980s, many houses were repossessed and many families became homeless. Along with the dream of home ownership came a parallel nightmare of negative equity. Thus, in the application of housing policy, one can detect the strong influence of the 'one nation' populism of traditional conservatism, according to which every citizen should benefit from popular capitalism. Yet the results were not those expected.

Not surprisingly, therefore, a considerable gap between what Mrs Thatcher said she was aiming at and what she actually achieved is to be observed. What was, however, most characteristic about Thatcherite policies was their almost crusading zeal. Yet, as can be seen in the above cases, overemphasising the influence of the New Right on Mrs Thatcher's policies must be avoided. In fact there is a great deal of continuity with regard to traditional conservatism. This difference between theoretical radicalism and practical policies can even be seen in the five tasks outlined in the 1979 Conservative manifesto:

1. To restore the health of our economic and social life, by controlling inflation and striking a fair balance between the rights and duties of the trade union movement;
2. To restore the incentives so that hard work pays, success is rewarded and genuine new jobs are created in an expanding economy;
3. To uphold parliament and the rule of law;
4. To support family life, by helping people to become home-owners, raising the standards of their children's education, and concentrating welfare services on the effective support of the old, the sick, the disabled, and those who are in real need;
5. To strengthen Britain's defences and work with our allies to protect our interests in an increasingly threatening world.

The general nature of the above priorities also applies to the three key Thatcherite policy areas considered and likewise influenced her cultural policy.

Mrs Thatcher's ideas on cultural policy

Mrs Thatcher denied that intellectuals or critics should have a leading role in cultural policy and proposed that free-market economics should also apply to cultural provision, that is to say market forces were to treat culture in very much the same way as any other leisure industry such as tourism. Firstly, Mrs Thatcher rejected the whole basis of the welfare state and the public good justification which had led to the postwar policy of saving highbrow culture. The public good simply means that every citizen has a right to certain public services that are deemed useful for the whole community. It is often used in the case of hospitals, schools, parks and sometimes culture. Secondly, she refused to accept the need to subsidise avant-garde art forms which could not attract large audiences in a commercial cultural market-place. This constituted a theoretical reaction against the various justifications for subsidising culture. Thirdly, she rejected cultural democracy in the form of community arts with its insistence on a person's right to cultural expression.

Mrs Thatcher's definition of cultural democracy was based on a commercial mass culture where supply and demand found a 'natural' equilibrium in the market-place. However, this encouragement of consumer culture was no 'neutral' project. It had significant implications in numerous areas. On the one hand, globalisation of the cultural industries meant that certain larger minority groups had more strategic power than smaller ones. These industries would meet the demand of large groups even if they were spread out throughout the world. Even if concentrated in one geographical area, the demand of a small group would not normally be met by the producers. Some economically poor subgroups, despite their numbers, would also be excluded from this market. On the other hand, consumer culture also encouraged new technical developments that have had a truly democratic influence by decentralising cultural practices. To give but one example, almost everyone can now make their own video films because production costs have been reduced due to mass markets and mass demand. Thus Mrs Thatcher's brand of consumerism also had a populist, democratic strand to it that compensated for the economic concentrations of the producers.

It must be stressed that the ideas of the New Right in general and Mrs Thatcher's in particular, seemed to sound the death knell of existing subsidised culture. Government spending was to be reduced and this was bound to affect cultural spending, often considered a luxury when compared to defence, law and order, education or the National Health Service (NHS). The Thatcher project was that cultural markets were to be regulated by the market-place, with no government interference. Put bluntly, she believed that culture should pay for itself. It is again the notion of an implementation gap which will explain the difference between Mrs Thatcher's cultural theory and her cultural practice. Moreover, these ideas were not the only ideas that gained popularity during the 1980s. In reality, rather crude New Right theoretical constructs had to compete with other cultural theories that tackle modern cultural phenomena in a more subtle way and propose more appropriate solutions to cultural problems. In fact, some of these cultural theories or some of their aspects were alternative sources of ideas for Mrs Thatcher's eclectic policies and this particular point needs detailed commentary.

Notes

1. M. Rothbard, *For a New Liberty: The Libertarian Manifesto* (New York: Collier-Macmillan, 1978).
2. R. Nozick, *Anarchy and the State* (Oxford: Blackwell, 1974).
3. quoted in *Woman's Own interview*, 31 October 1987.
4. Margaret Thatcher, *The Downing Street Years* (London: Harper Collins, 1993) 15.
5. Ian Gilmour, *Dancing with Dogma* (London: Simon and Schuster, 1993) 11.
6. A. Cooke, *The Revival of Britain: Mrs Thatcher's Speeches 1975-88* (London: Arum Press, 1989) 113.
7. This proposition has been made by Simon Jenkins, *Accountable to None: The Tory Nationalisation of Britain* (London: Hamish Hamilton, 1995).
8. Mrs Thatcher in R. Forrest, A. Murie, P. Williams, *Home Ownership* (London: Methuen, 1990) 55.

Chapter 2

A Comparative Approach to Cultural Policy - The case of the United Kingdom

In the postwar period, some form of cultural policy has gradually become accepted as one of the many functions of government. Very occasionally, the results of these policies catch the limelight as was seen in the media outcry over the minimalist sculptor Carl Andr,'s *Equivalent VIII*, that the Tate Gallery purchased in 1983, which was said to be an arrangement of bricks. On the whole, the rule is one of little public interest and culture being given a very low position on the political agenda. This can be seen in the fact that in Mrs Thatcher's memoirs a list of cabinets and major departments does not include the minister of the Arts and Libraries.[1]

The low priority that cultural policy has traditionally received in Great Britain has also existed in a number of other developed Western countries. Many different choices exist which can produce very distinctive reactions and results. It is vitally important to study the implicit values behind the different policy options that have emerged in these various countries. On the one hand, a certain administrative tradition, such as that of France, will produce a centralised high-profile Ministry of Culture. The former USSR represents the most extreme expression of this particular tradition. On the other hand, as in Britain, a low-profile, low-spending arm's length Arts Council with limited and elitist functions will produce very different results. Between the two extremes, come a wealth of different practices and priorities which all influenced Mrs Thatcher's decision making. The United States has a low-spending elitist definition that is compensated by a very high level of private patronage. The Federal Republic of Germany has a highly decentralised cultural system. The Swedish model is high-spending, relatively decentralised and has a very wide cultural definition. It is clear that different traditions not only result in different definitions of culture but that they also lead to the asking of two key questions in the assessment of all these national practices: How wide should the definition of cultural spending be? Which figures should be used?

A few methodological considerations

International comparisons produce many methodological problems, but they are necessary to arrive at some kind of evaluation. Basically, there are two conceptions of cultural policy in developed countries: the centralised approach which produces Ministries of Culture, and the arm's length approach, which produces Arts Councils. One can add that if there have been for a long time fundamental differences between the two models, now in the 1990s, they seem to be drawing closer together. A certain convergence would appear to be taking place. Yet this is not the only difficulty and methodological problems arise in other areas and particularly in the case of government statistics and figures. In addition, different countries have different government departments looking after a varying range of cultural affairs. Some statistics are quite simply unavailable or are not included in official figures. Added to this, national currencies vary over given time periods, making it extremely difficult to build up a precise comparative picture.

More generally, each developed country has its own cultural tradition. Some countries, such as Great Britain, may emphasise the need of a public library service, which reaches a large proportion of the population. Other countries, such as Sweden, insist on the importance of theatres and adult education, while for example, India, gives priority to national film production. All these cultural practices can be compared by taking one particular field and measuring the differences. The cultural policies that produce these characteristics reflect both the cultural priorities and the decision making processes that exist within these societies.

Another fundamental choice in cultural policy is whether to encourage cultural democracy or the democratisation of culture. The former allows all citizens to express themselves and the latter tries to make highbrow culture available to mass audiences. An example of the former would be community arts, which developed in the 1970s and 1980s, while the latter might be televising opera to make it more accessible to ordinary people. Before considering how Mrs Thatcher influenced cultural policy in Great Britain, it will be helpful to study the different cultural systems in the developed world to establish common denominators and specific features of particular systems.

These different choices in matters of culture are not only theoretical but have practical consequences. They sustain and give rise to different trends among the nation states, which have traditionally adopted two distinct types of reaction to cultural policy: they can either allow the increasingly international private sector to decide what cultural production should take place, adopting a free-market approach, or they can introduce protectionist measures and control the free flow of cultural products in the interests of national cultural identity. Such a general pattern has become noticeable in the last twenty years. In the 1980s, the pressure against protectionism grew steadily, while it is at present increasing. The recent GATT talks and the signing of an agreement in December 1993 by one hundred and seventeen countries have shown how important this trend will be in the future. However, even in this case a cultural exception (exception culturelle) was defined and finally accepted by the various countries.

Granted all these difficulties, the administrative structures and the funding patterns will be examined in five countries: France, the United States, the Federal Republic of Germany, Sweden and Great Britain. The first example shows a supposedly centralised Ministry of Culture with little private provision. The second example is famous for its decentralised system with high private provision. The third is a large, decentralised and high-spending European country and Sweden is a small one with a long tradition of local provision. It should be stressed that small countries find it difficult to preserve a cultural identity in a context of increasingly global cultural industries. This will then allow the British case to be placed into a context. Mrs Thatcher was determined to transform the approach and move towards the United States model. However, as the years went by, she increased government arts spending so as not to alienate voters and lose foreign tourists. She shifted her focus of attention away from negative attitudes to a more positive encouragement of the cultural industries.

The French model

The French model is particularly worth looking at because it offers a supposedly efficient, centralised system with a powerful Ministry of Culture. When the French Socialists came to office in 1981, they proposed a very broad definition of culture and Jack Lang, the then Minister of Culture, doubled his budget within two years of taking office. He claimed that: "culture is not limited to a market for privileged customers. For socialists all that concerns the human being is cultural, and from this point of view the entire Socialist plan is fundamentally a cultural project."[2] In this system a difference between what is pronounced in public and what is done in reality is evident. Here too an implementation gap is to be observed. Thus, in practice Jack Lang took a narrower definition and his Ministry mainly dealt with the performing arts, visual arts, museums, historic monuments, libraries, archives, cultural industries, cultural development, professional art training and popular education. This left twenty-two other French ministries to deal with cultural or sociocultural activities alongside the Ministry of Culture. There are in France twenty-two regional councils and at the local level, municipalities are playing an increasingly important role in cultural affairs. This is due to a process of decentralisation which the Socialist government launched in 1985 and that is continuing even now with Jacques Chirac after 1995. In reality cultural functions are in the process of being distributed to lower tiers of government and this process of devolution, when completed, will enable municipalities to play a significant role in cultural affairs.

For the purposes of this analysis, devolution means responsibility for culture at a lower level of administration, while decentralisation means that a central policy is merely implemented by a lower tier of government. Devolution produces greater cultural diversity, which some conversely consider to be administrative chaos and an uneven spread of services. Decentralisation leads to uniformity of provision and administrative clarity and this can encourage such philosophical concerns as citizens' rights to certain cultural services. The former encourages individualism and discourages debate, while the latter often tends towards equality and occasionally provokes democratic discussion.

The most common type of funding in France is that of the direct budget for operating expenses. It is, for example, the central government that pays for salaries. There are over 11,000 cultural officials or semi-officials on state salaries or permanent central subsidies. In addition, French governments have always been keen on 'Grands Projets', these taking up as much as a third of the total Ministry of Culture budget. This direct budgeting is becoming increasingly criticised, particularly in the case of the Paris Bastille Opera House that has consistently overspent due to state generosity and political networking. Under the Balladur government many of the recipients were told to find at least 20 per cent of their revenue from other than central sources.

A surprisingly low 29 per cent of cultural funding in 1983 was spent at the national level, 11 per cent at the regional level and 60 per cent spent at the municipal level. These basic figures make international comparisons possible. Italy and Great Britain are the most heavily centralised countries for cultural spending by the state. Not surprisingly, given their federal political systems and traditions, the Federal Republic of Germany and Canada are the least centralised of the countries. France is seen to be more decentralised than Great Britain which goes against the administrative stereotypes that are often circulated. The figures also give an indication as to the strength of regional government.

It works well in Germany, Canada and the United States, regional bodies playing major roles. However, it is rather weak in France and Italy, and quite simply does not exist in Great Britain. One criticism that might be levelled at the J. M. D. Schuster study is that considerable amounts of money were spent on the arts by Metropolitan areas and Regional Arts Associations and were not put under the category of regional spending. This was not wholly justified.

Furthermore if we are to examine the per capita spending for various developed countries we find two groups; one is formed by the United States, Italy, and Great Britain with very low per capita figures. The other group is all the other countries with $27-$35 per head. The French spent an estimated $32 per person on cultural activities organised by the state in 1983, that is the arts. The figure corresponding to the working definition of culture is, however, much higher when cultural industries are included. These tables give a broad idea of how much the selected states spend on arts policy, always remembering that different countries have different definitions of culture and the functions involved. The French state appears to be a high spender, taking into consideration that French cultural policy is only centralised in appearance, and in reality, increasingly decentralised.

In the second half of the 1980s, France, like many European countries, showed great interest in private support of the arts. The Association for the Development of Industrial and Commercial Patronage (ADMICAL) was set up in 1985 and estimated that five hundred French companies were participating in one form of sponsorship or another in 1987. An estimate by ADMICAL for the total value of cultural sponsorship came to the figure of 450-550 million francs for 1988. It was also discovered that bankers were the most enthusiastic sponsors among the service industries. Various tax changes were also introduced to encourage sponsorship. In 1987, the Development of Patronage Act became law. This introduced the idea of matched funding, that is the state putting up the equivalent amount as sponsors. It is the Council for Cultural Patronage that is responsible for this particular project. Thus even with a high-spending French government, sponsorship and private patronage have been strongly encouraged. Such trends were not a monopoly of Mrs Thatcher's Britain.

The United States model

Another model of cultural policy worth looking at in order to understand Mrs Thatcher's subsequent policy is that of the United States which is based on a mix of the arm's length principle and private provision. Various studies have been made on United States arts policy that can be added to that of J. M. D. Schuster.[3] The National Endowment of the Arts (NEA) is a 'quango' (as explained in the list of abbreviations) that is responsible for the distribution of government funds in a relatively restricted field of cultural activities. It supervises the performing arts, visual arts and museums while libraries are financed by another funding organisation as is the case in Great Britain. At the regional level, fifty-six State Arts Agencies (SAAs) encourage artistic activity with a wealth of different schemes. In 1989, many of these councils cut back on arts spending because of financial stringency and the oil states such as Texas were particularly affected.

The National Assembly of Local Art Agencies (NALAAs), with 585 members, estimated that there are in the region of 3,000 local arts agencies that cover around 80 per cent of the United States population. It also suggested a $500 million figure for the total budget of these local arts agencies. Many of these agencies receive money directly from the individual States, not from the Federal government, and often receive money from lotteries and a percentage from the Art tax. 20 per cent of NEA revenue has to be passed on to the State Arts Agencies. This type of administration can best be described as a devolved system with a federal base, stressing diversity rather than uniformity of services. The NEA is the best example of an arm's length cultural organisation, receiving money directly from Congress.[4]

In 1981, President Reagan tried to abolish the NEA but was defeated due to a public outcry. However, in 1989 Republican congressmen once again mounted a campaign to criticise this organisation using homo-erotic art as a pretence. Its future remains rather uncertain as the whole principle of federal arts funding is reconsidered regularly every five years. The funding level has been reduced over the 1980s as inflation erodes the rather static finance levels. This stable sum represents a real fall in true value due to inflation. However, the small amounts of money involved act as an official seal of approval and often unblock further funding from other official bodies. This is what Bourdieu would term symbolic power or cultural capital that can thence be converted into economic capital.

In 1983/4,[5] Federal expenditure on the arts was measured at 38 per cent, with the regional figure at 19 per cent, and local spending at 43 per cent. This is a surprisingly centralised result for a country that prides itself on its free market tradition and its liberalism. Per capita spending was only $13, but if private patronage and donations are included, a figure of $23 can be found. (See table 3.x on page xxx.) In addition, the tax deductions that accompany charity and cultural giving are in fact a hidden state subsidy. A low public figure on arts spending is made up for by a high private contribution. Here, appears the major difference between the United States and Western European cultural or arts practices. In the United States, there is a lot of indirect aid given in the form of foregone taxes. In this domain, the incomplete data that are available for Europe point to low levels of private patronage for culture in general, and for the arts more specifically, although this is now changing rapidly. It should be stressed that Mrs Thatcher was greatly influenced by her friend Ronald Reagan and his particular application of the United States cultural model. However, she can be said not to have followed the American example to the letter, as one simple example will immediately show: spending by the Arts Council of Great Britain, unlike the NEA, rose progressively throughout the 1980s.

The Federal Republic of Germany model

Historically, Germany was a collection of small states with a decentralised administrative system. The Second Reich, in 1871, brought with it the new idea of a national culture, and with the arrival of the Nazi regime in the 1930s, administration suddenly became radically centralised. The 1949 Constitution was a reaction against the dangers of centralisation and was founded on the idea of 'Basic Law'. It is the Lander (states) and Gemeinden (municipalities) that look after arts and cultural policy in general. The Bund (central government) only plays a very marginal role in this area.

The federal government spent only 1.7 per cent of total cultural spending in 1987.[6] In Berlin and Bonn a few privileged activities receive major federal support. However, most federal spending goes to paying for small proportions of Lander projects. For instance, federal finance has been very useful in funding the German film industry. The Film Promotion Institute (FFA) is partly financed by a levy that originated from cinema ticket sales; this functions very much like the Eady levy in Great Britain up until 1985. On top of this the FFA gets money from the two public television stations. It can, therefore, offer interest-free loans and co-production special financing is proposed by the television stations. In addition, tax incentives exist to make risk-taking involved in film production more attractive. The federal government has also set up panels, very much on the basis of the Arts Council, in order to distribute grants. For example, the German Literature Fund Inc. gives out individual grants and fellowships according to quality and supposed merit.

The second tier of administration is that of the Lander (states). The ratio of funding between the Lander and the municipalities varies considerably. In Bavaria for example, the ratio is 40/60 because of a long tradition of aristocratic patronage that has recently been replaced by local government. In the more heavily industrialised North Rhine Westphalia region, the ratio is 20/80. The administrative traditions are quite simply different. The 11 states have a Standing Conference of Ministers for Cultural Affairs (SCMCA) that defines priority areas for long-term planning. The Minister for Cultural Affairs who sits on this committee is responsible for education, research, science, the heritage as well as the arts. For this reason, precise figures for the arts are difficult to obtain. The Lander provide direct funding for arts associations and individual artists on top of financing the performing and visual arts.

The Gemeinden spend about 55 per cent of all cultural spending, especially on museums and the arts. Culture is often associated with local pride. A city's reputation can be improved by spending in this area. This is an example of the public good justification for cultural expenditure. Each citizen will supposedly benefit from the building of a museum, when museum-going often depends on class criteria or cultural level. Between 6 per cent and 8 per cent of total municipal spending goes to culture and about 70 per cent of this sum finances the performing arts. Theatres are heavily subsidised and even private theatres may receive subsidies. As in France, there is a great interest in sponsorship and private donations. However, little information is available and so grossing up figures is as yet impossible. One can mention the case of the Cologne Symphony orchestra that was told at the end of the 1980s to find at least 20 per cent of its income from sources other than subsidy. This was an attempt to make the orchestra more outward-looking and responsible for its financing. The orchestra rose to the challenge and has set a precedent against what may be described as 'over-subsidy'. This can be seen as a European trend aiming at a funding mix in order to avoid over-reliance on one particular funding source.

The three-tier German administrative system gave the following figures for 1987: the federal government spent 41 million DM, the Lander 2,150 million DM and the municipalities 4,311 million DM. This was the equivalent of œ23.96 per head for museums and the arts. German cultural policy would therefore appear to have a wide definition, to be very decentralised and patchy because of various local traditions. Above all, it is high spending, even by European standards. Concerning our investigation, Mrs Thatcher considered that the German cultural model promoted a dependency culture that was wholly undesirable in the United Kingdom.

The Swedish model

Swedish cultural policy is worth studying because of its relatively decentralised, high-spending and innovative form. On top of this, Sweden is a small European country and feels the negative effects of globalisation.

Historically, the Royal Opera and Royal Dramatic Theatre date from the 18th century. Indeed, there is a long history of royal patronage of the arts. In 1937, the government proposed a scheme whereby 1 per cent of the budget devoted to official buildings was to be spent on works of art. Since that year over 40,000 works of art have been produced thanks to the principle, even though the legislation did not follow. This can be considered as cultural policy through consensus, and is reserved for small, socially cohesive countries such as Sweden, Finland or Denmark.

In 1974, eight state cultural policy priorities were defined. They were designed to:

1. help to protect freedom of expression and create genuine opportunities for the utilisation of that freedom;
2. give people opportunities to engage in creative activities of their own and to promote interpersonal contacts;
3. Counteract the negative effects of commercialism in the cultural sector.
4. promote a decentralisation of activities and decision-making functions in the cultural sector;
5. make more allowance for the experiences and needs of disadvantaged groups;
6. facilitate artistic and cultural renewal;
7. ensure that the culture of earlier times is preserved and revitalised;
8. promote an exchange of experience and ideas within the cultural sector across linguistic and national boundaries.[7]

Various ideas in these general principles need to be stressed. The second point prioritises cultural democracy with the citizen's right of access to various cultural infrastructures, his or her right to participate. Mrs Thatcher's position was never as clear as this explicit statement. The third point is also worth considering as commercial, American-style culture has an obvious competitive advantage as regards minority cultures such as the Swedish one. The United States has the richest cultural home market in the world and Hollywood can export commercial products in a very competitive fashion. So do the Bombay films with a mass market in India and good export possibilities all over the world. The Swedish film industry clearly cannot compete on an equal basis. It has high overheads as Swedish actors and technicians cost more than American or Indian ones. Production costs are high because films are few and far between and distribution is limited to Scandinavian countries. The result is that Swedish films at present can only survive if subsidised. One should also add that the Swedish television service already uses a lot of British and foreign programmes. The only way to put forward a Swedish point of view is to subsidise, using national glory and pride as a justification.

A 1989 report by the Council of Europe was very enthusiastic about Swedish cultural policy, because it was clearly defined on a national level and also decentralised for local decisions. It would seem to have few disadvantages, except its high cost:

> It combines high public spending with a small national bureaucracy. Grants are administered in an exceptionally simple and economical way, with remarkably few strings attached. The division of responsibility between the Ministry and the NCCA (the National Council of Cultural Affairs) is another feature, which corresponds to the standard split in Swedish government between policy-making and implementation. [...] Sweden has made only limited use of legislation in the context of cultural policy, but exceptional importance has been given to the formulation of goals for national cultural policy, and to the creation of consensually based policies. The administration is centralised, but policy has been developed in a flexible voluntary partnership with the local authorities, both municipalities and county councils.[8]

If one considers central government funding, this represents about 30 per cent of all arts spending in Sweden. There is a strong tradition of adult education and yet most of the money spent on the arts goes to the performing arts and museums as in many other countries. Theatre has an extremely high level of subsidy with proportionally high audience levels. It is obviously an area where commercial foreign imports cannot compete and where local production has a naturally dominant position. In 1988, there were twenty nine producing theatres that included ballet and opera, to which can be added one hundred and twenty independent theatre groups. Classical music is the responsibility of the Swedish Institute of Concerts. Central funds financed ten major symphony and chamber orchestras and nineteen museums located mostly in Stockholm. Thus, in reality, in 1987/8, only 9 per cent of the income for these ten organisations came from the box office. This represents a very low figure. As for film production, the Swedish Film Institute is funded by the government and also by film and video levies. This is a novel idea that should be considered in other countries. As for literature, as far back as 1954, legislation was introduced to give financial compensation to authors whose books were borrowed from public libraries. This experience encouraged the introduction of the Public Lending Right in Great Britain in the 1970s. Subsidies are also distributed to encourage the publication of books and even to support bookshops. In addition, the literature fund also hands out grants and fellowships to encourage scholarship.

This highly subsidised Swedish system, designed to encourage Swedish production, has been criticised for being too expensive and representing bad value for money. Consequently, in 1987, the government asked the Visual Arts Fund to reduce the number of visual artists receiving subsidy. There were 1300 at the time and a year later the number had dropped to 129 artists receiving full salaries. In 1988, 200 authors, translators and illustrators received government grants. This whole idea of having artists who are in effect state functionaries was what Mrs Thatcher wanted to avoid at all costs. For her, artists might be subsidised but only as a small proportion of total income and preferably on a temporary basis. Even in Sweden, therefore, cultural experts were told that they could not have a blank cheque and needed to be more competitive in the increasingly international market.

As in all decentralised systems, local and regional authorities that spend about 70 per cent of total cultural expenditure show great diversity. In 1986, local and regional funds were split up between libraries (40%), schools and music (17%), adult education (12%) and museums and theatres (31%). 27 per cent of total spending on museums came from the municipalities and only 8 per cent from the county councils. Half of the museums were free which can help to explain the high attendance levels: in 1982, twelve million visitors went to Swedish museums and the figure rose to 17.3 million in 1987. Business sponsorship is another area that is being officially encouraged. In 1988, the Arts and Business Association for Cultural Sponsorship (ABACS) was set up. The levels, however, appear to be very low for the time being and precise figures are not available.

Total arts spending per head amounted to œ27.78 in 1987, which represents the highest level in the Policy Studies Institute comparison. All in all, the political and cultural situation being taken into consideration, the Swedish model in many ways represents the antithesis of Mrs Thatcher's idea of cultural policy.

The United Kingdom model

There is a long tradition of central funding in the United Kingdom. The British Museum was set up in 1753, and during the 19th century nine national museums were founded. The performing arts were left to private patronage until the Second World War and the setting up of the Council for the Encouragement of Music and the Arts (CEMA). In 1946, the Arts Council of Great Britain (ACGB) continued the job that CEMA had started and government support became accepted as normal practice.

In the United Kingdom, the Department of Education and Science (DES) was reponsible for the Arts Council and cultural policy until 1980. After this date, the Office of Arts and Libraries (OAL) was established as a junior department covering the Arts Council, the Crafts Council (CC), the British Film Institute (BFI), and the Museums and Galleries Commission (MGC). The OAL was also responsible for public libraries in England, Wales, Scotland and Northern Ireland. Most of United Kingdom heritage was left to the Department of the Environment (DOE). The ACGB funded fifteen Regional Arts Associations (RAAs) in England and Wales, there being none for Scotland and Northern Ireland. Nine other departments, such as the DES, the DOE and the Ministry of Defence, had responsibilities in cultural affairs as defined in a broad sense. In 1992, the new Department of National Heritage was set up with responsibilities in the cultural industries, heritage and the local organisations were given the title Regional Arts Boards (RABs). One discovers an administrative patchwork that caters for a limited elitist definition of culture in the United Kingdom.

During the 1980s, the ACGB wished to concentrate its efforts on the regions and away from its major companies in London. This was reflected in The Glory of the Garden (1984) strategy review. However, the abolition of the Greater London Council (GLC) and the resulting transfer of responsibilities to the Arts Council meant that the organisation became even more London-centred and elitist.

Efforts to help recipients of subsidy to diversify their funding sources were rather more successful in the United Kingdom than in other European countries. The Association of Business Sponsorship for the Arts (ABSA) distributed an estimated £30 million in 1988/9 and organised the Business Sponsorship Investment Scheme (BSIS). The Arts Council had its own Incentive Funding Scheme. In the case of museums, nearly all national museums now have entrance charges that were gradually introduced during the 1980s.

Local government involvement in cultural policy also goes back a long way in history. During the 19th century, many museums were set up. By 1939, 400 municipal museums and 200 theatres were in operation. After the war, cultural projects were considerably expanded. These were funded by the rates as well as the OAL. However, due to the rather imprecise figures, it is difficult to point to definite trends. Statistics that are available, such as those given by the Chartered Institute of Public Finance and Accountancy (CIPFA), tend to understate the real spending levels, because they are based on local authority estimates. About one half of cultural spending comes from central government and the other half from local government. Subsidy is low for a developed country and the system is surprisingly centralised.

The trend during the 1980s was one of arts organisations becoming less dependent on government funds. Ticket sales, and to a lesser extent private sponsorship and patronage, have filled the vacuum.

This trend provoked a certain professionalisation among arts administrators. Reliable attendance figures for museums are now available because of admission charges. In 1988, there were 24.3 million visitors to the government funded national museums. There were also 16 million visitors for local authority museums and 12.7 million for private ones. This gives a total of 53 million among which there were many foreign tourists. One can also mention 9 million spectators for the commercial London theatres and 1.9 million seats sold in the capital's principle classical music venues in 1987/8. The large number of foreign tourists means that one cannot compare the British cultural market with smaller ones such as in Sweden. These remarkable figures come with the proviso that there is overconcentration on London.[10]

Comparative distribution of government cultural spending

On the whole, two types of country emerge in the study conducted by J. M. D. Schuster on 1984 arts funding levels in developed nations.[10] The first group has a high level of government cultural spending on cultural affairs, with often a wide definition of what culture and the arts represents: Canada, the Federal Republic of Germany, France, the Netherlands, Sweden, which spend $27-$35 per capita. The second group spends much less in terms of a very restricted definition of culture: $10-$13 per capita. Great Britain is placed at the bottom of the cultural spending league table along with Italy and the United States. (various countries have different functions listed under culture and these functions can sometimes change rapidly over time.) Great Britain covers four main art functions. At the other end of the range can be found the Netherlands that cover nine.

In addition, many other interesting questions are brought up by J. M. D. Schuster's report which stresses the high level of government spending on cultural affairs in certain countries. What are the reasons for such a situation? The answer is that he who spends also controls. Western European nation states are very sensitive in the area of cultural affairs because of the long history of national identity. Some of these states, such as France or Sweden, adopt a protectionist and interventionist position when it comes to cultural industries such as the film industry or the Press. Most of the national identities concerned go back to the Renaissance period but the tradition is under threat because of a new European identity, globalisation and Americanisation in the cultural industries and also a parallel growth of very local identities. These considerations apply to the United Kingdom too, although the American form of English sometimes masks the threat of US cultural domination. Another example of high subsidy is the Swedish Press which received 17 per cent of total cultural spending in 1984.

Another question that is raised by the report is the low level of private sponsorship for cultural affairs in Western Europe. For example, corporate hiring of state subsidised cultural organisations led to protests from the Dutch government when the Concertgebouw was rented by Heineken for a private celebration. Volvo also proposed financing five string players for the G"teborg Symphony orchestra, but the Swedish government wondered who would pay for the positions after the five year period was over. The string players project was, therefore, not accepted. There seem to be social or psychological factors which act as a brake on private donations in Europe. One can also give a technical reason, because public sector accounting procedures often include a reduction of funds whenever alternative funds or savings are found. This disincentive discourages any sponsoring that might be seen as helping the state to save money. However, towards the end of the 1980s, the situation had changed considerably. Mrs Thatcher addressed the problem, as will be seen in Chapter Eight that deals with the Arts Council.

A more recent report on comparative cultural policies by the Policy Studies Institute (PSI), confirmed the conclusions of high private funding levels in the United States. (Table 3.4 on page 409 reflects a significant movement from the United States and British positions, through to the continental position). This table deals with arts spending by the state and shows that as a percentage of public expenditure there are three groups rather than two as suggested by J. M. D. Schuster. The high spenders are Germany and France, with a middle group such as the United Kingdom and Sweden. The United States spent considerably less than any of the other countries. However, if one takes total arts expenditure per head, the United Kingdom is placed much nearer the United States model than the Canadian or European norm. This second figure confirms the original 1984 Schuster hypothesis for 1987 and therefore the latter half of the 1980s. Britain comes closer to the United States model than to the European or Canadian models in expenditure terms and this must be accounted for as one of the key problems. A sudden change in attitude in Western European countries over private funding must also be pointed out. Sponsorship and patronage have become popular words even though the actual contributions are low. Mrs Thatcher's role in changing perceptions in Britain, and also in Europe, on this particular point is very important. This principle is now widely accepted and its symbolic value is great.

British Government figures and statistics

Before formulating her policies, Mrs Thatcher had to face the problem of incomplete cultural data. The present discussion over definitions is further complicated by the problem of which figures to use, and this is of particular importance concerning Great Britain. Various government statistics are published every year and provide a wealth of valuable information. Her Majesty's Stationary Office (HMSO) collects information on various government departments. The Central Statistical Office (CSO) also sets out figures in the form of Blue Books and the Family Expenditure Survey (FES). Despite this, there is no centralised information bank which can give overall figures on either arts or cultural spending. Such data have to be obtained from the individual government departments. This administrative practice also limits public discussion and involvement in the cultural debate. There are thirty departments that deal with cultural affairs, including the Office of Arts and Libraries (OAL), the Department of Education and Science (DES), the Scottish Office (SO), the Welsh Office (WO), the Northern Ireland Office (NIO), the Department of the Environment (DoE), and surprisingly, the Ministry of Defence (MOD) which in 1990 spent over œ50 million on cultural activities such as military music.

Local government spending must be scrutinised, and this is further complicated by the fact that there is no statutory obligation for local authorities to provide cultural services to the public. When the cultural spending figure is low, the amounts will often be put under various other headings. Many local authorities, for example, give rent reductions to charitable organisations and arts organisations are often placed in the charities category for administrative and taxation reasons. A look at charity organisations is therefore necessary.

The Census gives valuable information on social composition for cultural activities, but even here certain criticisms have been levelled against the reliability of these figures. Paradoxically, the Policy Studies Institute is the only independent organisation, with a staff specialising in cultural affairs, that brings together the mass of cultural information in the country. Many pressure groups are sources of information on very specific issues and the lack of public debate has encouraged their formation. These include the National Campaign for the Arts, the Association for Business Sponsorship of the Arts (ABSA) and even political pressure groups such as the Conservative Political Centre.

The need for extreme caution when dealing with facts and figures is demonstrated in the following example. Should the Retail Price Index (RPI) or the Gross Domestic Product (GDP) deflator be used, as a base for comparisons in government spending levels on the arts and culture more generally? If the GDP deflator is taken into account, the Arts Minister Richard Luce's claim, on 9th December 1985, sounds plausible: "in the past six years, we have more than doubled the amount of money given to the arts. The Arts Council's funds have increased by 7 per cent in real terms in the past six years."[11] However, the statement contradicts Mrs Thatcher's official policy of reducing red tape and state spending in general and particularly in the arts. If however, the Arts Council grants during the same period are taken into account using the RPI and excluding the money taken from Metropolitan Area spending and put back into central government spending, the result is a 1.4 per cent decrease. Moreover, if Housing the Arts is excluded, that is money spent on museum building and maintenance, a decrease of 4.7 per cent appears. The RPI can be criticised because it includes mortgage interest rates and the former rates or Community Charge. For this reason the GDP deflator is often used as the best available tool for measuring consumer spending trends. Certainly, most government Commissions use this method of comparison. One thing is certain, the advantages and disadvantages of the different figures available have to be carefully weighed up. Another problem is that the 1979-1990 time period does not provide us with handy comparative statistics and often tentative conclusions have to be drawn from the limited data available.

Official government statistics provide an estimate of overall consumer spending figures for culture. By the 1980s, culture had become a major economic sector in Great Britain. It represented, in the middle of this period, the same amount as total consumer spending on cars, motorcycles and other vehicles, or the equivalent of fuel and power sales, what is now termed the utility industries. A breakdown of the figures shows that one third of spending went on books, records and other cultural items for private enjoyment, one fifth on recreational and entertainment services, including spectator sports. One half went on musical instruments, video hire, television licences, electronic equipment. Another approach to this data gives the following breakdown: 8 per cent of the total went to museums, galleries, theatres and concerts, or what is usually termed the arts which is the area that government cultural policy has traditionally supervised; 29 per cent went on broadcasting and cinema; 36 per cent was spent on cultural items for sale, that is to say books, pictures, records, videos, crafts; a further 27 per cent was spent on ancillary spending specifically induced by cultural practices, that is to say stereo equipment or video equipment. There was, in fact, a doubling of private cultural spending during the 1979-1990 Thatcher years. These basic figures show how important arts and cultural spending in general are and the vital role they play in the economy. Mrs Thatcher certainly encouraged the private cultural sector through her policies.

The Multiplier Effect and its consequences

The basic figures on cultural spending have to be subjected to the multiplier effect which means that one cultural job stimulates additional ancillary service work. An example of ancillary services can be the serving by museum staff of drinks in plastic cups for thirsty museumgoers. S. Medlik has calculated this multiplier effect to be in the region of 1.7 per cent for cultural services.[12] In the £10 billion total for 1986 the multiplier effect gives a substantial £17 billion. However, Robert Hewison has pointed out that these figures have received a certain amount of criticism from various economists such as Gordon Hughes and Sir Alan Peacock and should not be used in an uncritical fashion. [13]

The popular view is that culture and the arts are heavily subsidised. This is clearly not true and the belief is due to the lack of public information and debate on the subject, which is largely the fault of successive British governments. In fact very little cultural spending is subsidised. In the case of the cultural sector that receives most of the government help, that is to say the arts, 81 per cent of total turnover comes from sales, while only 18 per cent comes from public subsidy, this representing both central and local government spending. Only 1 per cent comes from private patronage and even then the figures are difficult to determine. The most heavily government funded categories within the arts are museums and galleries, with 80 per cent of total revenue coming from public sources. These activities draw mostly from the middle classes and are also tourist attractions. Events and festivals got 51 per cent of their running costs from these sources.[14]

As for employment in the cultural market, the 1981 Census figures estimated that 450,000 people had direct jobs, but because of the seasonal nature of cultural employment, this is most probably an understatement. 50,000 jobs were provided in broadcasting alone and the multiplier effect has to be added to all these jobs. Thus for every £ spent by the state or by the private sector on cultural activities 70 pence are generated in ancillary services that often provide unqualified service employment. This is no small consideration when trying to deal with high levels of unemployment, especially as cultural employment also has the added attraction of needing low levels of investment and can often be located in run-down inner-city areas.

Mrs Thatcher's funding policy

In general, three types of policy are used by governments: (1) distributive policies which benefit all citizens, (2) redistributive policies which favour one group against other segments, (3) regulative policies which control the behaviour of members of the community. The first type of policies will produce, for example, sewage systems for all. In the cultural field one might take the example of subsidising opera or screening a production on the national television network. The second category will concentrate on, for example, subsidised social housing for those on low wages. This justification might result in theatrical performances in a factory or free admission for the unemployed at various concerts. The last category might represent censorship laws to decide what citizens may watch on television.

What was the position of various Conservative governments in the 1979-1990 period? At the beginning of the decade, Mrs Thatcher and her government argued the case for reducing state spending in general and subsidy to the arts in particular using monetarist justifications. In 1980 and 1983, the Arts Council suffered small reductions in its grant. This had great symbolic value, and yet in subsequent years, government cultural spending actually increased, although not as quickly as total consumer cultural spending. If one takes the 1979-1989 period, there was an overall increase of 22 per cent in central government spending on the arts, based on the GDP deflator. This takes into account the shift of functions from the Metropolitan areas to central government that took place after 1986.

Table 3.6 on page 411 shows a steady increase in arts funding levels during the 1980s, as can clearly be seen in the figures giving percentages of general government expenditure. This rose from 0.15 per cent in 1978/9 to 0.19 per cent ten years later. Table 3.6 also makes the point that within this increase, most was spent on tourist-attracting museums and galleries.

These figures again indicate an implementation gap in government arts policy. Private cultural spending more than doubled in money terms during the 1980s period and there was a 30 per cent increase in real terms, if 1985 constant prices are used as a basis. Government spending rose at a somewhat slower rate. Thus, in proportion, government spending declined. A rapid rise in the first half of the Thatcher decade took place up until 1986, with a levelling off in the later years. The extra money was spent mostly on museum building and museum staff salaries, as museums attracted and still attract many foreign tourists. Because the private market cannot pay for such enterprises, the government felt it useful and necessary to continue subsidising these projects.

Of course Mrs Thatcher did not give any detailed explanations to the general public as this justification did not fall in line with her official policy which was to reduce subsidy and let the market decide. A debate over the limitations of the market did not take place. The proportional decrease in arts spending levels was made up by higher ticket prices, higher levels of attendance, which in turn, made the arts more dependent on tourist support; this came out quite clearly after the Libya bombings in 1986 and later during the Iraqi war in 1991. One can therefore state that government spending on the arts in particular and culture in general increased during the period under consideration. However, government finance of cultural activities fell as a proportion of the total figure.

One of the great hopes of the successive Conservative governments was that the American model of private patronage might be applied to Britain. Enthusiastic efforts were made to stimulate business sponsorship and patronage. Sponsorship means an exchange of advertising for money. The Association for Business Sponsorship of the Arts (ABSA) was set up in 1976, under the previous Labour government, to distribute money to cultural organisations in a similar way to the Arts Council but on the basis of private funds. This system is particularly effective with the large high-profile museums, galleries, opera companies and international festivals. For example, the British Museum in 1987/8 received œ3.3 million in business sponsorship. This represents 10 per cent of all business sponsorship which ABSA estimated to be around the 30 million mark in 1990. Surprisingly, no precise overall figures are available. It can also be added that while this system of funding is useful during a period of industrial and economic expansion, recessions, on the contrary, bring reductions which administrators find difficult to manage.

Charity is also possible, meaning a straight gift. Corporate donations was one of Mrs Thatcher's great hopes in the field of the arts. She hoped to bring private contributions towards similar levels as those in the United States. Certain schemes were introduced to facilitate the giving of corporate gifts attracting tax relief. Figures are available via the Charity Aid Foundation, but nothing exists for the arts specifically. The biggest single tax expenditure in the cultural field is the £140 million of Value Added Tax (VAT) that were foregone in 1989 on book purchases, because VAT on books is zero-rated. The same also applies to newspapers, although this is currently under review now that the Press has started to show improved profits. This was not the case in the 1980s. Theatre owners quite rightly asked why theatre seat prices were not treated in a similar way. Overall figures for the private sector are difficult to assess because they do not always exist. Donations come somewhere between European and US levels. Thus one comes to a figure of £360 million spent on the arts by central government at the end of the Thatcher period.

Local Government figures

Central government policy has a strong influence on local government spending on the arts. The familiar problems over statistics, as there is no statutory obligation for local authorities to provide cultural services, are encountered. Local government cultural provision can be seen as a patchwork of different practices and activities. Stephen Mennell's report, on how cultural decision making is carried out by some local authorities, is vital in this respect.[15] In general, local authority expenditure increased up until 1984, and then levelled off. The figures that are available have to be treated with extreme caution. Several surveys carried out by the Chartered Institute of Public Finance and Accountancy (CIPFA), point out some major problems. For example the case of multi-purpose halls. Some function as bingo halls but also provide venues for live performances and concerts. It is this mix of entertainment, leisure and arts that causes the problems. There is also a lack of standardisation in local authority accounting procedures. In addition, local education authorities spend large amounts of money on cultural activities, but this is not included in local authority cultural spending statistics.[16] The rather imprecise figures that do exist show that by 1983/4 central and local government expenditure on the arts had reached similar levels in real terms.

The J. M. D. Schuster study calculated a 49 per cent arts spending level for central government and 51 per cent for local authorities. This assumption seems questionable: local authority expenditure on the arts was in the region of £300 million, if libraries are excluded; if the latter are included a total of 840 million were spent at the end of the period under consideration. This is considerably more than the central government total. If one turns these figures into proportions one arrives at 30 per cent for centralised institutions and 70 per cent for the local authorities. This would indicate that Mrs Thatcher succeeded in limiting government increases on the arts but found it difficult to do the same on a local basis. This reaction will be considered in Part Four.

After this watershed period, pressure was put on local authorities by means of rate-capping, local government reorganisation and the controversial Community Charge, to reduce local authority spending in all areas. By the end of the 1980s there had been a return shift back to the centre. Because of this, some local authorities, such as the conservative Westminster Council, refused to fund what they considered to be national cultural companies. In 1987, for example Westminster Council refused to subsidise the English National Opera (ENO) and English National Ballet (ENB) that were both located within its area. The figures indicate that arts organisations became less dependent on state subsidy in the 1979-1990 period. So in this domain, the move can definitely be said to have been significant.

Figures for the cultural industries

Mrs Thatcher's policy towards the cultural industries over the same period can be qualified as non-interventionist and laissez-faire. She wanted to encourage the private side of cultural production and consumption. The key idea here was that individuals were to decide how they should spend their money. This can be placed under the heading of cultural democracy if the prices charged are accessible to practically every member of the community. This is the very basis of pluralism. Statistics for the various cultural industries are available but are rarely analysed.

Cultural industries are those institutions which use the industrial corporation organisation to supply goods and services such as television programmes, television hardware, films, cinema distribution, newspapers, magazines, books and records. Although some areas may sometimes suffer heavy losses from time to time, the major motivation is profit maximisation. These cultural industries expanded greatly during the Thatcher years by using mass production and distribution techniques, divisions of labour and commercial criteria. There was a definite concentration of power in these cultural industries which benefited the multi-national, multi-media conglomerates in a worldwide trend. Internationally, these can be divided into two categories: the hardware producers such as Sony, Toshiba, Hitachi, Matsushita or Philips and the software producers such as Time/Warner, CBS, EMI, News International and Reed International. (Among the top 15 mass media conglomerates in the world, ten are American, two German, two Japanese and one Australian. However, the very idea of nationality as concerns multinational corporations is very dubious.) During the 1980s there was an increasing blurring of the distinction between hardware and software specialisation.

Mrs Thatcher's brand of popular capitalist ideology did not clash with this massive concentration of power. The Monopoly and Mergers Commission (set up in 1965) intervenes to prevent companies from having a monopolistic or oligopolistic position within a particular industry. This legislation led to diversification rather than overspecialisation in one area of the cultural industries. Mrs Thatcher, because of her belief in a free market, therefore, took no measures to stem the flow of Japanese video recorders and players during the 1980s. Non-intervention was the golden rule.

The key problem of the high costs involved in cultural production and the relatively low costs of cultural reproduction remains in the United Kingdom. It is only because of huge profits in cultural distribution that these very large corporations can invest in cultural production. Power and profit lie in cultural distribution and not production. It is for this reason that the unauthorised making and selling of video and audio cassettes, otherwise known as pirating, is such a lucrative business. Four such companies are Japanese, two American and the other four are German, Dutch, French and British.

All kinds of conclusions can be drawn from this assessment of Great Britain's cultural spending and the comparison with France, the United States, Germany, and Sweden. In general, Britain has a low level of public spending in this area, which can be compared with that of Italy, while the other countries have much higher per capita spending figures. During the 1980s, Mrs Thatcher tried to encourage private donations and sponsorship and she enjoyed a certain amount of success: Britain being situated between other European countries, which have very low levels of private funding, and the United States, that has very high ones. Generally speaking, British orchestras got little support from either private or central government sources. As a consequence, national British orchestras, although this applies to a lesser extent to smaller ones such as the Halle, fell between two stools. They attracted neither state support as in the case of German and French orchestras, nor private support as in Canada and the United States. The same clearly applies to British theatres which are however much closer to the commercial American model than the subsidised European ones. Great Britain seemed to get the worst of both worlds.

The British idea of a cultural policy is very limited and yet even when state support for the arts is low, it has a symbolic significance. In other words, a small grant may act as an official seal of approval for cultural organisations which may be totally disproportionate to the sums involved. An Arts Council grant can often unblock other sources of income. As for specific spending in Great Britain in the 1980s, the relatively small amount that was spent by the state was concentrated on the public libraries, the national museums, and the national companies. Local authorities spent more than central government because they often had a wider definition of culture than national government. The little that was left rarely went to minority group culture, such as, for example, ethnic or feminist culture. This typically British system also raised problems of accountability. Freeing the market was the watchword of the 1980s, and private cultural spending in fact doubled over the Thatcher period. Government spending on the arts rose at a much slower rate, thus declining as a proportion.

However, cultural policy cannot be limited to the arts. While the 1992 (just after the Thatcher period) change of functions in the new Department of National Heritage was a significant decision, a still wider governmental definition would have been even more useful. Cultural policy should have been extended to the strategically significant cultural industries. To take but one example, nothing was done to encourage a shift of resources on the part of the multinationals into cultural production. This was due to faith in free market economics and a failure to identify the importance of long-term strategic planning in this particular area. If the audio visual market is dominated by cheap foreign products, then it is part of a national identity that has disappeared. This paradox in Mrs Thatcher's cultural policy is one of the most important and is extremely difficult to explain. The result was a decline in cultural production in the United Kingdom and large increases in profits for the American and Japanese cultural reproducers. Such was the situation of the British cultural system in general international terms by the end of the Thatcher years.

Notes

1. Margaret Thatcher, *The Downing Street Years* 873-882.
2. J. M. D. Schuster, *Supporting the Arts: An International Comparative Study* (Boston: Massachusetts Institute of Technology, 1986) 4.
3. D. V. Shaw et al (eds), *Cultural Economics 88: and American Perspective* (Akron: Association for Cultural Economics, 1989). Milton C. Cummings jr et al (eds), *The Patron State* (Oxford: Oxford University Press, 1987).
4. Figures in this paragraph originate from *Cultural Trends No 5* (London: PSI, 1990).
5. Whenever the symbol / is used as in 1982/3 this refers to the full financial year ending on March 31st.
6. Most of the figures in this section originate from *Cultural Trends No 5*.
7. Kulturstatistik, (Stockholm: Statistics Sweden, 1987) 193.
8. *Examiners' Report on National Cultural Policy in Sweden* (Strasbourg: Council of Europe, 1989) 27-28.
9. For more detailed figures consult *Cultural Trends No 5*.
10. J. M. D. Schuster, *Supporting the Arts* 45.
11. Hansard, 9 December 1985. Richard Luce's speech in the House of Commons.
12. S. Medlik, *Paying Guests* (London: Confederation of British Industry, 1985).
13. Robert Hewison, *Culture and Consensus* (London: Methuen, 1995) 277.
14. These figures are taken from John Myerscough *The Economic Importance of the Arts in Britain* (London: PSI, 1988).
15. Stephen Mennell, *Cultural Policy in Towns* (Strasbourg: Council of Europe, 1976).
16. ibid.

Chapter 3
Cultural History in Great Britain

A considerable amount of high quality research has been conducted on the high arts in the period before that covered by the current study. One can mention the excellent series The Cambridge Cultural History edited by Boris Ford that starts with Early and Medieval England and ends with Modern Britain. The role of aristocratic and upper middle-class patronage has been discussed in Janet Minihan's stimulating book The Nationalisation of Culture. What has, until recently, often been ignored is the role of popular culture. An examination of the debate concerning popular culture in the recent past will be useful in helping one understand how its often contradictory processes functioned during the Thatcher years. In fact, the cultural paradoxes of the 1980s can only be understood as the most recent in a long line of cultural conflicts and manoeuvres.

British culture between 1800 and 1850

Some time in the 1800-1850 period, there occurred some profound changes within British society. In 1800, the general cultural values and practices were still and to a great measure of rural origin. Although the development of London is a special case, in the countryside the local gentry closely supervised popular cultural forms such as holiday processions, wakes and fairs. The gentry would often finance and actively participate in this traditional popular culture. Indeed blood sports such as cock-fighting, dog-fighting and bear-baiting were very widespread. Alcohol in the form of cider and beer, made on a local basis by farmers, was distributed without charge as part of a paternalistic system involving duties and rights that had been defined over many centuries. In the later phase of the Industrial Revolution many people had moved to the new urban centres to work in the factories. By 1900, very few people still worked on the land. The key issue that must be dealt with is not necessarily the precise dates of these transformations, but an understanding of the nature and cultural consequences of these changes. Popular blood sports gradually became less cruel in a process of middle-class incorporation or assimilation and recreation, in general terms, became more commercial with the move to urban centres.

Two different interpretations of these events have been made concerning the cultural consequences of urbanisation. E. P. Thompson, on the one hand, adopted a bottom-up approach to British social history by describing a unique 'plebeian culture' that was produced during the transition from rural to urban living.[1] J. H. Plumb, on the other hand, using a great deal of evidence from London, adopted a top-down approach and stressed the democratisation of elite culture in the 19th century. He, therefore, stressed middle-class appropriation of elite or highbrow culture and the development of the cultural industries.[2] It would appear that both points of view have a certain validity but need to be situated at different times, places and levels.

E. P. Thompson examines plebeian culture in a basically rural 18th century. He cites examples of rude sports such as wrestling, cudgelling, football, quoits, bell-ringing, bear and badger-baiting or cock-fighting. These activities often occurred around the traditional hiring fairs and markets. Labourers were hired at these vitally important economic and cultural events. The local gentry patronised these events and provided free drink as part of their duties. These fairs and markets moved about the country in a traditional fashion and procured a sense of community for those participating in them. They were also used as temporary escape-valves, allowing people to forget the harsh nature of labouring life for a few days. Michael Bakhtin has studied the general significance of this carnivalesque escape-valve.[3] Plebeian activity was group centred and based on an anonymous crowd that on occasion got out of hand. These traditional forms of control and temporary release were slowly weakened by increased commercialism. Labourers began to be hired for the day and no longer received any goods or services in kind. They received money wages only. As early as the mid-18th century, Henry Fielding, as a magistrate, described the consequences of this process on law and order:

> But nothing hath wrought such an alteration in this order of people as the introduction of trade. This hath indeed given a new face to the whole nation, hath in great measure subverted the former state of affairs, and hath totally changed the manners, customs and habits of the people, more especially of the lower sort.[4]

In the same line of thought, J. H. Plumb considered the emergence of a commercial leisure industry in urban 19th century Britain, but ignored popular forms of recreation and culture. He observed the development of spa towns, race meetings, the expansion of periodicals and newspapers. The emerging middle classes stimulated the new cultural industries. Yet J. H. Plumb seems to have generalised when only using London evidence. Even before, Henry Fielding had already noticed in 1751: "What an immense variety of places has this town and its neighbourhood set apart for the amusement of the lowest order of the people."[5] One should not, however, forget that the commercial pleasure gardens charged entrance fees and thereby excluded the labouring classes.

Both J. H. Plumb's and E. P. Thompson's findings can be used to describe a transformation of popular culture during the 19th century. The traditional rural culture of the 18th century gradually disappeared due to a variety of social and economic pressures. The process of enclosing common land removed the physical spaces that were traditionally used for fairs and festivities. Blood sports, street football, fairs were all discouraged by a number of additional influences such as Methodism, temperance societies and local authority regulation. The town of Derby, for instance, tried to ban its yearly football match during the 1840s:

> The assembly of a lawless rabble, suspending business to the loss of the industrious; creating terror and alarm to the timid and peaceable, committing violence on the person and damage to the properties of the defenceless and the poor, and producing in those who play moral degradation and in many extreme poverty, injury to health, fractured limbs and (not infrequently) loss of life; rendering their homes desolate, their wives widowed and their children fatherless.[6]

The tradition in Stamford was to let a bull lose in the streets. The local authority's decision to ban this popular practice met with resistance and had to be enforced by a troop of dragoons. The traditional country fair often lasted for several whole days. The new need for factory discipline and regularity meant that long periods of absence were no longer acceptable to the owners. This discipline of the cities was then exported to rural areas such as the tin mines of South West England:

> Desperate wrestling matches, inhuman cock-fighting, pitched battles and riotous revellings, are happily of much rarer occurrence than heretofore; the spirit of sport has evaporated, and that of industry has supplied its place. The occupations in the mining countries fill up the time of these engaged in them too effectively to allow leisure for prolonged revels, or frequent festivities, in the other parts of Cornwall, the constant pursuits of steady labour have nearly banished the traditional seasons of vulgar riots and dissipation.[7]

In 1833, cruel sports were officially banned for the lower classes, but not for the middle and upper classes. Fox-hunting was allowed to continue as a national sport. In 1835, street football was declared illegal. This slow process of erosion of traditional recreational forms was confirmed when a 1842 parliamentary enquiry showed the disappearance of all holidays excepting Christmas Day and Good Friday. There is also evidence that in rural parts the gentry attempted to civilise popular cultural expressions. A. Howkins has provided a certain amount of information about rural Oxfordshire.[8] The Lord's Day Observance Society and the Temperance Movement were very active and interventionist in the towns and provided alternative attractions such as marches, bands and teetotal festivals. Sometimes these were timed to coincide with the more traditional forms and events and cultural confrontations were provoked. However, the rougher side of popular culture merely moved to other sites and activities. Moreover, those who tried to combat the roughness of popular culture were far from united. The Methodists wanted a total ban. The employers wanted to introduce civilised activities such as day trips on trains in order to keep the workers happy and occupied. It was hoped that the workers would return refreshed and revitalised. Trade unionists wanted civilising activities in order to educate and uplift the workforce, so that it might organise itself and transform society.

What should be stressed is that traditional popular culture became more commercial in the move to the towns and that it lost much of its original roughness. J. H. Plumb described the commercialisation of middle-class leisure in 18th century London. The same process was at work throughout all the classes of 19th century Britain. However, paternalistic attempts at incorporation encountered a certain amount of resistance. One can cite the example of football clubs that were based on religious groups breaking away and becoming independent, or again teetotal Working Men's Clubs that were a singular failure.

British culture in the 1850-1900 period

The trend of cultural commercialisation intensified during the second half of the 19th century. The growth of very large cities meant that a certain specialisation took place. Towards the end of the 19th century in cities such as Liverpool, Manchester, Birmingham, Glasgow and especially London, highbrow culture split away from its vulgar and popular equivalents. In the case of the theatre, until the late 19th century variety acts were often used to attract as many customers as possible. Bear-baiting and horse shows would be followed by madrigals and sonnet reciting in what were termed variety performances. A new commercial culture emerged with the growth of urban populations. Yet local authority support, when it did come, was given to the quality end of the cultural market. The period was also characterised by the steady growth of cultural industries such as newspapers and book production that began to cater for the middle classes thanks to the development of the railway system.

On the popular side, the case of the music halls is particularly significant. In 1848, the first official music hall was set up under the name of The Surrey in Westminster Bridge Road. This was the result of the 1843 Theatre Regulations Act that had freed the market from the old monopoly-type situation. The Lord Chamberlain licensed establishments either on the basis of a theatre with strolling salespeople or a music hall with seats and tables at which to eat. In practice the difference remained blurred. For example the East End theatres often ignored these rules. By 1860, there were thirty large music halls in the London area. By 1870, the Era Almanac listed thirty large halls in the central London area alone. At first these were places where one primarily ate and drank. In the latter part of the century the quality of the entertainment improved and became the major attraction. Theatres were left to cater for middle and upper-class audiences and food was removed from the actual theatre. The high point of music hall came in the 1890-1914 period when songs such as Polly Perkins of Paddington and Two Lovely Black Eyes became popular favourites. The artists also became famous: Marie Lloyd, Harry Champion, George Robey. The latter was even knighted.[9]

As in all cultural areas, official bodies exerted pressure to remove the coarse and rough side of popular culture, and local authority support, when it did come, was granted to the better quality establishments. In the 1880s, fixed seats were introduced in an effort to attract richer customers. Once the cheeky vulgarity of music hall had been removed in the early 20th century, this popular and commercial cultural form suffered a slow but regular decline. The 1912 Royal Variety Command performance marked a significant turning point. Music hall had reached its popular peak and received royal (and thus Establishment) approval. As a consequence, the star Marie Lloyd was not invited to perform because of her vulgarity and her loose way of life. By being incorporated into the officially approved cultural system music hall had lost its adversarial content. Its soul was also lost in the process. It was music hall's disrespect for authority that won it success. Once it had become respectable the creative elements of the lower classes moved to other areas of cultural production and consumption.

This ever-present desire to control, license and regulate, led to the closing down of traditional fairs that moved around London in the first half of the 19th century. In 1850, Bartholomew Fair was stopped. In 1859, the Vauxhall Gardens were closed. Justifications of public morality and decency were given. There were also commercial pressures and interests; fixed locations were of course easier to control than ever-moving fairs. To illustrate commercial pressures one can take the example of gin palaces that did well in London by proposing sumptuous settings. After the 1820 legislation that authorised the licensing of beer houses, competition came from the new Victorian pubs that were located along commuter lines. When gin palaces were closed they often were transformed into music halls and, later in the 20th century, into cinemas, ballrooms and bingo halls. One form of popular culture replaced another but at the same location. As with the theatres and music halls, pubs started to cater for different social categories. Different rooms created different atmospheres. Popular entertainment was conducted in these pubs that did very well after the 1830 Beer Act, designed to reduce gin consumption. One should note the very commercial nature of these popular forms of culture and the ever-present hand of the authorities that wanted to avoid free revelling and disorder.

Between the 1850s and 1870s, union members founded co-operatives and building societies. Thomas Cooper, an ex-Chartist, disapproved of the petit bourgeois tendency of certain members of the working class:

> Wherever you go now, you will hear well-dressed working men talking, as they walk with their hands in their pockets, of co-ops and their shares in them, or building societies. And you will see others, like idiots leading small greyhound dogs, covered with cloth, on a string! They are about to race, and they are betting money as they go.[10]

This would suggest that the traditional rough blood sports were being replaced by dog and horse racing. Popular interest had been forced away from bear-baiting to these, despite the hostility of Methodists and temperance societies.

The cultural industries took off during the second half of the 19th century. In 1855, Stamp duty was removed and in 1861, paper duties were abolished. A considerable brake on commercial culture was thereby removed:

> This day should henceforth be a red letter day in English calendars. This day the chief obstacle to the dissemination of knowledge among the people is renowned. This day the tax which was imposed with the direct object of putting fetters upon public writers who expose the abuses of government and of the governing classes [...] is swept away for ever.[11]

Magazines became popular as in the case of Tit Bits, founded by George Newnes in 1881. The steady increase in middle-class sales of newspapers continued. In 1896, Alfred Harmsworth launched the Daily Mail, the first mass circulation popular newspaper that showed the way for developments in the 20th century.

Of course, the cultural elitists were not satisfied with the cultural level of mass and popular products. They were quick to criticise the quality of railway literature in the mid 1850s: "On the assumption that persons of the better class who constitute the larger proportion of railway readers lose their accustomed taste the moment they enter the station."[12] By the end of the century the differentiation was very clear concerning novel reading. It is G. K. Chesterton (1874-1936) who insisted on the difference between high and low culture. George Gissing, however, both admired and hated cosmopolitan London. He analysed the new cultural developments: "Literature nowadays is a trade [...] our Grub Street of today is quite a different place: it is supplied with telegraphic communications, it knows what literary fare is in demand in every part of the world, its inhabitants are men of business".[13]

The development of a commercial and mass newspaper culture would not have been possible without improvements in education. The

1870 Education Act was a fundamental piece of legislation. It was an attempt by the state to define an officially approved national culture. Once again one encounters the desire to control and regulate content. It insisted on the 3 Rs, reading, writing and arithmetic and made school compulsory for boys up to ten in 1876, to eleven in 1893 and twelve in 1899. W. E. Forster (1819-1886), William Arnold's brother-in-law commented:

> civilised communities throughout the world are massing themselves together, each mass being measured by its force; and if we are to hold our position among men of our own race or among the nations of the world we must match up the smallness of our numbers by increasing the intellectual force of the individual".[14]

As for H. G. Wells, he was not so enthusiastic about the educational project, claiming that it was second-rate and used 'inferior teachers'. Whatever the quality, the result was a mass reading public that had to be satisfied by commercial cultural industries.

The Victorian state was keen to define the limits of popular culture. It was, however, rather mean in its financing of officially approved highbrow culture. Various remarkable individuals such as Henry Cole (1808-1882) and Lyon Playfair (1819-1898) set about democratising it. The former was in large part responsible for the Great Exhibition in 1851 and he also founded the South Kensington Museum. Cole used statistics to show that high arts were reaching more and more people. The Albert Hall was opened in 1871, and Penny Subscriptions were introduced in 1872 "to enable all classes to enjoy music".[15]

The Public Libraries Act of 1850 allowed town councils to finance public libraries. The 1849 Museums Act meant that museums might be financed too. Thus Birmingham, Liverpool, Leicester, Leeds, all opened museums in 1867, 1877, 1885 and 1888 respectively. The Recreations Grounds Act of 1852 allowed local authorities to set up middle-class parks to compensate for the loss of common land. A social historian, C. Ehrlich, has noted that English people at the turn of the century had ten times as many pianos as Americans and thirty times as many as Germans. Piano playing was very popular because of cheap lessons and cheap sheet music, this providing further evidence of the development of the cultural industries based on economies of scale.[16]

The Victorian state did not encourage the elitist arts with lavish state subsidies. It mostly tried to promote voluntary bodies. This was to inspire Mrs Thatcher's pronouncements during the 1980s. The Royal Academy of Music was, therefore, always underfunded after being founded in 1823. Another example of state meanness can be found in Henry Tate, who became so exasperated by the long negotiations for the financing of a gallery to house his paintings that he had it built himself. There was talk of a national theatre but it came into existence only one century later, in 1976.

An interesting example of both popular and highbrow culture and its smoothing out can be seen in the Welsh Eisteddfod. The usual pressures to transform rough content into more socially acceptable forms were put on the Welsh national festival. In 1860, alcohol was banned and in 1880, vulgar and popular demonstrations were excluded. In an attempt to offer an officially approved alternative to gambling, prizes were introduced. This added popular excitement to the proceedings. However, the use of English was forbidden at festivals in the 20th century and only Welsh was henceforth allowed. An exception was made for festivals in America and Australia. This is a good example of popular and highbrow culture co-existing in the interests of a minority national culture and was probably due to the rural nature of Welsh society. It is reminiscent of the variety acts that were performed in theatres in the early half of the 19th century.

The second half of the 19th century can be considered as a period when the mass cultural industries can really be said to have started their modern development. Highbrow arts were made available to an ever increasing number of middle-class people. Popular culture such as music hall was rendered safer and cleaner by public authority pressure. However, popular creativity also offered a certain amount of resistance and merely moved to other less controlled areas of expression. Victorian cultural policy can be considered as a desire to organise voluntary groups and give official support to a very few elite art forms. However, even commercial culture remained a minority taste.

There was no attempt to integrate the lower classes into middle-class or official culture. It was in the 20th century that technological progress brought a mass democratic culture to the commercial market.

British cultural history in the 1900-1945 period

This period can be characterised as one of continuing growth in the popular press and development in the cultural industries. While the elite end of the newspaper market did well because of the need for high quality advertising, the new cultural industries needed mass products and this tended to squeeze out highbrow content. Popular culture such as the showing of musicals and comedies in Odeon cinema chains flourished in the 1930s. Leisure and recreations for all classes expanded considerably throughout the period.

Popular culture developed steadily. Wages increased for the lower classes of society, despite periods of economic recession as in the 1930s. The pub remained the place where people could discuss social and political issues. Societies such as Odd Fellows and the Foresters organised discussions. Darts and dominoes became popular pub activities. However, during the First World War, opening hours were limited and these restrictions were maintained after 1919. In 1930, beer consumption actually fell.

As far as wireless or radio ownership is concerned, by 1939, there were nine million licences and nine out of ten homes had the new technology. Although radio programmes could not be described as popular, they did transmit late-night dance music from London hotels. Dance halls also did very well throughout this period. The most significant development of the first half of the 20th century was the arrival of talkie movies. Al Jolson's The Jazz Singer was the first film to have sound in 1927 and it sparked off the cinematic love affair that stretched through the 1930s, 1940s and 1950s. Old music halls were transformed into cinemas. Cheap seats could be had for one shilling and in 1937, twenty million seats were sold every week. The Hollywood dream factory produced mass and popular products that were distributed throughout the world. Mrs Thatcher mentions her sense of wonder when she would go every week to watch the films of the time: "I was entranced by the romantic world of Hollywood".[17] The styles and images portrayed were often used in personal lifestyle:

> Girls copy the fashions of their favourite film star. At the time of writing, girls in all classes of society wear 'Garbo' coats and wave their hair ... la Norma Shearer, or Lilian Harvey. It is impossible to measure the effect that films must have on the outlook and habits of the people.[...] Certainly today the cinema is par excellence the people's amusement.[18]

Outdoors, workers now had Saturdays off and took to bicycling and hiking. The Youth Hostel Association (YHA) was set up in 1930 and Butlin's first holiday camp opened in Skegness in 1939. Day excursions were still popular occasions. Motorcycles were also sold as the working-class equivalent of the middle-class car. Football stadiums were built and working-class football stars were cheered. Here is a classic example of middle-class incorporation. Street football was declared illegal in 1835 but a new cleaner version, stressing team spirit rather than individualism, was invented to replace it, using lower-class heroes. It was also played in very safe locations with a minimum amount of violence. i. e. in football stadiums. In a further popular development, by 1938, ten million people would fill in the football pools every week.

This period saw the arrival of mass entertainment for the lower classes and the continuous development of the Press. In the 19th century, culture had been the preserve of the middle classes in the form of newspapers and books. However, despite resistance from elitist elements of the middle classes, popular and mass culture were grudgingly accepted as part of life. The sacred Victorian work ethic was watered down in order to accept this new leisure industry and thereby generate mass profits from a mass market.

In 1851, newspapers had annual sales of 85 million. By 1920 this had risen to 5,604 million. Popular dailies were set up: the People in 1881, the Daily Mail in 1896, the Daily Express in 1900, the Daily Mirror in 1903. Most commentators agree that there was a certain deradicalisation of the Press. If popular dailies were to survive, they had to either achieve mass sales and therefore move towards the centre or find alternative funding sources. Thus the Daily Herald, in order to survive reduced sales, became the official organ of the Labour Party in 1921. In the 1880-1918 period, most of the current national daily and Sunday papers came into existence. Three categories were developed: mass, middle-market and specialised. Already, by 1925, one could make higher profits with a specialised product: "A very limited circulation, but entirely among the wealthy [...] may be more valuable than if the circulation were quadrupled."[19]

Another phenomenon was the depoliticisation of the national press under the influence of the press barons. In 1921, Lord Northcliffe owned The Times, the Daily Mail, the Weekly Dispatchand the London Evening News. Lord Rothermere ran the Daily Mirror, the Sunday Pictorial, the Daily Record, the Glasgow Evening News and the Sunday Mail. On top of these two press barons can be added Lords Camrose and Kemsley. By 1937, these four owners sold 13 million newspapers every day. The eccentric styles of the barons led to many stories. Beaverbrook was aloof, while Northcliffe meddled personally, sacking many of his employees. The increasingly commercial nature of newspaper production can be seen in the circulation wars that led to free gifts being given with subscriptions in the 1930s. In order to survive, newspapers had a choice of either specialising or increasing their circulation figures.

The main consequence of the control of these press barons is that newspapers could break away from political and establishment controls. The barons acted as independent pressure groups and organised the Anti-waste League or the Squandermania campaign in the 1920s. The development of market research also showed that the lower classes were considerable consumers and had to be taken into account.

The Press, cinema, radio and television, therefore, moved towards the mass market. Asa Briggs has written about a 'mass entertainment industry'.[20] However, both radio and later television, were highly controlled. Lord Reith (1889-1971) supervised the BBC in the inter-war years, giving it a distinctive and elitist character. He was a cultural elitist and believed in raising standards, even if this was unpopular. This gap between highbrow and lowbrow culture was temporarily bridged due to a unique national event: the Second World War. It was a total war in which all Britons had to take part. 300,000 civilians died in the bombings and many had to work in the factories or on the land. There was a strong sense of unified purpose that certain old people are still nostalgic about today. For these reasons a common culture evolved during the war years accepting both highbrow and lowbrow cultural expressions because they were British. The Entertainments National Service Association (ENSA, 1940-1945) proposed jazz concerts as well as opera productions for factory workers. This was a truly remarkable time due to an exceptional national emergency.

By the end of the Second World War, there were mass sales for the Press, a vigorous cinema industry and a highly controlled broadcasting system. Radio was split up into the Light Programme for the lower classes, the Home Service for middle-class audiences and the Third Programme for the upper classes. This was supposed to mirror Britain class divisions. The whole of the first half of the 20th century can be summed up as one of development among the cultural industries and increased commercialism. The second half is a period when highbrow culture was in retreat and where middlebrow culture was to triumph.

British cultural history in the 1945-1979 period

The postwar period is well documented and can be considered as one where the cultural industries flourished and started to compete one against the other. After the golden age of the cinema in the 1930s, 1940s and 1950s, it began to suffer from the competition of television in the 1960s and 1970s. The Press also suffered from reduced sales. The record business flourished by proposing low cost mass products that catered for many different tastes. In fact the example of the record business shows that the commercial and popular culture of the 1950s and 1960s was a democratic one. With rising affluence and increased leisure time citizens of all classes could participate as consumers in this popular culture. Mrs Thatcher, in the 1980s, was to promote this particular type of privatised, commercial cultural consumption.

One of the major cultural trends of the postwar period was that social stratification was increasingly based on cultural differences rather than economic ones. More leisure time and the growing numbers involved in service industries rather than manufacturing, meant that social identity tended to be expressed in how one spent one's leisure time rather than in work relations. Culture assumed a greater significance than previously and so did the necessity of government cultural policy.

The postwar period was one where the lower classes gained a certain degree of confidence. As everyone had participated in the war effort, everyone also wanted to benefit from the economic recovery. Clement Attlee's government set up the National Health Service (NHS) and the Welfare State. Various pieces of legislation such as the 1944 Education Act, the 1945 Family Allowances Act, the 1945 Distribution of Industries Act, the 1946 National Insurance Act, the 1947 Town and Country Planning Act, the 1948 National Health Service Act all helped to set up what became known as the Welfare State. Mrs Thatcher was to argue against this safety net, claiming that it led to inertia and a dependency culture.

There was also what can only be termed a leisure explosion. All cultural levels experienced significant development. Books, plays, photography and concerts, all became much more popular. In the 1960s, Independent Television (ITV) was held by many to become the people's television. Working-class youth split up into different tribes such as mods, rockers, greasers, rastafarians or skinheads. The case of the Sports Council is particularly significant. It was set up in 1965 and was supposed to encourage national competitiveness in international sports. This elite justification was quickly watered down and, by the end of the Wilson period, the official justification had been transformed into 'sport for all'. Therefore, between 1972 and 1978, the number of municipal sports centres had increased ten fold, from thirty to 350 and the number of indoor swimming pools had gone up from 500 to 850.[21] However, while the official discourse was sports for all, the policy mostly favoured middle-class white males. In this domain, Mrs Thatcher was to try and target specific groups in need rather than give blanket provision.

In the area of attitudes and values significant cultural changes and discussions took place. The 1960s were the decade where people discovered a consumer society. Gone were the days of rationing and restrictions. Goods were mass produced and then advertised in order to create a demand. The term 'keeping up with the Joneses' was used to describe a process of emulation that seemed to capture the spirit of the time. One had to have the same kind of car, house and garden as one's neighbour. The lower classes started to go on package holidays and became considered as an important segment of the market. However, along with consumerism came the so-called permissive society. During the 1960s, legislation was passed on the subjects of abortion, family planning, homosexuality and divorce laws. A certain amount of hypocrisy was taken out of official policy. However, Mary Whitehouse along with Malcolm Muggeridge and the supposed 'moral majority' fought a rearguard action against the mass media and television in particular. Mrs Thatcher was to side with the moral majority in this particular debate.

Another issue was that of woman's role in society. Women's liberation and feminism challenged the traditional patriarchal model. Germaine Greer wrote The Female Eunuch in 1960. The magazine Spare Rib highlighted certain problems such as the unjust salary differentials between men and women. Virago Press published books written by women. On this particular subject, though Mrs Thatcher sided more with tradition, she, as a woman must also have had a certain amount of sympathy towards some of the issues.

One of the important changes of the 1960s and 1970s, was the realisation that small was beautiful.[22] This was a reaction against the soulless systems of mass production and mass society and the resulting alienation. This attitude led to various movements such as alternative life-styles, or in other domains, the Campaign for Real Ale (CAMRA), organic farming, small craft industries. Later, Mrs Thatcher's economic views were not impervious to these arguments and she tried to encourage small businesses, realising that it was a good way of creating jobs with low overheads. This was an ideal instrument with which to fight the dependency relationship as regards the state.

The 1950s and 1960s were also a period when other cultures started to become visible in England. The Notting Hill riots of 1958 brought to the fore racial tensions. Discrimination was practiced in almost every area: education, jobs, housing. However, the various ethnic minority groups living in Great Britain were never really included in cultural policy and Mrs Thatcher continued this tradition. In fact, culture tended to move away from the public domain as represented in community activities and became more privatised and individualised.

Thus the cultural history of the last two centuries in Britain shows a continuous development of the significance of culture. Culture had become one of the most important elements of social stratification and for this reason lower- class cultural expressions were increasingly incorporated into more acceptable middle-class practices. Mrs Thatcher allowed the expansion of the cultural industries with all the implications that this has in the area of cultural democracy. New technology had and has allowed large sections of the lower classes to participate in cultural activities. However, this review of British cultural history shows that Mrs Thatcher's cultural policy was only the most recent expression of a cultural evolution that saw the dominance of the highbrow arts at the beginning of this century and their progressive decline in the postwar period.

Notes

1. E. P. Thompson, *The Making of the English Working Class* (London: Pelican, 1972).
2. J. H. Plumb et al, *The Birth of a Consumer Society. The Commercialisation of Eighteenth Century England* (London: Hutchinson, 1983).
3. Michael Bakhtin, *Rabelais and His World* (Cambridge: MIT Press, 1968).
4. Henry Fielding, *An Inquiry into the Causes of the Late Increase of Robbers etc.,* (1751) xi.
5. ibid., 9.
6. E. and S. Yeo (eds), *Popular Culture and Class Conflict 1590-1914* (London: Harvester, 1982) 90.
7. R. Burt (ed), *Industry and Society in the South West* (Exeter: Exeter University Press, 1970) 71.
8. E. and S. Yeo (eds), *Popular Culture and Class Conflict 1590-1914* 188-194.
9. For a full account see Gavin Weightman, *Bright Lights, Big City* (London: Collins and Brown, 1992).
10. Boris Ford (ed), *Victorian Britain* (Cambridge: Cambridge University Press, 1992) 6.
11. Boris Ford (ed), *Victorian Britain* 29.
12. ibid., 29.
13. ibid., 37.
14. Boris Ford (ed), *Victorian Britain* 35.
15. ibid., 31.
16. This is explained in Boris Ford (ed), *Victorian England* 31.
17. Margaret Thatcher, *The Path to Power* (London: Harper Collins, 1995) 14.
18. Eric Hopkins, A *Social History of the English Working Classes* (London: Hodder and Stoughton, 1992) 255.
19. James Curran, *Power Without Responsibility* (London: Routledge, 1991) 40.
20. Asa Briggs, *Mass Entertainment: the Origins of a Modern Industry* (Adelaide: Griffin Press, 1960).
21. *Sports Council Annual Report* (London: Sports Council,1983).
22. E. F. Schumacher *Small is Beautiful* (London: Sphere Books Limited, 1980).

Chapter 4
The Nature of Popular Culture

Popular culture and its implications are at the heart of Mrs Thatcher's cultural policies. She wished to privilege the commercial part of the cultural market, and yet there are many contradictory aspects that had unforeseen consequences in her endeavours.

Popular culture is a relatively recent area of study and has to reconcile two fundamentally contradictory functions. Firstly, the production and selling of cultural products in what are termed cultural industries that are organised on a commercial basis. Corporations spend large amounts of time, money and effort, trying to convince consumers that a product is worth having. It is a singularly risky business as no product is guaranteed mass sales. Mrs Thatcher had no trouble with this part of popular culture. Secondly, after the point of sale, one has to consider the way in which these cultural products are used. Is there in fact passive consumption as certain mass theorists, such as the Frankfurt School, suggest? Or is there a remarkable degree of creativity on the part of active consumers? Far from being passive, are not the lower classes in fact engaged in a permanent rejection and challenge of authority? Those who argue the former are the mass society theorists and some pessimistic democratic pluralists. Those who argue the latter are writers such as Mikhail Bakhtin, Michel de Certeau and Umberto Eco on the left and the optimistic pluralists in the centre ground. This is obviously a much more debatable aspect of Mrs Thatcher's action.

One can use the blue jean to illustrate the processes involved in popular culture. Large corporations produce and market their goods throughout the world market. The blue jean is a very popular cultural product that is sold all over the world, and yet it has different meanings in different settings. It is a popular cultural product because it is used on a symbolic level and does not have one fixed meaning. It is polysemic. Basic jeans are rugged, cheap, natural and are marketed as youthful and hard-wearing. Designer jeans are sexy, sophisticated and more expensive. Then there are faded denims that are supposed to show sympathy for the poor and the ragged. They can be associated with an apparent rejection of standard middle-class values. The fashion industry quickly produced pre-faded jeans in order to satisfy demand. This is yet another example of incorporation. A potentially subversive trend is integrated into mainstream fashion and therefore rendered inoffensive. Blue jeans are sometimes deliberately torn or slashed. This can be considered as a creative element on the part of some consumers: they fashion the product in their own personal way. This is sometimes referred to as excorporation, a process of rendering a product offensive and dangerous to the established social order. These 'Western' trousers have been used as symbols of revolt in the former Soviet Union and Iran. The blue jean is, therefore, a good popular cultural product that shows the double nature of the processes involved. Passive consumers can suddenly be seen to be creative and indeed subversive.

By encouraging middlebrow and popular tastes Mrs Thatcher also stimulated the commercial side of the market. At the same time, she unwittingly encouraged certain tendencies that were subversive. How these tendencies were combated will have to be considered.

The contradictions of popular culture

Popular culture can be observed from either the supply or the demand angles. On the supply side, production can be disrupted for various reasons such as bad industrial relations, weak technology or bad management. On the demand side, consumers can freely accept or reject a certain product. The basic commodities are industrial and therefore produced by a hierarchical system. No item can count on guaranteed success: it has to be massively approved of if it is to be a real success. Popular culture is, therefore, not imposed from above in a top-down process of manipulation. Crude hegemonic explanations cannot explain this phenomenon. It is a two-way process that is always volatile. Fashions change ever more quickly and may be resurrected after only a few years. De Certeau has emphasised the subversive nature of everyday life.[1] He has likened popular lifestyles to 'guerrilla warfare' against the dominant system. The weak can be considered to be mobile, flexible and constantly playing tricks on the system. The powerful are, by contrast, over-organised and lack imagination. This lack of flexibility leads to a certain degree of vulnerability.

John Fiske has illustrated the point by giving the example of young males in a shopping mall in Australia. They spend time in the place and occupy the space, but do not spend any money. It is a free spectacle for them. The representatives of the official system, the private security guards, try to discourage their presence there because of their negative effect on sales. Drinking alcohol on the premises is not allowed and alcohol is, therefore, sometimes put into soft drink cans but the young men may pretend to be drunk while actually having soft drink in their cans. They often gather in front of shop windows and prevent customers from seeing the goods. The gang also gives a feeling of insecurity to the regular customers. A game is played with the representatives of authority based on trickery and evasion. The groups are highly mobile and split up very quickly to regroup in another part of the building. These are techniques that are also often used by football hooligans. This strategy makes the life of the security guards difficult and stressful.[2]

The pleasures of popular culture can be split up into two sections. Firstly, the productive and creative side of making one's own culture. Secondly, the evasive and the offensive pleasures of resisting the structures of domination. Middle and upper class pleasures, by contrast, are both based on deferred gratification and self discipline. Evasion is often centred on the body. Mikhail Bakhtin and Roland Barthes both emphasised this aspect, giving the body a positive value while Kant and Schopenhauer had insisted on the opposite. Barthes distinguishes between two types of popular pleasures.[3] 'Jouissance' is a temporary loss of self identity and control. This can be seen when the reader of a book gets a sense of catharsis on finishing a book. Drugs and alcohol can also provide bliss and 'jouissance'. This loss of self identity can best be seen in popular wrestling where crowd behaviour dominates. Youth cultures have also insisted on ecstatic evasion. Acid House raves in the 1980s were organised around repetitive, loud music, drugs and alcohol. As in previous centuries, the modern version of popular culture can act as a threat to middle-class and established order.

Mikhail Bakhtin has a positive interpretation of bodily pleasures. His idea of the carnivalesque is that normal rules and controls are temporarily inverted and evaded. These temporary inversions provide physical pleasure in the communal and public domains. One can cite the rural English wakes and revels as historical examples of the carnivalesque. However, Bakhtin also insists on the fact that these temporary inversions are escape valves that allow the system to continue unaltered in the long term. He suggests that the carnival consists of laughter, excessiveness, bad taste, offensiveness and degradation: "Carnival celebrated temporary liberation from the prevailing truth from the established order: it marked the suspension of all hierarchical rank, privileges, norms and prohibitions."[4] Its aim was to "consecrate inventive freedom, to liberate the prevailing point of view of the world, from conventions and established truths, from cliches, from all that is humdrum and universally accepted."[5] The grotesque is then linked to an earthy realism and is opposed to the 'aesthetics of the beautiful'.

Bakhtin thus controverted the former views of Kant and Schopenhauer who both considered the body and its pleasures as inferior to those of the mind. For Kant, sensuousness is natural and consequently low. In this sense, art that appeals to the senses has to be considered as pleasant rather than beautiful. Schopenhauer also makes a similar distinction between the 'charming' and the 'sublime'.[6]

If one turns to the world of the music hall, the first group of theorists would have considered it as an evasion where middle class rules were rejected. Bakhtin would have seen the carnivalesque in bodily excess and temporary inversions of authority. By contrast the two German philosophers would have seen music hall as quaint and vulgar.

For them the sublime could only be found in high art forms. Thus popular art forms have been and still are liable to two absolutely contradictory assessments. In a way the debate between the cultural elitists and what would now be classified as the culturalist approach assumes the same importance as the former confrontation between the ancients and the moderns.

Bodily Controls

According to certain views of traditional Christianity the body has always been dangerous and potentially sinful. The soul has always been under threat from sensuousness. Michel Foucault has insisted on the fact that the body has long been the site of a struggle for social control. Upper and middle class bodies are clean and unthreatening. In this, Mrs Thatcher was very much in line with tradition. She used the phrase: "cleanliness is next to godliness" in the LBC interview on page 11. By contrast, the lower class body is considered to be dirty and threatening, even if many suggest that excessive bodily pleasure, as seen in carnival type behaviour, is a strategy of containment that allows the system to continue. Popular culture is often accused of being bad for the mind and body. To give just one example: soap operas were considered by a doctor in the United States to have a bad influence on normal people. "In March 1942, a New York psychiatrist, Louis Berg, told the Buffalo Advertising Club that listening to soap operas caused acute anxiety state, tachycordia, arrhymias, increases in blood pressure, profuse perspiration, tremors, vasomotor instability, nocturnal frights, vertigo and gastrointestinal disturbances."[7]

Throughout the 19th century, public authorities tried to exercise control over excessive bodily pleasures. Many warned against portraying bodily pleasures in popular culture. The whole history of popular culture is one of challenge or excorporation and gradual incorporation or assimilation by the powers that be.

Some examples of popular culture

In 1984, Janice Radway conducted a study on housewives and the kind of books they read. She found that the typical book was one that their husband would disapprove of. The housewives tended to read evasively, favouring books whose overall values were anti-patriarchal. The readers were found to empower themselves by rejecting patriarchal power.[8]

Another example can be observed in Michaels' study of Rambo.[9] He found that this film was very popular among aborigines in Australia. These aborigines read the text in an oppositional fashion siding with Rambo in a primitive and successful struggle against the whole of modern white society. It seems strange that President Reagan, as a representative of institutional authority should also have enjoyed the film for its active individualism. This is one of the characteristic strengths of popular cultural texts. They can be read in different ways. They can empower, be oppositional and also strengthen the social order.

The Madonna phenomenon is yet another example of popular culture. The artist's songs and shows can be considered in various ways. Many feminists see her provocative behaviour as a way of reinforcing patriarchal values. She is just another 'sexploiter'. Indeed many males derive a great deal of voyeuristic pleasure when they see Madonna's clips and performances. On the other hand a certain number of young girls gain a sense of power and independence from these same clips because according to them, Madonna parodies and criticises patriarchal values and therefore criticises them. Part of the public therefore remains at the surface level, while another enjoys the sensuous and hidden side of her clips and appreciates the oppositional nature of Madonna's work. In this way the star can satisfy large and diverse sections of the pop music market.

These examples show that popular cultural products are those that are consumed in a mass way but tend to gain critical disapproval. They often use oral rather than literary language. They are not bothered with language and correctness. Popular culture is usually excessive and parodic: it is vulgar and obvious and because of this its effects appear to be out of control. The popular Press, using cliches and puns challenge the common sense of dominant explanations. Another aspect of popular culture is repetition and seriality. The texts are not finished objects that are to be consumed in their entirety. They can be used again and again and can be 'nibbled' from time to time. Popular serials can be seen occasionally. The serial form was invented by the Victorians and the technique is currently widespread in television work.

To sum up:

> "Bourgeois tastes are contrasted with popular tastes not only in terms of their valorisation of distance and absolutes, but also in their absence of fun and a sense of community. Participation brings with it the pleasures of revelry and festivity, of self-expression and the expression and experience of solidarity with others."[10]

Folk culture

Popular culture can be contrasted with traditional folk culture. The former is the product of an industrialised society. The latter is the result of a stable traditional social order. G. Seal has listed four characteristics of folk culture:

> 1. Folklore defines membership of a particular group with regard to other groups. Folklore is a group experience rather than a privatised one. Popular culture is very different in this respect;
> 2. Folk culture is transmitted orally and informally. There is no clear difference between transmitter and receiver;
> 3. Folklore operates outside the Establishment of the Church or the education system;
> 4. There are no standardised versions of sacred texts.[11]

Folklore and pop cultures are the cultures of the middle and lower classes. Both experienced growth during the 1980s. If we take the example of the 'gay community', folk music often provided a meeting point for this culturally diverse group. This folk music expression has sometimes been turned into a popular product as in the case of the pop group Village People. It encouraged a feeling of community that came in reaction to globalisation and despite Mrs Thatcher's encouragement of purely commercial culture. This trend and evolution continued during the Thatcher years. Her promotion of purely commercial culture was only one force amongst many others which were left unchanged if not exacerbated by reaction and refusal.

Sport

While the process of incorporation has been ever-present in sport, there has also been a certain amount of resistance. Popular games such as football, cricket and rugby have been the site of a struggle for control and redefinition. Middle-class institutions removed the uncontrolled carnivalesque aspects of sport during the 19th century and introduced the idea of Queensbury rules and gentlemanly conduct. Team spirit was encouraged as opposed to individual activity.

By contrast, wrestling, seems to have avoided such incorporation, still remaining firmly in the popular carnival world and is often given as an example of genuine popular culture. As in any carnival activity the normal rules are ignored and subverted. Wrestling is a parody of sport. The referee is often challenged, disregarded or even attacked. The distance between audience and participant is very small, and spectators are often involved in the fighting. The wrestlers occasionally ignore the limits of the ring. Theirs' are the contrary of the 'aesthetics of the beautiful'. Their performances often parody normal social relations and swearing, that is often termed billingsgate, is ever present. This would appear to be one of the few popular cultural activities that continued despite the opinion of Mrs Thatcher and any other politicians. Another popular activity is the white knuckle rides in various fair grounds. They provoke a loss of self and a 'jouissance'. Everyone is reduced to being a mere body that is flung around. Hierarchy is suspended: one no longer exists as a stockbroker, a teacher or a student.

All of these are classic forms of popular culture in the domain of sporting activities. Of course Mrs Thatcher, along with the vast majority of the middle classes, discouraged the oppositional character of such activities as can be seen in the case of football hooligans or the smashing of instruments and seating in pop concerts. However, despite her efforts, the anarchy and latent violence in popular culture survived.

The debate concerning popular culture clearly places Mrs Thatcher in the cultural pluralist camp. Her ideas on culture were based on free market economics and the development of private consumption with individual consumers spending as they wished. On the content side, this meant an emphasis on middlebrow tastes because highbrow arts and lowbrow cultural products tend to attract fewer people and lower profits. However, there were also many unforeseen subversive reactions to this official support of commercial popular culture. All in all, one is inclined to think that the prime minister encouraged commercial culture so that the state might gradually disengage itself from the process of subsidy. Parts Two and Three of the research will measure to what extent Mrs Thatcher actually did reduce British state subsidy in the cultural field and the means she used to expand the cultural industries.

Notes

1. Michel de Certeau, *L'invention du quotidien* (Paris: 10 18, 1980).
2. John Fiske, *Understanding Popular Culture* (London: Routledge,1994)37-41.
3. Roland Barthes, *The Pleasure of the Text* (New York: Hill and Wang,1975).
4. Mikhail Bakhtin, *Rabelais and his World* 10.
5. ibid., 34.
6. *Chambers Bibliographical Dictionary* (Edinburgh: Chambers, 1990) 1193.
7. R. Allen, *Speaking of Soap Operas* (Chapel Hill: University of North Carolina Press, 1985).
8. J. Radway, *Reading the Romance: Feminism and the Representation of Women in Popular Culture* (Chapel Hill: University of North Carolina, 1984).
9. E. Michaels, *Aboriginal Content*. Paper presented at the Australian Screen Studies Association, Sydney, December 1986.
10. John Fiske, *Understanding Popular Culture* 141.
11. G. Seal, *Play*. Paper presented at the Gender and Television Group, Perth, 1986.

Chapter 5
The Role of the State - The debate prior to Mrs Thatcher

English monarchs and aristocrats have always been major patrons of the arts and theirs would have been a total monopoly but for the influence of the Church of England and the commercial classes. As the aristocrats gradually lost their financial predominance during the 19th century, the upper-middle classes took over. In fact a mass market developed catering first for the middle classes and later for more and more of the lower classes. This mass cultural market began to develop at first through the newspaper and book industries and then through the entertainment business. After the Second World War, the state gradually took over the patronage of the high arts as private individuals disengaged themselves from the process. In such circumstances, during the 1940s and 1950s, a broad consensus could be observed around the idea of saving the 'jewels' of a mostly English national identity and it was very rarely challenged. Thus, until 1979 and Mrs Thatcher's coming to power, postwar cultural policy can be seen as the preservation of elitist national cultural identity and one of democratising highbrow cultural forms.

Cultural production and consumption before the 20th century

The distinction between popular and high culture already existed in 16th century England when William Shakespeare wrote and performed his plays. Bear pits were used for performances of Shakespeare's drama. Tragedy or comedy would follow bear-baiting or cock-fighting on the same premises and this for an audience which can be said to have been the same. Up until the second half of the 19th century one can talk of a national culture in which both popular and elite forms were often expressed in the same physical setting. It is in the latter half of the 19th century that the physical separation of popular culture and the high arts took place and the two domains became more and more autonomous.

In the second half of the 19th century (as described in Chapter 4) various pieces of legislation were passed that tried to control the subversive nature of popular culture. It was argued that pubs and inns led to rowdy behaviour and revelry. Fairs encouraged promiscuity and attracted people away from the churches. It is for these reasons that the Fairs Act of 1871 was introduced, regulating the opening hours of fairs. The 1870 Education Act defined an officially approved and safe culture of national writers. This legislation is vital in defining the emergence of a national culture in the 20th century. There was during the whole of the 19th century an acrimonious debate over whether the urban masses should be educated. Some in the middle classes argued that education would produce model citizens, while others suggested that revolutionary ideas might result. This particular debate has a familiar ring to it as it announces the different points of view of the Marxists with their definition of false consciousness and cultural hegemony and the optimistic pluralists who believed in ever improving cultural levels. The 1888 and 1894 Local Government Acts gave local authorities the powers to build theatres, reading rooms, museums and libraries.

Paul Di Maggio's hypothesis, that the division in cultural production was possible because of a new kind of organisation, reflects the importance of late 19th century legislation. Urban concentration and new technology produced a commercial popular culture industry. In contrast to this development, the growth of the big industrial cities also led to a new private or semi-private, non-profit type of cultural institution, based on corporations and trustees. Di Maggio maintains that towards the end of the 19th century, Boston's industrial entrepreneurs established cultural corporations which were to cater exclusively for the upper classes. Prestige came from these socially-exclusive events as defined by Bourdieu. Between 1870 and 1900 the physical settings of high and popular culture became separate. Buildings became specialised in one or the other cultural forms and civic pride was used as a standard justification:

> The broad charters of Boston's major cultural organisations permitted their missions to be redefined with time, and enabled their governors to claim (and to believe) that they pursued communitarian goals even as they institutionalised a view and vision of art that made elite culture less and less accessible to the vast majority of Boston's citizens.[1]

By the end of the 19th century, the two cultures in Great Britain had also been separated. On the one hand could be found serious, government approved culture such as museums, libraries and theatres. On the other hand was to be found all forms of popular culture that were considered subversive; the music halls, pubs and fairs. Henceforth the authorities would stress the negative aspects of popular culture, claiming that pubs and the like led to boisterous behaviour and the breakdown of law and order. Such views were widespread and introduced an implicit agenda into cultural policy which was never fully debated. Thus did popular or lowbrow culture become a threat to officially approved highbrow culture.

New technology and interventionism in the inter-war period

The state became more directly involved in cultural policy during the inter-war period and especially in the postwar years. The high or performing arts in Great Britain adopted an increasingly defensive posture towards the evident success of popular culture. Newspapers, photography, radio, television, video, records, all in turn revolutionised cultural consumption, which became increasingly personal and individual rather than community-based. The 'noble' arts, as a result, turned to being more restricted and more elitist. Consequently, arts auditoria have been built on a smaller scale in recent years, and are now often multi-functional, being used for ballet, concerts, as well as plays.

Gradually, central government was pulled into cultural provision. The setting up of the British Broadcasting Corporation (BBC), in 1922, meant that the state had a formidable tool for educating citizens away from the extremes of communism in the 1920s and fascism in the 1930s. The British Council started its activities in the 1930s, playing a crucial role in promoting a positive image of the United Kingdom while criticising extremist propaganda. During the Second World War, the government again felt forced to intervene to boost the morale of British troops in the fight against Hitler's Germany. The Entertainment National Service Association (ENSA) was set up to provide entertainment of all sorts, mixing all cultural forms. State intervention was no longer considered a dirty word and it actually became a duty in the fight against the Nazi regime. Token admission fees were charged for cultural activities in barracks and factories. In this way popular culture was officially encouraged. Another organisation was set up, the Committee for the Encouragement of Music and the Arts (CEMA), to prevent cultural deprivation on the home front.[2] The first director of CEMA was John (later Lord) Maynard Keynes, the economist, who made sure that it concentrated on classical music, drama and the visual arts.

The birth of the Arts Council and a cultural consensus

From the seeds of CEMA was born the Arts Council of Great Britain in 1946. The more popular ENSA was ignored once the emergency of the war years had receded. One can now state that the exceptional circumstances that had united the two cultures no longer applied to postwar Britain and the elitist definition retook its dominant position. In the same year, the Royal Charter was introduced and its main objectives were:

> to develop and improve the knowledge, understanding, and practice of the fine arts, to increase the accessibility of the arts to the public throughout Great Britain; and to advise and cooperate with government departments, local authorities and other bodies on any matters concerned whether directly or indirectly with the foregoing objects.[3]

The advice contained in the Charter was supposed to colour all the actions of the future Arts Council of Great Britain. Keynes commented:

> I do not believe it is yet realised what an important thing has happened. State patronage of the arts has crept in. It has happened in a very English, informal, unostentatious way; half-baked if you like.[4]

Hence, the Arts Council turned out to be a small club of like-minded friends who wanted to save everything that they personally considered to be the best of a mostly English highbrow culture, which could not survive the pressures of the market-place. In this effort the influence of the elitist theorists such as Matthew Arnold and T. S. Eliot can be clearly detected. The national companies and the Royal Opera House (ROH) especially have always dominated discussions at the Arts Council since its inception. After the Second World War the Royal Opera House (ROH), the Royal Shakespeare Company (RSC) and the English National Opera (ENO) all started to receive grants because they were structurally unprofitable and losing money. Successive governments, whether Conservative or Labour, never talked in these terms but defended subsidy by calling these English institutions 'flagships of excellence' which acted as cultural ambassadors abroad. One can note the nautical reference contained in the term. The sense of national pride mirrors the local authority justification of civic pride to subsidise elitist cultural practices. In fact, there has always been a hidden cultural agenda which has remained implicit. The present day consequences of this restricted definition of the arts is that the Arts Council, on average spends around 40 per cent of its budget on the national companies and around 80 per cent on music and drama alone. This has led to excellent cultural provision in the capital for a lucky minority of tourists and Londoners. The crucial second part of the Royal Charter dealing with accessibility to all members of the British public has simply not been dealt with.

In its original form, the Arts Council was supposed to be an arm's length distributor of funds in the cultural field. Originally, its members were appointed by the Chancellor of the Exchequer. In 1967, the Royal

Charter was slightly modified and the members and the chairman were appointed by the Secretary of State for Education and Science, after consultation with the Secretaries of State for Scotland and Wales. In its present form, the secretary-general is chosen by the Council with the approval of the Secretary of State. Various unpaid panels assist the Council in certain specific areas such as music, art, drama and literature. The arm's length principle was designed to avoid having state approved art. In reality, whenever the Arts Council gives a subsidy, whether big or small, it also gives an official stamp of approval, which in turn generates further funds for the organisations concerned. As a consequence, the Arts Council wields infinitely more power than at first meets the eye and it is a good example of the symbolic power that exists at the heart of all cultural affairs.

Another drawback of this organisation is lack of accountability. Secretaries of State in practice issue a blank cheque to the Arts Council, which then distributes the money on the basis of often secret criteria. On the one hand, this allows a certain independence in the determination of quality, but on the other hand, problems arise over who is responsible for a particular situation.

During the 1950s, the regional offices which had tried to encourage cultural activity in the provinces were closed down. Excellence became the new priority and the task of providing cultural experiences for all was forgotten. The Royal Charter was only half applied: This is in marked contrast with Andr, Malraux's idea of bringing culture to the people, but it nevertheless became official Arts Council policy as:

> the Arts Council believes then, that the first claim upon its attention is that of maintaining in London and the larger cities effective powerhouses of opera, music, and drama, for unless these quality institutions can be maintained, the arts are bound to decline into mediocrity.[5]

The secretary-generals, E. N. Williams and Kenneth (later Lord) Clark in the 1950s and 1960s argued for centres of excellence. Kenneth Clark admitted that "the poet and the artist are important precisely because they are not average men; because in sensibility, intelligence and power of invention they far exceed the average".[6] E. N. Williams at first insisted on 'few but roses' before wanting to 'raise and spread' arts provision. The Arts Council, therefore, developed into a reactive organisation, acting in a piecemeal way to demands on an individual basis: there seemed to be no long-term aim. The 'club' would bail out the bastions of national culture that found the market-place too competitive. In the postwar period, up until 1979 and the first Thatcher election victory, there was a remarkable continuity in the cultural patronage of the state. Relatively small amounts of money, but possessing a totally disproportionate amount of symbolic value, were distributed by establishment administrators, such as Lord Goodman in the 1960s or Sir Roy Shaw in the late 1970s. Elitist English culture was propped up, and because the funds were limited, ethnic and minority art, new art forms and popular culture were totally excluded. The second part of the Royal Charter was definitely not a priority for the Arts Council. These implicit policies empowered the upper strata of English society to act in national cultural affairs using the idea of national pride as a justification, while disenfranchising and disapproving of the lower strata. Thus did the cultural Establishment define what postwar cultural policy should be while politicians kept a low profile on the issue.

The only potential challenge to this cosy consensus on highbrow cultural subsidy and democratising elitist forms came in 1965, with Labour's A Policy for the Arts. Jennie Lee became Minister for the Arts and announced her aim to "bring the best of the arts within reach of a wider public". In the meantime, the organisations were to keep a "jealous regard for the maintenance of high standards".[7] The amount of money devoted to the arts was trebled under the Labour Wilson government but the spending criteria remained the same. Highbrow culture was to become available to the man in the street. Many local authorities built theatres, which of course attracted middle-class audiences: it is known as a 'bricks and mortar' approach to cultural policy. The modern equivalent of the music hall was not proposed to lower class audiences.

In the end it was left to the private sector to bring a 'cultural revolution' by marketing the Beatles and Carnaby Street. During this period the Arts Council continued to sell its highbrow wares to a cultural elite while officially proclaiming that it was trying to reach every citizen. The Labour Party missed an opportunity of bringing cultural democracy to the average citizen, not realising that different policy options were actually possible. In fact elitist culture could have been popularised by showing it on television, as has been seen in recent years with opera or ballet for example. The arts could have been brought to the factories as was done during the Second World War. Theatre could have equally been performed in the street. These three points are examples of the democratisation of culture, which is what the Labour government vaguely hoped to do but did not. An even more radical proposition would have been the encouragement of cultural democracy in which everybody would have been able to express himself or herself at different cultural levels.

The case for increased subsidies

During the 1960s, economic pressures developed that put strains on labour intensive arts organisations. At a time of increasingly automated production, theatres, for example, could not replace actors with mechanised robots or cheap labour as in car factories. It was argued that mass production techniques could not be introduced into theatres which demanded high manning levels. Trade unions also dragged their feet over productivity rates and these restrictive practices led to Tony Richardson, an outstanding film director, refusing to shoot films in Great Britain. Two American economists, W. J. Baumol and W. G. Bowen, argued that these economic trends inevitably led to a reduction in arts production, because of the inherently labour intensive nature of arts provision. According to the Baumol and Bowen thesis, arts organisations had certain fixed costs and economies of scale could not be achieved. It was difficult to cater for large increases in demand without having to build a larger theatre for example, thus involving very high costs. They also argued that increased ticket prices led to audience size reductions. The only solution was for the state to step in and subsidise the loss-making operations as a socially responsible response.[8] The Baumol and Bowen thesis was widely used as a justification for state intervention in arts activities in the 1960s and 1970s and as a major reason for the setting up of the National Endowment for the Arts (NEA) in 1965, the equivalent of the Arts Council in the United States. Yet many analysts have since criticised the theory for being simplistic. In a nutshell, consumers can cope with increased ticket prices and private sources of funding can also perform the proposed job of the state in subsidising arts enterprises.[9] It is also argued that new technology can be used to improve productivity and reduce labour costs. Counterclaims suggested that state subsidy can lead to inefficiency and a smug attitude which does not sufficiently take into account the tastes of the audiences. Further, it must be pointed out that the evidence used by Baumol and Bowen applied to a comparison between manufacturing industry and arts organisations. Other service industries were not considered. The evidence was based on orchestra costs in the United States and thereby excluded theatres and museums. Lastly, this theory could only have worked in a period of low inflation, which was certainly not the case in Great Britain during the 1970s. So it appears that the theory was seriously flawed and only served to support the top-down policy favoured by the governments of the period.

The case for efficient subsidies

It was left to the American, Richard Netzer, to construct a coherent theory that contradicted many of the Baumol and Bowen claims.[10] He argued that artistic creation needs change to stay dynamic and that subsidy leads to a protection of the status quo. Bureaucracy causes a lack of accountability both to the state and to arts consumers and the inevitable result is inefficiency and complacency. Netzer collected evidence in the United States showing that a 10 per cent rise in ticket prices in the performing arts led to a mere 2.5 per cent fall in audience levels. He also argued that demand might be stimulated by improving educational levels, or showing arts products on television which is a much cheaper way of popularising culture than subsidising a large number of companies. Netzer's views coincide with Pierre Bourdieu's idea of the distribution of cultural capital through the education system and he added that increased income did not necessarily lead to increased consumption of cultural services and products. In reality cultural demand is stimulated by educational level. He was particularly critical of subsidised art and what has been termed the New Class, a group of bureaucrats and artists who have supposedly got rich on state subsidies.

State help has several additional undesirable side-effects. Subsidising ticket prices merely provides money for the entertainment of high income groups. Subsidy often leads to a 'bricks and mortar' approach, where buildings are constructed rather than spending on arts activities and companies. Moreover, state financing means a seal of approval to certain companies and certain activities, with a similar implicit disapproval of other companies, thus causing a lot of bitterness and a sense of injustice. The solution that Netzer proposes is to find an optimum level, based on maximum efficiency. Museums or theatre companies have to calculate various cost levels to determine how much is needed. Grants to individual artists have also been suggested, as has the idea of once-off subsidies. All these ideas seemed valid in the 1980s when monetarism became fashionable, but the findings of the Priestley Committee, which were made public in 1983, showed that underfunding was in fact the rule in Great Britain and that the objective of maximum efficiency and an optimum level were both a long way off in many publicly funded cultural organisations.[11]

Perhaps the clearest economic commentary on the arts came from C. D. Throsby and J. D. Withers.[12] They argued that there is an 'income gap' in arts organisations, that can be combated by increasing the demand and by reducing costs. Two justifications were proposed for public subsidy. Firstly, the government is responsible for the enhancement of a nation's cultural life, this being called the 'merit good' argument. Secondly, the government can intervene 'temporarily' in the pursuit of market efficiency, this being called the 'externality' argument. If state subsidy is necessary, then the government has a duty to be explicit in its criteria for intervention in the market, explaining what is meant by national identity, the pursuit of excellence, the idea of democratising the arts or the role of education in creating future cultural demand among the generations to come. Decisions have to be justified and governments accountable. In Great Britain during the 1980s, these ideas fell on deaf ears, because there was no public debate over cultural policy in general and arts policy in particular. In theory, the great Thatcher project was to save public money and to look for greater efficiency. In fact, a secret style of policy making was maintained and state spending on cultural affairs increased in the absence of either public debate or official justification.

Two Labour Ministers for the Arts before 1979

Hugh Jenkins, a former Equity official and founder of the Theatre Advisory Council in 1962, became Minister of Arts and Libraries under Labour in the 1974-76 period, proposing some radical measures such as a Wealth Tax and a Public Lending Right (PLR). He also argued for greater accountability and democracy within the Arts Council. The Labour party election manifesto had mentioned all these proposals[13] and yet none of them were voted through Parliament because of the small Labour majorities at the time. The Labour party simply could not gain enough support for innovative measures such as a Wealth Tax, and the Public Lending Right had to wait for Mrs Thatcher's term of office. Cultural policy was low down on the political priority list before Mrs Thatcher came to power.[14] However, Hugh Jenkins did manage to appoint a few of his allies onto the Arts Council such as Raymond Williams and Richard Hoggart.

The next Labour Arts Minister was the discreet Lord Donaldson, who in 1977 declared to the House of Lords:

> As a member, however humble, of this government, I do not feel that I can
> quarrel with my leaders, so long as they maintain and do not decrease
> Government support for the arts.[15]

Lord Donaldson was a low profile junior minister who did not rock the
boat and brought no change to the official cultural system, thus
strengthening the cultural status quo or Establishment.

The administration of the arts in 1979

In 1979, roughly half the money spent by the state on cultural
affairs was spent by local authorities. No statutory obligation was
imposed on these local authorities, so cultural provision varied greatly
from one area to another, this representing a devolved policy.
Metropolitan areas spent much more than county councils. Table 6.1
(on page 418) describes the administrative structure and gives the
names of the Arts Ministers, the chairmen and secretary-generals of the
Arts Council since 1970. Broadcasting and the Press came under the
Home Office, the British Council under the Foreign Office (FO),
architecture under the Department of the Environment (DoE). Crafts
was the business of the Crafts Council, design that of the Design
Council and films that of the British Film Institute (BFI). The Arts
Minister got what was left: public libraries, national museums, classical
music, opera, theatre, dance, literature and art. He had limited powers, a
small budget, half of which was spent by the Arts Council. In 1979, the
Arts Minister was, however, given full minister status within the
cabinet, but when the Conservatives came to power Norman (later
Lord) St. John Stevas, a so-called 'wet' because of his moderate
political opinions, took on the function and announced what was to
come:

> The arts world must come to terms with the fact that government policy in
> general has decisively tilted away from the expansion of the public to the private
> sector. The government fully intends to honour its pledges to maintain public
> support for the arts as a major feature of policy, but we look to the private
> sphere to meet any shortfall and to provide immediate means of increase.[16]

There was a certain amount of turbulence in the early 1980s and early 1990s. St. John Stevas and Paul Channon did not stay in office very long and the same applied to David Mellor who was forced to resign for personal reasons and Peter Brooke who had a bad media profile.

Mrs Thatcher, as prime minister, was certainly aware of the economic issues involved in the cultural debate. The fact was that state funding levels were already very low when she came to head her first Conservative government and only marginal reductions could be made. Inflation in the 1970s had forced companies to become more efficient and move towards the optimum efficiency position that Richard Netzer had discussed. A large proportion of public funds was spent on the London based 'flagships of excellence', that attracted large numbers of foreign tourists. Reductions in this area could be a dangerous exercise for politicians, as Mrs Thatcher was only too aware. She probably remembered her time as Education Secretary in the Heath government when she was almost forced to resign over her removal of free school milk in primary schools in 1970.

In the period before 1979, one may say that all in all, there was no public debate about cultural policy. Arts policy up to the arrival of Mrs Thatcher can be summed up as a minimalist and elitist arts subsidy based on implicit value judgements. Broadcasting, by contrast, was treated in a different way with a mix of private and public monies accompanied by tight government controls. Nevertheless, as soon as Mrs Thatcher became prime minister she sent a clear message to the public by stating that she wanted to roll back the state, which had obvious implications for cultural policy. This public statement was intended to launch a public debate that never occurred. On the one hand the prime minister announced the reduction of state subsidies on culture. On the other hand she had to defend Britain's national identity in an increasingly world-oriented cultural market. There was thus an incompatibility between two of her policy aims, the second having to prevail in the last analysis.

Notes

1. Paul Di Maggio, "Cultural Entrepreneurship in 19th century Boston" in Richard Collins (ed), *Media, Culture and Society* (London: Sage, 1986) 200.
2. A list of the aims of CEMA is to be found in John Pick, *The State and the Arts* (London: City Arts, 1980) 10.
3. ibid., 3.
4. Richard Netzer, *The Subsidised Muse* (New York: CUP, 1977) 197.
5. John Pick, *Managing the Arts? The British Experience* (London: Rhinegold, 1986) 22.
6. Roy Shaw, *The Arts and the People* (London: Jonathan Cape, 1987) 88.
7. Robert Hutchison,*The Politics of the Arts Council* (London: Sinclair Brown, 1981) 60.
8. W. J. Baumol, W. G. Bowen, "The Future of the Theatre and the Cost Disease of the Arts" in M. Hendon, J. Richardson, W. Hendon (eds), *Bach and the Box* (Akron: Association for Cultural Economics, 1985).
9. Mulcahy and Swain, *Public Policy and the Arts* (Colorado: Boulder, 1982).
10. Richard Netzer, *The Subsidised Muse* . This book is very critical of indiscriminate subsidies.
11. *The Financial Scrutiny of the Royal Opera House Covent Garden and the Royal Shakespeare Company*, Cabinet Office, 1983.
12. C. D. Throsby and J. D. Withers, *The Economics of the Performing Arts* (New York: St Martin's Press, 1979).
13. See the Labour Party manifesto for 1974 and particularly the 1977 The Arts and the People that wanted the abolition of the Arts Council.
14. For a full account of this period consult Hugh Jenkins, *The Culture Gap* (London: Marion Boyars, 1979).
15. *Hansard,*10 February 1977.
16. Roy Shaw, *The Arts and the People* 40.

Chapter 6
Mrs Thatcher - a Sociological Assessment

Two versions of what Mrs Thatcher represented from the cultural point of view were circulated during the 1980s. Members of the cultural Establishment claimed that she was and still is a Philistine who wanted to cut spending levels on everything from education to national heritage. Furthermore, she was the incarnation of lower middle-class arrogance, a reincarnation of Charles Dickens's Mr Gradgrind who had an obsession with work and production. Yet others claimed that Mrs Thatcher was the representative of the new entrepreneurial class that believes in private cultural patronage by the 'very rich', whatever their class origins, and is very much centred on the self-made ethos. Her supposed conception is thus interpreted as a kind of return to the situation when state subsidy did not exist. This line of argument holds that culture is a very personal affair. A sociological assessment of Mrs Thatcher's background should help with placing her somewhere within the two extremes, establishing a true picture of her personal cultural preferences.

For her cultural development, Mrs Thatcher's formative years were crucial. Mrs Roberts, her mother, was a dutiful housewife, who did her work conscientiously and was not interested in decision making. It was her father who, by contrast, was interested in power and after building up his grocery business, went into local politics. Both her parents were keen and active Methodists, a religion that has traditionally attracted upwardly-mobile working-class people. Methodism insists on hard work, frugality, Sunday observance and negligible alcohol consumption. Mrs Thatcher's father became Mayor of Grantham during the war years. In 1943, she got her A levels and went to Oxford to read chemistry.

Most of the minority of working-class students who go to Oxbridge, the two traditional universities, get assimilated into the dominant cultural mode. In social terms it means that they lose their original, regional accents, they start attending classical concerts and they lose their working-class roots. Edward Heath is a good example of this process of cultural assimilation. He was a carpenter's son who while at Oxford, travelled widely across Europe and learned to appreciate and play classical music. Margaret Roberts, although having a more middle-class background, did not travel, but instead worked diligently and went to the Conservative Association for relief. She just did not want to spend time on what she saw as rather frivolous cultural activities. She did, however, read widely and made political contacts that were to be useful in later years. Thus she wrote in her memoirs: "I made friends in university politics who, as in the novels of Anthony Powell, kept reappearing in my life as years passed by".[1] In fact she discovered a burning political ambition during her student days and she consequently established the necessary networks with men such as William Rees-Mogg, Robin Day or Edward Boyle.

All the same, branding Mrs Thatcher a philistine, as the cultural Establishment has regularly done, is incorrect and unfair. She was simply more interested in middlebrow culture than in the highbrow one. There exist several examples of British prime ministers who were much more critical of highbrow sensitivity. Jim Callaghan or Harold Wilson, Mrs Thatcher's immediate predecessors, were proud of their total lack of musical appreciation and flaunted their working-class backgrounds and lifestyles. Harold Wilson's raincoat and HP sauce were perfect examples of such working-class pride. According to Miss Roberts, culture was fine as long as it cost the taxpayer very little or preferably nothing. She sang in the Bach choir and played the piano tolerably well. Before marrying, she worked in a cake factory for J. Lyons. She married a rich industrialist, Dennis Thatcher, who was wealthy enough to be able to pay for her legal training and then to finance her political career. Dennis was a member of the Church of England and Mrs

Thatcher moved from her Methodist roots towards a more Anglican outlook on life. In cultural terms this can be seen as a move away from the lower end of middlebrow culture towards a more upper-middlebrow approach. The Anglican tradition reflects the values of the middle and upper classes of southern England, as opposed to the northern and lower middle-class values of Methodism. Hugo Young enumerates Mrs Thatcher's preference in her spare time for religious philosophy, detective novels and government reports.[2] Above all she was a fanatic of the work ethic.

Conservative MP for Finchley

When Mrs Thatcher was first elected to Parliament in 1959, it was to represent Finchley, an upper middle-class suburb of north London, with a large Jewish community. The Jewish outlook on life insists on self-help and this did not fall on deaf ears. Mrs Thatcher became firm friends with Immanuel Jakobovitz who, as Chief Rabbi from 1967 onwards, argued that hard work was the best way of dealing with social deprivation and poverty. Mrs Thatcher's first job in government was as Parliamentary Secretary at the Ministry of Pensions. She met her first civil servants and from the start disapproved of their methods. In the 1960s, she stated that civil servants followed the politicians too closely: "I came to the conclusion that the Civil Service tend not to put up advice that they think the minister will reject."[3] All in all, Mrs Thatcher found civil servants to be spineless, unprincipled individuals who changed positions according to the political circumstances. What irritated her the most, was the civilised way of wasting time, the implicit understatement that permeates all Civil Service activities and the cultural trappings of the 'mandarins' all based in London and reflected in their subsidised cultural practices.

Secretary of State for Education and Leader of the Opposition

Mrs Thatcher did not join in the controversies of the 1960s between Premier Edward Heath and Enoch Powell. Mr Powell put forward the idea that the British way of life was being undermined by a wave of immigration from the former colonies. British cultural practices were under threat and, curiously, such an argument has been used consistently in the European debates since this period. In the Heath government, Mrs Thatcher was Secretary of State for Education at the Department of Education and Science. Paradoxically, in view of her future policy statements as prime minister, she successfully kept a high spending level for her department. There was a wide consensus in the Heath government that state intervention and the European dimension were both solutions to Britain's relative economic decline. It was only later that Mrs Thatcher invented the U-turn myth, arguing that Edward (later Sir) Heath had bailed out Rolls Royce and Upper Clyde Shipbuilders, contrary to election pledges. Right up to Heath's problems as Conservative Party leader in 1975, Mrs Thatcher never expressed herself openly, probably because of her political ambition. Her political pragmatism forced her to keep her personal reactions a secret. Suddenly in 1975, after being elected leader, she revealed a more personal position at the Conservative Party Conference. Everyone had "a man's right to work as he will, to spend what he earns, to own property, to have the state as servant and not master".[4] However, Conservative Party documents, such as the The Right Approach to the Economy (1977), were all pragmatic papers designed to attract voters rather than worry them about the fundamental principles of monetarism. Once in power Mrs Thatcher adopted a more right-wing tone.

Building on image

In 1979, Mrs Thatcher started 'appropriating the universe of discourse', to use a term coined by the Frankfurt School. Her political image was projected in an efficient and effective way by Saatchi and Saatchi, her advertising consultants, and Bernard (later Sir) Ingham, her faithful Press Secretary. Mrs Thatcher's image was improved on by using American presidential style techniques. Gordon Reece, an ex-television producer, lowered Mrs Thatcher's voice to make her sound more statesmanlike and improved her elocution. By contrast, Michael Foot's discursive, rambling style compared badly with the clarity of Mrs Thatcher's populist messages. She talked of the state as an 'extravagant good fairy'.[5] She tried to project the image of a direct and frank, no-nonsense northerner, when in fact, she had been assimilated into a rich southern family. When she heard of the Toxteth riots in Liverpool, she exclaimed: 'Oh those poor shopkeepers'.[6] She always tried to relate to the average citizen, the mythical man or woman in the street. Hers was a middlebrow style of discourse that was not too flowery or complicated and yet at the same time never vulgar. She insisted that she would not have 'beer and sandwiches at Number 10',[7] this being a reference to her Labour predecessors.

Above all, Mrs Thatcher and her aides invented catch phrases for media consumption, the most famous of which was 'there is no alternative' (TINA for short). This phrase was used in the 1983 elections and effectively excluded other types of discourse. There were of course, a whole range of solutions to economic and social problems other than the Conservative proposals. The mass media retained TINA to the Conservative Party's benefit. In the battle for linguistic domination, Mrs Thatcher did extremely well because clear messages come over well in the mass media while complicated ones, even if correct, are often rejected. Therefore, in a 1984 Daily Telegraph article, she argued: "I am in politics because of the conflict between good and evil, and I believe that in the end good will triumph".[8] This clarity appealed to the popular vote and included the average person in a process of communication, which had been until then, largely monopolised by the upper-middle classes and the quality newspapers.

In addition, Mrs Thatcher was opposed to Foreign Office style. This is where the culture clash between Mrs Thatcher and the Civil Service was at its most evident. After a visit to Washington, Lord

Carrington, with an Eton background and at the time Foreign Secretary, was asked how it had gone and answered: "oh very well indeed. She liked the Reagan people very much. They are so vulgar."[9] She herself admitted the same to Bernard Ingham. They both lacked smoothness and she considered this to be a positive quality. Her roughness, however, was in reaction to the cultural Establishment and did not represent the subversive lower class roughness referred to in chapters 4 and 5. In foreign policy, Mrs Thatcher often ignored the most elementary diplomatic rules and she systematically ignored Foreign Office advice and its 'mandarin' art of implicit, hidden meanings. For electoral reasons, she believed in being explicit and clear, refusing to have anything to do with 'intellectual' and 'Frenchified' language. Her style could be appreciated by the popular Press and can best be described as middle-class frankness.

All the people whom Mrs Thatcher selected to serve in her governments tended to have similar sociological backgrounds. They were mainly self-made men, who had not necessarily gone to university and had earned large quantities of money as entrepreneurial businessmen. Cecil Parkinson, Norman Tebbit and John Major are all examples of this selection process. They all belonged to a new generation which had had nothing to do with her predecessor, Edward Heath. Norman (later Lord) Tebbit never lost a chance of vilifying the universities and criticising the cultural Establishment. This group was opposed to inherited wealth and whiggish paternalism and especially disliked left-wing intellectuals living in ivory towers. In business, Lord King (Chairman of British Airways), Lord Weinstock (Chairman of GEC) and Lord Hanson (of the Hanson Trust) are all examples of self-made men. In fact very few intellectuals were attracted to the Thatcher camp. The economist Sir Keith Joseph, the writer Kingsley Amis, the historians Hugh Thomas and A. L. Rowse are the notable exceptions to this particular rule.

The aristocratic Gilmours and St John Stevases took a superior attitude to the Iron Lady (Mrs Thatcher became known as the Iron Lady after her anti-communist speech in 1977). Other members of the cultural Establishment had some extreme reactions. Baroness Warnock spoke of a 'kind of rage' whenever she as much as thought of Mrs Thatcher. Angela Carter commented on Mrs Thatcher's voice: "It is her voice which sums up the ambiguity of the entire construct. She coos like a dove, hisses like a serpent, and bays like a hound."[10] Moreover, Mrs Thatcher even succeeded in alienating the Church of England and Dr. Runcie, the then Archbishop of Canterbury. The only Bishop who gave Mrs Thatcher his entire support was the Bishop of London who was appointed with her approval and later joined the Catholic Church in 1993, after the decision to ordinate women. Mrs Thatcher alienated large sections of the Establishment and patronised a very select band of nouveau riche, self-made men, with all the symbolic significance that this had on Conservative party politics.

The Arts Council can be considered as a perfect example of the type of establishment organisation that Mrs Thatcher came to hate. Robert Hutchison collected some interesting sociological data on the top positions of the Arts Council:

> The somewhat incestuous world of opera house politics can be characterised further: 13 of the 46 male members of the Royal Opera House Board since the war went to Eton, and over half to one of five public schools; most went to Oxbridge; most were members of one or more of three London clubs, the Athenaeum, Brooks, and the Garrick.[...] This overlapping and multiple-holding of trusteeships, directorships, and advisers, is characteristic of the national companies, national galleries and the Arts Council.[11]

This metropolitan world was entirely male-dominated and between 1945 and 1966, there were only thirteen women members of the Arts Council. Between 1967 and 1980, only nine women were appointed out of a total of sixty six. Ethnic minorities were and still are almost totally excluded. Mrs Thatcher must have particularly disliked the fact that this opera class was protected from the pressures of the market-place by a system of public subsidy and trusteeships. This ran totally against the grain of her free-market ethos.

Given such socio-political prejudices, Mrs Thatcher and her circle of allies were determined to define the cultural debate according to their agenda and on their own terms. She wanted to develop commercial and middlebrow culture as well as a certain definition of national culture. At the same time, she insisted on conveying her populist message in simple terms, which conflicted sharply with the Civil Service and Establishment ways of doing things. However, she skillfully manipulated the mass media, imposing boundaries on the universe of discourse and restricting the nature of public debate by careful use of her Press Secretary. The sociological factors show that she did belong to a definite milieu with very specific reactions, and yet her policies, if partly explained by this, cannot be reduced to it. In the end, it was her ability to know how far she could go at a particular time that made her a winner, and implicitly shaped her arts and cultural policies.

Notes

1. Margaret Thatcher, *The Path to Power* 43.
2. Hugo Young, *One of Us* 409.
3. ibid., 48.
4. Hugo Young, *One of Us* 104.
5. Hugo Young, *One of Us* 147.
6. ibid., 239.
7. ibid., 368.
8. *The Daily Telegraph*, 18 September 1984.
9. Hugo Young,*One of Us* 252.
10. Hugo Young, *One of Us* 411.
11. Robert Hutchison, *The Politics of the Arts Council* 30.

Chapter 7

Mrs Thatcher, the Arts Council and the British Council

The cultural agenda for the conservative governments between 1979 and 1990 is characterised by two policy priorities. The first was a long-term policy of reducing government spending levels in all state controlled areas in general and in the arts in particular. The question then is to what extent was government arts spending reduced? The less noticed second objective was to reinforce a national cultural identity while at the same time attracting tourists with their foreign currencies. It is thought that British or rather English cultural products, such as English novels or the playing of English music, can enhance an international reputation that tends to create a certain amount of goodwill. Pushed to the limit, it is argued that an influential foreigner who appreciates the best of English civilisation will become an Anglophile and can be a useful ally in the commercial domain. This is how the British Council usually tries to justify its expenditure. In fact, it is because subsidised highbrow culture attracted foreign visitors that the argument for arts subsidy was won. These are contradictions with entailing tensions that are of great interest and are to be observed very closely.

The British way of administrating the arts

The British model of administrating the arts is unique. Up until 1967, the Department of Education and Science looked after arts policy, but this changed with the arrival of Jennie Lee as Labour's Minister for the Arts under Harold Wilson. The Office of Arts and Libraries (OAL), up until 1979, was run by a junior minister, who supervised cultural spending by the state, using a very restricted arts definition. After this date the Minister of Arts was a full Cabinet member. In 1992, this situation changed with the setting up of the Office of Arts Libraries and Heritage. This new body added the functions of media policy and the preservation of buildings of historical importance. The original Office of Arts and Libraries, before 1992, was responsible for the national museums that took up about 25 per cent of total resources, in the form of direct support. The public library service, likewise, was another important responsibility. Roughly 40 per cent of total funds went to the Arts Council, over which the minister had very little direct control. There were some other arm's length bodies, which were also financed by the Office of Arts and Libraries: the Crafts Council, the British Film Institute, the Museums and Galleries Commission, the National Film and Television School, the British Library, the Acceptance in Lieu Scheme (this scheme allows death duties to be paid for in kind) and the National Heritage Memorial Fund. The new Office retained these functions, while taking on additional ones.

Between 1978/9 and 1988/9 there was a 5.5 fold increase in state spending for museums and galleries. The other two major beneficiaries of the period can be identified as the Arts Council and the British Film Institute. They both experienced a tripling of resources. Similar increases ocurred for both Scotland and Wales. These countries had four times as much spent on the arts at the end of the Thatcher period than at the beginning. Northern Ireland benefited from a mere doubling of revenue which is due to fewer classical orchestras, opera performances and fewer official cultural activities. Statistics show a tripling in arts spending by the state, but part of that increase can be explained by the transfer of certain local authority responsibilities to central government in 1985, with the disappearance of the metropolitan authorities. Inflation also has to be taken into account, thus reducing the figures to a still significant 22 per cent increase, in adjusted terms, for the 1980s period. In the following analysis the whole of the United Kingdom, that is to say England, Wales, Scotland and Northern Ireland will be considered wherever possible. When this is impossible, figures for Great Britain, or England and Wales, will be used and stated.

As mentioned before, British cultural policy is characterised by low spending and relative centralisation, although this should not be over-emphasised. The United Kingdom was the first country to adopt the arm's length system when the Arts Council was formed by Royal Charter in 1946. Other Anglo-Saxon countries have copied the arm's length approach, emphasising some of its particularities. The Arts Council chairman is named by the prime minister. It is the chairman who then chooses the committee that organises the work of the Arts Council. Once the Council is in place, the government has very little say in the day to day business, except when the allocation of money is decided every year and also when there is media controversy over public money being spent as in the case of avant-garde art. Specialist panels decide how money should be spent, according to available resources and mostly on quality considerations. Various criteria are used in determining who should get a grant and preference is given to stable customers who have already been given previous grants. In this way the arm's length system allows criticism to be directed away from government onto the Arts Council, while maintaining overall government supervision.

A large proportion of total Arts Council spending (between 30 per cent and 40 per cent) goes to the big national companies that are almost invariably based in London. There is a considerable conflict of interest between the big, visible, London-based companies and the smaller, lower profile, provincial companies. One should not forgot that the Arts Council had regional offices that were closed in the mid 1950s. Provincial companies were therefore both symbolically and in fact given the cold shoulder. In the 1960s, independent arts pressure groups were set up in the provinces to fill the gap that had been left by the closure of the regional offices. It was hoped at first that a large proportion of funds would be of local origin but they did not materialise with the subsequent Regional Arts Associations (RAAs). These organisations resemble miniature Arts Councils, but with local knowledge and sensitivity, as will be shown below. Like the centralised organisation they have a preference for quality, rather than comprehensive services. The Arts Council of Great Britain also delegates power and resources to the Scottish, Welsh and Northern Irish equivalents. (A total of £600 million was spent for the United Kingdom for both central and local governments.) The total, of course, excludes monies spent on the excellent and mature public library service that exists in Great Britain. The resulting system is one of overall administrative diversity leading to a wealth of local practices and arrangements and areas of very poor official cultural provision.

Nine other state departments spent an estimated 200 million on the arts in 1989, the Department of the Environment, the Ministry of Defence and the Department of Employment being the major spenders. Large increases benefitted the British Museum where spending almost doubled in the space of three years. The Urban Development Corporations (UDCs) also spent significant amounts on museums within their areas. 4.2 million were spent in 1986/7 in the Merseyside urban development scheme. The Department of Employment's Community Programme (CP) and Enterprise Allowance Scheme should also be borne in mind as they often applied to small crafts organisations. University museums and galleries doubled their expenditure in five years. Surprisingly 55 million were spent on military bands.

As has already been mentioned, the fact that the Arts Minister had low cabinet status, that there was much fragmentation in culture in general and in the arts in particular, meant that arts interests had little political weight in the British political system. The same cannot be said for example, about the road lobby, which has considerable influence and deals with one government department, namely, the Department of the Environment (DOE). The latter of course has large hierarchical organisations such as car producers and road makers that are very visible and wield considerable political power. John Myerscough argues that the road industry and the culture industry have the same economic weight, but do not have the same political muscle.[1] The arts, therefore, remained very much on the periphery of British politics during the 1980s.

Mrs Thatcher's initial dealings with the Arts Council

When she came to power, Mrs Thatcher was caught between her wish not to alienate too many potential electors and the desire to teach the Establishment a lesson. As early as 1976, she had met the Chairman of the Arts Council and told him that it made no sense for the government to: "look for candle-end economies which will yield a very small saving, whilst causing upset out of all proportion to the economies achieved".[2] St John Stevas, as shadow Arts Minister, argued in a similar vein in 1977 and asked for increased spending by the state on the arts. A Conservative Political Centre paper that was written by St John Stevas claimed that "the arts can genuinely be said to pay for their way" and finished by calling for beauty "and the advancement of things of the spirit".[3] It is in 1979 that the tone changed significantly, the Conservative Political Centre issuing a paper by Kingsley Amis under the title of An Arts Policy? In it Amis wrote that: "public taste may not be the best taste but it is the best available, certainly better than the critic's taste or the expert's taste or the bureaucrat's taste".[4] This represented the first serious challenge to the arts consensus.

Grant cuts in the Arts Council

One year later, despite her previous assurances to the contrary, Mrs Thatcher executed her first recorded U-turn and reduced the Arts Council grant for the first time in its history. This was the first stage in what Mrs Thatcher intended to be a thorough attack on the postwar cultural consensus. St John Stevas was informed of the decision, apparently, very late in the day. It was seen as a personal sop to him as he had previously argued forcefully against cuts in the arts. It was also considered as a challenge to the arts Establishment and yet it was the logical outcome of the way the Conservative Party was moving. Everyone, it was argued, had to make an effort in the fight against deficits which were due to an increasingly ageing population, taking up high cost medical care and pensions and to increased unemployment and social security benefits, all of which the state had to pay for. The cut in itself was only a small one and thus, was merely of symbolic value, but it did represent the first cut in thirty-five years and was therefore a change of direction. Tony Field, the financial director of the Arts Council at the time, decided to maintain the existing level of subsidy to its major recipients, with the result that forty-one of the minor ones saw their grants withdrawn. The cut had two major consequences. Firstly, it sent a clear signal to the arts Establishment, showing that the arts world could not count on subsidy as a right. Secondly, it unwittingly brought to light the problem of Arts Council accountability.

The Arts Council experts had until then tried to maintain a secret and implicit definition of quality. Decisions to subsidise a company were made according to undisclosed criteria, such as financial competence, useful contacts and the quality of the products. The recipients who had their grants withdrawn reacted in a foreseeable manner. They all considered the withdrawal as an official sign of disapproval. Just as a relatively small allocation from the Arts Council to an arts organisation often acted as a key to other sources of funds, a withdrawal, no matter how small, was considered a stamp of disapproval and yet, of the forty-one cuts, many were made on geographical or strategic grounds rather than quality reasons. The Arts Council found it easier to stop subsidising London-based companies, where supply was at a high level and also to cut a few subsidies in a long list of names. One beneficial result of these cuts was that, in 1984, the Arts Council finally set out its public criteria for granting subsidy, although it did not give a specific order of priority. These were:

> a. quality of artistic product;
> b. actual and potential creative strength;
> c. the extent to which stated aims and objects are realised;
> d. the fullest practicable use of facilities and widest provision of the arts to the community;
> e. education policy in relation to the artistic programme;
> f. the employment and other opportunities extended to members of the ethnic minority groups;

g. overall value for money;
h. box office and attendance returns;
i. the company's success in raising local authority support and other income;
j. the efficiency shown in using available resources and the accuracy and control of budgeting;
k. the urgency and nature of any fundamental financial problems;
l. the adequacy and security of tenure of premises;
m. the balance of provision between London and other regions;
n. the Council's existing declared policies.[5]

The government cut had a very useful effect in clarifying the criteria on which the Arts Council chose its beneficiaries and a clear picture was set out for potential applicants. Companies had to provide good value for money to a wide public, if possible involving ethnic minorities and the young, while at the same time, stressing quality and creative strength. It could be considered as a statement of policy. The policy application was a different matter and will be dealt with later. This was a very clear signal to artists from the Arts Council and it certainly had Mrs Thatcher's approval.

Mrs Thatcher and her Arts Ministers

Her first Arts Minister, St John Stevas, had felt the tide turning in 1979, when he admitted that the arts world "must come to terms with the situation and accept the fact that government policy in general has decisively tilted away from expansion of the public to the enlargement of the private sector".[6] For the rest of his one and a half year period as Arts Minister, he admitted that he was more "a sort of fund raiser than a minister". In a government reshuffle in 1980, he was replaced by Paul Channon, whose prime concern was to stimulate private sponsorship. In 1983, Lord Gowrie was appointed Minister for the Arts and Libraries in the second Thatcher government. The Arts Council grant was cut a second time, this time with the full consent of the Arts Minister. He argued that 'the landscape (had) changed' and 'the limits of hospitality' had been reached.[7] The Arts Council issued a document on the cuts that were made in 1980, but failed to explain that the cuts, repeated in 1983 for a second time, were due to arbitrary decisions based on monetarist principles.

Richard Luce took over in 1986 and continued the Conservative efforts of increasing private sponsorship and patronage. But at the same time he discreetly increased state spending on the arts. He stayed on until after the study's time period. This was proof that Mrs Thatcher had changed her priorities in the course of her eleven year premiership. At first she was keen to cut and show that everyone had to make an effort in keeping down government spending. In the latter half of the decade when the prime minister realised that increased government spending did not necessarily produce inflation, she implicitly accepted the economic value of government spending on the arts. The length of office of Lord Gowrie and Richard Luce reflect a rather less conflictual and more relaxed atmosphere in the second half of the decade.

Mrs Thatcher, the secretary-generals and the chairmen of the Arts Council

Such was the evolution in the policies followed by the various Arts Ministers who were appointed to serve in the successive Thatcher governments. These changes were reflected in the Arts Council appointments too. Mrs Thatcher was allegedly always asking the question: "Is he (or she) one of us?".[8] Obviously she gave preferment to people who shared her kind of ideas, but not always. She was also a realistic and practical politician. As the number of people who closely shared her opinions was rather limited, she had to appoint the people who were available. During the period of cultural consensus before Mrs Thatcher, the secretary-general of the Arts Council was the dominant personality, while during the Thatcher years the chairman increasingly took over power. The reason for this change was that Mrs Thatcher appointed the chairmen.

The secretary-general in the 1975-1983 period was Sir Roy Shaw, a man of working-class origins, who came into the Establishment through a life in adult education. He was a self-made moderate, which is why he survived so long. However, in 1979, he was only just re-elected by the Arts Council. His successor, Luke Rittner, formerly chairman of the Association of Business Sponsorship (ABSA), replaced Shaw as secretary-general in 1983. In 1981, the Labour-appointed Kenneth Robinson was replaced by Rees-Mogg as chairman of the Arts Council. Rees-Mogg (later Lord) was definitely 'one of us'. He waxed lyrical over Shakespeare being a Thatcherite Tory and in 1985, published a booklet called The Political Economy of Art. He believed that the role of the Arts Council should be very limited and argued that he would never support its creation if it were to be re-organised. In 1980, St. John Stevas suggested that Alastair Mc Alpine, a captain of British industry who later became the Treasurer of the Conservative Party, be appointed to the Arts Council. Both Kenneth Robinson as chairman and Roy Shaw as secretary-general, opposed the nomination. The minister countered: "I think you will appreciate that this nomination comes from a very high source".[9] Mc Alpine did become a member, but not for a long time as he hated the atmosphere of the organisation.

Another example of political influence came in 1982 when Paul Channon, Minister of Arts and Libraries, forced Richard Hoggart's resignation as vice-chairman of the Arts Council. Channon justified the decision by stating that 'Number 10 doesn't like him'.[10] In 1986, the conservative Rees-Mogg was replaced by Lord Joel Barnett, a Labour peer, thus showing that Mrs Thatcher could be practical as well as interventionist and doctrinaire in her approach to appointments. One of the results of this kind of partisan patronage was that the arts lobby, instead of working with the Arts Council as it had done before, moved to being an independent pressure group. The National Campaign for the Arts, for example, was set up in 1985. All these examples of political influence in appointments raise the problem of accountability. Should arm's length organisations be accountable to the prime minister, to Parliament or to the voters in whatever form that may take? This question was particularly relevant throughout the 1980s with the expansion of the cultural industries.

Three enquiries on the Arts Council

Until Mrs Thatcher came to office, enquiries on the Arts Council were made regularly over its forty year life span and they were just as regularly ignored. In 1976, Lord Redcliffe-Maud produced a report entitled Support for the Arts in England and Wales that argued that amateur art should become the priority of the Arts Council. It suggested that this organisation should function like the Sports Council which deals only with amateur sport.[11] Although this report came under a Labour government, the recommendations were completely ignored by both Labour and Conservative parties.

In 1982, a Parliamentary Select Committee on Education, Science and the Arts, issued a report Public and Private Funding of the Arts that focussed on an over-emphasis of provision in the metropolitan areas in general and in London in particular. It also deplored the level of underfunding encountered by most major arts organisations. This report surprisingly had some effect and encouraged the Arts Council to produce an important document on its own policy called The Glory of the Garden - A Strategy for a Decade (1984). The very preface clearly stated the most acute problem: "We live as two artistic nations: London and everywhere else." Curiously, the document made no distinction between the terms devolution and decentralisation:

> In administration the Arts Council wants to carry forward the existing programme of devolution of assessment and funding to the Regional Arts Associations. This document announces the largest single programme of devolution in the history of the Arts Council. It is a genuine and major act of administrative decentralisation, a step back from centralised bureaucracy as a mode of administering the arts in Great Britain.

Four major aims were set out:

> Firstly raising the quality and increasing the quantity of arts provision in the regions to bring it nearer the standards of provision in London;

Secondly in identifying new developments in the regions for direct support from the Arts Council itself, focussing on the dozen or so areas within England where the population is most densely concentrated;
Thirdly making a start to redressing certain historical imbalances in funding which favour some art forms at the expense of others;
Fourthly in appropriate cases, basing the Council's own subsidy decisions more consistently and deliberately than in the past on the availability of matching funds locally.[12]

This appears to be the clearest, most unambiguous statement of policy of Mrs Thatcher's period and yet it lacks clarity as both terms, devolution and decentralisation are used in the same paragraph to describe the same conditions. Indeed the Arts Council did decentralise its money to the RAAs, while at the same time devolving its policy decisions. In addition, the excluded art forms are not specifically mentioned. Curiously, two years earlier, the Policy Studies Institute (PSI) had published a paper showing that Arts Council expenditure per head of population in the London area in 1980/1 was three and a half times as great as the next best-provided region (Merseyside Arts) and nine times as much as the worst region (Eastern Arts). The paper proposed a 6 million reallocation of resources to the RAAs and the regions. In turn, The Glory of the Garden document came to a similar figure of 6 million to be transferred to the regions. It also paid the by now habitual lip-service to business and industry.[13]

A closer look at The Glory of the Garden reveals several further points of Mrs Thatcher's stance. Riverside Studios, while producing adventurous works of an extremely high quality, was not considered to be sufficiently rigorous in its financial affairs. The Arts Council "is therefore issuing a warning to the company, that if in 1984/5 it fails once more to operate within available resources, its subsidy will be withdrawn". In opera, Glyndebourne Touring and Kent Opera were praised for their high artistic standards and could therefore count on a continuing grant. Opera 80, a small touring company, however, did not "represent the wisest artistic or strategic choice. The nature of the operation therefore precludes it from providing in the areas which it visits, the educational and outreach work to which the Council attaches increasing importance". In fact, Opera 80 as a small company was a much better tool for educational purposes than the hugely elitist Glyndebourne company. What is not explicitly stated is that opera was taking up too much of a proportion of total funds, as compared to other spending areas. Given the various criteria for choosing recipients, and taking into consideration the subsidy levels per ticket, it is striking to note how much opera was absorbing in terms of financial resources. This had little educational value and subsidised the 'very rich'.

The strategy review also mentioned the proposed reorganisation of the metropolitan areas. Such an openly political move, led to the reallocation of spending from the old metropolitan areas to the Arts Council and the RAAs. The proposed decentralisation of the policy review was in part contradicted by the actual centralisation caused by the reorganisation of the metropolitan areas. Subsequently, it explains why in 1986 there was an apparently marked rise in arts spending, when in fact a large proportion of the increase was caused by this administrative reorganisation.

The 1979-1985 period

During the 1980s, no grand policy for the arts based on a specific political philosophy emerged. The Arts Council remained unaccountable and the arm's length policy remained in place, albeit with the top jobs taken by Mrs Thatcher's nominees. It continued to publish annual reports for citizens to admire. Sir Hugh Willat, secretary-general in the early 1970s, had justified his decisions by calling them a policy of response. The Arts Council had also acted as a pressure group for increased state funding of the arts. In the 1980s, these major roles were ignored. In fact, the organisation seriously wondered what its role was throughout the 1980s. The chairmen openly argued for a reduced, even residual role and less money. Two government enquiries did not consult the Arts Council, thus implying a reduced role for the quango.[14] In 1985, the drama panel resigned en masse, while in the same year the commercial theatre directors declared that they no longer had any confidence in the Council's ability to defend their interests. Marghanita

Laski, the vice-chair of the drama panel said that she 'felt impotent' and confidence reached an all-time low. The mid-1980s can be described as years of very low morale and self-doubt.

In the later years of the decade, Mrs Thatcher began to realise that the arts had a significant economic role to play. The British Tourist Board, for example, printed a leaflet in 1985, which claimed that: "the arts are to Britain what the sun is to Spain". Many American tourists claimed in opinion polls that they came to Britain in large part because of the cultural richness. This was particularly true for the private theatres of London's West End, which became increasingly dependent on foreign tourists throughout the 1980s. Many of the commercial plays were tested in the subsidised theatres before coming to the commercial circuit, so state subsidy actually reduced risk-taking for the private sector. What completely transformed the public/private debate was the publication of thoroughly researched figures on arts spending by Muriel Nissel in 1982, and by John Myerscough in 1988.[15]

The emergence of organisations such as the Policy Studies Institute (PSI), financed by various public and private bodies, can be seen as part of a general trend towards professionalism in the cultural sector, a response to the flagrant lack of official government information on the cultural industries. Both authors showed that the arts were a major industry which gave Great Britain a net benefit in its balance of payments. Arts loss leaders, that is to say arts services which are subsidised by the state because unprofitable in the open market-place, could be justified by the large number of tourists that they attracted: these in turn all needed accommodation, restaurants and a whole range of entertainment and services. It should be remembered that the multiplier effect plays a significant role in this process. In this context Myerscough examined London theatres and concert halls and found that sometimes over 50 per cent of the tickets went to foreigners. Arts subsidy in London could therefore be rightly justified as an indirect subsidy to the hotel industry. Conversely, in the provinces, local residents formed the biggest proportion of consumers for museums, galleries, theatres and concerts.

Figures that had previously been split up between different government departments, were finally put together thanks to the efforts of various pressure groups. Museums and galleries had a œ230 million turnover for 1986, of which 113 million were spent on the national museums. Total spending on theatre for both public and private sectors was calculated to be 422 million, providing work for 103 resident companies and 350 touring companies. As for music, this sector of the arts economy represented œ194 million in 1986, providing work for twenty-two orchestras and five opera and dance companies. As a result of this pioneering research work on cultural spending, the successive Thatcher governments dropped their doctrinaire talk of the early years. Government spending on the arts was increased, business sponsorship was encouraged and projects such as a national lottery with proceeds going to the arts were given official approval.

The middle period of the 1980s was dominated by a heated debate over funding levels in the arts. The Policy Studies Institute (PSI) figures provided information that could be used to challenge the previous monopoly position of the government. Lord Gowrie claimed an 18 per cent increase in Arts Council expenditure in the 1979-1985 period. In a House of Commons official report dated 9th December 1985, Mr Richard Luce claimed:

> In the past six years, we have more than doubled the amount of money given to the arts. The Arts Council funds have increased by 7% in real terms, in the past six years. I am satisfied that we are maintaining our support for the arts.[16]

By then the debate had become public and Simon Crine, chair of the National Campaign for the Arts, challenged these claims. According to him, the first figure was false, and the second one was dubious. The government figures were based on the GDP deflator, which in this case was inappropriate. The Peacock Report in 1983, had recommended the use of the RPI and using this as a base, (as mentioned earlier) a 1.4 per cent reduction could be found. If Housing the Arts was included in the total, then a five per cent reduction could be shown. The main point about the debate on figures is not so much the different calculations, but the fact that discussions occurred at all. Whereas before official figures had to be accepted without criticism, the new arts pressure groups started counterbalancing government monopoly. In fact, these new groups reflected the growing economic importance of cultural activities as a whole and the move towards the professionalisation of an arts world that had previously been staffed by well-placed amateur administrators. During the 1980s, administrative amateurism with its vague and incomplete figures was progressively eliminated by the appointment of professional arts administrators with proper training, and Mrs Thatcher played a vital role in this process. In fact, it was this new team of arts administrators which actually introduced the cultural debate.

The 1985-90 period

The first part of the period was characterised by a break with the postwar tradition of a steady rise in arts spending. In the second half deeper structural reforms were introduced to make the arts more privately funded and to make them less elitist. This was clearly stated by Richard Luce, Minister for the Arts and Libraries in 1987: "Our aim is to ensure that public expenditure takes a steadily smaller share of our national income [...]. The arts cannot be seen in isolation from this dramatic change in the political and economic climate." He also claimed in what became a famous catch-phrase: "Give a person a fish and you feed him for the day; teach him how to fish and you feed him for life."[17] The second half of the Thatcher decade was most definitely about teaching fishing techniques. Richard Luce also wanted to fight the anti-business ethos:

> "there are too many in the arts world who have yet to be weaned away from the welfare state mentality - the attitude that the taxpayer owes them a living. Many have not yet accepted the challenge of developing plural sources of funding. They give the impression of thinking that all sources of funding are either tainted or too difficult to get. They appear not to have grasped that the collectivist mentality of the sixties and seventies is out of date."[18]

By the end of the Thatcher period all arts organisations, even the big national companies, were busy earning money through commercial activities. Thus 'incentive funding' was introduced in November 1987, with 5, 6, 7 million earmarked for 1988/9, 1989/90 and 1990/1 respectively. This meant that arts organisations that successfully attracted private funding would also gain an equivalent sum from the government. The scheme produced an Enterprise Fund and a Progress Fund based on the National Endowment of the Arts model in the United States. These two funds were later amalgamated into one. The use of incentive funding was direct government interference in a supposedly arm's length body. What should also be stressed is that the earmarking of funds during a period of financial contraction meant that other recipients had to make do with less.

Another manner of making public money go further was to reduce administrative costs. Business practices, as in all the Civil Service, were introduced into the Arts Council. One can safely say that the Arts Council throughout the Thatcher period suffered from administrative overload. It is largely for this reason that the RAAs were left to take on most of the extra work. In 1984, a management consultant was called in to find ways of improving organisational efficiency. This led to a certain amount of restructuring and the introduction of what were termed 'modern business techniques'.

A Management Team under the secretary-general was organised to co-ordinate the work of the panels within the Arts Council. A Finance and Policy Committee was resurrected and placed under the control of the chairman. In practice, this committee met only rarely because there was no dissent among the top managers. A Marketing and Resources Department was constituted to improve contacts with the outside world. In fact this department took on a public relations role. A Planning Department was also made responsible for co-ordination with other public bodies dealing with the arts. Of course the consultant suggested staff cuts and retraining. This resulted in training schemes that transferred personnel from administrative responsibilities to more financial tasks. The three year rolling programme was the logical continuation of these changes. It set out provisional grants over a three year period, thus allowing recipients to have longer-term planning than before.

This new business attitude in Arts Council management did lead to a reduction of administrative red tape. It was part of a more ambitious project to make the whole of the Civil Service more efficient and market-oriented. However, trying to make unpaid panels more efficient was impossible and by 1988 even Rees-Mogg agreed that the Arts Council had reached an optimal point that could not be bettered.[19]

Towards the end of the Thatcher period an attempt was made to extend these business practices to the RAAs. Thus in December 1988, Richard Wilding, the Civil Service head of the Office of Arts and Libraries, conducted an enquiry into the funding structures in England. The Wilding Report (1989) proposed that the administrative structures of the RAAs be examined and modern business methods were suggested. This introduction of the business ethic was to be extended to all the administration of the arts in the United Kingdom. All kinds of administrative duplication was to be removed. Lord Goodman claimed that it was "a plan that for practical purposes spelt the end of the Arts Council".[19] He was very close to the mark. By 1994, the Arts Council of Great Britain had become the Arts Council of England and only funded fourteen major national arts bodies.

Another trend of the Thatcher governments was to work outside the Arts Council. Arts Marketing Grants were established as was Business for the Arts, a scheme sponsored by IBM. One can also mention the Foundation for Sports and Arts, that is financed by the pools companies and delivers part of their takings to good causes in the cultural domain. These are concrete examples of what Mrs Thatcher hoped would happen to arts funding in Great Britain throughout the 1980s in a move that was meant to make them less dependent on the public sector.

Making the arts more accessible

One of Mrs Thatcher's aims was to make the arts more accessible and popular. In this sense she wanted to apply the second half of the 1946 Royal Charter, whereas all the previous postwar governments had encouraged elitist practices. Thus in March 1986 Richard Luce, the then Arts Minister, announced:

> The arts are not quite clearly for the many, not for the few [...]. I welcome the desire of so many in the arts to see an expansion of arts facilities and even wider public access to the enjoyment and enlightenment the arts can provide. The theory that the arts can or should only be appreciated by the few, I find thoroughly repugnant. We, in the arts world, should not be like dragons slumbering contentedly over hoarded treasures.[21]

Despite these ambitious aims, little was actually done to popularise the arts. The strategic policy change encouraging a shift in the allocation of resources to the regions, announced in The Glory of the Garden (1984), was finally abandoned in 1989 due to the effects of the Wilding Report. However, various schemes were set up to promote touring. The Controller of Touring was appointed to encourage regional touring in an attempt to counterbalance the natural tendency of large organisations to stay in one place. 'Upstart Productions' was also set up to assist touring and it was hoped that it would receive private funding after an initial government grant. Finally, a Touring Fund was constituted to help the arts move to the people. All these schemes reflect Mrs Thatcher's desire to democratise the arts, as seen through the populist messages of her Arts Ministers.

Thus, if the first half of the Thatcher decade was one of stopping the rise in government spending and thereby challenging the cultural Establishment, the second half was characterised by more efficient administration and teaching arts organisations how to fish. Business practices were transferred to the Arts Council. Various methods of encouraging private financing were introduced and by the end of the decade, no single arts organisation could avoid the logic of this new system. Not even the large national companies could now count on increased state spending to cover rising costs. In fact, it was after 1987, when Mrs Thatcher had a 140 seat majority, that she had the greatest possibilities for change and that many of the measures proposed throughout the 1980s were finally implemented and applied to arts administration.

Four questions about the Arts Council

The tensions between amateurism and professionalism as reflected in the Arts Council throughout the 1980s provoked grave criticism of the organisation: weak management, too much secrecy, lack of accountability, an 'incestuous' relationship with grant recipients, lack of ability to deal with new activities, over-concentration of provision in London, duplication of administration. In 1981, Graham, Norman and Shearn carried out a study on opera subsidies and accused the Arts Council of weak management, a charge that is often made against British industry in general:

> Decision making for opera subsidy is fragmented in the Council. The roles of the various committees and panels are not clear in practice and there is confusion on the part of the Music Panel members as to what is expected of them. There is still disagreement within the Arts Council as to the role of financial detail in the overall assessment of companies and whether the panel members should, or even can, take it into account. Information provision to be used as a basis of policy evaluation is limited. Although Council and the Music Panel sometimes spend considerable amounts of time discussing individual clients, there does not appear to be any routine evaluation of the overall effect of opera subsidy in Great Britain; the last time such an overall analysis took place in a formal and observable way seems to have been in 1972 when the Opera Report was published.[22]

The successive chairmen and secretary-generals during the Thatcher years did not have faith in subsidy as a system for the arts. They believed in giving to the private sector all possible responsibilities to keep the big national non-profit making organisations going. However, this narrow vision of the arts economy was far too restricted and the lack of a coherent plan was surprising. As for secrecy and lack of accountability, they were also left unresolved. The arm's length principle, by its very nature, caused problems of accountability. To do the Arts Council justice, it did set out its criteria of evaluation in 1984, but despite this improvement, many of its applicants still felt that choices were made according to 'unofficial' criteria, such as personal contacts or outright favouritism. The problem went beyond Mrs Thatcher's new policy. A lot of work needed to be done to establish confidence between the Council and potential recipients who clamoured for a fairer system, especially in view of the additional funding resulting from Arts Council backing. The last major criticisms of the Council, namely of concentrating arts provision in London and not being able to help new art forms, seemed too difficult to remedy. The Council was aware of the problem, but unless there existed a statutory obligation for local authorities to spend on the arts and decentralisation was imposed, there would always be a wealth of local practices. This was the inevitable price to pay for a devolved system of administration. In 1984, the Council could have corrected the imbalance with a considerable shift of resources to the regions. This was, however, largely undermined by the reorganisation of the metropolitan areas in 1986. (A full account is given below.) As far as administrative duplication is concerned, the Wilding Report (1989) announced what was to come. In 1994, the Arts Council was left with a residual role for England, the RAAs, or Regional Arts Boards as they were termed, being given all the remaining responsibilities.

So, as in other domains, many important questions were left unanswered by Mrs Thatcher. New art forms are difficult to subsidise because they are often controversial and generate bad publicity for the arts bureaucracy. They are also often short-lived and arts administrations encourage long-term projects. One solution to this problem would have been to subsidise individuals with non-renewable grants, as proposed by Richard Netzer, thus giving them a chance without creating a dependency relationship. However, the administrative centralisation that occurred in other areas of government did not apply to the Arts Council. After the 1979-90 period, most of the council's functions were transferred to the Regional Arts Boards.

The British Council

The second of the cultural bureaucracies in the United Kingdom, the British Council, which is responsible for culture overseas, now needs considering. It has the same sociological composition as the Arts Council and uses similar recruitment networks. It also employs reactive policies, that is to say reacting on an individual basis to particular requests, and concentrates on the elitist end of the cultural spectrum.

Mrs Thatcher's desire to reduce government spending levels applied to the British Council. It was felt to produce wooly ideas rather than goods for sale. In August 1979, the Foreign Secretary Lord Carrington, informed officials concerned that there were to be reductions of 3 per cent in 1979/80, 7.5 per cent in 1980/1, 12.5 per cent in 1981/2 and 17.5 per cent in 1982/3. The proposed cuts provoked a public outcry. Academics and Members of Parliament wrote to the Council to make their views known. Henry Moore, the most talented of Britain's postwar sculptors wrote a personal letter to the prime minister:

> The council continues to support young artists in the way it has supported me in the last thirty years - many of our painters and sculptors will benefit from its encouragement and practical help, and will bring credit to the cultural life of our country (as well as income from abroad). I feel sure, Prime Minister, that money spent on the full support of the British Council is financially profitable to the nation.[23]

On 3 June 1980, the chairman, Sir Charles Troughton, had a personal meeting with Mrs Thatcher. Following the discussion, both agreed on an 18 per cent cut over four years rather than the 25 per cent cut that was initially proposed. The British Council had made a case for reduction and had survived.

Lord Seebohm was appointed to conduct a wide-ranging review of the cultural organisation. The terms of reference were the following:

TO EXAMINE
1. The role of the Board (and its advisory bodies), its relationship with the sponsoring Department of State and the chief executive of the Council and the extent to which it should monitor the attainment of agreed Council objectives;
2. The financial management and funding of the Council;
3. The Council's manpower recruitment.[24]

The report was published in March 1981 and contained 85 recommendations: 6 on the council's relations with government departments, 10 on the Board, 5 on advisory committees, 12 on management, 31 on financial procedures and 21 on manpower. Criticism was made of relations between the Foreign and Commonwealth Office (CFO), the Overseas Development Administration (ODA) and the Council. Subcontracting, as in the case of Paid Educational Services (PES), was highlighted for lack of monitoring and a source of potential liabilities. Clearer management procedures were also suggested. The review was an attempt at justifying the continued existence of the British Council and was a partial success.

The impact of the proposed cuts was limited by three factors: (1) The increase in revenue from English teaching; (2) The reduction in costs due to withdrawal from Iran, Malta and Argentina; (3) The long-term nature of the cuts, that allowed voluntary redundancies.

In fact the funding levels, in the 1979-1984 period, rose from 109 to 173 million. This was achieved through savings in manpower and an increase in non-subsidy revenue. English teaching through the Cambridge examinations expanded considerably and will continue to do so in the future. Commercial patronage was also encouraged during the decade, in line with government cultural policy in general. The British Council did not prove to be an exception in the Thatcher government's challenge of the cultural Establishment. It too had to 'fish' for scarce resources and commercial practices were adopted:

From the Corporate Plan downwards, Council documents seem to be couched more and more in management-speak. "Corporate", "business", "products" and other unlovely terms have become as much part of our vocabulary as "cultural manifestation", "functional" and "specialist tourist". So all-pervasive is this new terminology that an impression has been created that the Council is little more than a commercial firm with the same purposes as, say, Marks and Spencer.[25]

In 1991, the Thatcher Foundation was created and in many ways acted as a lowkey private competitor to the British Council. Its aim is to spread the spirit of Thatcherism around the world and especially in Eastern Europe. By 1994 it spent about 300,000 a year on projects that Mrs Thatcher considered worthwhile. Mark Worthington, its director stressed three projects of particular interest for 1995:

> 1. Training 40 Russian librarians in modern techniques at the Library of Congress in Washington;
> 2. Helping foreign language teachers in Poland switch from Russian to English;
> 3. Training craftsmen in the skills required to restore ancient buildings in Prague, skills lost during the communist years.[26]

All these areas touch on the work of the British Council and the Arts Council. In this particular case, Mrs Thatcher is now applying the principles that she drew up in eleven years of cultural policy.

Why did Mrs Thatcher keep the Arts Council and the British Council? Perhaps because in spite of her liberal talk of letting the market decide, she actually found the system useful in handing out official approval. The system was a very convenient way of favouring highbrow and middlebrow English culture. It thereby officially excluded other kinds of more disruptive culture, such as popular, minority or ethnic ones. The process encouraged an official national culture which in a way answered some of her aims. By using arm's length organisations, the government could claim that it was impartial while at the same time appointing dependable friends to key positions. In this way both organisations moved in what she considered as the right direction and any controversial decisions did not unfavourably affect the government's reputation. However, the lack of accountability, along with the diffuse nature of arts administration created a smokescreen which the newly established arts pressure groups and the general public found hard to pierce. In this way Mrs Thatcher kept public debate to a strict minimum. As a consequence of her policy, The British Council was given a reduced role and by 1992 numerous staff had been made redundant. The Arts Council of England was all but abolished in 1992 and given a very residual role. Such was the logical outcome of eleven years of Thatcherite indirect use of the institutions as a lever for undeclared political aims and action.

Notes

1. John Myerscough, The Economic *Importance of the Arts in Britain* 35.
2. Roy Shaw, *The Arts and the People* 13.
3. ibid., 36.
4. ibid., 87.
5. *The Glory of the Garden* (London: The Arts Council of Great Britain, 1984) 6.
6. Roy Shaw, *The Arts and the People* 40.
7. Roy Shaw, *The Arts and the People* 40.
8. Hugo Young, *One of Us* 338.
9.   Roy Shaw,*The Arts and the People* 42.
10. ibid., 44. This report was financed by the Gulbenkian Foundation.
11. Roy Shaw, *The Arts and the People* 24-25. This report was financed by the Gulbenkian Foundation.
12.   *The Glory of the Garden* 6.
13. *A Hard Fact to Swallow* (London: PSI, 1982).
14. Lord Priestley, *Report on the Royal Opera House and the Royal Shakespeare Company* (London, Cabinet Office, 1983). Lord Rayner, *Report on the National Theatre* (London: Cabinet Office, 1985). Both concluded that there was serious underfunding by the state.
15.   Muriel Nissel, *Facts About the Arts* (London: PSI, 1982). John Myerscough,*The Economic Importance of the Arts in Britain*.
16. Simon Crine, *National Campaign for the Arts*, Number 1 Spring 1986.
17.. Anthony Beck, "The Impact of Thatcherism on the Arts Council" *Parliamentary Affairs* (Oxford: Oxford University Press, 1988) 369.
18. Robert Hewison, *Culture and Consensus* 259.
19. Anthony Beck, "The Impact of Thatcherism on the Arts Council" 374.
20. Robert Hewison, *Culture and Consensus* 260.
21. Anthony Beck, "The Impact of Thatcherism on the Arts Council" 374.
22. Graham, Norman and Shearn, *Cost Effectiveness and Opera Subsidy* (University of Sheffield, Final Report, Division of Economic Studies, July 1981) 15.
23. Frances Donaldson, *The British Council* (London: Jonathan Cape,1984) 311.
24. Frances Donaldson, *The British Council* 322.
25. B. Vale, "The Council in the Age of Thatcher", *Connect No. 55*, Spring 1991.
26. *The Sunday Times*, 22 October 1995, 3.

Chapter 8
Centralisation, Decentralisation and Devolution

As has been mentioned before (see pages 62-63), most public policies can be placed under three categories: (1) distributive policies which benefit all citizens indiscriminately; (2) redistributive policies which favour one section of the population at the cost of another; (3) regulative policies which control behaviour. Had there been a proper public debate on cultural policy, it would have been centred over the distributive and redistributive continuum. As it was, any discussion that did occur was often built around certain terms that were popular during the 1980s: centralisation, decentralisation and devolution. The last two terms in fact often represent a means of reducing public spending for a cost-cutting administration. Functions are devolved without the necessary accompanying resources. In this way the local authorities soak up criticism for inadequate financial provision from the national government.

Decentralisation means that a central policy is merely implemented by a lower tier of government, this leading to a certain uniformity of provision. Devolution, on the other hand means passing on policy decisions to a lower tier of government, thereby leading to a great multiplicity of practices. Mrs Thatcher's policies, and especially her cultural policy, were particularly paradoxical. Her official statements insisted on less red tape and a reduced government role as long-term aims, along with the re-establishment of state authority as a short-term goal. The clash between these two different aims led to contradictory policy realisations.

In practice, from 1984 onwards, central government took on a greater role through rate-capping. The aim was to cut local government spending by fixing an arbitrary limit. This interference in local government affairs is an area of policy which goes against the grain of what Lord Blake defines as four key traditions in British Conservatism: opposition to centralism, defence of national interests, opposition to egalitarianism, the avoidance of internal splits.[1] In this case, Mrs Thatcher felt that she had to reassert the authority of the state: she therefore played down the conservative tradition of opposing centralisation. In reality, the Conservatives stayed in power throughout the 1980s and one simple way of attacking the opposition parties and thereby rallying the Conservative voters, was to attack those local authorities that were under opposition control.

The growth of the Regional Arts Associations

Before the Thatcher years, the Arts Council had clearly defined its role in British cultural life. The crucial period was that of the mid 1950s, during which the implications of the second part of the Royal Charter were ignored (to increase the accessibility of the arts to the public throughout Great Britain). Decisions were made on the basis of quality and metropolitan standards. In the 1960s, the idea of regional offices was resurrected when the Regional Arts Associations (RAAs) were set up over several years and began to fill the void. The result of the administrative measures was a kind of patchwork of organisational styles, set up on a very organic, grass roots basis. The dominant organisational form, however, was one of regional Arts Councils, insisting on a policy of popularising quality culture. The goal was a democratisation of highbrow culture using elitist justifications.

During the 1970s, there were three official enquiries into local, regional and central government relations with regard to public subsidy for the arts, the most important of which was that of Lord Redcliffe-Maud's Support for the Arts in England and Wales (1976). It stated that: "we must look to local elected councils, at district and county level, to become the chief art patrons of the long term future".[2] A move away from centralised spending towards regional and local devolution was advocated. However, local authorities still had no statutory duty to spend on the arts and after the RAAs were formed very little local authority money actually went to them. This is one of the reasons why metropolitan areas spent much more on the arts than county councils. The 1982 Commons Committee on Arts Funding also recommended a shift of funding from London to the regions and the reaction of the Arts Council to these proposals was to print The Glory of the Garden (1984) policy review. £6 million were allocated to the regions, which then acted in a very similar manner to the Arts Council, distributing subsidies to quality productions rather than to organisations whose primary aim was to reach a wide audience. Over the Thatcher years, the RAAs saw their budgets grow from £5.2 million in 1978/9 to £29.1 million in 1988/9. This was indeed a significant move from the centre to the regions. (there was a doubling of RAA revenues in the 1983-1988 period.)

One of the highest spending RAAs, as might be expected, is London. More surprisingly, comes Northern, with the highest level per head of population. Merseyside Regional Arts Association also received significant sums of money, perhaps because of its economic and political problems. If this was the justification used, then why did South East Wales get only 40 pence per head of population in 1989/90? Cardiff experienced as high levels of unemployment as Liverpool during the period. The explanation can only be found in the Arts Council's reactive policy, which provided most of the regional funding. Where contacts and good liaison existed, projects were considered and encouraged. Low levels of grants for RAAs do not reflect low artistic levels. They rather show poor administrative organisation. It can therefore be assumed that Cardiff and the surrounding area had bad administrative contacts during the 1980s.

The national companies received 14 per cent less in the 1983-1989 period at constant prices, but in reality the shift was not as great as had been expected. These national companies were quite justifiably hostile to the idea of devolution, suspecting that local authorities would have less regard for national cultural institutions. This opinion was vindicated when rate-capping was introduced in the 1980s, in order to reduce local authority spending. The example of Westminster Council deciding not to support the English National Opera (ENO) has already been mentioned. However, it appears that these national companies were not the only losers during the 1980s. While Arts Council spending increased by 22 per cent during the latter half of the Thatcher period, that of the Welsh Arts Council went down by 2 per cent and that of the Scottish Arts Council decreased by 4 per cent.

Throughout the 1970s, relations had been strained between the Arts Council and the directors of the RAAs. At a meeting in June 1978, it was argued that:

> a RAA is not just 'another' Arts Council of Great Britain funded organisation. Unlike most organisations the Arts Council supported, RAAs have to fulfil many of the same functions as the Arts Council itself. In addition they have areas of work and responsibility which the Arts Council has either handed over or has never dealt with at all. The pressure on RAAs to initiate and to respond to new conditions is far greater than that experienced by the Council.[3]

One of the real strengths of the RAAs, namely the potential of being close to a local population and being able to respond to local cultural needs and demands, is observable. After the June 1978 meeting, a paper was produced called The Arts in the 1980s, that was followed by a working party paper with the title Towards a New Relationship. The RAAs won the power struggle by default because the Arts Council did not wish to take on any more functions and the former, by contrast, seemed more ambitious and inventive. In fact the Arts Council throughout the Thatcher period was in a permanent condition of administrative overload. It just could not deal with any more requests. This is why devolution began in the arts even before Mrs Thatcher assumed power and was continued throughout the 1980s.

Moreover, RAAs were more democratic: they are composed of a mixture of local councillors and elected representatives. Despite being more democratic than the Arts Council, this system sometimes led to constitutional conflicts. RAAs are neither local branches of the Arts Council, nor purely local authority associations. Sometimes, they are both partners with local authorities and supplicants of funds from those same local authorities. For example, a constitutional crisis was provoked in 1980 within the Merseyside Arts Association where members of the Arts Association successfully managed to elect the executive. This conflict between the Arts Council and local authorities led to the setting up of a trust to carry on the work, while a new constitution was defined.

The quality of local government decision making in the arts is often criticised, but perhaps it is because the arts are a relatively new function for the local authorities that errors have been made. A local authority is much closer to the local community than an Arts Council, if only because it is elected every four years while Arts Councils are accountable only to the government once a year. RAAs can support artistic work which the Arts Council would not even consider, such as community arts or ethnic minority culture, depending on local circumstances. Some remarkable work in this area can be found in Camden and Thamesdown, for example. There is evidence that local authority spending on the arts and libraries increased considerably at the end of the Thatcher period. Capital expenditure on theatres, that is building or maintenance work, was reduced especially in Wales. This suggests that local authorities considered that they had enough theatre provision under their responsibility. However, spending on theatre productions and libraries went up considerably, while that on museums and galleries was less spectacular. Museums and galleries had been given considerable increases during the first half of the period. One should also point out that Scottish local authorities spent much more than Welsh ones.

The abolition of the Greater London Council

In total contradiction to this movement of devolution, Mrs Thatcher's removal of the metropolitan tier of local government took money away from the regions back to the Arts Council, which then redistributed it to the RAAs. The consequence of this move was that the redistribution of funds away from London to the regions was slowed down. The Local Government Act of 1985 was a messy and expensive administrative blunder, justified on partisan political grounds. In the case of London the functions of the metropolitan authorities were divided between thirty-two London boroughs, the City of London, the Inner London Education Authorities, various 'quangos' such as the Thames Water Authority, the Arts Council, thirty-six metropolitan district councils, nineteen newly elected Joint Boards, one London-wide body for waste and various statutory waste disposal bodies for other areas. The result of this policy was that while the big national arts companies survived, because they could turn to alternative sources of funding such as those offered by the private sector, small, amateur and ethnic companies were eliminated. After 1985, for example, sixty organisations that had been funded by the Greater London Council (GLC) and the Greater London Arts Association (GLAA) did not receive replacement funds.

All things considered, Mrs Thatcher's cultural policy with regard to central and local government was highly ambiguous. The Arts Council decentralised some of its powers to the RAAs during the 1980s. At the same time the reorganisation of the metropolitan areas in 1985-1986 led to a significant move towards centralisation in arts spending by central government. Thus a discrepancy between what was intended and what actually happened is visible. As before, with other aspects of cultural policy, an implementation gap appears due to contradictory policy aims. On the one hand, Mrs Thatcher continued to argue that the consumer should decide, and yet, on the other hand, she centralised and decentralised at will, implementing apparently contradictory policies. In fact, her priority in this policy area was to re-assert the authority of the state. With such an aim in mind, she decentralised in an uneven way, with partial success in the case of the RAAs and partial failure in that of the re-organisation of the metropolitan areas.

Notes

1. Andrew Gamble, *The Politics of Thatcherism* (London: Macmillan, 1990) 157.
2. Robert Hutchison, *The Politics of the Arts Council* 127.
3. Robert Hutchison, *The Politics of the Arts Council*

Chapter 9
The Positions of the Different Parties

It is surprising how little the various arts policy proposals of the major political parties in Great Britain during the 1980s differ. In fact there existed a remarkable consensus on the matter. All the parties believed in the principle of the democratisation of elitist culture. This consensus is all the more astonishing as various European countries during that period had totally different cultural policy traditions. These alternatives were never discussed during the Thatcher period. The all-party agreement over arts policy was only dented by the Liberal Democrats proposing several innovative ideas.

The Conservative position on the arts

For the Conservative Party, cultural policy is an area of government where the agenda is left as muddled and vague as possible. This is in line with the traditional liberal position of keeping legislation to a minimum and resorting to short-term, reactive policies. In 1959, a Bow Group document entitled Patronage of the Arts best described Conservative Party cultural policy before Mrs Thatcher's term of office. "Britain has the lowest financial contribution to the arts of any civilised nation", was its introductory phrase. It was followed by an appeal: "Provision for the arts should be removed from the political sphere. The arts should become a utility service: like education, available for all, and indeed as a logical extension to education."[1]
The Prime Minister at the time, Harold (later Lord) MacMillan, was stating that people had 'never had it so good'. In practice it meant that

the state should assume an ever increasing number of functions. In the Heath period, the government did not reduce the amount of money spent on the arts which had tripled during the Wilson years (1964-70). What most people remembered was the charging of entrance fees to museums, which Lord Eccles, the then Minister for the Arts, unsuccessfully tried to introduce in 1970 under Edward Heath, but failed because of fierce public opposition and high running costs. This political miscalculation was reminiscent of Mrs Thatcher's school milk fiasco in 1970, when she was accused of being a 'milk-snatcher'. After this period, the Conservative Political Centre produced the last consensus type cultural document in 1978. In it, St John Stevas argued that state money on the arts was a good investment: the arts "can genuinely be said to pay their way". Paradoxically, at the time, this claim could not be backed up by any body of available evidence.

Henceforth, official Conservative policy shifted and Kingsley Amis, through the Conservative Political Centre, became its advocate. In 1979, the document An Arts-Policy? argued very much against any idea of a need for government to popularise art. Amis argued that "more (would) mean worse". In reality, this kind of general proposition was very much in line with the idea of a previous mythical golden age and declining standards much beloved of cultural elitists. He wanted the consumer to decide:

> In fact central government has traditionally had only a junior role to play in supporting the arts; public expenditure as a whole is, and always has been, only a fraction of total expenditure on the arts. We believe that that is right, and that it is right for the consumer rather than public expenditure on the arts to be the major determinant of the market.[2]

Nonetheless, Amis attacked all kinds of government cultural policy in the mass media. For him, the Arts Council was "pathetically pretending that some external obstacle has hitherto stood in most people's way. Most people aren't truly accessible to art and never will be and we shouldn't try to make them."[3]

Lord Gowrie, who was both Minister for the Treasury and Minister for the Arts, used the same kind of language: "It is the concern of all levels of government to deal with materialistic things. As a Conservative I believe that governments with the loftiest ideals tend to do the most damage."[4] This was another example of a politician trying to restrict the political agenda and have a minimum amount of public debate. Gowrie further confused the issue by arguing that anyone who was any good would read for him or herself. Pierre Bourdieu's claim, that the bourgeoisie tends to think of culture as a 'natural' activity, as if it is normal for civilised people to have a certain cultural level, this functioning as an excluder of lower strata which have less cultural capital, seems to be vindicated in Gowrie's assertion. However, even conservatives know that cultural progress is usually a slow and sometimes painful process based on long and time-consuming education. Thus, Sir William Rees-Mogg also argued against public subsidy, as it 'weakens the sinews of self-help'.[5] Many of the conservative back-benchers agreed with this position and applauded Simon Jenkins' claim in The Economist that subsidy "keeps its victims cocooned in a 1960s time warp of jaded radicalism".[6] However, both the Priestley Report and the Rayner Report, in 1983 and 1985 respectively, having looked at real case studies, came to quite opposite conclusions. Despite this evidence, the Conservative Political Centre continued to argue that money was being squandered: "Where standards have fallen, the Arts Council should take a stricter stance towards support; their limited funds should be concentrated on providing excellence and encouraging promising talent rather than subsidising the stale."[7]

Thus, during the Thatcher period, Conservative Party policy on the arts, although never clearly stated, was primarily based on a reduced role of the state and a significant increase in private patronage, sponsorship and charity. It recalled the Victorian period, where values such as paternalism, civic pride and duty to one's community dominated public policy. These deeply influenced Mrs Thatcher's political credo. Premier Gladstone's claim, that "the higher instruments of human civilisation are also the ultimate guarantees of public order,"[8] was an inspiration again.

Conversely, in the 1980s, opposition parties saw in cultural policy a quick and easy vote catcher. The then director of the National Theatre, Peter Hall claimed that "well over 90 per cent of the people in the performing arts, education and the creative world are against her".[9] The opposition, therefore, defined their counter-arguments to Conservative Party policy in the arts in the same reactive and short-term fashion. The various parties were themselves forced to adopt Mrs Thatcher's pragmatic approach to arts policy.

The position of the Labour Party

The Labour Party position on the arts before 1979 was simple: everyone should have access to high art forms. This was its basic idea of the democratisation of culture. On the far-left wing of the party, the idea of cultural democracy was pushed to the limit. People involved in community arts argued that cultural expression was a basic human right and that people should express themselves in the form that made them feel most comfortable. This constituted the only ideological threat to the cultural consensus that came during the Thatcher period. Su Braden, a prominent spokesperson for Community Arts wrote: "The great artistic deception of the 20th century has been to insist to all people that this was their culture. The Arts Council of Great Britain was established on this premise."[10] Her implication was that it was unacceptable to have an official Arts Council culture, a view which paradoxically coincides with the conservative libertarian tradition. Thus the left wing of the Labour Party, which became known as the New Left, attacked the Arts Council for being a 'tool of the ruling class' and of being a means of producing 'cultural imperialism'. In this controversy, the right-wing Conservative back-benchers and the tabloid press were surprisingly joined by the left wing of Labour in their criticism of the cultural Establishment. However, the radical wing of the Labour Party was brought to heel by the then leader Neil Kinnock, who successfully excluded Militant supporters from party membership in 1986 and after and directed the party towards the consensual centre. Henceforth, the Labour Party proposed some reasonable and unrevolutionary changes in cultural policy.

The election manifesto, in 1983, contained proposals for a new ministry of broadcasting and the arts. Zero-rating VAT for the arts was also suggested. Resources were to be switched from the centre to what would be called Regional Arts Development Boards. These new boards were to replace the old RAAs. In addition to the proposed changes, the Labour Party wanted to introduce a mandatory minimum level of spending on the arts for local authorities: 1/2p on the rates was suggested but the idea was later dropped on political grounds. Although this measure would have had a beneficial effect in starting to redress the imbalance between various local government funding levels for the arts, the idea of obliging people to spend money on the arts when there might be no local demand or tradition in the field was a major political problem. Thus, the anti-consensual Conservative ideas, but also their consensual practices, were countered by Labour moderation and the radical left's suggestions were firmly excluded by Neil Kinnock. Both Labour and the Conservative Party continued in the elitist cultural tradition. For that reason, the idea of cultural democracy, close to the modern culturalist way of considering artistic expression, was marginalised and kept on the periphery of the political agenda.

The positions of the Liberal and Social Democratic Parties

At the time, the most innovative and imaginative suggestions came from the two other major national British political parties, the Liberal Party and the Social Democratic Party, which in 1988 were to come together in the Liberal Democratic Party. In 1982, the Liberal Party produced its Manifesto for the Arts. Like the Labour Party, it proposed a new ministry for both broadcasting and the arts. It also wanted zero-rating VAT for arts activities and added tax deductibility for arts donations. A scheme was proposed for a voucher system, that would give money collected on the sale of blank audio and video cassettes to live cultural events. A similar project has functioned in

Sweden over many years. This was an excellent idea because it would have taken resources from private cultural consumption to live cultural events. Its aim was to transfer money away from the cultural reproducers to the less profitable cultural producers. Its drawback was that the scheme would have been complicated to put into practice. (The Liberal Party manifesto for 1987, even proposed a Ministry of Arts, Communication and Heritage.) The Arts Council was to be scrapped and RAAs funded directly by the new ministry. It was hoped that endowment trusts, based on capital funds, comprising Treasury stock or local government bonds, would be the main source of funding.

The Social Democratic Party adopted a different line of argument, calling for a reform and not for a scrapping of the Arts Council system. It proposed that all ministerial nominations were to be subjected to a House of Commons scrutiny committee. This was a direct response to Mrs Thatcher's partisan nomination practices, and represents a political problem encountered in all advanced centralised industrialised states. The SDP also proposed that the Arts Council's annual accounts be subjected to Parliamentary scrutiny. An Arts Bank was suggested, to help artists set up their own businesses, as was an advertising levy to raise an estimated £250 million a year for the arts.

Deciding for or against political proposals is a difficult task for the arts because there is relatively little experience in the field. However, the implications and the probable consequences of these proposals can be meaningfully discussed. The process is similar to that of staging new plays. It is the audience that decides and ultimately, 'the proof of the pudding is in the eating', when the policy proposals are applied. Under the Conservative governments in the 1979-1990 period, the Arts Council came under a lot of pressure and the whole arm's length principle seemed to be about to collapse. In such circumstances, direct government funding of the national companies would have been administratively cheaper and the remaining distribution of funds might have been transferred to the RAAs. The idea of creating a large ministry dealing with the arts, broadcasting and heritage was excellent, as it would have permitted a clarification of policy and better strategic planning, contrasting with current short-term decisions and little public debate. In 1992, the Conservative government under John Major created a Department of National Heritage. Both the Press and broadcasting then came under the responsibility of the new minister in a £1 billion ministry. However, David Mellor, the first Heritage Secretary, failed to include the British Council and the BBC World Service. By 1994, further changes meant that the Regional Arts Boards took over practically all the responsibilities of the newly-renamed Arts Council of England. One project on which all the political parties agreed was the proposed National Lottery with proceeds going to the arts and heritage. This was in fact created in 1994, after much discussion and controversy. Another area of agreement for all the major British political parties was the rejection of the French concept of Maisons de Culture et de la Jeunesse. The French idea of cultural democracy, a citizen's right to various cultural activities, did not even get onto the political agenda. community arts was considered by all major parties as a luxury which post-Imperial Britain could not afford, and Mrs Thatcher was in large part responsible for this conceptual shift in the direction of the market economy.

All three major political parties agreed on democratising elitist and national culture. The only real challenge to this consensus came in the form of the community arts movement and its proposal of cultural democracy. And as the inner-city riots of the early 1980s receded, Mrs Thatcher naturally reduced the grants for community arts. Thus were political and security problems disposed of. Once again, the cultural debate was effectively smothered.

Notes

1. *Patronage of the Arts* (London: Bow Group, 1959) 12.
2. *The Arts: the Next Move Forward* (London: Conservative Political Centre, April 1987).
3. Roy Shaw, *The Arts and the People* 111.
4. Roy Shaw, *The Arts and the People* 107.
5. ibid., 35.
6. ibid., 90.
7. *The Arts: the Next Move Forward.*
8. Roy Shaw, *The Arts and the People* 25.
9. Hugo Young, *One of Us*

Chapter 10
Sponsorship and Patronage

The centre piece in Mrs Thatcher's cultural policy was business sponsorship and patronage. While the state was supposed to pull out of subsidising arts activities, it was hoped that the businessman would gradually fill in the vacant space. She hoped to push Great Britain significantly in the direction of the American model of private cultural provision, bringing entrepreneurial vigour and business rigour to the whole arts market. One can also regard it as a move back to the Victorian past when private patronage was the major form of cultural subsidy. Although the Victorian state was particularly mean in the cultural domain, it was the local authorities that provided the most imaginative examples of cultural encouragement.

The Association of Business Sponsorship for the Arts (ABSA) was set up in 1976 by large tobacco companies that were trying to find advertising space in the face of increasing difficulties with billboards in the street and in sporting events. Most significantly, Luke Rittner, the Chairman of ABSA, in turn became secretary-general of the Arts Council in 1983. In the previous year, the British Tourist Board had provided a frank booklet, explaining to organisations how to go about gaining business sponsorship. There was an "increasing awareness of smoking and health, tobacco companies' sponsorship of sport (was) being questioned and a move towards arts sponsorship (was) a way of overcoming this".[1] The leaflet suggested that the potential arts sponsor should "know the chairman's hobbies". In 1985, Mr Rees-Mogg maintained that sponsorship was "a selective form of high quality advertising". By 1985/6, ABSA claimed to have distributed 15-20 million of subsidy to various arts organisations. In reality, it acted in much the same way as a private Arts Council, only it had no obligation to publish figures and had a much higher media profile than the state organisation. One half of the relatively large amount of money collected by ABSA was in fact corporation tax that was not collected by the state, this representing a hidden government subsidy. However, the large size of ABSA's income in 1985 can only be regarded as proof of its effectiveness and success.

Three problems with sponsorship

Although ABSA did provide a large amount of money, there were and still are three major drawbacks to this innovation: a moral problem, a possibility of instability of funding and difficulties over quality of production and risk taking.

The way business sponsorship came to be accepted is an excellent example of reactive policies. Past arts administrators such as Lord Goodman, the former chairman of the Arts Council, argued that any money going to the arts was useful, no matter what the source: "Sir, I would accept money for the arts from anyone, even murderers and rapists."[2] Others, such as Sir Roy Shaw, argued against, claiming that a coherent position needed adopting. On the one hand, government health warnings were put on all forms of cigarette advertising. On the other hand, in the early 1980s, banners of cigarette companies were seen proudly unfurling above symphony orchestras. The London Symphony Orchestra even offered free cigarettes at some of its concerts as a result of pressure from its tobacco sponsor. In the absence of any action by the Health ministers of the time, Paul Eddington and Warren Mitchell, two well known actors, set up a pressure group called Actors Against Tobacco Sponsorship (ACTS). By 1986, the Labour Party agreed on a ban on cigarette advertising if the party came to power. However, none of this pressure produced a ban on cigarette sponsorship and the cigarette companies continued to get cheap and up market advertising space in the arts. It should not be forgotten that Mrs Thatcher is even now a consultant for the tobacco company Philip Morris in the United States.

The second problem over business sponsorship was its inherent instability as a form of funding. A company uses its funds to get maximum coverage for a minimum price. In 1985, Mr Colin Tweedy, director of ABSA, put it in a nutshell: "sponsorship may have begun as a prestigious form of public relations, but it has increasingly moved towards selling".[3] Moreover, what was given one year might be withdrawn in the course of the next. In contrast, the Arts Council, despite its drawbacks, provided a relatively stable form of funding. ABSA financing rarely lasted for more than a few years, before the company changed to another arts organisation. Business sponsorship therefore provided valuable money for the arts but it could only form the icing on the cake and not the very basis of arts funding. It could only be considered as a short-term measure for certain high-profile arts organisations.

A similar kind of problem came in 1986, when Luke Rittner, the Arts Council secretary-general, approved various budget changes on tax exemptions to charities and payroll deductions. His reason for such changes was that arts organisations would have to go out and search for money. There is nothing wrong with going out into the market-place and selling yourself if you are an arts organisation, but arts administrators complain that they spend a lot of time and energy trying to obtain temporary money from business companies. Brian Nicholson, then joint manager of the Observer, made a significant remark about the point of view of the advertisers. "You should be absolutely ruthless in breaking off any sponsorship that doesn't fit your present needs."[4] So, from the point of view of the arts organisations, business sponsorship was far from the panacea that Mrs Thatcher and the Conservatives hoped it would be, especially when recession hit the British economy at the end of the 1980s and the early 1990s.

The third major problem over business sponsorship is the kind of work it encourages. Victor Head pointed out that "controversy is usually bad for business".[5] Although recent Benetton advertisements show that controversy can sometimes be beneficial (in the case of the Aids adverts in 1993), this is clearly the exception to the rule. In general, sponsors will be attracted to safe, mainstream cultural forms and will tend to shy away from experimental or avant- garde art forms. Given this situation, it is often left to state organisations, in view of their less direct links with the market-place, to take risks on innovative art forms. In the theatre, plays are often tested in fringe theatres before being transferred to the commercial West End theatres. Dario Fo's Accidental Death of an Anarchist is a good example of this procedure in the early 1980s. Therefore, when it comes to risk taking, commercial sponsorship is no match for state subsidy. Thus the two cannot be said to be interchangeable, as Mrs Thatcher and the Conservatives argued in the 1980s. They should rather be considered as complementary.

Curiously, ABSA was set up in 1976 with the blessing of the Labour Government. It was given enthusiastic support by the successive Conservative governments and it adopted a high profile media style. American-style award ceremonies were organised every year and, in the 1977-1987 period, one hundred and three awards were handed out, such as Best Commission of New Art or Best Sponsorship of Arts and Disabled People. By 1983, it counted one hundred members and, in 1987, that figure had doubled with ABSA spending an estimated 25 million. In 1983, the organisation published its own sponsorship manual. ABSA has therefore been a relative success story, with only a few reservations. Nonetheless, the Conservative rhetoric and praise is out of place, as the House of Commons debate on business sponsorship of February 1984 shows: "There have been outstanding acts of patronage, gifts made purely for the love of the arts, with no thought of a return. It is disinterested giving as distinct from the interested giving that is business sponsorship."[6] This refers to the 1984 British Sponsorship Investment Scheme (BSIS) that matched private contributions with government money.

In 1986, further changes were made to try and imitate the United States model of donating to culture. Deeds of Covenant were kept, but on a more simplified basis and up to 120 were tax exempted through the Pay As You Earn (PAYE) scheme that was introduced in 1980. The changes that occurred due to these tax modifications are difficult to measure, once again because government figures apply to all charitable organisations and do not give a specific breakdown for the statistics relating to the arts. Only estimates are available. John Myerscough calculated the amounts of money given in Glasgow, Merseyside and Ipswich and grossed up a 40-50 million donation level on a national basis. Although this is not a very scientific form of calculation it is the only way of gaining an overall idea of sponsorship levels. The 2 million that were measured for Glasgow, Merseyside and Ipswich were multiplied to give an indication of national levels.

In conclusion, ABSA was a very successful organisation for the contributors from the business and media coverage point of view, but caused problems for the recipients of private patronage and sponsorship. The amounts of money generated were and still are substantial, but part of that money is government tax foregone, and private patronage and sponsorship levels inevitably declined with the onset of recession in 1990.

Mrs Thatcher and the Conservatives had hoped that by encouraging private patronage and sponsorship Great Britain would follow the United States's model of cultural spending. Although ABSA and sponsorship were a significant success, the private mode of cultural funding was never able to replace that of the British public mode. The two types of funding were in fact complementary and exercised different functions. This thrust placed Britain somewhere between the Western European high-subsidy tradition and the United States high private spending model. Thus, despite eleven years of premiership, Mrs Thatcher did not succeed in making Britain emulate the American position as closely as she would have liked.

Notes

1. Roy Shaw, *The Arts and the People* 71.
2. Roy Shaw, *The Arts and the People* 72.
3. Roy Shaw, *The Arts and the People* 67.
4. ibid, 62.
5. ibid, 62.
6. ABSA, *A Celebration of 10 Years of Business Sponsorship of the Arts* (London: Telegraph Publications, 1987) 12.

Chapter 11
An Overview of the Museums, Performing Arts and Libraries

Museums and galleries

Museums and galleries did surprisingly well out of the 1980s decade. This came as a surprise as prospects in 1979 were rather gloomy. The first Thatcher government threatened reductions in government support due to financial stringency. In actual fact, museums and galleries were given top priority in the allocation of government funds, and private patronage and sponsorship were both areas that could be successfully exploited in the case of high-profile national institutions. The Thatcher period is therefore one of stable funding levels. The three most significant changes that occurred were the generalisation of museum charges, a certain professionalisation in museum administration and a reduced role for local authorities.

An important and politically sensitive change in cultural policy comes when admission charges were officially encouraged on a voluntary basis. This is another example of the British voluntarist tradition. Many art galleries and museums introduced charges during the 1980s, this causing a slight reduction in the number of visitors. By January 1990, the House of Commons Select Committee on Education, Science and the Arts was recommending that "all national museums and galleries should consider introducing compulsory admission charges". Most followed this advice but there were exceptions such as London's Victoria and Albert Museum, that kept to its system of voluntary donations started in 1985, or Bradford's National Museum of Photography that did not charge entrance fees. Tim Renton, Minister for the Arts, summed up the situation in 1991, one year after Mrs Thatcher's resignation: "Those museums where admission charges have been introduced have reported that, after dropping initially, attendances have generally picked up and in many cases, have returned to previous levels."[1] Official figures show a near doubling of the British Museum's attendance levels between 1982 and 1991. The figures before 1986, for both the National History Museum and the Science Museum, are unreliable. The respective levels of 1.5 and 2.5 million visitors are surely more realistic for the years after 1986. The National Gallery and the Tate also experienced a significant increase in the number of visitors. Taking into account the unreliable nature of the pre-1986 figures, it would seem that there was a gradual increase in the number of people going to national museums throughout the 1980s.

A complex and heated political debate arose over museum charges. Some saw them as the terrible result of Mrs Thatcher's policies of rolling back the state, a return to Victorian meanness. The minister for Arts and Libraries, Lord Eccles, had tried to introduce admission charges under the Heath government in 1970 and was forced to back down under public pressure. Many others claimed that it was a good idea to charge foreign tourists for the services they used. The quality of the debate was largely spoiled by the lack of reliable statistics. However, despite the sharp and often doctrinaire exchanges, a universal benefit favouring a mostly middle-class and often foreign audience was difficult to justify in the harsh economic climate of the 1980s. The introduction of charges did lead to a reduction in the number of visitors, but as the previous estimates were unreliable, no accurate comparisons could be made. Given the precedents, the fact that a public debate took place over this cultural issue was an achievement.

The economic climate of the 1980s encouraged administrators to be more rigorous in the handling of resources and more adventurous in finding revenue. For such purposes, information was suddenly available to the public and league tables were printed showing how various museums were doing. Publicity also encouraged a greater sense of public accountability among the administrators. Catering services and shops were added to many of the national museums and galleries.

Choices became more commercial and clear financial policies had to be presented. Management of personnel and resources became increasingly based on the criteria of efficiency. All these changes were of the kind that Mrs Thatcher approved of.

These trends during the 1980s did not only affect the national galleries. After 1986, local authorities experienced a government squeeze and had therefore to improve their performances. Local authority museums and galleries introduced admission charges and this did not have a significant effect on visitor numbers. This was only to be expected as few museums cater for the lower income levels. Middle-class users could, therefore, afford to pay for this type of culture especially as their tax levels were reduced during the Thatcher period. This slight but steady increase in numbers mirrored the trend for national museums.

The revenue shortfall had to be found somewhere, so this encouraged innovation and all types of alternative funding sources. In fact, both national and local authority museums and galleries moved in the direction of those policies followed by the independent (private) museums. This sector has always depended on admission charges and imaginative services for its survival. It is interesting to note that the largest category, that drew 27 per cent of the total for independent museums, was that of industrial museums. The museum at Ironbridge is a very successful example of this type of project. The second most popular category was the transport museums with a vast range covering steam engines, buses, trams, cars and motorbikes.

In the Thatcher years there was an increase in the number of museums which meant that the average number of visits per museum fell. In 1978, there were 72,000 visits per museum. The figures for the years 1982, 1986 and 1988 are 61,000, 51,000 and 48,000 respectively. Long-term growth in museum attendance levels seems to be unlikely. The effect of rate-capping by central government on local government was that some councils decided to withdraw funds for local museums. A vivid example of this policy can be seen in the closure of the Exeter Maritime Museum in December 1991, despite very high attendance levels.

Most statistics on the subject point to a natural limit on the visiting levels of museums and thus one way of introducing more efficiency would be to reduce their number. This trend will probably be confirmed in the 1990s. However, given this situation, another solution would be to increase the number of visitors. Various cultural blockages exist on the content and the presentation of galleries and museums. Potential visitors are put off from going to them. One survey came to the conclusion that lower social classes and ethnic communities saw museums as 'dingy places of white culture.'[2] Another one confirmed a decline in attendance among older age groups and among lower social grades.[3] Innovative ideas can help only slightly. For example, the Geffrye Museum in London tried to serve a local multicultural community. It launched a specific programme for ethnic minority groups and old people. In 1990, exhibitions of Chinese design and its influence on British homes, and some on Indian culture on British homes, were real attempts to attract new visitors. In 1991, a report by Her Majesty's Inspectors pointed out that too few museums had specialised in young people, which constituted another solution for increasing attendance levels. However, a definite specialisation in what certain museums offered reflected a multiracial and multicultural society and emerged as a significant trend of the 1980s.

Globally speaking, the Thatcher decade saw an increase in the amount of money and central government spending on museums and galleries. This was primarily due to the significance of this form of recreation in attracting foreign tourists, and the important economic role of the varied services that they require. However, on assuming power, Mrs Thatcher gave a clear signal to museum administrators that local government should be squeezed and that central government spending would proportionally decline, although this actually happened only after 1986. She encouraged museums and galleries to be more businesslike, more efficient and more professional. During the 1980s, both series of institutions rose to the challenge and improved their services in all the areas concerned.

Opera

Opera, classical music and museums can all be put in the same category as they receive the heaviest level of arts subsidy in the United Kingdom. When Mrs Thatcher took office in 1979, it was expected that opera would be one of the areas most affected by the process of rolling back the state. Yet again a discrepancy between the long-term objective of cutting state expenditure and shorter-term objectives became evident. Thus for example, maintaining an international British musical reputation and attracting high quality American tourists, both long and short-term objectives, prevailed. In that case it was national pride that justified high subsidy levels.

Examples from other countries influenced British politics in terms of subsidy levels. In Europe, La Scala in Milan is subsidised to the tune of 70 per cent, while at the other extreme the Metropolitan Opera in New York gets only 20 per cent subsidy. Both have excellent international reputations and stage imaginative productions. Mrs Thatcher was not surprisingly attracted by the United States model. Thus ticket prices more than doubled over the Thatcher years and audiences increased despite a temporary decline in 1986, as shown in Table 12.4 on page 429. This table provides evidence that all the major opera companies in Great Britain significantly increased their box office takings in the second half of the Thatcher decade. Both Scottish Opera and English National Opera more than doubled their takings in the five year period under consideration. This is mirrored in the figures of percentage capacity. Means were found for selling higher levels of tickets and filling the theatres to greater capacity. This is clear proof of better marketing, higher productivity and more efficient organisation in the major opera companies during the latter part of the 1980s. There was also a slight increase in the number of performances from 690 in 1984/5 to 747 in 1988/9. This confirms the fact that the Baumol-Bowen thesis (see pages 107-108), as seen in their book in the 1960s, no longer applies, if it ever did, to certain performing arts. Another reason for the higher audience figures undoubtedly is television coverage on BBC 2 and

Channel 4, with twenty-eight operas shown in 1988 getting up to 800,000 viewers.

In 1979, there were seven principal revenue funded opera companies in Great Britain: the Royal Opera, English National Opera (ENO), Opera North, Kent Opera, Welsh National Opera (WNO), Scottish Opera and Glyndebourne. Opera North became an independent company in 1980, and Opera 80 was set up in 1979 as a small touring company for the whole of England. There also exists Opera Northern Ireland which combines the talents of the Northern Ireland Opera Trust and the Studio Opera Group under the supervision of the Arts Council of Northern Ireland. The Glory of the Garden (1984) policy statement claimed that opera was concentrated on London and taking up too large a proportion of Arts Council funds. This had to be corrected. In 1985 and 1986, a spheres of influence policy was therefore introduced to give a maximum amount of opera provision to the English regions. This provision was a great success: nationwide touring seasons attracted high subscription levels. Immediately, the Arts Council Touring Department spent substantial sums on helping local touring, especially with Kent Opera and Opera North. Nonetheless, the Arts Council Opera Study Group also produced a pessimistic report on regional touring in the early 1990s. This undoubtedly was for strategic and political reasons, as the cultural results were remarkable during the whole Thatcher period.

During this period, central government and local authority subsidy declined as a proportion of total revenue for opera companies. In 1983/4, 60 per cent of total revenue came from subsidy while in 1987/8, that proportion had fallen to 51 per cent. This was a significant change and a result of political decisions. If one takes the example of Opera Northern Ireland, one finds a 69 per cent subsidy level and a high 12 per cent sponsorship proportion of total revenue. This reflects the fact that the best profits are to be made in London with its international reputation and its teaching possibilities. It is extremely difficult to build up an international reputation when one is placed on the periphery of the British Isles. A parallel development was the increase in sponsorship revenue: from 6 per cent to 8 per cent in the same period. Furthermore, other trading activities were developed, such as catering in order to earn straightforward cash.

One major problem with this more accountable system where opera companies relied more heavily on ticket receipts, is that risk taking was reduced. If the public pays proportionally more, it has a greater say in what is staged. The inevitable result is commercially safe and unadventurous programming with little contemporary music. One can establish a kind of Top Ten and Bottom Ten list of opera for the year 1983/4. Number one would be Die Fliedermaus (with 50,197 seats sold). Number two was Don Giovanni (49,234 seats). Carmen was number three with 32,412 seats. Then follow La Boh^me, Fidelio, Madame Butterfly, The Mastersingers of Nuremberg, La Traviata, Rigoletto and the Magic Flute. The worst scores went to War and Peace, the Beggars Opera, Parsifal, From the House of the Dead, The Seraglio, I Cappuletti et I Montechi, Jenufa, Katya Kabanova, La Clemenza di Tito, and Toussaint respectively. Thus the table shows that Michael Tippett's music was absent and modern composers such as Maxwell Davies got only 55 per cent capacities. Completely modern works attracted the lowest audience levels. In 1984, Janacek's Mr Broucek, a very imaginative London production, only attracted a 60 per cent audience capacity. This increased dependency on commercial and middlebrow culture led to the taking of fewer artistic risks in the overall programming.

Curiously, Mrs Thatcher personally liked opera and this may be one of the reasons why this area of the arts did so well during the 1980s. Government subsidy was certainly reduced as a proportion of total income, but the shortfall was more than made up for by a mix of higher ticket prices and other commercial activities. As in the case of museums, it was an attractive area for commercial sponsors and patronage. Thus despite Mrs Thatcher's rhetoric of rolling back the state and encouraging middlebrow and commercial content, opera remained one of the cultural priorities as had been the case throughout the postwar period. In this particular case the prime minister's action was in total continuity with her predecessors'.

Classical music

In Britain, classical music is in a similar position to opera. It too attracts international audiences and gives the country an international reputation that is the envy of many other European countries. Mrs Thatcher's policies in music were similar to those in other high arts areas. The state continued to finance the most prestigious and loss-making highbrow end of the market, while at the same time encouraging the profit-making part of the business.

In consequence, the classical music business remained remarkably stable throughout the Thatcher period. The number of performances did not vary much during the middle years of the Thatcher period. In fact they went down slightly from 2002 in 1982/3 to 1832 in 1987/8 for the major orchestras, excluding the BBC ones. When the Arts Council decided to implement The Glory of the Garden (1984) policy, it decided to encourage the transfer of two orchestras. The Bournemouth Symphony and Sinfonietta was to move to Bristol, while one of the London orchestras was to move to the east Midlands. Nothing came of these proposals because Arts Council funding was only a small element of total income and thus Council advice could effectively be ignored. Another important reason for musicians staying in London is that they supplement their meagre incomes through recording work, which is almost invariably done in London. These same musicians also have a considerable amount of teaching work in the capital that would be lost in the provinces. Mrs Thatcher's laissez-faire policy, therefore, encouraged the natural tendency of the market to produce centres of excellence.

At the same time, Mrs Thatcher's political declarations on reduced government spending on the arts compelled the orchestras to become more efficient. Orchestras simply had to fill their empty seats and keep safe concert programmes attracting mass audiences. The 1986/7 season was bad because Libyan terrorist threats and fear of Chernobyl caused a certain number of American tourists to stay at home. It should be noted that the percentage of capacity increased significantly over the 1980s period. Still, in the meantime, ticket prices were increased without reducing demand. Indeed, Simon Rattle and the Birmingham Symphony Orchestra (BSO) showed that new demand and excitement could be stimulated by adventurous programming. Likewise, when the London Symphony Orchestra (LSO) had financial problems in 1982, they were solved by adventurous programming and by attracting younger audiences.

Among contract orchestras, all increased the number of recording sessions in 1987/8 compared to 1984/5. The effect of the abolition of the metropolitan areas and the consequent move from local authority funding to Arts Council funding was being felt. One can also note that recordings and overseas touring increased for most orchestras. This can be regarded as one aspect of the globalisation of culture. All these orchestras were trying to raise revenue without asking for increased subsidy. Sponsorship and other private income increased slightly up to 1986, but the figures are surprisingly stable. The regional contract orchestras relied heavily on income from live performances. (yet this is not the case for the London orchestras.) The London orchestras were in a good position to develop other activities in order to raise money. They could turn to education, film sessions, film music, recordings, touring. These orchestras were much less dependent on subsidy than regional ones but at the same time had to respect commercial rules.

The BBC orchestras have a tradition of providing classical music outside the capital. In 1987/8, the BBC spent œ8.5 million on its own house orchestras, making vital contributions for the Ulster Orchestra and the BBC Welsh Symphony Orchestra, which a deregulated market would have excluded. The classical music policy of the BBC has been one of trying to educate, by bringing serious music to the provinces despite higher costs. This policy was in the public service tradition and functioned in a way similar to the risk taking that occurs in the subsidised part of the theatre business. The BBC contract orchestras also played more contemporary music than the London ones. Thus, the BBC was able to be more adventurous, in its programming, than the more commercially oriented orchestras. As a consequence, the Arts Council suggested that grant aid would be more closely tied to risk-taking. However, the London based organisations could not be both innovative and at the same time more commercially successful. This contradiction was never resolved.

The Arts Council wanted to encourage both contemporary and early music, during the Thatcher period. Four period instrument groups emerged from this initiative: the London Classical Players, the Orchestra of the Age of Enlightenment, the English Concert and the Monteverdi Choir and Orchestra. Nasseem Khan conducted a study on ethnic music in 1976 entitled The Arts Britain Ignores. This laid the groundwork for an Arts Council survey into ethnic classical music that was conducted in 1985. The Report came out in 1986 and recommended an increase in subsidy. In 1984/5, 17,500 were spent on classical music from the Caribbean, Pakistan, India, and Africa. In 1987/8, the figure had increased to 170,000 and by 1989/90 it had reached 300,000. This was official recognition that a multi-ethnic Great Britain existed, but the actual sums given to ethnic music can only be considered as symbolic. In any case, it will take many years before reaching the proportional government subsidy levels which the ethnic minorities deserve according to their numbers.

The BBC has a vital role to play in popularising music. In the various radio channels (Radios 1, 2, 3, 4 and now 5), it devoted 63 per cent of air time to both classical and popular music in 1987/8 and the television stations gave 1 per cent of total viewing time to music. For example, Omnibus at the Proms (BBC 1) had a 750,000 average audience in 1988, with a very even spread of social categories. 60 million were spent on classical music and arts features for 1987/8. Slightly more (67.1 per cent) was spent on popular music and variety shows. This financial breakdown clearly shows that the BBC had a preference for the highbrow end of the market during the 1980s. Index-linking the licence fee and keeping costs down inevitably worked in favour of commercial and popular content against elitist content. Mrs Thatcher clearly tried to squeeze the BBC by keeping the licence fee in line with the cost of living. Nonetheless, the results were productivity increases, better value for money for the viewer and the continued presence of classical music.

Another area of the music business which is very difficult to analyse is that of music publishing. It would seem that there was a certain amount of concentration in this area in the 1980s as can be seen in the 1987 Chappel takeover by Warner, which in 1988 became Time/Warner. Figures that were collected by the Monopolies and Mergers Commission show considerable amounts of money that the general public are not usually aware of. In fact, the figures show a doubling in the value of music sales between the years 1982 and 1990. This was a market that expanded considerably during the Thatcher period. Two societies collect money for composers and musicians: the Performing Rights Society (PRS) and the Mechanical Copyright Protection Society (MCPS). A 1986 White Paper recommended a few modifications in this area, but none were in fact implemented.[4]

The classical music business thrived in the face of the challenge posed by reduced government subsidy. It had a world-wide high-profile reputation that could successfully attract alternative funding arrangements, despite the high costs of musicians. The classical orchestras found the right balance between adventurous programming and the need to fill up their auditoria. Serious music did remarkably well during the Thatcher years.

Theatre

The fundamental difference between museums, opera, classical music and theatre is that the last category has a commercially viable sector in the form of the West End which takes up 1/3 of total spending. Theatres experienced the same kind of pressures as the other performing arts, but this activity being much more diversified than that of the other categories, it reacted differently. In many ways the commercial end of the theatre business was the best prepared for the commercial trend that was encouraged by the prime minister. There were also many talented amateur or semi-amateur groups that played in arts centres or unofficial venues and there was a considerable increase in their numbers during the 1970s and 1980s.

The 1980s were a decade of continuing government support for the Royal Shakespeare Company (RSC) and the National Theatre (NT), two of the 'flagships' of British culture. Politically, the idea of national pride meant that Mrs Thatcher could not cut subsidies to these companies. However, there were many and varied contradictory pressures at play during her period in power. The Arts Council's The Glory of the Garden (1984) strategy document had announced a shift of emphasis away from London to the provinces. This was unwelcomed news for the two national companies as they spent long periods of time in London. In 1983, the Priestley Report, contradicting the business ethic that Mrs Thatcher was encouraging, asserted that the Royal Shakespeare Company (RSC) was underfunded and needed some form of additional revenue. The same applied to the Raynor Report in 1985. At about the same time, in 1986, the metropolitan tier of government was removed, transferring resources away from bodies like the GLC to the Arts Council and then on to the Regional Arts Associations. The RSC understood that because of the reorganisation it could not expect increased subsidies from the government, and so, it had to consider other sources of revenue. As a result, other sources of finance were exploited to the full, such as William Shakespeare tee-shirts and various tourist products. Ticket prices were also increased.

Despite all these efforts, sponsorship could not be exploited as easily as with classical music or opera. Theatre has a lower media profile because it is language bound and therefore difficult to sell in Europe and around the world. Consequently, it is less commercial a proposition. Music on the contrary can be understood by everyone. Thus despite a considerable increase in subsidy levels and box office takings, both companies found it difficult to make ends meet. To give an order of comparison, four touring companies in Scotland cost under 1 million to run in 1987/8. The RSC cost seventeen times as much for the same year. Even with these apparently generous revenue levels, the end of the 1980s was a difficult period for the RSC because it had to deal with a combination of fewer American tourists and a change in production policy. The financial strain led to the temporary stopping of Barbican productions in the early 1990s.

During the Thatcher years, the national companies, the grant-aided producing theatres and the university theatres were all pulled in the direction of the commercial sector. Local authorities and universities were squeezed and had to spend less. An example of this can be seen in Newcastle, where the university theatre had to be closed in 1989. As, for electoral reasons, cultural spending is politically easier to cut than hospital provision, there were three major consequences. The number of performances was reduced, attendance figures rose, and box office receipts increased.

Reducing the number of performances to 30 weeks for example is an easy way of reducing costs, salaries making up about 50 per cent of theatre costs. Some theatre companies also reduced the number of actors. Thus many actors got unemployment benefit and income support, which increased government spending in other areas. One survey of small theatre companies came up with a median earning for actors of 3,750, which proves that many actors are not in the profession for money's sake but for love of performing.[5] Artists living in poverty is obviously not just a 19th century, romantic myth. It would appear to have been very present during the Thatcher years, but this does not represent a new trend.

The 1980s saw a significant increase in the number of small drama companies. This was encouraged by the Manpower Services Commission which financed the Community Programme (later the Training Commission). It is likely that this source of help for actors will disappear in the long-run. The fringe theatre and the radical side of the theatre business are probably heading for hard times in the 1990s. Many gifted actors have gone into teaching or other professions because their families needed a regular and reasonable income. The removal of the metropolitan tier of government also moved subsidy away from certain radical companies to more mainstream ones. This was in line with the prime minister's desire to encourage middlebrow culture.

It is the commercial West End sector of the theatre business that felt the influence of Mrs Thatcher's cultural policy the most. There was considerable expansion in the number of seats sold, and revenue from tickets almost tripled. But even with the highly successful commercial sector, it is the subsidised theatres that take the risks. Indeed many transfers are made between the fringe and the commercial sectors. Examples such as Les Miserables or Me and My Girl come to mind. The report Theatre is for All (1986) stressed this point: "this development marks the way in which the publicly funded sector has become a research and development operation for theatre in England in general".

Theatre was made more commercial by Mrs Thatcher's policies. Plays had to appeal to a mass audience if they were to break even or make a profit. Theatrical shows therefore aimed at the middlebrow and tourist markets in order to maximise profits. This was all the more feasible as the large private sector had already developed commercial and efficient running practices such as stand-by tickets that are sold at the last minute. Mrs Thatcher merely intensified a trend that already existed before her. However, commercial orientations in this domain clearly led to less risk taking. Here one encounters the implicit nature of Mrs Thatcher's cultural policy. Commercial practices and middlebrow content are inextricably mixed in this particular example.

Dance

Dance constitutes the last element of the performed or performing arts. A so called 'dance explosion', in the early 1980s, was followed by a gradual decline in the second half of the decade. In reality Mrs Thatcher's dance policy had much the same effects as with opera and classical music, the major difference being that ethnic dance was officially approved and encouraged by the Arts Council and the Regional Arts Associations. This is all the more difficult to justify as ethnic music, theatre or literature were not given the same kind of official approval by government organisations.

There are six English dance companies and one Scottish: the Royal Ballet, Sadler's Wells Royal Ballet, Rambert Dance, English National Ballet, London Contemporary Dance Group, Northern Ballet Theatre, and Scottish Ballet. Box office takings increased significantly during the Thatcher decade. However, subsidy levels remained higher than with the other performing arts, while audience levels remained remarkably stable.

It was in contemporary dance that there was a sudden boom in the early 1980s. Some have explained this as part of the aerobics and keep-fit explosion. In the same fashion, when there was a decline in these healthy activities, contemporary dance was also affected. Most probably, this reduced enthusiasm was due to bad programming especially in the case of Ballet Rambert, where there was a significant fall in audience levels. There was also a shortage of first rate choreographers. On top of this, others claim that the Baumol-Bowen theory now applies to the relatively young audience of contemporary dance and that they were effectively squeezed out. The proponents of the theory argue that Mrs Thatcher's cultural policy failed to take into account the weaknesses of the market, thus excluding certain relatively poor people. However, the previous criticisms that were made about the Baumol-Bowen thesis still apply.

One area where there was sustained growth was in small-scale dance and ethnic dance. These companies often had a transient existence and it is the local authorities and the Regional Arts Associations that helped finance them. For example, West Midlands Arts spent 149,000 on dance and mime, of which œ41,000 went to New Midlands Dance for performances and workshops, 25,000 to Lanzel African Dance Co-op, 37,000 on Kouma Performing Arts and the Black Dance Development Trust, œ14,500 on new work and 31,000 on dance animateurs. A survey by the PSI showed that average income levels for dancers in dance companies were slightly higher than those for the theatre at about œ4,000 per annum during the period under consideration. This survey found very low administrative costs, most of the company income going on salaries. In 1987, the Arts Council published a report on African dance. It pointed out that audiences were mostly white, female and in the 25-34 age range. The late 1980s saw a remarkable increase in the subsidy of Afro-Caribbean dance groups.

The impact of television in stimulating demand for live dance should not be overlooked. Ballet and modern dance on television can attract from 300,000 to one million viewers. The two genres have different audiences which do not mix. For example, Pina Bausch and Dame Margot Fonteyn each got one million viewers. During the 1980s, there were about 25 dance programmes on BBC 2 and Channel 4 a year. However, one trend has been confirmed by recent television figures: contemporary dance is losing its popularity both in terms of live performances and in terms of recorded viewing figures.

Mrs Thatcher's policies produced little change in this particular area. The 1980s can be seen as a rather stable period for dance as a particular art form. Subsidised national companies continued much as before but ethnic dance groups made a breakthrough. However, this subsidy of ethnic companies can be considered as a continuation of the traditional responsive or reactive cultural policy of the Arts Council. As public interest for ethnic dance increased, the Arts Council responded by allocating various funds. This came in contradiction with other ethnic cultural areas which were not treated so favourably, perhaps because music was more esoteric, and theatre and literature potentially more dangerous.

Amateur Arts and Crafts

One area of the arts where government cultural policy could only have had a minimal impact was that of amateur arts and crafts. The Sports Council was set up to encourage amateur activity in the domain, in opposition to the Arts Council which only supports professional individuals and organisations. However, this can be said to be an error because amateur arts often function as a breeding area for future professionals. Most professionals have to be amateurs before moving on to successful commercial careers. In fact, without such activities, cultural life in Great Britain would be considerably the poorer.

During the Thatcher decade the difference between amateurs and professionals became increasingly blurred. As in almost all cultural areas one generally starts off as an enthusiastic amateur before becoming a professional artist. The General Household Survey (GHS) gives an overall picture of arts activities among the British population. It shows a 66 per cent arts activity level for the 16-24 age group and also a 50 per cent plus level for all categories up to sixty-five years of age. One general tendency for the 1980s was a steady ageing of the amateur arts population, although this varied considerably among the various categories. In addition, more women were active in the arts and crafts, while men tended to dominate in the playing of individual musical instruments.

Another phenomenon that emerges from the statistics is that arts activity is based on family and not class. During the 1980s, musical families produced musical children. Parental interest was seen as vital if children were to play an instrument:

> Contrary to some expectations, the findings on local musicians and their backgrounds in Milton Keynes in the early 1980s did not reveal any class dominated patterns for involvement in music generally. [...] Many of those engaged in classical music were from reasonably affluent, educated, and privileged families, but not all [...] neither rock music nor brass bands could be said to be exclusively or even primarily 'working class'; nor was folk music (indeed if anything, it was mainly favoured by the highly educated practitioners); while jazz and operatic activities were particularly heterogeneous in terms of social and economic background.[6]

This has been confirmed by other studies in other countries.[7]

Although most amateur arts practice goes on at home on an informal basis, there are also official organisations known as 'umbrellas' that try and co-ordinate efforts and encourage particular artistic activities. In 1990 a PSI survey gained information on the 30 largest umbrella organisations that had 10,780 affiliated groups and a total of 552,000 members. Only a few of these organisations had full-time staff such as the English Folk Dance and Song Society, the Traditional Music and Song Association of Scotland, the Royal Scottish Country Dance Society and the Royal Scottish Pipe Band Association. Most, such as the Morris Ring, the Morris Federation, Open Morris or the Welsh Folk Dance Society had volunteers. Most amateur arts and crafts activities come outside these umbrella organisations and represent well over one million regular participants. This was a very large creative source for the end of the Thatcher period.

From 1979 to 1990, there was a considerable diversification in the arts activities practised in different areas of the United Kingdom. Scottish country dancing moved considerably south of the border. Welsh folk dancing likewise, moved eastward. Ethnic art forms also sprung up such as Greek folk dancing or American Kilk Kickers in Aberdeen. Multicultural art forms became readily available in large cities all over the United Kingdom. Another trend was the arrival of brass bands in the south east, whereas this activity had previously been limited to the north of England. One can regard the trend as a consequence of Mrs Thatcher's economic policies that developed areas in the south and east of England thereby attracting skilled workers from Scotland, Wales, Northern Ireland and the northern parts of England.

One should not underestimate the indirect help that local authorities often give to local amateur arts groups. Choirs often get free rehearsal space, the loan of musical instruments and concert halls. This often takes place in schools or adult education centres. Sometimes grants are given for musical activities in parks that are run by the local authorities. Mrs Thatcher's policy of rate-capping had little effect on this type of help, as it was based on buildings that would continue to exist come what may. It should also be stressed that most amateur activities are self-financing and thus had Mrs Thatcher's entire approval. In this way they were largely unaffected by her cultural policy. If anything, the policy of discouraging state subvention probably encouraged this type of arts activity. It recalls the Victorian age with its encouragement of voluntary bodies, with the state merely co-ordinating and not intervening directly. The cultural diversity that exists in amateur arts activities can be seen as a sign of the multicultural reality of modern Britain and this is a trend which no government, even Mrs Thatcher's, could possibly change.

Mrs Thatcher's policies had little direct influence on the level of amateur cultural activity. It may even be claimed that people reacted against commercial culture and moved towards direct participation. What figures are available point to an increase in amateur arts participation levels. This can be seen in the number of musicians taking the Associated Board Examinations organised by LEAs. Official figures show an almost doubling of candidates taking the official music examinations between 1974 and 1989. It would appear that arts activities, like entertainment and leisure in general, have good prospects for future years. Actually, this expansion was partly encouraged by Mrs Thatcher's promotion of the middlebrow and commercial definitions of culture, allowing increasing numbers to participate in these art forms.

The public library service

This can be considered as one of the jewels in the crown of British cultural policy. It is a free library service which is available to every citizen and has one of the highest user rates in the whole world. Most middle-class children have vivid memories of going to the library and borrowing books. Mrs Thatcher did not challenge its continued existence, making sure, however, that expenditure did not increase in any significant way.

The decision to build a new British Library on the Euston Road site was one made before Mrs Thatcher's term of office. Work was started in 1982 and it would have been very difficult for her to have blocked the project. The current use of the old British Museum Library was reaching saturation point and an efficient library service is one of the pillars of cultural policy in the United Kingdom. The new library (BL) is now open and has eighty computer terminals from which to select books and documents. Spending on the British Library represented 21 per cent of total Office of Arts and Libraries spending in 1987/8. This can be considered as a significant effort on the part of a cost-cutting administration. Expenditure for the British Library, the National Library of Scotland and the National Library of Wales far from being cut during the Thatcher years was in cash terms more than doubled, with a quadrupling for the national library of Scotland. It should also be noted that the province of Northern Ireland did not have a national library during the Thatcher years.

The local library service also fared rather well during the 1980s. There are 4,000 libraries in the United Kingdom with a total of 145 million books, sound and video recordings. On average, spending in Scotland went up higher than in England. The exact opposite is true for Northern Ireland. Local libraries cover a vast range of activities. These ancillary activities were developed throughout the 1980s. Not surprisingly, it was found that old people were heavy borrowers of books and also took out few records, cassettes and videos. By contrast, young people used the library for studying and getting information. In its different activities the local library service met the needs of various segments of the local community. In this way all sections of the community were taken into consideration.

While Mrs Thatcher was keen to maintain a government commitment on the free public library service, a 1988 Green Paper proposed financial improvements: "it wants to make it easier for library authorities to increase their income by joint ventures with the private sector, and by charging specialised services."[8] Practices varied considerably according to geographical location. In the south east of England, nearly all the additional services were paid for, while in Scotland and Northern Ireland, only half the libraries made people pay for them.[9] Borrowings per head dropped somewhat. An increase in the number of books bought on the commercial market and a reduction in the opening hours of libraries caused the level to drop. This fall in the level of borrowings therefore was only to be expected. Total book stock remained remarkably stable during the 1980s while book prices dropped considerably for popular books. One third of the market is shown to be served by the public service, and this represents a considerable effort on the part of the government and the local authorities.

One area which was a victim of reduced government spending was the university library service. Specialised hard-back academic book costs increased rapidly during the 1980s and education services were made to function within arbitrary limits. Between 1982 and 1986, the book index went up by 40 per cent while the funding level only increased by 16.6 per cent. This represented a real financial squeeze and the result was a marked reduction in the number of books available and a 5 per cent reduction in the number of librarians.[10] Since university libraries are vital for the cultural and intellectual life of a country it would appear to have been a means of punishing the intellectual elite for the supposedly ideological resistance that it offered Mrs Thatcher.

Clearly, the British public library service is a great British institution. Many other industrialised countries are jealous of the high levels of service that are offered. Funding levels are among the highest in the world and the model has been duplicated in the United States. Mrs Thatcher maintained this basic system while encouraging the use of payments for any additional services. University libraries, on the other hand, were given clear signals to reduce costs and this part of the public service was considerably reduced.

Mrs Thatcher had two contradictory policy priorities in her overall arts policies. The first one was to free the market by removing public subsidy. State was supposedly to be replaced by private patronage. Her pronouncements of the early 1980s certainly bear this out. The second priority was to encourage business in Great Britain by whatever means possible. Because elitist national culture attracted many foreign tourists and could not be paid for by the private sector, Mrs Thatcher, in the late 1980s, started making pro-arts speeches, enthusing about the sculptor Henry Moore, for example. Although never explicitly admitting it, she realised that market failure could, in certain cases, justify state help and intervention. This is a clear example of the often implicit nature of her cultural policy. The first half of the period is marked by arbitrary cuts and open conflict with the arts Establishment. A more understanding and realistic or pragmatic outlook towards the arts characterises the second half of our period, along with the encouragement of private funding. In addition, arts subsidies by the British government represented excellent value for money for the tax-payer. A third priority that was more implicit lay in Mrs Thatcher's desire to stop subsidising politically radical arts groups and move production to middlebrow and commercial areas. She was successful to a large extent and yet these changes might well have occurred even with a Labour government in power.

One should also stress the diffuse nature of Mrs Thatcher's arts policies. One cannot really write about a coherent arts policy since the results of these fragmentary decisions concerning the arts form a patchwork. Ethnicity was encouraged in the case of ethnic dance and left unaided in the case of ethnic literature. Traditional Welsh music was not on the agenda, with the exception of the national festival, while large sums were spent on the Welsh National Opera. These were contradictory decisions which do not seem to have much logic in them. Arts policy during the 1980s is characterised by its diffuse and reactive nature. This ambiguity and lack of clarity can be observed in Mrs Thatcher's own writing. In the second part of her Memoirs she argues that she steered a middle course between the extremes of a totally free market and an overly interventionist state:

> I was not convinced that the state should play Maecenas. Artistic talent - let alone artistic genius - is unplanned, unpredictable, eccentrically individual. Regimented, subsidised, owned and determined by the state, it withers. Moreover the 'state' in these cases comes to mean the vested interests of the arts lobby. I wanted to to see the private sector raising more money and bringing business acumen and efficiency to bear on the administration of cultural institutions. I wanted to encourage private individuals to give by covenant, not the state to take through taxes. But I was profoundly conscious of how a country's art collections, museums, libraries, operas and orchestras combine with its architecture and monuments to magnify its international standing. It is not just or even mainly a question of revenues from tourism: the public manifestation of a nation's culture is as much a demonstration of its qualities as the GDP is of its energies. Consequently, it mattered to me that culturally as well as economically Britain should be able to hold its head up to comparison with the United States and Europe. And indeed we did. London is one of the world's great centres of culture. We have, in the West End, one of the most vibrant commercial theatres in the world. We have probably the widest variety of museums of any city, ranging from the intimate and yet magnificent Wallace Collection to the glories of the British Museum. The performing arts, whether theatre, music or opera are represented in astonishing diversity.[11]

Traditionally the United Kingdom has placed itself somewhere between the American position of leaving the private sector to provide arts funding, and a certain European position in which the state pays for everything. Mrs Thatcher tried to push Great Britain's arts policies in a decidedly American direction with its insistence on private patronage and sponsorship. However, the proportion of state funding did not decline in a dramatic fashion and it would appear that many European states are now imitating such a syncretic approach and moving in the same direction towards plural funding.

Notes

1. *Hansard*, 1 July 1991.
2. *Dingy Places with different kinds of bits. An attitude survey of London museums amongst non-visitors.* (The London Museums Consultative Committee, London Museums Service, 1991.)
3. *Omnibus Arts Survey* (London: Arts Council of Great Britain, August 1991).
4. *Intellectual Property and Innovation*, Cmnd 9712, April 1986.
5. Barry King, *Equity Survey* (Ealing College of Higher Education, 1988) 46.
6. Ruth Finnigan, *The Hidden Musicians - Music making in English towns* (Cambridge: CUP, 1989) 312-314.
7. See for example William Morrison and Edwin West, "Child Exposure to the Performing Arts" *Journal of Cultural Economics*, Vol 10, No 1, June 1986.
8. *Financing our Library Service: 4 Subjects for Debate,* House of Commons Green Paper, 1988.
9. David Bartlett, "Public Library Charging Policies", *Public Library Journal*, Vol. 3, No. 6, 1988.
10. *Library and Information Statistics Unit*, University of Loughborough.
11. Margaret Thatcher, *The Downing Street Years* 632.

Chapter 12
The Press

The Press is one of the most important cultural components of modern societies and British society in particular. In general, the mass media are often treated as a single cultural phenomenon but this study will separate the Press from broadcasting. They will be analysed differently, since they both have their own specific ways of functioning and sometimes have different logics. To give but one example, the Press in Britain is zero-rated for the purposes of VAT and the whole policy tradition is one of non-interference and free-market principles. Such low-profile state leadership led to union abuse of power during the 1970s, before Mrs Thatcher's premiership, and this the prime minister wanted to put right. Broadcasting, on the other hand, because of the limited number of frequencies available, was closely supervised by the state, right from its inception. Thus the first broadcasting organisation was state controlled and was called the British Broadcasting Corporation (BBC), being based on the public service model, in contrast with the free-market attitude favoured for the newspapers. In the late 1950s, broadcasting production was split between the public and private sectors, but even then, the private sector was heavily taxed and controlled by the state. Levies were paid to the state and quotas had to be respected if private companies wished to operate. The whole policy tradition was markedly different from that used for the newspaper industry.

The Press can be considered as the most ancient cultural industry. By cultural industry is meant the industrial division of labour, where mass produced cultural hardware and software products are made for maximum profit. In Britain, the Press also happens to be a political 'sacred cow', because it accompanied, from the very beginning, the development of Parliamentary democracy.[1] It is therefore a potent symbol of individual liberty. In the 20th century proper, traditional government policy towards the Press has been to let proprietors get on with the job of printing their papers and allow them to maximise profits in a free fashion. Among the serious newspapers, only the Observer, the Independent and the Guardian criticised Mrs Thatcher's policies. But even these titles at times of national crisis such as the Falklands' War, brought editorial content into line with government opinions as is shown by Michel Morel's article on Guardian editorials.[2] In 1979, therefore, the Press was overwhelmingly pro-Conservative. Even when Mrs Thatcher was forced to leave office at the end of 1990, national newspapers remained supportive of Conservative rule. This is one area of cultural policy where change was not asked for by the successive Conservative governments and Mrs Thatcher's policy on the Press can only be termed as one of remarkable continuity with the past.

The most recent of a series of Royal Commissions on the Press, the Mac Gregor Commission of 1977, examined ways of financing the newspaper industry, arguing from the traditional liberal point of view. The state was supposed to let the market decide which papers were to survive. The commission criticised the restrictive practices of the print unions, that abused their monopoly over the distribution of newspapers, and it was likewise critical of the high manning levels for production. It insisted on the need to introduce new technology, in order to reduce costs, in an industry where economic recessions could rapidly put the newspapers into deficit, due to reduced advertising revenue. After all, it was argued, new technology had been successfully introduced in other countries. In the long term, it was hoped that reduced costs would open up the market and lead to more competition and more titles.

The reorganisation of Fleet Street

One of Mrs Thatcher's main political objectives was to reassert the authority of the state in this sector. Above all, she wanted to be seen teaching the unions a lesson. In 1980, the first of her governments passed an Employment Act, later followed by another Employment Act (1982), outlawing the crucial practice of secondary picketing. It was this piece of legislation that allowed the long overdue modernisation of the Press in the United Kingdom. In 1982, for example, the national Press, that is to say all broadsheets and tabloids, lost a total of œ29 million.[3] It was Eddie Shah who took on the improbable role of saviour of the British Press in 1983. He was a freesheet tycoon who in 1986 set up a new newspaper, Today, using new technology located in the East End of London. The new technology used computer typesetting instead of the old manual typesetting, thus cutting out a lot of unnecessary, old-fashioned and slow, manual work. The East London premises had much lower running costs than those on Fleet Street, which is in the centre of London. Mr Shah also refused to accept a National Graphical Association (NGA) closed shop requirement for his Warrington site. A six month protest, that finished in early 1986, producing many cases of violent confrontation and testing Mrs Thatcher's new union legislation, ended in a Shah victory. The courts forced the NGA to pay several fines including an œ11 million one, that resulted in its assets being confiscated. However, despite the new technology, the Today newspaper remained unprofitable and another tycoon, Rupert Murdoch, bought it up in 1987. Nonetheless, Shah had broken Fleet Street's and the unions' grip on the newspaper market by using Mrs Thatcher's legislation.

Murdoch, a keen supporter of Mrs Thatcher, followed Shah's successful struggle with the unions and transferred production of his titles the Sun, the News of the World, The Times and the Sunday Times, over to Wapping. He also sold the Fleet Street sites at handsome prices, as City property values rose ever higher throughout the 1980s and more especially at the end of the decade. The unions refused to accept no strike contracts, and 5,500 personnel were sacked in 1985.

Murdoch then used his own transport company to distribute his News International (now News Corporation) newspapers. He proceeded very quickly and as this strategy was seen to succeed, the other newspapers were forced to follow, due to cost differentials and competition. By 1989, the last of the Fleet Street printing presses was closed down. In this fashion, the British Press was modernised, in large part due to Thatcherite policies backing modernisation against union resistance. It was Mrs Thatcher who introduced the legislation on employment that strengthened the positions of the newspaper magnates. She also obliged the police to intervene in cases of secondary picketing and insisted on the notion of a right to work. In the same vein, private verbal agreements were almost certainly made on the subject by the parties concerned.

It had been hoped that the newly modernised Press would expand due to reduced costs. Nevertheless, launching costs still remained very high and newcomers needed about œ20 million to set up a modern newspaper in the 1980s, although production costs represented a mere 21 per cent of the total costs. Despite this fact, a number of new titles were launched. Two quality newspapers appeared, the Independent in 1986, and the Independent on Sunday in 1987. Another newcomer, Sport on Sunday, was at first intended to be a new, radical, left-wing tabloid. After going bankrupt, it was transformed into a pornographic, right-wing tabloid. For its part the London Daily News, a Murdoch funded project, could not generate enough profits and it disappeared after only a few months of printing.

In the newspaper market of the mid-1980s, the break even point for a quality newspaper was around a 400,000 daily circulation figure, for a tabloid 800,000. A few new titles, therefore, provided more choice in areas that were already well served. No radical new newspaper emerged and socialist sympathies were only represented in the Guardian and the Daily Mirror and perhaps the Observer. Overall, the national and Sunday Press in fact contracted over the 1980s. Most newspapers experienced a slow but steady downward movement in their sales figures with the Daily Star losing half of its readers. The Times, the Guardian, the Financial Times are all exceptions to this general trend.

Their success showed that the quality end of the market could expand. This expansion potential was confirmed by the arrival of the Independent in 1987. Among the Sunday newspapers the News of the World was the only one that managed to increase its sales during the 1980s period, which strengthened Rupert Murdoch's position within the market. Thus the Thatcher Employment Acts did encourage the arrival of new titles, but the market in fact contracted in spite of this political support, and national newspapers had to fight for smaller market shares.

Concentration of ownership

One area of the British Press about which Mrs Thatcher did not express too much concern, was concentration of ownership. During the 1980s, five groups controlled 90 per cent of the national market. The market was supposed to be self-regulating according to the prime minister's liberal brand of economics. In 1947, the Royal Commission on the Press had concluded that concentration posed no threat to the accuracy of the news. In 1965, the Fair Trading Act was introduced to regulate market distortions like ownership concentration, but of the one hundred and twenty-five press acquisitions it dealt with, only five were in fact refused. In reality the Monopolies and Mergers Commission, that was the result of the 1965 Act, was given remarkably few opportunities to intervene. The Australian magnate Rupert Murdoch should have been scrutinised by the commission over the purchase of The Times and the Sunday Times in 1981. The same should have occurred with the acquisition of Today in 1987. Likewise, Robert Maxwell acquired Mirror Newspapers in 1984 and was not investigated. Due to the various groups' financial predicaments, the Conservative government cast a blind eye on these affairs, leaving owners such as Rupert Murdoch and Robert Maxwell as lords of the 'global village' (using Marshall McLuhan's phrase[4]) to fight for supremacy. These managers and owners bought up loss-making companies for strategic reasons, as part of their global communications strategies. Such conglomerate structures gave the Murdoch and Maxwell companies enough financial security to weather the storms of recession and allowed them to lose large amounts of money in order to have a strategically dominant market position. Mrs Thatcher allowed the concentrations of the market to remain.

This internationalised market led to ownership changes. In 1981, the Observer was bought up by Tiny Rowland of Lonrho, an international conglomerate once described by Edward Heath as the 'unacceptable face of capitalism'. The Daily Telegraph and the Telegraph Group were taken over by the Canadian Conrad Black in 1985, to the tune of 85 per cent. Likewise, in 1985, Fleet Holdings was sold to United Newspapers. However, Murdoch defended conglomeration by stating that it was good for customer choice: "cross ownership of the media is a force for diversity".[5] In contrast to this view, left-wing political scientists such as Graham Murdock and Peter Golding,[6] contended that this concentration of ownership was proof of capitalist owners exercising greater control over the media than before. On the other hand, Jeremy Tunstall levelled criticism at the evidence used by Murdock and Golding, arguing that anecdotal accounts point to an attitude of resistance rather than subservience on the part of the journalists.[7] Tunstall also claimed that national concentration did not really take place during the 1980s and that regional and local companies challenged the so-called hegemony of the big multinationals.[8]

The biggest companies in the British market, had such commercial weight as to be able to discourage potential newcomers. Mrs Thatcher did nothing to increase competition in the name of a free market. In addition, in the regions, many cities had newspapers that exercised local monopolies. There was a slight reduction in the number of local titles, but this was compensated by a 'freesheet explosion'. In 1975, there were 185 freesheets and this figure had risen to 896 by 1988. The whole idea of the freesheet is a typically commercial concept, its only aim being to promote consumption. It pays for itself and is wholly financed by advertising. However, while encouraged by Thatcherite policies, freesheets expanded considerably all over Europe throughout the 1980s and this progression is not limited to the United Kingdom.

If one looks at the figures for the 1976-1988 period, there is little evidence to show a concentration of the market in favour of the three leading corporations. If anything, the total share using the various measures of the table, point to a remarkable stability. Murdoch's News Corporation bought The Times and Sunday Times in 1981, along with Today in 1987. Tiny Rowland's Lonrho bought up the Observer in 1981, while Conrad Black's Hollinger acquired the Daily Telegraph and Sunday Telegraph in 1985. However, in the early 1990s many of these conglomerates recentred their strategies on their major activities and sold off their peripheral interests. Pergamon Holding Foundation was the most dramatic example of this process when in 1993 the sons of Robert Maxwell were forced to sell off many of the company's interests to stay in the market after the financial collapse caused by the owner's death. It seems that competition was not kindled by new technology in the provincial urban centres in Great Britain during the 1980s. Local newspapers such as the Manchester Evening News or the Liverpool Echo remained virtual local monopolies. Thus, a concentration of ownership, with only a few new entrants, vindicates to a certain extent the case of the Marxists over the pluralists in this particular area. However, the power of the transnational conglomerates should not be over-exaggerated, as the demise of Robert Maxwell's empire proves that they too can collapse if overstretched.

The effects of commercialism and advertising

Mrs Thatcher saw only advantages in using advertising revenue to finance newspapers. After all, businessmen paid for the privilege of gaining access to readers and the newspapers made profits from it. There were only benefits to be reaped from this process by both parties concerned. This was the the kind of logic behind Mrs Thatcher's commercial definition of culture. Yet the implicit side of advertising has great significance in the shaping of the Press. Examples of overt control by advertisers, as was the case over certain Guardian advertisements during the Suez crisis in 1956, are rather rare. However, advertising pressures are usually exerted in more subtle and indeed implicit ways.

According to James Curran, advertising leads to a press structure that legitimises the inequalities of the social structure. Advertising forces the quality Press to go up-market, because it is there that the highest advertising rates are to be found, and therefore seventy per cent of its revenue comes from this source. Conversely, the sales of the tabloids command low rates as they have to specialise in everyday items such as soap powders and food. This is also due to the social composition of the audience, and advertising produces a mere forty per cent of total tabloid revenue. Most advertisers do not like controversy, so they have a de-radicalising effect on the Press. This is a similar process to commercial sponsorship in the arts.

Generally speaking, the commercial newspaper market caters well for the young and the middle classes which represent 5.5 million consumers, while failing to satisfy the old and the lower classes, which form 16 million rather less affluent consumers. It is for this reason that the News Chronicle went out of business in 1960, despite a 1.162 million daily sales figure, as did the Daily Herald with 1.265 million sales. They failed to attract the readers that the advertisers were interested in. Popular dailies have also felt television competition more keenly than the quality dailies, as television advertising concentrates on everyday goods. This polarisation of the Press in Britain can in part be attributed to the role of advertising. Mrs Thatcher was not in the least concerned by such trends. She believed that the market should decide and find a 'natural' point of equilibrium. However, in the analysis of the effects of advertising on the structure of the Press, the Marxist arguments appear more relevant than the pluralist ones.

According to Curran and Seaton, the Press has been deradicalised and depoliticised, in large part, due to the influence of advertising. A study of content analysis in the years 1936, 1946 and 1976 is used as evidence in support of this argument. The editorial content of the popular Press has shrunk during the last forty years. There has consequently been a marked reduction in the amount of public affairs news and analysis published in all popular papers.[9]

However, Ralph Negrine points out certain methodological weaknesses of Curran and Seaton. Furthermore, politics and ideology are no longer the fashionable subjects that they used to be. People's tastes have changed and newspapers have merely reflected this change towards leisure interests. The Daily Mirror adapted to those changes and survived, while the Daily Herald failed to do so. Newspaper owners are certainly very sensitive to sales figures, which is not a capitalist trick or plot, but a sociological and economic fact. The depoliticisation of the Press and the reduced role of ideology in general are sociological trends of the 1980s and 1990s. Newspaper proprietors could once sell their political ideas, and the press barons certainly did so in the late 1920s. But in the 1980s, they had to give entertainment to their various audiences and if they strayed too far from the audience's tastes, reduced sales inevitably followed. The disappearance of the magazine Punch at the end of the Thatcher period is a good case in point. The magazine alienated its traditional readers and did not pick up new ones quickly enough, so quite logically went bankrupt. Therefore, in this particular case the critical theories are less appropriate than the pluralist ones.

Mrs Thatcher also encouraged the development of advertising to finance the Press. In fact, the 1980s saw a freesheet explosion in which newspapers with nothing but advertising did remarkably well. This trend had a logic of its own and produced policy consequences which are mostly hidden and remain implicit. It cannot be denied that the use of advertising excludes certain subjects from being treated by the Press and includes various others. The logic of advertising in fact creates a dreamworld in which the consumer is king in a classless society, existing only in terms of what he consumes.

Few criticisms of this dreamworld have been made, one of the most striking being Sillitoe's novel The Loneliness of the Long Distance Runner. Certain subjects, which middle-class readers would find unsavoury, were excluded, such as poverty, social injustice, or homelessness. By contrast, advertorials, that is to say advertisements masquerading under the guise of editorial space, were positively encouraged, as seen in the motoring columns, the travel columns, or the eating out sections. To back up this assertion, it can be pointed out that there was a 40 per cent increase in pagination during the 1980s among the quality papers and a generalisation of both Saturday and Sunday supplements.[10] The logic of advertising also means that advertisements placed near 'good stories' are the most attractive. Good stories are those of policemen catching criminals, sports heroes breaking records, natural and unnatural disasters and other such apolitical events. In fact, a good case can be made for the way advertising influenced the Press during the Thatcher period. The supposedly free market had hidden implications that Mrs Thatcher did not properly explain to the British citizens.

Newspaper owners become more interventionist

In the same way, another important aspect of culture which did not overly concern Mrs Thatcher while she was prime minister was the interventionism of newspaper proprietors. Throughout the 1980s, owners of publishing groups became more interventionist over editorial content in their newspapers. This is where the link between ownership and ability to do what one wants with one's private property clashes with the need to inform the general public, that is to say the public service spirit. Owners became much more interventionist, while journalists sometimes offered less resistance. This was not really a new phenomenon. In the 1930s, when the press barons mounted the 'Empire Crusade' campaign against prime minister James Baldwin, they were acting in a similar fashion. However, the 1970s were characterised by weak newspaper managements and so the strong, new managements of the 1980s were difficult for the journalists and employees to accept.

Just as Mrs Thatcher wanted to strengthen the authority of the state, there was a similar movement among newspaper owners exercising more power within their businesses. Examples of Messrs. Murdoch, Rowland and Matthews changing editorial content are legion. Lord Matthews, head of the Express Group from 1977-1985 dismissed Peter Grimsditch, editor of the Daily Star, in 1979, because of the latter's pro-Labour opinions. When asked about Watergate-style political scandals in Britain, Lord Matthews replied: "I would find myself in a dilemma about whether to report a British Watergate affair because of the national harm. I believe in batting for Britain."[11] The nationalistic, patriotic cricket imagery is noteworthy. Conrad Black, the Canadian owner of the Telegraph Group, publicly complained about the stance taken by the editor of the Daily Telegraph in 1989.

Naturally, Mrs Thatcher preferred this attitude to that of the watchdog role or a more open style of government due to the pressure of journalists. Press conglomerates also posed the problem of international law, and different legal systems that are sometimes incompatible. Rupert Murdoch, with his Australian background, is probably the best example of a meddling owner in Britain. He acquired the Sunday Times in 1981 and in the following five years, 100 of the 170 journalists left his paper because of the owner's style and political leanings. The editor of The Times, Harold Evans, resigned in 1983 rather than "be subjected to a thousand humiliations, challenged on every paperclip".[12] At the News of the World (Murdoch owned), Stafford Summerfield resigned, and another editor, Barry Askew, claimed that "he would come into the office and literally rewrite leaders which were not supporting the hard Thatcherite line".[13] In such circumstances, all that the journalists could do was to refuse to sign their modified articles, as did the labour editor of the Sunday Times during the miners' strike in 1984-1985.

Robert Maxwell is another good example of an interventionist owner. When he bought the Mirror Group in 1984, he stated his aims clearly: owning newspapers "gives me the power to raise issues effectively. In simple terms, it's a megaphone."[14] Although Maxwell was not a Thatcherite, he certainly benefited from her policies. The Third Viscount Rothermere, who took over the Express Group in 1985, was an exception to the rule, keeping a low profile and sticking to the 1960s and 1970s tradition of non-intervention.

As the Press was massively in favour of the Conservative party, Mrs Thatcher left it alone. It would have been extremely difficult to legislate against interventionist owners acting on newspaper content, even if Mrs Thatcher had been inclined to do so. However, it is possible to use state subsidy to put over alternative points of view, as is done in Sweden in the name of plurality of opinions. Yet this was, quite simply, not in the interests of the various Conservative governments, as the Press was massively in favour of Mrs Thatcher and her policies. In fact, the political leadership style that was adopted by Mrs Thatcher was not very different from that of the newspaper owners. She actually proudly proclaimed her belief in leadership rather than consensus.

Resistance against the owners

In practice, the power of the owners is counterbalanced by various other pressures. Owners remained very sensitive to sales figures and therefore could not disregard the views of their readers. An example of this kind of logic is the appointment of Simon Jenkins as editor of The Times in 1990. Its purpose was to staunch the haemorrhage of readers switching to the Independent.. Each newspaper in Britain also has a history and a certain tradition, which the owner cannot change over a very short period, because losing old customers would mean financial ruin. Punch magazine, as mentioned previously, went out of business in 1993, because it did not respect this most elementary rule. Change is better effected over several years, giving the newspaper the time to attract new readers. Most important of all was the fact that journalists could fight against the intrusiveness of the owners by using commercial pressures or the threat of adverse publicity.

One of the best examples was the Observer editor's threat of resignation over various articles on Zimbabwe. Lonrho, the company which then owned the Observer and directed by Tiny Rowland, had business interests in this country. In 1984 Rowland tried to stop the publication of an article critical of Joshua Nkomo, who was the presidential candidate favoured by Lonrho. In the end Rowland had to give in, because the newspaper's reputation would have been badly affected.

In the middle of the 1980s, another example of journalistic resistance could be observed in Lonrho's attempts at blackening the name of the El Fayed family, which bought up the Fraser Stores Group. A special mid-week issue was seriously criticised by the newspaper journalists who then refused to print false accusations of supposed British Aerospace bribery in Saudi Arabia. David Leigh, leader of the Observer investigation team, resigned rather than publish Lonrho's desired version. The power of the owners is therefore counterbalanced not only by the market, the tradition, and the journalists, but also by the fact that no single individual can personally manage all the details of these multinational conglomerates.

The power of the journalists, or what is termed the professional responsibility model, is, in effect, easily counterbalanced by the pressures that the owners exert on their newspapers. However, Mrs Thatcher did not encourage the professionalisation of journalists. In fact, her anti-union legislation had the effect of undermining the power of the profession. Most professionals, such as doctors or lawyers, must study for many years before being given the official stamp of approval by a professional body, such as the British Medical Association (BMA) or the Law Society. Standards within that profession are maintained by that body which can exclude any members who are not up to scratch. In the case of journalists, they do not have to do any prescribed type of study before exercising their profession and content was, until recently, only partly regulated by an independent body called the Press Council. Some journalists, in 1989-1990, by-passed the National Union of Journalists (NUJ) and signed individual contracts with their employers. This example shows the weakness of the journalistic profession regarding both government and proprietors. These very same problems were encountered in the relations between Mrs Thatcher and the public service BBC. (To be studied in chapter 14.)

The limits of press freedom

Mrs Thatcher's policies participated in the definition of the limits of press freedom. Just like culture, the Press is many things to different people. It is a source of profits for the owners. However, sometimes, these profits turn into losses, as in any free enterprise. It is also a source of employment for the journalists, the technicians who produce the newspapers and the distributors who sell them. It transmits information to a reading public, that can choose from different ideas. Investigative journalists supposedly act as public watchdogs, by rooting out political corruption, dishonesty and incompetence. Opposition parties invariably want this watchdog role to be given priority, while the government in power always aims at maximum secrecy. During the Thatcher years, the Conservative governments favoured non-intervention and left the market to find its point of equilibrium since it was favourable to the Conservatives.

Yet the state clearly did intervene in what could legally be said and printed and what sanctions applied when someone stepped over the legal limits. Information was still carefully controlled, especially when it was that of the state. Since 1911, the Official Secrets Act has made revelation of practically all state information a crime. It was originally introduced to cover spying during the First World War, but continued in peace time, covering all civil servants from deputy secretary to tea boy. The Conservatives clarified the situation by modifying the Official Secrets Act in 1989. The notoriously wide definition of Section Two was reduced and this is to the credit of the Conservative Party in general and Mrs Thatcher in particular.

In 1979, the Williams Committee on censorship, had recommended the modification of the notoriously vague Obscene Publications Act (1857 and 1959). The committee proposed a liberalisation of the previous law. However, despite these suggestions to clarify the law towards the end of the 1980s, various pieces of legislation in fact extended the powers of the Obscene Publications Act to broadcasting. The Press Council, which was set up in 1963, did not have the necessary power to limit the excesses of the tabloid Press. The enforcement of libel laws was too expensive for individuals and rogue tabloids could cover the costs of the few cases taken to the courts. In fact, the Press Council worked well during the period of consensus, but was inappropriate in a society where sectional interests dominated, as was the case in the 1980s. The Calcutt Report (1990) recommended the use of voluntary controls yet again, which could only encourage the tabloids to more titillation and encroachment on the personal lives of both public and private individuals. This is another example of the typically British voluntarist approach. It gives an illusion of government non-interference, when in fact the government can intervene at any moment. After all, a truly hegemonic project has to be unseen to be really effective.

On the whole, the Thatcher governments maintained a strict control over pornography by extending the Obscene Publications Act, and yet in practice they did nothing to deal with the excesses of the tabloid press. Since Trafalgar House, United Newspapers and Pearson all contributed large sums of money to the Conservative Party, this inaction was not so innocent. Mrs Thatcher could be interventionist at times, as in 1986, when she pulled out of UNESCO over the flow of information controversy and the question of journalists' cards. On the whole, however, she left the Press to get on with its work. In fact, the prime minister got on well with the self-made tycoon Rupert Murdoch and encouraged him in his Sky satellite channel venture. She even made an appearance on the first Sky satellite programme which was of great symbolic significance.

These particular points are always stressed by Marxist interpretations of the British Press, and one can only say that this habit of financial wheelings and dealings poses a major problem for democratic practices in Great Britain. The issue of buying goodwill from political parties was further aggravated by the massive use of patronage in unelected quangos, a system that was greatly developed during the Thatcher decade. Put crudely, individuals paid contributions to the Conservative Party, which then distributed legislative favours, appointments and honorary titles in exchange. This particular case of the limits of press freedom is another example of Mrs Thatcher avoiding the neo-liberal stance of a totally free market in a key cultural industry.

The lobby system

One way of controlling the flow of information, that Mrs Thatcher used to perfection, was the lobby system. Of course, her predecessors had used it, but by appointing Bernard Ingham as her Press Secretary, Mrs Thatcher made the system even more effective. Bernard (later Sir) Ingham manipulated information, which helped her cabinet work, allowing her to divide and rule. The lobby system gave the House of Commons and the prime minister a great deal of influence. It is the Press Secretary who defines the agenda and the timing of the news releases, who invents the short pithy phrases that appear in the media. The journalists, meanwhile, are not allowed to name their sources and, during the time that they are in the House of Commons, are unable to interview civil servants or businessmen who may give different accounts of the situation or problem. Only once did Ingham falter in 1985, claiming that the pound would not be held up by the Bank of England, with disastrous consequences for the British currency. Because the lobby system was so carefully orchestrated and managed, the journalists of the Guardian decided to leave it in 1986, while those of the Independent never ever joined. In time, journalists found that they could not do their work properly within the lobby. Many politicians also criticised the system, most notably Sir Ian Gilmour.[15]

Nonetheless, Ingham did a very effective political job, feeding out snappy phrases and creating myths to allow an interpretation of history which was favourable to Mrs Thatcher and her changing positions. Phrases such as 'no beer and sandwiches at Number Ten' or 'the Lady's not for turning', were snapped up by the Press and were extremely effective. The first was invented after Mrs Thatcher refused to meet the unions at Ten Downing Street. The latter referred to her determination not to make any political turnabouts. However, Mrs Thatcher did execute a turnaround in the case of human rights violations in the USSR, when she decided to help Mikhail Gorbachov politically. 'There is no alternative' (or TINA) was an example of a myth that was invented to exclude any alternative policy options, of which there were of course plenty. The image of the 'Loony Left' managed to wash off on the whole of the Left. In fact, Goldsmith College's Media Research Group (University of London) found that many of the press stories that were circulated were untrue. On the whole, the lobby system was skilfully used as a tool for defining the terms of reference of the political discussion between the Conservative governments and the Press. News management was so carefully planned by Mrs Thatcher and her Press Secretary as to make the Press loyal to the Conservative prime minister almost without overt effort.

Despite the influence of Westminster on the Press, Mrs Thatcher failed to convince the British people that her radical ideas for reform were right. In the mid-1980s, British Social Attitudes surveys showed that the citizens of Great Britain were still in favour of the National Health Service and suchlike collectivist institutions of the postwar period.

Press criticism of Thatcherism

Newspapers rarely played the public watchdog role during the 1980s. One exception was when the Guardian was given information about cruise missiles in 1983. A civil servant, Sarah Tisdall, leaked information about the government's intention of withholding information about the future installation of American cruise missiles at Greenham Common. Mrs Thatcher was furious because the revelation coincided with the United States' invasion of Grenada. She was not informed of the invasion, and she thought that it was intolerable for a big country to invade a small island without the request of the inhabitants as had happened in the Falklands. Large scale demonstrations against cruise missiles were provoked by this leak and the public was shocked when the civil servant was sent to prison for six months in 1986.

Mrs Thatcher was particularly sensitive to Grenada and the cruise missile furore because it touched on what was known as the 'special relationship'. Britain was supposed to have a special friendship with the United States that was due to historical, cultural and economic reasons. Mrs Thatcher and president Reagan also got on very well together on a personal level. The prime minister found it difficult to deal with the anti-Americanism that was caused by these incidents. At the end of 1983, Rupert Murdoch and Paul Johnson both criticised the Tory leader, writing that she was tired and needed a rest. However, the criticism did not last long. Another instance when the Press felt that her resignation might be forced, was over the Westland affair. In the end, it was Michael Heseltine who left office and not the prime minister. When asked why the newspapers were so positive towards her, Mrs Thatcher replied: "That's because I've been so kind to them".[16]

Other political reactions

The Labour Left reacted by proposing structural reform of the Press and an integrated approach to policy making. A Media Enterprise Board was suggested, which was to cater for small publications and minority tastes. By its very nature, the market excludes certain minorities, such as feminists, gays, blacks, Asians or regional minorities. This can be considered as the same process of exclusion that emerged in official national culture in the arts. The Media Enterprise Board was to allocate resources, so that a broad spectrum of views was represented, not just the profit making ones. This project actually functions well in Sweden, where a large section of the Press is subsidised by the state. It also works in France for the smaller regional newspapers. Certain cultural forms, such as opera or libraries, are also subsidised by the state, so it is argued, why should the Press not be included in the United Kingdom? In this justification, the Left wanted the Press to be a mirror of society and this in turn would have led to informed, democratic discussion.

More radical ideas were proposed by such politicians as Tony Benn or David Meacher. The former wanted the Press to follow broadcasting in having a public service justification. According to him, it should have a requirement to inform, educate and entertain, just like the BBC. The latter proposed an Independent Press Authority, much on the lines of the Independent Broadcasting Authority (IBA), that would have regulated newspapers. All the above proposals justified state intervention by arguing that the market was decidedly unbalanced.

Surprisingly, traditional left and right-wing politics do not apply to attitudes to the Press in a straightforward fashion. Because the Press is supposed to play such a crucial role in modern society, it challenges the logic of party politics. In the Labour Party some believed that newspapers should be left alone while another large group preferred franchising the newspapers, much in the public service tradition. Yet a third group believed that competition and diversity should be promoted by subsidising minority publications. The Labour Party was split over whether to have strict anti-monopoly laws or whether to have a freedom of information law to allow greater access to official papers.

The Conservatives had both 'libertarian' and 'paternalist' supporters, the former wanting more open government and the latter wanting more protection of peoples' private lives. Some neo-liberal Conservatives wanted a strict enforcement of anti-monopoly laws. For the centre parties, the Press was to represent a greater diversity of ideas, this being very much in the pluralist line of argument. The Liberal Democrats also expressed a wide range of views within their party, and this diversity shows that political parties are profoundly divided over such issues, with a consensus forming around the traditional British non-interventionist policy. This is the line that Mrs Thatcher adopted and which is in keeping with the laissez-faire tradition in the United Kingdom.

How to influence government policy? An example of a pressure group

The 1980s saw a dramatic increase in the influence of pressure groups as the postwar consensus became increasingly challenged. Pressure groups such as Greenpeace or Friends of the Earth found effective ways of influencing government policy. During the Thatcher years these groups learned to control the flow of information, in much the same way as the Thatcher governments managed news out of

Parliament through the lobby system. A good example of a high profile campaign was the Campaign for Lead Free Air (CLEAR). Des Wilson, the director of CLEAR, wanted to use London-based quality newspapers and tabloids to influence the general public in this area and thereby put pressure on Parliament to legislate. CLEAR's predecessor, the Campaign Against Lead in Petrol (CALIP), was a low profile campaign, that lacked the resources necessary for coverage in the mass media. It was set up in 1974, had produced a symposium report that looked at the scientific evidence, and claimed that lead pollution in children was due to environmental conditions, such as car fumes, rather than to food and drink. Lead pollution has the unfortunate disadvantage of retarding brain development in children. This CALIP report led to the Lawther Committee being set up by the Labour Government. The resulting report was published in 1980 but nothing was done by the new Thatcher government.

CLEAR started in January 1982, and Des Wilson decided to drip-feed information to the Press regularly, using his personal contacts and his working knowledge of the press world in the campaign. Every month a news event was stage-managed in order to keep CLEAR in the public eye. The Yellowlees Letter, a very controversial document, was leaked giving information that apparently contradicted the findings of the Lawther Committee Report. Sir Henry Yellowlees was Chief Medical Officer of the Department of Health and Social Security and was not at all happy about the way his letter was made public and used out of context. CLEAR organised surveys, glossy brochures, made a report for city analysts and organised another symposium. CLEAR's aim was the outright banning of lead in petrol.

As a result of the campaign, the Thatcher government was forced to act. It reduced the permissible amount of lead in petrol from 0.45 grammes a litre to 0.15 grammes. The conflict between the petrol lobby, which argued that lead in petrol did not cause brain damage in children, and CLEAR was resolved by this compromise solution. In addition, pressure from the European Community meant that lead-free petrol had to be available all over Britain, but the aim of having leaded petrol totally banned was not achieved. This example proves that public opinion and news management did influence government policy, despite the lobby manipulations. The compromise solution defused the situation politically and allowed successive governments to ignore action on a total ban on lead in petrol. Moreover, environmental issues tend to attract cross-party support and articles published in various quality newspapers can put pressure directly on Parliament. But there were also counter pressures, such as the petrol lobby, the car makers and the scientific evidence proving no clear link between lead in petrol and brain damage in children.

This is an interesting example of Mrs Thatcher bowing to public pressure as represented by a pressure group with contacts in the quality Press. One cannot accuse her of being a doctrinaire ideologue. In fact, this case shows the exact opposite. She was a prime minister who knew when to bend and by how much. She upheld the general principles of the free market, but she also knew when legislation was necessary in order to avoid politically disastrous public reactions. Here can be seen an example of a pragmatic politician acting when necessary. It also represents another case of reactive politics rather than co-ordinated political programming.

Magazines

In general, the magazine sector held up well despite the reduction in newspaper sales. In particular, the 1980s experienced a spectacular rise in the number of specialist publications. The specialist magazine sector is a good example of a cultural industry that was allowed by Mrs Thatcher to develop in a significant fashion. This was due to three basic reasons. Firstly, the Thatcher years witnessed a rise in the number and influence of pressure groups. Secondly, the service industries expanded considerably and became more professional. Thirdly, specialist magazines were a perfect means for targeting specialist advertising groups in an increasingly fragmented and individualistic society. According to Jeremy Tunstall, there were over 10,000 magazines in Britain in 1982, if one included the 2,500 magazines for employees and the various trade union publications.[17] This market experienced a certain amount of concentration, being dominated by such companies as IPC and VNU.

If one takes the example of the highly specialised literary magazines in Britain, one can compare the figures for 1979 and 1985, in Table 13.6 on pages 458 and 459. In 1979, there were forty-three literary publications. By 1985, this had gone up to sixty, representing an increase of one third. One should note Granta with particular interest for its very high sales and its marketing methods. This publicaation has a global vision and modern packaging and sales techniques. Specialist magazines was an area of fast growth, targeting very specific market demands. Therefore, increases in the number of titles can be noticed among professional categories such as medical journals or the newly privatised utility companies. The same occurred in all the leisure industries throughout this period. Specialist advertising kept the magazine sector buoyant during the Thatcher decade. This is yet another example of both a democratisation of culture and at the same time cultural democracy. Both phenomena occurred in the same movement. More market choice came with Mrs Thatcher's encouragement of commercial culture.

On the whole, Mrs Thatcher strengthened the Conservative bias of the Press by allowing newspaper owners to re-acquire a dominant position, as had previously been the case with the Beaverbrooks. Non-intervention was the official rule, but behind the scenes negotiating occurred without any public debate. This is a singularly undemocratic way of governing a country. The structural inequalities of the system were maintained and even increased. On the positive side of the equation, Mrs Thatcher allowed the newspaper industry to modernise and free itself from the unreasonable blockages of the print unions. New technology was introduced and a few new titles came onto the market. These structural changes allowed the industry to become highly profitable, thus forcing the Major government to consider charging Value Added Tax (VAT) on newspapers in 1994. This was the logical outcome of Mrs Thatcher's commercial outlook regarding the cultural industries. In another recent development the tabloids and The Times have decided to reduce their cover prices. Both these developments could not possibly have occurred without the legislative changes on unions introduced in the 1980s by Mrs Thatcher. Any legislation that was brought in to control the freedom of the Press, such as the Official Secrets Act of 1989, was passed on a reactive basis depending on particular circumstances. One should also stress the voluntarist tradition that was upheld by Mrs Thatcher throughout her premiership. Newspapers were allowed to continue their self-regulatory processes. Voluntarist controls were maintained by the industry, very much in line with Mrs Thatcher's free-market principles. This gave the impression of a free Press when in fact there are limits that were more clearly defined by the prime minister than before, especially in the political domain. It is certainly true that the most effective forms of hegemony are the ones that remain invisible.

Notes

1. Jack Goody (ed), *Literacy in Traditional Societies* (Cambridge: Cambridge University Press, 1968) 48-49.

2. Michel Morel, "Falklands: Le Guardian et la Guerre", in *Lez Valenciennes* No. 7, Universit, de Valenciennes, 1982.

3. James Curran, *Power Without Responsibility* 101.

4. See for example M. McLuhan, *Understanding Media* (London: Routledge, 1964).

5. Mac Taggart Lecture (London: News International, 1989) 9.

6. See Chapter 1 "Culture, Communications and Political Economy" in James Curran and Michael Gurevitch (eds), *Mass Media and Society* (London: Edward Arnold, 1991).

7. Jeremy Tunstall, *The Media in Britain* (London: Constable, 1987) 186-187.

8. ibid., 173-175.

9. Ralph Negrine, *Politics and the Mass Media in Britain* (London: Routledge, 1989) 83.

10. *The Guardian*, Monday 19 July 1993.

11. James Curran, *Power Without Responsibility* 89.

12. ibid., 87.

13. ibid., 87.

14. ibid., 90.

15. Ian Gilmour, *Dancing with Dogma*.

16. Hugo Young, *One of Us* 510.

17. Jeremy Tunstall, *The Media in Britain* 105.

Chapter 13
Television and Radio

Mrs Thatcher's successive governments intended to question the justification of the public service model and wished to make the British Broadcasting Corporation (BBC) more responsive to market forces. From the start, Mrs Thatcher had a social market attitude towards sound broadcasting and television, which placed her in a rather paradoxical position. She wanted, on the one hand, to control broadcasting in the interests of the state, and on the other hand, wished to make the public service more open to market forces. Once again the paradox of Margaret Thatcher's policies reappears: in the short-term, she intended to strengthen the authority of the state and yet, in the long-run, she also wanted to open up the market, thus reducing the role of the state. A clash between short-term and long-term objectives was inevitable and it is the former necessities which won out in the end. As in other areas of cultural policy, she urged far-reaching changes, but one may affirm that there was more continuity than change in government broadcasting policy during the Thatcher period. It appears to be one of the best examples of an 'implementation gap' in the cultural industries.

One of the most significant changes that was introduced by the prime minister in this field, was the modification of the franchise system for the private sector, represented by Independent Television (ITV) in the 1990 Broadcasting Act. The BBC licence fee was kept as the main source of income for the public service, despite Mrs Thatcher's desire to do away with it. She then used the threat of privatisation to try and bring the BBC into line with her Conservative wishes. Such threats, however, were never actually put into practice and the basic duopoly system was maintained. The consequence was that commercial culture was not allowed to function in a totally free market, but remained constrained by the influence of the public service.

The BBC

At first sight, the BBC seems to represent the greatest of the 'cultural bureaucracies',[1] along with the British Council and the Arts Council of Great Britain. Before Mrs Thatcher's arrival at Ten Downing Street, the concept of a public service was justified in terms of scarce airwaves and the mostly paternalist, liberal argument that broadcasting had a role in educating as well as entertaining the whole nation. British broadcasting has a long tradition of supervision by the state. Right from the beginning, the BBC could not broadcast objective information about union activities and demands during the General Strike of 1926 because, as Lord Reith, its first Director General, put it, the BBC was not "entirely a free agent".[2] The Reithian BBC was elitist and had a strong sense of the public good.

The introduction of ITV, in 1959, put an end to the monopoly position of the BBC. Threats of government interference and legislation were used to influence ITV on programme quality. This part of broadcasting history indicates that government interference was a stick that had been well used before the Thatcher period. The market was split into two parts, with both halves having to be responsive to pressures from the other. In this way, the excesses of commercial television were avoided, while the public service was obliged to be less elitist so as not to lose its viewers to the other channels. BBC 2 was added to BBC 1 in 1967, representing a high quality public service channel which was supposed to cater for minorities too. This highly supervised system, with its checks and balances, functioned rather well until the end of the 1970s.

Over the years, the BBC gained a certain amount of autonomy from the state, despite the fact that it is a state-run television service. Conflicts came at times of national crisis, when the governments wanted it to give wholehearted support to national interests. But the BBC always argued that a public service had a duty to present various points of view. In normal times, the BBC was politically neutral and gave an accurate and fair reflection of the different views expressed in society. In a time of political consensus and a two party system, this simply led to social democratic views for Labour and conservative opinions for the Conservative Party. During the 1980s, when politics became more ideological and partisan, the BBC had more difficulty in giving impartial coverage to all views. Its inbuilt bias towards the centre was almost natural in this vast, mostly middle-class, cultural bureaucracy. The Conservative governments of Mrs Thatcher were irritated by such a neutral tone, especially during moments of national crisis. Right from the moment the Conservatives took office in 1979 (after the Carrickmore incident as described on page 209), Mrs Thatcher gave the BBC very clear warnings. By 1982, she told the television channels to "put their houses in order".[3]

The television incidents

One of Mrs Thatcher's primary aims was to reassert the authority of the state in strategic areas. Broadcasting did not prove to be an exception. During the 1960s and 1970s, this vital part of the modern mass media had gained a certain amount of autonomy with regard to political power. This right of the television companies, justified in the name of a public service and a need to educate, was indirectly challenged by Mrs Thatcher in a series of conflicts. However, it should be stressed that such incidents were far from the first that had occurred in this domain, but that the prime minister merely intensified the process of government exerting pressure. The tensions built up and culminated in October 1988, when Mrs Thatcher decided to draw the line and made direct interviewing of Northern Irish terrorist groups illegal. Here was a clear example of the prime minister defining the role of the state, using special powers to ban direct broadcasting in the case of paramilitary groups. What is surprising is that Mrs Thatcher took so long before directly intervening, being apparently very respectful of British broadcasting traditions.

Some commentators, such as Tom Burns, suggest that the BBC has always been faced with 'liberty on parole'.[4] This theory suggests that government pressures have always been present, forcing the organisation to adopt safe and uncontroversial policies. Traditionally, it was the BBC governors who protected the journalists from direct political pressure. However, during the 1980s, tensions built up until the government decided to define official limits to broadcasting freedom in 1988, and banned the direct broadcasting of terrorist organisations. John Birt, the BBC deputy director-general, and a Thatcher supporter, claimed in the same year that the move would destroy "some of the most cherished elements of a free society - freedom of expression and independence of the media".[5] In contrast to Birt's analysis, the current research maintains that a democratically elected government has a duty to clearly define the limits of broadcasting freedom and that broadcasting organisations, which after all are not elected, should not exercise that role. The three main groups of players in these conflicts were the Conservative governments, the governors, the programme producers and top management. The tensions sometimes showed differences of opinion between the managers and the governors. On the other hand, some of the cases are examples of differences between governments and both managers and directors. All the incidents show a steady rise in government pressure.

Criticism of top managers in the BBC was not limited to the Conservative governments of the 1980s. In 1972, prime minister Heath had asked for A Question of Ulster not to be shown. The governors of the BBC refused to stop the broadcast and this moment marks the end of a period of understanding that had existed between television producers and politicians during the 1950s and 1960s. Managers became critical of all forms of authority and tried to push away the limits of television freedom. In 1977, Lord Annan claimed that broadcasters had become "an overmighty subject" and an "unelected elite".[6] The report concluded that the governors were not intervening enough in deciding what might and might not be shown.

During the 1980s, the governors had the invidious task of either siding with the managers and therefore being accused of defying government proposals, or siding with the government and being branded as paper tigers. When Conservative patience ran out, the government gave a clear political statement. However, up to this point the Thatcher governments showed remarkable respect for the institutions and only exercised informal pressure to encourage the BBC to follow the line. The various incidents show a whole range of different reactions to the vitally important issue of broadcasting freedom.

A) The Carrickmore incident (1979) and At the Edge of the Union (1985)[7]

In the first incident, a BBC Panorama team filmed Northern Irish terrorists and many conservative politicians accused the state broadcasting service of giving free publicity to the terrorists. In fact, BBC referral procedures had not been respected and neither Lady Faulkner, the BBC governor for Northern Ireland, nor the BBC Northern Ireland manager, had been shown the film before broadcast. The result was that Roger Bolton, the editor of Panorama, was temporarily removed, but later reinstated. Some of the governors expressed deep concern over the decision not to punish the editor of the programme. Mrs Thatcher openly criticised the BBC and stated in the House of Commons that it had to tighten up on its procedure systems. In this particular case, tensions arose between a management that did not follow normal procedures and the governors of the BBC.

In the second incident the BBC commissioned a series called Real Lives that produced a documentary entitled At the Edge of the Union. This incident seriously damaged the BBC's reputation for political independence. In the interests of the BBC's implicit policy of balance, two supporters of violence were interviewed: Gregory Campbell of the Democratic Unionist Party (DUP) and Martin McGuiness of Provisional Sinn Fein (the political wing of the provisional IRA). The usual referral procedures were followed and the assistant director- general gave his approval in the name of Alasdair Milne, the director-general, who was away on holiday. One week before the scheduled broadcast, a Thatcher interview in New York was published in the Sunday Times. In it the prime minister argued that interviews involving IRA chiefs should not be broadcast. Michael Checkland, the deputy director-general, consulted senior managers and decided that the film should be shown. The Home Secretary, Leon Brittan, wrote a letter to the chairman of the BBC governors, Stuart Young, claiming that the film gave terrorists free publicity. The letter cited a speech made by Mrs Thatcher in the summer of 1985, that condemned a Palestinian hijacking and asserting that "terrorism thrives on the oxygen of publicity". The governors, contrary to usual practice, decided to screen the film before broadcasting. The top managers of the BBC were outraged by the decision as the directors had agreed with the government position, despite their claim of independence. In this specific case, the tensions were between top managers and the governors who were accused of bending to official pressure. The governors agreed on several cuts before the programme was finally screened.

B) The Falklands War (1982)

The BBC was placed in a delicate situation over its treatment of the Falklands War. It was caught between the need to give objective information to the British public and government pressure to generate popular support for a costly and strategically difficult enterprise. The Newsnight presenter Peter Snow was accused by the conservatives of being too even-handed when he dissociated himself from the official British point of view: "until the British are demonstrated either to be deceiving us or to be concealing losses from us, we can only tend to give a lot more credence to their version of events".[8] Mrs Thatcher reacted in the clearest possible manner: "[...] many people are very concerned indeed that the case for our British force is not being put fully and effectively. I understand that there are times when it seems that we and the Argentines are being treated almost as equals and almost on a neutral basis [...]. I can only say that if this is so, it gives me offence and causes great emotion among many people." [9]

A Panorama programme also aired the views of various anti-war Members of Parliament, thereby giving an impression that the war was unpopular. It provoked an outrage among backbench conservatives who demanded an explanation from George Howard, chairman of the BBC governors, and Alasdair Milne, the deputy director-general. The usual BBC defence was stated, arguing that different points of view had to be expressed in order to give a balanced picture of events to the public. However, despite this groundswell of conservative outrage, the BBC weathered the storm and came out of this particular conflict without having impaired its reputation for political independence. On the contrary, it came out of the conflict with apparent serenity.

C) Zircon (1986/1987)

The BBC commissioned a radical journalist, Duncan Campbell, to make a Secret Society series. In December 1986, under Ministry of Defence pressure, the spy satellite film Zircon was withdrawn by Alasdair Milne. The Attorney General granted an injunction against Zircon and the police then searched the Glasgow offices of the BBC, removing everything concerning the whole of the series. In October 1987, the threat of charges was withdrawn and five of the original six programmes were shown. Meanwhile, in January 1987, Alasdair Milne was dismissed by the directors of the BBC and a more Thatcherite successor was found in Michael Checkland. This was an unprecedented move that showed the effect of pro-Thatcher appointments among the directors. John Birt, a manager from the ITV networks, was appointed as deputy director-general. Yet, despite these new appointments, far from disappearing, conflicts continued to dog relations between the BBC and the conservative governments.

D) *My Country Right or Wrong (December 1988)*

In this incident the BBC decided to stand firm on a matter of principle over a radio programme. The correct procedures were followed and the secretary-general informed the D Notice committee, the organisation that cleared all official information. However, the Attorney General questioned a possible breach of confidentiality over interviews with former spies. The BBC refused to give copies of the interviews to the Treasury solicitor. A subsequent court injunction forbad the broadcasting of the radio programme and yet, six months later, the programme was finally authorised after the transcripts had been listened to.

Both Zircon and My Country Right or Wrong can be seen as examples of the government using temporary injunctions against broadcasting programmes with alleged offences. They are examples of Thatcher government intimidation, yet both programmes were subsequently aired and the charges dropped.

E) *Maggie's Militant Tendency (1986)*

This Panorama programme showed that two conservative back-benchers had associations with neo-fascist organisations. The government took the BBC to court for libel and the governors decided to pay for damages of £500,000 in a move that infuriated managers within the corporation. Such an out of court settlement seemed to show that the BBC was implicitly admitting guilt. This particular incident is an excellent example of the tensions that existed between the top managers and the governors within the BBC.

F) *Death on the Rock (1988)*

According to the Thatcher government both the BBC and ITV stepped over the acceptable mark in their treatment of the shooting of an IRA gang in Gibraltar by Special Armed Services (SAS) soldiers. ITV produced Death on the Rock and the BBC dealt with the subject in a programme of the Spotlight series specialising in current affairs in Northern Ireland. Government pressure was exerted for the programmes to be shown after the inquest. Both IBA and BBC chairmen refused to comply with the request. Mrs Thatcher then warned the broadcasters in the Commons that: "one cannot agree with the rule of law and flout its conditions".[10] Finally, a Thames Television enquiry conducted by Lord Windlesham, concluded that there was nothing illegal in the programme and it was shown. It is this losing of face that prompted the Thatcher government to ban direct political broadcasting of terrorist organisations in Northern Ireland. The government, in this case, clearly set out the limits of broadcasting freedom in a formal way. What is the significance of the various incidents between broadcasters and the Thatcher governments? Mrs Thatcher's aim was to establish the official limit to political broadcasting. She redefined the Official Secrets Act in 1989 and she tried to assert the primacy of her political authority. Conversely, the BBC and ITV tried to continue in their supposed right to give a balanced view on issues of national security, using the public interest justification. When the self-censorship of the voluntarist tradition was seen to fail, Mrs Thatcher acted in a more direct manner and reasserted the authority of the state. This was indeed a legitimate claim as her government was democratically elected. Organisations such as those involved in broadcasting could be said not to have the legitimacy of elected bodies and to be partly irresponsible, despite the often inflated rhetoric of the top managers and governors. All in all, the various broadcasting clashes that occurred during the 1980s, show that the BBC was 'on parole' and that the hard-earned privileges that had been granted over the years were not limitless, and might be withdrawn by a determined (in this case Thatcher) government if public opinion allowed it to happen.

Programming

In the Thatcher decade the content of the programming was also problematic. In ITV broadcasting during the period, news, current affairs and general factual programmes increased from 22 per cent to 28 per cent. Entertainment and light music also increased, while education was greatly curtailed, from 14 per cent to 4 per cent. This can be explained by Channel 4 coming into service in 1982, taking on a lot of the education programmes and those destined for minority tastes. News output increased and education was reduced. Between the financial years 1983/4 and 1988/9 there was a halving in production of plays, series and television movies. Entertainment and light music were likewise halved. Sport was increased as well as feature films and education. These are remarkable achievements given the limited resources. It would appear that Channel 4 accepted to take on education in much the same way as did BBC2 with the Open University.

The BBC significantly increased news, documentaries and feature films. The big losers between 1978/9 and 1988/9 were children's programmes and education that were cut by half because of high costs and relatively small audiences. Production costs for drama were high and documentaries and arts programmes comparatively cheap. It is remarkable that ITV gave 10 per cent of output to the arts and 21 per cent to documentaries, especially when one bears in mind the political problems that were associated with programmes such as Death on the Rock. Increasingly minority tastes were catered for by independent producers, thus costs were reduced for the BBC. Most of these trends point to a definite move towards more commercial programming. This was in line with Mrs Thatcher's ideas on commercial culture and allowing individuals to choose.

During the 1960s, broadcasting was dominated by the idea of public good. For example, the Open University started showing lectures on BBC2. In the 1970s, this idea was replaced by professionalism within the in-house production structures. The 1980s can be defined as years when feature films and repeats replaced education and where commercial considerations took over, albeit within a carefully controlled duopoly system. According to James Curran, the 1980s were years of professionalism to be replaced by a new wave of enthusiasm for the public service in the 1990s. This now appears to be a vain hope.

Increased competition certainly led to a reduction of expensive programmes and the expansion of middlebrow content. Drama and education were the most expensive products and as a consequence suffered cuts. Sports, along with news and entertainment, represented very good value for money, and were therefore expanded considerably. With Mrs Thatcher's financial pressure on the public service, the BBC had to reduce costs, and inevitably had to follow the trend. Moreover, broadcasting policy decided in the 1980s, had clear implications for the 1990s. International markets and exporting cultural products became the primary focus of interest. National markets and national culture became background issues. Cheap American or foreign products were imported and home production, as a proportion, was reduced. This should not be exaggerated, as the latter was four times as large as American imports in 1988.[11] Mrs Thatcher's policies, certainly encouraged this commercial trend which could only influence content quality. Throughout the 1980s, in this domain as in the preceding ones, there was a permanent slide towards middlebrow content.

Financing Television

In Britain, as elsewhere in the developed world, finance plays a particularly important part. Many aspects of the question are closely related to the financing of the British Press. The licence fee finances the services offered to the public by the BBC. ITV makes profits through advertising part of which goes to the state through the levy. Ian Haldane, head of the Independent Broadcasting Authority (IBA) research department summed up the consequences of this arrangement: "If the suggestion is that advertising has some impact or influence on ITV programmes, that is not so: the two are absolutely separate as laid out in the IBA Act under which we broadcast, and neither has any influence on the other."[12] However, Haldane's assertion is based on a narrow definition of what influence represents. He considers influence to be akin to direct intervention or action. Advertising, however, has a much more subtle, indirect influence on broadcasting content, which means that there is a natural tendency towards the lowest common denominator. This is the implicit agenda which lurks behind commercial cultural policy in many other areas. Nonetheless, the duopoly system tends to pull commercial television up market.

Mrs Thatcher wanted to encourage commercial and middlebrow culture. This inevitably meant a strategic advantage for ITV, in the case of broadcasting. Curran has convincingly demonstrated the influence of advertising on the British media in general. During the early 1960s, a great deal of advertising moved from the popular Press to the commercial television companies and it was only government restrictions imposing profit limits that slowed down this process. The levies managed to make private television less attractive than it might have been in a totally free market. Up to the end of the 1970s, television became the clear leader as a medium for advertising everyday articles such as food, drink and household products.

This competition between popular newspapers and commercial television meant that profit margins were reduced for both. Advertisements generally applied to mass markets and excluded specialist audiences in broadcasting, while the Press catered for particular tastes, by having specialised magazines. Advertising meant that risky subjects were avoided and safe programming became the norm. All the public service could do was to align itself with the commercial sector, as measured by audience ratings. Tom Burns added that this obsession with the ratings figures was somehow like medicine being practised by watching a thermometer, that is to say, using far too crude an instrument. However, it seems difficult for the public service BBC to specialise in only minority taste, quality and prestige arts programmes or education.

Although Mrs Thatcher did not wish to have a totally deregulated broadcasting system, her emphasis on value for money and commercialism, to a certain extent squeezed out highbrow and minority tastes from the market in the 1980s, and these were increasingly replaced by middlebrow entertainment. However, the British duopoly has produced a few prestige productions, such as The Raj Quartet and many Channel 4 productions in the 1980s. In the Press, an unregulated market has produced quality and tabloid extremes. This, however, did not occur in broadcasting, the quality side being provided by BBC2 and Channel 4 and the middle ground being catered for by BBC 1 and ITV. The tabloid equivalent did not come into existence as many had predicted. Burns' criticism of audience research is nonetheless valid.[13] Hardly any research is carried out on levels of satisfaction and why potential viewers do not watch a particular programme. Another problem with advertising is that the largest single buyer of television advertisements in 1989 was the public sector. Thus, the state played its part in legislating, but also exercised great influence as the biggest single advertiser in Britain.[14] While Mrs Thatcher gave an edge to the commercial broadcasting sector by indexing the licence fee for the BBC, the considerable implications that this had on the finely balanced duopoly system have also to be stressed.

The funding practices of the BBC and ITV are fundamentally different. The BBC was and still is financed by the licence fee, that governments find very difficult to increase. This licence fee was index-linked and because production costs increased faster than the rate of inflation, the effect was that of a squeeze on the BBC. ITV, on the other hand, was financed by advertising and was dependent on the economic cycles. There was a doubling of ITV advertising revenue between 1983/4 and 1988/9 which reflects the improving economic climate of the time. It should also be noted that Channel 4 had a large increase in revenue, from £75 million in 1984/5 to £256 million in 1988/9. This represents a three and a half fold increase in money terms. A significant increase in production was due in part to a more commercial attitude to broadcasting and a loosening of union manning levels. It can also be seen that Channel 4 broadcast almost as much as ITV in 1988/9, this representing a remarkable achievement considering the resources available. Given the financial disadvantage of the BBC during the 1980s, the improvement in the share of audience from 47 per cent in 1985 to 51 per cent in 1989 is undoubtedly a success. The leaner BBC of the late 1980s was more competitive and did so through more commercial practices.

TV-am

In 1983, the evening news duopoly of the BBC and ITV met with a serious challenger. The Independent Broadcasting Authority (IBA) decided that TV-am was to provide a serious morning news service. Five stars were engaged as news presenters; Anna Ford, David Frost, Peter Jay, Michael Parkinson, Angela Rippon. This rather good idea was in fact a ratings disaster, as those who wanted early morning news did not want this particular format. An actor's strike lost a significant amount of advertising revenue for the news programme and a further mistake was made when Mission to Explain, organised by John Birt and Peter Jay, was given an unsuitable time slot. Not surprisingly, the BBC breakfast television experience was much more popular. Jeremy Tunstall suggests that this was due to a "lack of appropriate producer experience and direction".[15] The infrastructure was quite simply not sufficiently well thought out.

In May 1983, under the guidance of Greg Dyke, TV-am made a rapid recovery by offering soft news in order to attract large enough audiences for the advertisers. The trade union and technicians were locked out, as part of the Thatcherite pressure to reduce union abuse of power. During the later part of the Thatcher period, TV-am gained high audience figures and became very profitable. However, the tabloid content displeased the ITV hierarchy and the licence was finally withdrawn in 1991 and the formula dropped at the end of 1992. This is a good example of the tension that exists between the need for mass audiences in order to satisfy the advertisers, and also the need for quality in order to get a licence. In this particular case Mrs Thatcher was an advocate of commercial middlebrow culture and yet it could only function under certain conditions. The British broadcasting model is certainly not a purely commercial one as in the case of the United States. Mrs Thatcher did not deregulate as demanded by the neo-liberals. In fact, many of the existing regulations were maintained and once again one can observe reactive and voluntarist policies at work.

New technology and ownership

During the 1980s, it was thought that new technology could have an influence on union power in broadcasting, as it did in the Press. However, because market penetration levels were very low during the 1980s, this was not the case. Mrs Thatcher put forward neo-liberal justifications and threatened the deregulation of the broadcasting system and a more American-style television. Yet again, the tension between short-term and long-term aims emerges: either to control broadcasting for political reasons or to liberate the market. According to J. G. Blumler in deregulated broadcasting systems, as seen in the United States, specialist and minority programmes disappear and are replaced by fast moving, emotional products, which exclude cognitive or logical skills.[16] This particular analysis ties up with the ideas of the Frankfurt School and the limiting of 'the universe of discourse'. If cable and satellite television are not controlled, there could be serious effects on television quality. Advertising revenue might be spread more thinly, leading to cost cutting, forcing the companies into the vicious downward spiral of the lowest common denominator. This was predicted in the Peacock Report (1986). In Great Britain, Mrs Thatcher started the process, by squeezing the BBC, reducing state expenditure on broadcasting and supporting satellite television.

As the market for broadcasting increasingly became a global one, national governments found it more and more difficult to influence ownership patterns and Mrs Thatcher had to accept this simple truth too. Multi-media corporations are termed conglomerates, or transnational corporations (TNCs) and they currently represent $250 billion. Therefore, Time and Warner Brothers merged in 1988 and presently have a $10 billion turnover while employing 340,000 people worldwide. As far as content is concerned, the American style seems to dominate the world market and local versions are often adapted from the original American programmes.

The free flow of cultural goods is controlled by trade barriers or protectionism. The third Thatcher government removed the system of import control through quotas on foreign films. Brazil, India, and Iran, are the best examples of countries that block foreign imports. At the present moment, the large American companies consider Europe to be an excellent market for American cultural exports because of the high disposable incomes available. Mrs Thatcher did nothing to try and slow down the trend to world conglomeration. She did, however, accept the 1983 European Union 86 per cent European-made quota system, which protected the local market from foreign competition until 1987. In the 1990 Broadcasting Act, the prime minister introduced a 25 per cent independent production minimum for both the BBC and ITV. This had been the case for Channel 4 since 1982 and for ITV since 1987.

Anti-protectionist conservative attitudes and policies meant that the big conglomerates survived, while the independent producers disappeared during the periods of recession, which occurred in the early and late parts of the 1980s. Conglomeration weakens the strength of national governments and the concentration of ownership in a few American and Japanese companies has to be seen as a somewhat worrying trend. During the 1980s, Mrs Thatcher allowed the market to find its own balance and did not interfere in the area of ownership concentration. This policy of non-interference allowed TNCs to concentrate on global strategy plans. Thus, free-market principles in the case of media conglomerates are similar to those observed in the Press. In these global movements, individual government policies not only have little effect, but non-interference may be said to have actually allowed if not actually helped such an evolution.

Appointments and Accountability

Perhaps the biggest change between Mrs Thatcher and her predecessors was a difference in style or degree of influence in the appointments in broadcasting organisations. The previous consensus had always ensured that moderates were appointed to the top posts of the BBC. The director-generals during the Thatcher period were Lord Trethowan (1977-1981), Mr Milne (1981-1987), who was forced to resign by the board of governors, and Sir Michael Checkland (1987-1992). Alasdair Milne, in his memoirs, complains of Mrs Thatcher's partiality:

> Time and again, the BBC put forward what seemed to us perfectly proper names for consideration by the government [...] time and again such names were rejected, usually, we were told, by Number 10, and people of obviously political complexion appointed.[17]

Mrs Thatcher had a 'one of us' attitude to appointments. Of the eighteen directors or Governers who were appointed to the BBC during the period, eleven were pro-Thatcher. Many critics accused her of Conservative bias and of not respecting the gentleman's agreement on balanced representation. The Board of Governors is often accused of having acted as government censors during the Thatcher years. However, the evidence is rather thin when trying to justify such a claim. Only once with the At the Edge of the Union programme did the board bend to government pressure in refusing to show a programme. Of course the removal of Alasdair Milne was a patently political decision and was executed by the Thatcherite directors. In all the other cases the governors continued to help the professional broadcasters against government pressures.

The huge pool of social democratic middle managers meant that the whole system was weighted to the centre.[18] So the tip of the iceberg appeared solidly pro-Thatcher, while the hidden part was actually hostile to monetarism and the ideology of the New Right. Despite the appointments of conservative governors, frictions between government and governors did not suddenly disappear as might have been expected. In fact, Mrs Thatcher's nominations were not necessarily disliked by middle management. The City accountant Stuart Young was appreciated in 1983, when he became chairman. He died in 1986, and Marmaduke Hussey was appointed after a long career at The Times. Sociologically these were not the self-made men that Mrs Thatcher was supposed to promote. The vice-chairman William Rees-Mogg came as no surprise, and later Lord Barnett, a former Labour MP, was also appointed.

In the private sector, the Independent Broadcasting Authority (IBA), was traditionally recruited from the centre. Sir Brian Young (1970) and Lord Thomson (1982-1988) were both moderate director-generals. Since 1990, it would seem that there has been a move back to the centre in broadcasting appointments. George Russell became the director-general of the Independent Television Council (ITC), which replaced the IBA.

The question of nominations is closely linked to the problem of accountability. As with all cultural bureaucracies, it was a matter of deciding whether the BBC should represent a pluralist mix of opinions, or reflect government opinions thereby theoretically reducing the friction between state and the public broadcasting service. The end of consensus politics seemed to point to the end of consensus appointments. Yet different political views were expressed among the directors of the BBC. The problem was that a right-wing government found it difficult to appoint left wingers.

Therefore, Mrs Thatcher did try to put the BBC's house in order, but only managed to change parts of the roof. Broadcasting administration, in general, remained heavily biased to the centre, despite her attempts at change. Informal pressure was brought to bear on the BBC by conservative back-benchers who were given wide tabloid coverage when the public television service was too outspoken. Thus Press pressure was used to keep the BBC in check. As in other areas of the cultural industries, the voluntarist approach prevailed. In her struggle to bring the independently minded BBC to heel, Mrs Thatcher wielded the privatisation stick. Here too, short-term interests won out against long-term policies. Ultra-liberal political scientists even argued that the BBC should be broken up and advertising used to replace the licence fee. Cento Veljanovski, director of the Institute of Economic Affairs, proposed total deregulation: "Beyond the minimum constraints, the market should decide." [19] The Adam Smith Institute agreed with this type of proposition. In 1988, Mrs Thatcher seemed to agree too, when she declared at a Press Association address that "free movement and expression of ideas is guaranteed far better by numbers and variety than it can be by charters and specific statutes".[20] Imminent changes were promised and yet, as the years went by, she realised that a public broadcasting service was useful in controlling the flow of information. Despite the rhetoric, Mrs Thatcher, in fact, played safe because she recognised the cultural significance of an institution as prestigious as the BBC. This was continued after her departure. Since 1990, the Broadcasting Act (1990) has maintained the current form of the BBC until 1995, while proposing a new system of franchising to the highest bidder in the commercial sector.

The 1981 Broadcasting Act

Typically, broadcasting policy is based on a Royal Commission, which is used as a means of consultation with interested groups. The commission acts as a basis for the ensuing legislation that comes a few years later. The influential Annan Report (1977) led to the Broadcasting Act of 1981, that produced Channel 4. Mrs Thatcher continued the tradition, by setting up a Royal Commission, that produced the Peacock Report in 1986, which in turn provided the basis of the 1990 Act that maintained the duopoly system. The Commissions produced a wealth of evidence that was thoroughly discussed by interested parties and the government. In sharp contrast with this long consultation period, minimalist legislative papers were often produced as seen in the 1981 extension of the BBC, that covered 15 years of continued existence for the BBC in 14.5 pages.

This rather lengthy procedure explains why Mrs Thatcher did not block the arrival of Channel 4 in 1981. She did not approve of a minority interest channel because it might cater for uncommercial interests. However, she allowed the channel to come into existence due to pragmatism and her practical nature. She also introduced the novel idea of the publisher relationship in broadcasting. This was part of a more ambitious move to make broadcasting more competitive and more commercially responsible. Both the BBC and ITV had, up until then, used in-house production services that gave the unions concerned considerable strategic power. By encouraging subcontracting and independent production a new mode of production was invented, that was to be generalised in the second half of the 1980s. Channel 4 was to be comparable to BBC 2, but based on advertising revenue from the 15 regional ITV companies. It came as a short-term success for the various broadcasting unions: NATTKE, EEPTU, SOGAT, ITCA, Equity, ACTT, the Musician's Union (MU) and the National Union of Journalists (NUJ).

The 1981 Act put a 14 per cent limit on foreign films, that is to say, all films made outside the EEC. A Welsh 4th Channel was also set up, Sianel Pedwar Cymru, thereby officially recognising the need for cultural diversity of a traditional nature within the United Kingdom. The act also reallocated the franchises in the private sector (see Chronology on page xxx for a full list of franchises). Among the network companies, Thames, London Weekend, Yorkshire and Granada stayed unchanged, while ATV became Central. Among the regional companies, Westward TV became Television South West, Southern TV became TVS and breakfast television was provided by TV-AM. This allocation of franchises gave considerable power to the prime minister and the Home Secretary as they could personally influence decisions.

The Peacock Report

In the period between the 1981 Act and the 1986 Peacock Report, another mode, the private mode of policy making, was used. This involved the use of hastily formed committees, whose reports led to White Papers, which were then transformed into government bills, thereby involving very little consultation. The process can be likened to the use of an inner cabinet or to increased centralisation. One example is the Hunt Report on cable television, that led to the setting up of the Cable Authority in 1985. The intention was clearly to impose minimum constraints and call for very little consultation in order to come to swift decisions. This was an example of legislation introducing a third mode of broadcasting production. The first was the in-house model used by the BBC and ITV. The second was the publisher mode of subcontracting as seen in Channel 4. The third was the packaging mode as seen in satellite and cable broadcasting, which did not get involved in production. All three systems were allowed to co-exist, but it would seem that the first type of production will be gradually phased out because of high costs. These were potentially significant changes that were made possible by Mrs Thatcher.

The Peacock Committee was, by contrast, a much weightier affair. It was supposed to decide whether the old duopoly should be replaced or not. The previous Royal Commissions on broadcasting had all three advised against the commercial American model, arguing that it restricted choice. The Beveridge Committee in 1951, and the Pilkington Report in 1960, both held that a solely commercial television "restricts the range of programmes".[21] The Annan Report (1977) claimed that "the strength of British broadcasting lies in the creativity of the people who make programmes".[22] Annan stressed the quality aspect of broadcasting. Peacock, like previous commissions, warned against a deregulated broadcasting system: "The BBC and the regulated ITV system has done far better than any purely free market system financed by advertising could have done."[23]

The Peacock Report was, therefore, not a neo-liberal document in that it believed in the free trade approach, but that in the short-term a social market approach was necessary to give consumer choice. Its main conclusions were that the duopoly was an excellent system, that the licence fee for the BBC should be phased out gradually to be replaced by a pay-per-view system and that advertising should not be used to fund the BBC as there were insufficient resources to go round. The Peacock Report stressed the problems of peak time advertising in the United States, Italy and Australia. It recommended the ending of censorship and the use of contracting out production work in order to make the producers more sensitive to costs. Three phases were suggested:

1. A period where independent production was to be encouraged;
2. The BBC was to be funded by individual subscriptions;
3. Broadcasting regulations to be abolished.

Of the eighteen recommendations, eight were accepted, four were undecided, three were rejected and three were partly rejected by the 1988 White Paper entitled, Broadcasting in the 90s: Competition, Choice, Quality.

Samuel Brittan, a neo-liberal member of the committee, lucidly pointed out the difference between the rhetoric of the Conservative government and its actual policy proposals:

> Peacock exposed many of the contradictions in the Thatcherite espousal of market forces. In principle Mrs Thatcher and her supporters are in favour of deregulation, competition and choice. But they are distrustful of plans to allow people to listen and watch what they like, subject only to the law of the land. They espouse the market system, but dislike the libertarian value judgements involved in its operation: value judgements that underlie the Peacock Report.[24]

The neo-liberals would have liked the privatisation of BBC's Radio 1 and Radio 2, the introduction of auctioning for radio franchises and the establishment of a Public Service Broadcasting Council. The insistence on quality considerations may well see the duopoly system continue into the late 1990s. Mrs Thatcher therefore, maintained the BBC/ITV duopoly system, despite her liberal rhetoric, proving her political realism and her sensitivity to public opinion which was not ready for a totally deregulated market.

The 1990 Broadcasting Act

The free marketeers of the New Right were disappointed by the 1990 Act, that merely modified the old system. The 1988 White Paper had already given hints of this, by insisting on the term 'standards'. The viewer was to have more choice, but this was not to result in lower standards. In the light of this argument, the Obscene Publications Act (1857 and 1959) was extended from the Press to broadcasting too. A fifth terrestrial channel was recommended and was supposed to run on a commercial basis. The other main proposals of the 1990 Act were the gradual introduction of subscription television, the need to have a 25 per cent minimum independent production and the introduction of an Independent Television Commission (ITC) to replace the IBA. In fact Mrs Thatcher toned down the more radical aspects of the Peacock Report such as the abolition of censorship. The most controversial aspect of this surprisingly mild Broadcasting Act was the idea of having highest bid auctions for ITV franchises. In October 1991, the result was that Thames was replaced by Carlton, TVS was replaced by Meridian, TV-AM by GMTV, and TSW by West Country TV.

One of the main reasons for this gradualist Conservative policy towards television is that the BBC is one of the major institutions of British cultural life. The BBC plays a major role in the shaping of a national cultural identity. It has a world-wide reputation and gives excellent value for money. In 1987, a survey showed that 75 per cent of the people interviewed, agreed with the principle of the licence fee. Because of the question of government control, Mrs Thatcher decided not to deregulate either on a large scale or rapidly. In any case cable and satellite were deregulated, except for taste and decency purposes and therefore proposed an alternative. The prime minister managed to protect national identity against the effects of a totally free market in the case of broadcasting.

Mrs Thatcher allowed the private broadcasting sector to expand if it so wished, but new technology and the European dimension had in fact already limited British Parliamentary control over broadcasting. In 1989, a Council of Europe decision proposed a fifteen per cent time limit on advertising, a twenty per cent limit in every hour and a fifty-one per cent minimum of television fiction and documentaries coming from European Community countries. This was accepted by the British government, but Mrs Thatcher was clearly worried about the problem of declining standards and it is for this reason that she set up the Advertising Standards Authority (ASA) and the Broadcasting Standards Authority (BSA) in 1988. In this sense Mrs Thatcher's policies towards television can be considered to have been a defence of a safe middlebrow culture that   was meant to strengthen family values. Peacock showed where the prime minister's heart lay, while the 1990 Broadcasting Act showed her practical policy applications. In this particular case, Mrs Thatcher cannot be considered a neo-liberal, but has to be seen as a social market free trader.

The consequences on employment

Mrs Thatcher's general encouragement of a commercial culture had numerous consequences. Working practices changed considerably. By the end of the period, in 1990, there were an estimated one thousand independent producers trying to gain individual contracts.[25] A parallel can be seen in the case of arts organisations having to 'fish' for funding. This considerable loosening of the television market was in large part due to the setting up of Channel 4 and the financial squeeze imposed by index-linking the television licence fee. As production moved to independent producers, excess studio capacity was shed. Another consequence was the reduction of labour. ITV lost 6000 employees in the 1987-1993 period. The official total went down from 17,000 to 11,000. This represents a reduction of a third. The BBC preferred to remove excess personnel in small operations and mostly in the post-Thatcher period.

These reductions in personnel had an immediate effect on the unionisation of television technicians. The various unions amalgamated into the Broadcasting, Entertainment, Cinematograph and Theatre Union (BECTU). The tighter financing meant that over-manning could no longer be tolerated. Producers had to speed up their work schedules and cost all the details in a precise way, something that had not been done in the 1970s. Once again can be observed one of the common themes of Mrs Thatcher's cultural policy. She wanted to reduce union power and costs, and in broadcasting as with the newspapers, she succeeded in a spectacular fashion. Her aim of better value for money displeased cultural elitists, but the basic structures of broadcasting were left intact.

Radio

If Mrs Thatcher was very careful with television, she was slightly more adventurous in her radio policy. Expenditure on BBC radio remained remarkably stable throughout the period as can be seen in Table 12.9. As a proportion of total BBC spending, radio went down over the decade from 28 per cent to 26 per cent. Those private radio stations that had authorisations to function made significant amounts of money in 1990, with Capital Radio the most successful performer. There was a steady rise in the number of independent licences granted to private radio stations throughout the 1980s. Between 1979 and 1983, the Foreign Office (FO) contribution to the BBC World Service was cut arbitrarily and systematically by a total of £3 million. This was part of the monetarist strategy to reduce government spending whatever the department. A plan to reduce the number of foreign language sections from thirty-nine to sixteen was defeated by a public outcry. Here can be observed consumer resistance to cost cutting, a pressure that Mrs Thatcher was sensitive to because of its vote-catching importance.

In fact, apart from the cost to the Treasury, the radio services were to become very useful to Mrs Thatcher. In 1982, in conformity to article nineteen of the BBC Charter, a transmitter was taken over by the Ministry of Defence and official information was beamed at South America for the duration of the Falklands conflict. Audience figures decreased dramatically and BBC journalists refused to participate in this propaganda exercise and thereby resisted. The opposite was to be observed in the case of the Press, where most journalists eventually supported the patriotic line for sales reasons.

In 1990, the Broadcasting Act maintained Radios 1 and 2, despite demands by neo-liberals for deregulation. Mrs Thatcher preferred a gradualist approach with regard to public service radio. Only Radio 5 was added to the range of radio services offered by the BBC. This station covers sports and general interest subjects.

It was in the commercial part of broadcasting that deregulation went the furthest. The 1990 Act introduced the same rules for radio franchises as for television franchises. The present situation is that there are fifty-five radio franchises available and the companies have to prove financial solidity, as well as being in tune with local needs while also increasing listener choice. Following the Thatcher period, but also as a consequence of Thatcherite cultural policy, the first national commercial radio station was launched in September 1992, under the name of Classic FM, and is specialised in classical music and not in pop music. The station was supposed to make classical music more accessible to the average radio listener and thereby democratise highbrow culture. This may be in large part due to the prime minister's personal dislike of pop music. Another station, Jazz FM, has also followed, while a new Radio Authority had powers to prevent the introduction of exclusively pop music radio stations. By contrast, the supposedly centralised French state allowed all-pop radio stations during the 1980s. Therefore, commercial success was not the only criterion used by Mrs Thatcher and her governments in radio policy. There was also a lot of implicit policy in the insistence on quality and elitist tastes. This hidden agenda was never fully explained to the public.

Even in radio policy, where she was more energetic than in television, Mrs Thatcher showed great caution and, far from transforming broadcasting in the sense of freeing the market, maintained the basic structures that had existed previously. The American model was not copied and the market was not allowed to decide for itself but was given a certain amount of new flexibility. One explanation may be that the Peacock Report showed that there were not significant amounts of advertising revenue to be generated by freeing the market. The private sector was given encouragement but in an elitist direction. It would seem that Mrs Thatcher in her later years started to recognise the dangers of excessive commercialism on the content side.

Mrs Thatcher's policies in broadcasting were characterised by their fragmented nature and this gave her great influence in co-ordinating overall policies. Such a practical short-term approach also gave her strategic power because it was difficult to criticise piecemeal changes that did not appear to form a coherent plan. Contrary points of view could not be quickly developed in such circumstances. Once again, her radical rhetoric, namely the abolition of the BBC licence fee, led to rather unadventurous policies in practice and maintained a centralised broadcasting system.

Undoubtedly, Mrs Thatcher felt that too much was at stake: she was sensitive enough to public pressure in this domain and she knew in fact that broadcasting played a very useful role in upholding the authority of the state. One of her main objectives being to reassert the authority of the British state she may have considered that television was a good enough tool for putting across her messages, and preferred to keep it unreformed, leaving the government controlled market to act mostly in her favour. However, the gradualist approach did produce slow structural changes during the period under consideration. The prime minister's encouragement of independent producers meant that the business became very competitive and work conditions less secure. This can be seen as a quiet revolution where the old model of in-house production was replaced by independent production. Once again, short-term aims leading to the preservation of the old system won over the longer-term one of market deregulation. Thus broadcasting policy provides another example of Mrs Thatcher's political pragmatism winning out against dogmatic ideological change.

Notes

1. Tom Burns, *The BBC, Public Institution and Private World* (London: MacMillan, 1977) 1.

2. For a critical discussion on Reith and politics see James Curran, *Power Without Responsibility* Chapter 8.

3. Ralph Negrine, *Politics and the Mass Media* 130.

4. Tom Burns, *The BBC,Public Institution and Private World* 189.

5. John Birt, "Gagging the Messenger" *The Independent* 21 November 1988.

6. *Report on the Committee of the Future of Broadcasting* (HMSO 1977, Cmnd 6753) 14-15.

7. Both these incidents are examples of tensions between managers and governors.

8. Peter Walters, "The Crisis of Responsible Broadcasting: Mrs Thatcher and the BBC" *Parliamentary Affairs* (Oxford: Oxford University Press, 1989) 382.

9. Peter Walters, "Mrs Thatcher and the BBC" 328.

10. Peter Walters, "Mrs Thatcher and the BBC" 388.

11. *Cultural Trends* No 6, 58.

12. James Curran, *Power without Responsibility* 309.

13. Tom Burns, *Public Institution: Private World* 137.

14. S. Valechesky, *Broadcasting Choice* (Hobart Papers on Liberal Economics, June 1989) 7.

15. Jeremy Tunstall, Television Producers (London: Routledge, 1993) 52.

16. Jay G. Blumler, " The New Television Marketplace" in James Curran, Michael Gurevitch (eds), *Mass Media and Society* 211.

17. Alasdair Milne, *D G: Memoirs of a Broadcaster* (London: Hutchinson, 1988) 82.

18. Jeremy Tunstall, *The Media in Britain.* See Chapter 15 for a sociological breakdown.

19. Cento Veljanovski, *Competition in Broadcasting* (London: Institute of Economic Affairs, 1989) 24.

20. Alistair Hetherington, "The Mass Media" in D. Kavannagh and A. Seldon (eds), *The Thatcher Effect.*

21. James Curran, *Power Without Responsibility* 321.

22. ibid., 317.

23. ibid., 321.

24. Samuel Brittan, "The Fight for Freedom in Broadcasting*" Political Quarterly* No 58, 1 March 1987.

25. Jeremy Tunstall, *Television Producers*, Chapter 9.

Chapter 14
Cable and Satellite

When the Conservative Party won the elections in 1979, a Cabinet Information Technology Advisory Panel (ITAP) was set up to discuss new technology. This committee comprised specialists and industrialists who gave their views on probable trends and strategic needs. It was they who decided that cable and satellite should be entirely self-financed and that there should be no state subsidy. Contrary to this view, in other European countries such as France and Germany, it was decided that providing basic infrastructures such as sewers, railways, roads and also information networks came in the state's sphere of action. In France, for example, the Minitel system was state financed in the 1980s. In Germany, cable systems were paid for by the state. However, in Britain, it was hoped by Thatcherites that the new technology of cable and satellite would prove to be a glowing example of free-market economics. In short, new broadcasting technology would prove the superiority of the laissez-faire system.

During the 1980s, cable was quite successful in the US, because of bad picture quality and poor reception for the other television stations. In Britain, however, the national networks were well accepted by the majority of viewers and picture quality was of a high standard. During the Thatcher period there was a boom in the number of people using video recording machines, who either recorded late-night programmes or watched rented videos. This is one of the main reasons why the rather commercially unattractive cable market developed slowly. Statistics show that there was a considerable amount of consumer resistance to cable broadcasting systems. By March 1990, 9.5 million homes had theoretical access to cable services. Of these only

1.6 million actually had a service on offer from a cable operator. Because of low consumer interest 300,000 homes were in actual fact connected to United Kingdom cable companies. To give an order of comparison, the highest take-up rate of cable facilities in Europe is the Netherlands with a 10 per cent level. Already in 1989, the Cable Authority (set up in 1984), expressed its dissatisfaction with the bad results:

> Because of the necessary length of the franchising and licensing procedures, coupled with the time-consuming nature of cable construction, little of this new interest in cable had found its way into physical cable systems by the end of the year. The small amount of cable in the ground continued to be a disappointment to the authority.[1]

Most of the companies involved in cable distribution are American or partly American owned. United Artists Entertainment and Maclean Hunter are two of the major distributors. Why did these companies do well in the US and yet encountered very slow progress in the United Kingdom? One obvious reason is the high costs involved in the initial outlay. Economic considerations are based on long-term policy objectives. Streets have to be dug up and it takes time and money. Another reason may be consumer resistance because cable companies often offer cheap American imports that are not much appreciated despite their competitive pricing. Yet another reason could be boredom concerning the television medium itself. Viewing figures for the decade showed a drop of 2.75 hours in the average weekly total.[2] British viewers prefer doing other activities such as watching videos, and television is often now considered of secondary interest (this will be dealt with in chapter 17). Others have suggested that there was not enough money and potential profits in an already well provided broadcasting system.

Cable has the undoubted advantage of being potentially interactive in the case of fiber-optics. Satellite is the most important competitor to cable. Satellite dishes, however, are a much more flexible and cheaper method of providing access to broadcasting channels. During the 1980s, cable operators were forced to offer more choice due to competition from the satellite channels. In 1989, Rupert Murdoch launched his four Sky channels based in Luxembourg. All that one needed was an Astra satellite dish and a subscription for the film channel to be able to view these rather down market, lowbrow products. Mrs Thatcher encouraged Murdoch in his schemes. British Satellite Broadcasting (BSB), the home-grown British product, was launched a year later using a different system, squarials and not round dishes. BSB was then bought up by Murdoch, who worked in collaboration with Granada, Pearson, Reed International, and Chargeurs, a French textile company. This combined company became known as B Sky B and Murdoch had to wait patiently for four years before starting to make a profit from his satellite television venture.

Continuous risk-taking over long time periods before making a profit demonstrates the dangerous nature of cultural entrepreneurship. Only multinational conglomerates can afford to lose such large amounts of money over several years. Even these sometimes pull out of the market, as shown in the BSB example. The consumer may also lose out with changes in technology. Squarials suddenly became obsolete and the consumer was left holding the baby i.e. he had a useless aerial. In this fast moving information world there is no guarantee that the services attracting the consumer initially will stay on the market. In general, profit margins in satellite are very low. However, the companies that find themselves in an oligopolistic (that is to say a quasi-monopolistic) position can dictate their own terms later on. Therefore, many brakes to the growth of both cable and satellite television in Great Britain existed during the 1980s, risks and potential profits being equally high. This is what logically happened even with Mrs Thatcher's blessing of this new cultural industry.

Although initially slow, sales of Astra dishes (dishes for European stations) increased steadily during the last years of the decade. Sales of satellite dishes such as Astra started taking off at the end of 1989. By May 1990, 800,000 were sold over that particular month. It should be added that consumer reluctance was combated by reducing prices, thereby reducing the initial risk of buying new technology. Most of the channels available were in English or German. These included four Sky channels, MTV which is a pop music channel and two W. H. Smith channels called Lifestyle and Screen Sport. Different dishes proposed different kinds of channels. The first five channels are Murdoch owned and totalled 1 million subscribers in Great Britian by January 1990. One should also add that some channels such as Screen Sport and Lifestyle experienced negative growth. This is evidence of the risks involved in new technology.

The strategic positioning that occurred during the 1980s over technical definitions and standardisation is of great importance. Various systems are used for broadcasting throughout the world. Mrs Thatcher insisted on a D2 Mac standard for television definition. The whole of the European Union agreed to this standard in 1985 and later on in 1989. The first high definition televisions started rolling off the assembly lines in 1990 and yet the standard was finally abandoned in 1993. Mrs Thatcher had imposed her will on the European Union but made the wrong commercial and strategic decision. This is the very opposite of a voluntarist approach.

The example of cable and satellite can be contrasted with the video explosion. During the 1980s, video recorders were first rented and then bought as prices were reduced. Many independent video rental shops were set up in what was a democratic cultural phenomenon. In that domain, one can certainly talk in terms of a democratisation of culture in both production and consumption. By contrast, the cable and satellite companies marketed their products at the higher end of the market offering rather mediocre services in a centralised system.

With the future introduction of Channel 5, it would seem that advertisers might in fact have too much space available in 1996. It might even be that the new broadcasting market has reached saturation point and can expand no further. Mrs Thatcher hoped for a self-financing technological revolution that simply did not take place in either cable or satellite. The prime minister made some strategic decisions that later proved to be based on incorrect or insufficient information. During the 1980s, these new broadcasting forms found it very difficult to compete against the sleeker production of traditional television and the new video industry. The market was simply not resilient enough to develop in a free unconstrained manner and one may add that if it does occur in the future, it will not be before the late 1990s.

Notes

1. *Cable Authority Annual Report* 1988/9.
2. MORI/NOP poll, *Satellite Television and Family Viewing*, Jan 1990.

Chapter 15
The Book Industry and the Music Business

The Book Industry

The book industry, like the Press, had a special place in Mrs Thatcher's cultural policy. A literate and critical citizenry is one of the main bases of Western democracy. It is for this reason that British state support of the public library service has never been criticised by the conservatives, excepting the most extreme libertarians.

Mrs Thatcher did not question the principle of the public library service. She in fact made full use of the publicly financed Her Majesty's Stationary Office (HMSO). Her governments also kept a brake on institutional purchasing of books, while at the same time maintaining spending levels on public libraries. The innovative Public Lending Right Act was put into service in 1983. The prime minister also encouraged the private side of the market by maintaining zero-rate Value added tax (VAT) on paper print, and was rewarded by a 50 per cent increase in private spending on books in the 1980-1988 period. She therefore maintained the public service, while also encouraging the private sector.

There is a long history of English central and local government support for public libraries, dating back to actions such as the founding of the British Museum in 1753. It is in the first two decades of this century that local public libraries became the accepted norm. The justification for public expenditure in this area was that an educated and reading citizenry would not succumb to extremist propaganda and would enjoy life to the full. Public intervention in this area has widespread public approval and the British Library (BL), despite its current problems, will certainly become the jewel in the crown of the library service, like the British Museum Library previously.

Two major sources of information exist to measure the progress of the book industry in this period. The government has a Business Statistics Office, which produces the Business Monitor, and the publishing business has its own Publishers Association Statistics Collection Scheme (PASCS). As with other areas of cultural practices, the figures often present difficulties of interpretation. The Business Monitor does not get any information on companies which have fewer than twenty-five employees, this representing a major problem because of the large amount of subcontracting that goes on in publishing. PASCS, on the other hand, bases its figures on voluntary responses from members of the Publishers Association. Both types of figures give an incomplete picture and one has to resort to grossing up, based on estimates of various missing elements. However, despite the approximate nature of the figures, a general picture of the importance of the book industry in the Thatcher years can be established. The Business Monitor statistics give an idea of the scale of book sales in the United Kingdom.

A large increase in book consumption in the private sector during the Thatcher decade is revealed by official figures. Hardback and paperback sales went up by over fifty per cent in the 1983-1988 period. Within the hard-back category, school textbooks and Bibles did not expand as much as the others. At the top of the list came reference books, followed by adult non-fiction and fiction/literature/classics. Within the paperback category, children's books almost tripled and no one category did less well than any other. They all did well in sales terms. It should also be stressed that in 1988, 30.5 per cent of sales went abroad. The book market, just like most of the cultural industries, is increasingly a global one and must think in terms of global strategies. A 1989 Mintel survey confirmed this general impression of expansion. It found a sixty per cent increase in retail book sales between 1983 and 1988. This improvement, however, was offset by a decrease in institutional purchases, such as universities and schools.

It would appear that in general terms, the British book industry is not in a very healthy position, because it produces as many titles in the United Kingdom as are produced in the United States, whose market is five times as large. The 40,000 titles lead to lower profit margins than in most other parts of the economy. As a consequence, distribution chains have a considerable strategic advantage in negotiating bulk orders from the publishers. During the Thatcher period there was considerable growth in the number of shops belonging to chains. Very slim profit margins remained unchanged over the Thatcher decade despite a doubling of sales per person. In this case higher productivity did not increase profits because of rising costs. This resulted in the quasi-disappearance of the independent book shop. Among the publishers, much restructuring occurred during the 1980s. Many permanent staff were laid off and self employed part-timers were used instead, in order to reduce costs. New technology also meant that sub-contracting could be done at home rather than in expensive offices.

One area of great controversy in the book industry was encountered over the usefulness of the Net Book Agreement (NBA). It was referred to the Office of Fair Trading in 1989, for imposing artificially high book prices. This agreement made retailers sell books at the publisher's recommended retail price. Paradoxically, this British policy was similar to former French Socialist Culture Minister, Jack Lang's law on book pricing. Whether this led to over-high prices, or whether it encouraged diversity in the publishing industry has not yet been resolved. The debate on pricing, however, could not put into the same category a £50 hardback research book and a £2.50 mass paperback. They were clearly two very different products. A recent Peat Marwick McLintock survey showed that mass market paperback sales doubled in the 1981-1986 period. Other book categories' costs rose very marginally. The profitable part of the market was shown to be the mass sales side.[1] One can also add that the NBA was finally removed in September 1995, allowing publishers and retailers to fix their own pricing policies.

Another report by Dr. Fishwick dealt with a marginal increase in the cost of all books when compared with the Retail Price Index (RPI).

What is certain is that the publishers did not significantly widen their profit margins during the Thatcher period, but they increased the volume of sales in the profitable end of the market. Mrs Thatcher therefore maintained the NBA, deliberately choosing not to free the market. This policy measure was in marked contrast with the arguments used by her in other areas of the cultural industries. Controls were maintained in the book industry while they were removed in the film industry. Both cultural industries have foreign multinationals that dominate the market. Mrs Thatcher, therefore, gave the book industry a privileged status within the cultural industries. Conversely, the film industry got very little help against international competition. One can only infer that Mrs Thatcher considered reading as an essential cultural activity, while going to the cinema was a luxury option that could be done without.

One area where cultural policy in the arts, as seen in the ABSA awards for private sponsorship, was mirrored by the book industry, was over the enthusiasm for high profile book awards. About £1/3 million were distributed in 1988, generating a considerable amount of publicity. The mass media covered the awards and the interest guaranteed mass sales. This is a good example of symbolic power being transformed into economic success. To use Bourdieu's language, cultural capital in these cases hit the jackpot, which is rarely the case. The Booker Prize became the most striking example of this phenomenon and various other schemes, such as the Whitbread Prize, coexisted together throughout the 1980s.

Most significantly, on the public side of the book industry, the high spending levels for public libraries were maintained by Mrs Thatcher. Expenditure in fact rose considerably both in real money and constant price terms. Local authorities were unwilling to reduce services and Mrs Thatcher did not take the appropriate action to reduce spending. Either the prime minister turned a blind eye, or she implicitly approved of this added expenditure.

The Thatcher government allowed the introduction of the Public Lending Right (PLR), that gave royalty payments to authors whose books were in public libraries. A similar project has been working in

Sweden for many years. This novel idea fixed a £6000 limit for successful writers such as Agatha Christie or John le Carr, and allowed authors of expensive children's books, to enjoy a small income. The latter were virtually excluded from the private sector because of the high prices of their products which involved a combination of many colour pictures, good quality paper and small print runs. The amount of money spent on this scheme increased from £2 million in 1984, to £3.5 million in 1989. This would appear to be a project that Mrs Thatcher wholeheartedly agreed with. In this case the prime minister did not approve solely of the private sector of the market. She also wanted to encourage the public library service and showed a preference for the social market approach rather than free market economics.

The official representative of the government in literary affairs is the Office of Arts and Libraries (the Department of National Heritage as of 1992). The Arts Council had a literature panel during the 1980s, which resigned in 1985. This was because the panel had hoped to subsidise the highbrow end of the market, much on the lines of the British Film Institute (BFI) in the cinema business. However, the government disapproved of highbrow content in this particular area, while approving of such popular and commercial writers as Jeffrey Archer or John le Carr,. On the other hand, the Welsh Arts Council literature panel had an important role to play in printing Welsh language books in order to keep the written Welsh heritage alive. One can therefore find examples of officially approved book subsidies.

The book industry remained a special case throughout the 1980s and strong links between the public and private sectors were allowed to continue. The situation in this domain mirrors that of the theatre business. Mrs Thatcher did not cut back on public spending on public libraries and maintained levels in line with inflation. The NBA was not abolished until 1995 under John Major. Her overall policies benefited the private retailing end of the business, at the same time reducing institutional spending by schools and universities. Just as with broadcasting, state intervention was maintained and reoriented in this particular area of the cultural market-place.

The Music Business

The music industry has many different components: the artists and singers, the recording studios, the producers of cassettes, records and videos, the producers of hi-fi equipment and the producers of musical instruments. It now covers a wide range of music which goes through classical, rock, disco, country, blues, jazz, pop, easy listening. As Mrs Thatcher believed in free-market economics, she encouraged the commercial side of the music business and ignored certain measures such as the imposition of quotas for foreign and especially American pop music. In France, regional types of music tradition have long been subsidised by the state. This was certainly not the case in Britain during the 1980s.

Mrs Thatcher helped the serious sector of the music industry in much the same way as her predecessors, thus maintaining London as one of the classical music centres of the world. Since the music industry is good for exports and produces a high level of invisible earnings in the form of copyright fees and royalties, her reasons for continued subsidy are obvious. In addition, musical products also have the advantage of being exportable without needing subtitles as in the case of films. Music can be understood by everyone as there is no language barrier. Although contrary to her reading tastes, Mrs Thatcher personally preferred the elitist end of the market and disliked pop music, she continued to support commercial music by leaving the market relatively unregulated.

The record business has an international structure and it is therefore difficult to obtain figures for one particular country. However, by 1987, 42 per cent of sales on the British market involved UK based companies, such as EMI or Virgin. North American based companies, such as Warner Brothers or Polygram, held 32 per cent of the market, while European ones took 25 per cent. During the 1980s, there was a significant restructuring of the business. The recession, at the beginning of the period, had an impact on United Kingdom sales. Concentration of compact disc production on a few mostly German sites also took place around this time. British factories came at the end of the 1980s period.

This process was similar to the concentration that was carried out in the same period in the car business, thus leading to significant economies of scale.

In Great Britain, the 7 inch single record grew less popular as the decade progressed. This was not the case in the United States, however, where it made a comeback in the late 80s. Long player (LP) sales picked up on the British market in the latter half of the 1980s. Compact disc sales rose steadily throughout the Thatcher decade, but not in such a spectacular way as in some European countries. This might be explained by the relatively high-price policy of the record companies in the United Kingdom compared with much cheaper equivalent products in the United States.

A Coopers and Lybrand survey, on behalf of the Association of Professional Studios (APRS), assessed the turnover at £49 million and the workforce at approximately 1000 people. As for recording equipment manufacturers, turnover was estimated at £66 million (seventy-six per cent was exported), and employment at 1600. Another aspect of the music industry is music publishing. In this domain the British Phonographic Industry (BPI) estimated that $560 million were earned for British artists in the form of invisible exports in 1987. The whole of the 1980s were years of both vertical and horizontal integration in the music publishing business. The merger of Chappell and Warner in 1987 and EMI's buying of SBK Entertainment World demonstrates this tendency.

Sheet music sales do not generate much income, but the opposite is true of mechanical and performance royalties. Considerable amounts of money are involved in the work of the Performing Right Society (PRS) that distributes copyright money to its musical members. There is a similar organisation, the Mechanical Copyright Protection Society (CPS) that deals with royalties for records, films and advertisements. One should mention the high administrative costs due to the complicated procedures and calculations involved. In 1990, £23.75 million were spent on administration with a total œ49 million going to writer members in Britain, £34.7 million going to publisher members and £22 million going to foreign payments.

A 1986 White Paper, Intellectual Property and Innovation, recommended the abolition of the Statutory Recording Licence (SLR) that allows the sale of music by a record company without the consent of the artist, but no legislation was produced. Mrs Thatcher clearly approved of individual private property, but did not have enough time to legislate before introducing the 1987 wave of privatisations. Total figures for the music publishing industry were £98.7 million in 1986.

Yet another aspect of significance to the music trade is musical instruments. The business had 2060 VAT registered music shops in 1987/8 and forty per cent of its production was exported in 1987. An even higher proportion was imported. By 1990, the United Kingdom exported £45 million worth of musical instruments and products. Competition against Asian production will be difficult in the future due to a mixture of technical innovation and low labour costs. No measures were taken to limit the imports of cheap Asian musical instruments in the interests of free trade and market efficiency. In this case, the free market model was maintained by Mrs Thatcher.

By the end of the decade, profits from television copyright alone had become higher than those from direct sales. Therefore, it is difficult to take only one strand out of a music business that has international ramifications and works closely with practically all the cultural industries. One successful private company such as Virgin, during the 1980s, dealt with films, videos, video clips, recording and record distribution, but also, surprisingly, air travel. Virgin can be considered as one of the most successful enterprises of the decade, with the very entrepreneurial and high-profile Richard Branson at its head. The company was later bought up by EMI in 1992. The British music industry is a small component of the various international cultural industries. It is difficult to talk only of the musical dimension when, for example, dealing with music channels such as MTV that combine television and pop music. The Thatcher years were a period of restructuring that was certainly encouraged by free-market policies. Yet the music business does not seem to have evolved at all differently from other countries though the governments might have contrasting political orientations.

Notes

1. Peat Marwick, *McLintock, Book Prices in the UK* (London: British Library, 1989).

Chapter 16
The Cinema and Video Industries

Cinema and video stand apart in so far as they show different results despite similar policies. The contrasts are very striking and difficult to explain and justify. Concerning the British cinema business, Mrs Thatcher's period can be described as one of improvement followed by decline as regards film production, and as one of decline and renewal, as regards film consumption. The video industry, by contrast, expanded steadily throughout the 1980s, and is a clear example of Mrs Thatcher's cultural policy in a new cultural industry.

The cinema industry

In France, the Socialist governments protected the French film industry from foreign, and especially American competition, by subsidising home production. Mrs Thatcher, by contrast, did little to protect the British film industry. It is true that she allowed Channel 4 to come into existence, and this resulted in a mini revival in independent film production in the first half of her decade. The contents of this revival will be studied in a separate chapter later. However, the major change that Mrs Thatcher instituted was the removal of the Eady Levy which was a protectionist tool for helping home-grown production. To a large extent, she freed the market-place from government control and feature film production suffered a severe decline.

The Eady Levy

The Eady Levy was the kind of protectionist mechanism that, in the long term, Mrs Thatcher wanted to remove. It was a means of taking a proportion of box office receipts from the distributors to hand money back to the producers. A similar scheme functions in the Federal Republic of Germany. In 1985, the levy was replaced by British Screen Finance Limited, which was a private consortium offering loans to British film talent. Also in 1985, came the end of the 100 per cent capital allowance on production deficits, thus making film production an even riskier business than it already was. The following table shows the remarkable decline in United Kingdom film investment that occurred after 1985 and which was a direct result of this measure. In the latter part of the 1980s, low budget television films became the norm. Investment in full feature films declined progressively after 1985, the stagnant figures representing actual reductions if constant prices are used. By contrast, television spending on films rose in a spectacular fashion. However, one should also make the distinction between the significant rise in spending on television series and an actual reduction in television films. This shows the necessity of looking at the details of the charts and figures. It would appear that money was moved from film production to advertising production. If the total of these two categories is made, £434.8 million were spent in 1984, while £433 million were spent in 1989. Of course, if one measures in constant price terms, this represents a slight drop. If total United Kingdom films are considered, the level stayed about level because the feature film drop was compensated by an increase in television production.

For this remarkable reduction in United States investment in United Kingdom film production, David Robinson puts the blame squarely on the government's shoulders: the ending of capital allowance directly provoked this decline.[1] Peter Harcourt, a Canadian commentator, takes the same view:

When the 100 per cent Capital Cost Allowance was in place, it was possible, although still difficult, to raise funds from private investors. But in 1987 [...] the CCA was reduced to 30 per cent over a two year period and the private funds immediately disappeared.[2]

One should also add that restrictive practices by unions contributed to make Great Britain an unattractive location for international film companies.

If the top twenty films in the United Kingdom in 1989 are taken, fifteen were of United States origin and only three were purely British. This shows that culturally speaking, the British have a special relationship with their successful American cousins. American commercial culture is regarded with a mixture of both admiration and envy. What is even more striking, was the absence of European films in the British cinemas. This ties up with the strong anti-intellectual streak that exists in Britain today and that was encouraged by Mrs Thatcher's pronouncements and was reflected in her cultural policies that tended to reject the highbrow, elitist end of the market. However, with American companies adopting global strategies, the whole idea of national production seems to be redundant. British film directors now shoot American films on foreign locations using global strategies. To illustrate the point, no less than seventeen American films were shot in Ireland last year.[3] Thus, as concerns film production, the Thatcher strategy was to significantly deregulate the market.

In 1990, her government announced a belated plan for providing £5 million of public money for European co-productions. Mrs Thatcher was accused of giving too little too late. She certainly dealt a harsh blow to the ailing feature film sector through her non interventionist measures. One can thus measure the significance of the implementation gap in other domains which were protected from such voluntarist interference.

Film Distribution

On the consumption side of the British film industry during the Thatcher period, one can paint a more optimistic picture. While there was a general decline in cinema audiences in Western Europe, admissions to British cinemas almost doubled between 1984 and 1989. This is confirmed by 17.3 b that shows a doubling according to various age ranges. In the second half of the 1980s, a slow recovery started in the United Kingdom. This can best be explained by the rise of the multiplex cinema complexes, that combine a large number of screens with ancillary services such as restaurants and bars. Because of the diversity of services offered, profit margins are higher than in the classic single-screen cinemas. American companies such as Multi Cinema started the trend and the first multiplex was opened at Milton Keynes in October 1985. Other companies joined in: Cannon, CIC which later became UCI, Maybox and National Amusements. At present, there are three United States exhibitors in the United Kingdom: UCI, Warner, and National Amusements. The main British companies are Rank and Path, House, the latter including Cannon and Granada.

Multiplex cinema screens currently account for a third of all screens that are available in the United Kingdom and it may be that the novelty value will wear thin in future years. However, the use of various sizes for cinemas means that exhibitors can now cater for specialist needs or minority tastes, whereas the old cinemas had to cater for general tastes. This added flexibility led to the closing of many independent cinema clubs during the Thatcher period as managements found it too expensive to reorganise the single-screen cinema into multi-screen houses. Increased competition certainly pleased Mrs Thatcher as many of these independent cinemas showed politically radical films that sharply criticised the status quo. The cinema distribution market became increasingly dominated by the major companies during the 1980s. There was a certain amount of concentration for Path,, Rank Leisure and UCI. As for the independents, after a decline in the early part of the decade, there was a slight recovery began in the second half of the period. Throughout the period, ticket prices for cinemas remained remarkably stable in real terms and the fact comes as a great surprise since it is known that all the performing arts companies increased their ticket prices during the period. The bottom of the trough came in 1984 and the market had almost returned to 1980 levels by 1989.

As in other areas of cultural policy, government responsibility was shared out between various government departments thus leading to reduced accountability: among those, the Department of Trade and Industry (DTI), the Home Office, the Office of Arts and Libraries (OAL), the Northern Ireland Office (NIO), the Welsh Office (WO), the Scottish Office (SO). This spreading out of responsibilities also meant a weakened opposition, while concentrating strategic importance on the prime minister. The official government representative in the film industry is the British Film Institute (BFI), that started as a voluntary body and now uses government funds for the National Film Theatre in the South Bank complex, the Regional Film theatres, such as the Cornerhouse in Manchester, and the 280 film societies that exist around the country. Despite Mrs Thatcher's populist discourse and middlebrow personal tastes, this institution had a considerable increase in subsidy. It is somewhat paradoxical as the British Film Institute and the National Film Finance Corporation (NFFC) put forward money for the quality end of the market and highbrow films. In other cultural areas such as literature, the highbrow form was not encouraged in the same way, the Arts Council literature panel having very little influence. In the case of the BFI the cultural Establishment gained what it wanted despite Thatcherite opposition.

In conclusion, British feature film production was not propped up by government policy or money, true to the ideas of the New Right. The 1980s saw the industry transformed from a producer of major feature films involving large sums of money, into a producer of low-budget television-style films. This was not necessarily a bad thing, but the high quality big budget feature film end of the market came to remain under the domination of the American companies with only a few European productions. The exceptions to this rule were Chariots of Fire in 1981, and Gandhi in 1983, which both won Oscar awards and sold well internationally. Various capable directors, such as David Puttnam or Simon Perry, left the United Kingdom for Hollywood. In 1984, in the middle of the Thatcher period, sixteen of the Top 20 films were of United States origin.[4] By the end of the decade, the figure had increased slightly to seventeen.[5] The flight of investment out of Britain can be directly attributed to government taxation policy. Yet this non-interventionist attitude in the mass commercial market was not maintained in the highbrow end of the market where government funds were greatly increased during the Thatcher period. Mrs Thatcher's policy in the British film industry can be characterised as one of encouraging the commercial end of the market by removing protective legislation, and heavily subsidising the highbrow side. There appears to have been a two-tier policy in this particular cultural area with tensions that were never fully debated by the general public.

The Video Industry

The government's low budget policy that was the feature of British film production in the 1980s contrasts with the British love for videos. The decade saw a spectacular boom in the video industry that affected all classes of people and encouraged a private mode of cultural consumption. Just as the private car was the Thatcher ideal in transport, for the prime minister, the video represented individual choice in cultural consumption. It is an example of a cultural industry where Mrs Thatcher was in wholehearted agreement with British citizens. It can also be seen as an encouragement of cultural democracy.

On the hardware side, 64 per cent of British households had a video cassette recorder (VCR) in 1988, and 10 per cent had two or more VCRs. The latter figure shows how the VCR market had reached maturity, and people were increasingly buying rather than renting machines in the late 1980s. The percentage of households with machines rose in an uninterrupted fashion throughout the 1980s, from 38 per cent in 1984, to 60 per cent in 1988.

As with most new technology, the British prime minister was enthusiastic, but had paternalistic reservations over what individuals should be allowed to view. The government was not interventionist, except for taste and decency. The highly profitable video industry was allowed to develop according to free market forces, with only a minimum amount of censorship on the content side. The Thatcher government could have put limits on VCR imports from far Eastern Asia, as was the case in Socialist France, but it decided against such protectionism. It could have put a levy on blank video cassettes as is common practice in Sweden, or introduced quotas, but this was not done either. Because the market was highly profitable, VAT was maintained on both hardware and software. The effect of this free market was to strengthen the position of the multimedia transnational companies, which had a strategic advantage, right from the start of the video boom. Sony, for example, produces hardware in the form of VCRs but also software, in the form of prerecorded videos and blank videos. Thus it makes most of its profit from the cultural redistribution end of the market. It is extremely difficult for new entrants to compete in a field where the large corporations such as Sony or Philips can sustain heavy losses for strategic reasons over long periods of time. The same logic applies to all new technology, whether it be in the Press, in satellite broadcasting, or high definition television.

In the early part of the decade, the rental market developed very rapidly, most rental shops being independent and non-specialist. Towards the end of the period, the 7500 video software shops, of which 70 per cent dealt with video rentals, became more specialised and increasingly dominated by chains such as Video Magic, Clearview and Cityvision, the last mentioned having 164 outlets in 1989. As far as consumers were concerned, various figures show that the rental market was and still is dominated by feature films and humour. The late 1980s trend of buying videos meant that certain categories such as child videos or music videos experienced considerable development. It would seem that children and music videos were the most popular categories for purchasing. Video is a truly democratic product and for this reason, Mrs Thatcher liked encouraging this end of the cultural market. The evidence for the early 1990s shows that the boom of the 1980s is over and that the market is coming to maturity. Three explanations come to mind: (1) Later consumers appear to be more marginal and discriminating viewers; (2) The novelty value of video, as with television, is wearing thin; (3) Satellite television is now competing against video viewing. All three are plausible reasons and now combine to act as a brake on what can only be described as a video explosion.

It is over censorship that Mrs Thatcher showed the limits of her free market philosophy. There were a series of what became termed 'video nasties' that showed children being tortured or even killed, the latter being termed 'snuff movies'. The media reflected the revolt of the vast majority of British citizens. Legislation was drawn up and the Video Recordings Act made law in 1984. Existing legislation merely prosecuted producers and viewers when the material was judged by the police to be offensive. The new legislation introduced censorship that was slow and administratively heavy to implement. In the interests of protecting the public, red tape was introduced, which was paradoxically one of the areas of government that Mrs Thatcher had hoped to reduce.

In conclusion, the video industry, as a new cultural industry, provides one with a very clear picture of Mrs Thatcher's cultural policy ideal. The successive Thatcher governments allowed the free market to operate, giving an advantage to the transnational corporations on the hardware side and to the chains on the software side. These observations bring out the implicit and hidden nature of Mrs Thatcher's cultural policy that encouraged middlebrow content. The kind of products that came to dominate the video market were very much of the middlebrow sort, mostly in the mass entertainment category, such as Crocodile Dundee, that attracted a remarkable twenty million viewers. This free market attitude was only limited by questions of taste and decency when legislation was introduced in response to a specific problem. A minimalist legislative attitude was adopted and maintained throughout the eleven year period. Finally, cultural reproduction proved highly profitable while cultural production often lost large sums of money. A coherent cultural policy should have taken this into account, and yet, Mrs Thatcher seems to have ignored this particular aspect. One may affirm that a very clear picture of Mrs Thatcher's cultural and economic preferences can be seen in the video industry. It is one of the few cultural industries where free-market economic policies were fully applied and where results were as successful as expected.

Notes

1. David Robinson, "Fading of a False Dawn" *The Times*, 3 December 1989.
2. Peter Harcourt, *Cultural Economics 88: A Canadian Perspective* (Ottawa: Association for Cultural Economics, 1989) 83.
3. *BBC Radio 4, Woman's Hour*, Friday 14 April 1995.
4. John Myerscough, *Facts About the Arts* Vol 2 (London: PSI, 1986) 225.
5. *Cultural Trends No 6* (London: PSI, 1990) 25.

Chapter 17
The Art Trade and Heritage - A Heritage Industry?

The art trade

In her memoirs Mrs Thatcher explained her disappointment at not being able to secure the Thyssen collection of grand masters for the nation. It might have been purchased for a fraction of the estimated market value. Even the reduced price, however, proved too high for the Thatcher state. This gives a hint of how the prime minister regarded art. She did not necessarily see the aesthetic qualities but she certainly noticed the market value. Her definition of art was based on the economic principle of supply and demand and as the grand masters were by definition limited on the supply side, they were of great value. Thus, for the prime minister, culture was rather a set of valuable objects than unique group or community experiences. This explains the prominence assumed by the art trade in the cultural policies followed by the different governments of the period.

The 1980s were years of constant expansion in the art trade and London became the world centre of this multi-million pound market due to favourable legislation. This period was immediately followed by the catastrophic 1990-1991 years that particularly affected the auction houses' trade. The reason for this dramatic drop in sales was that the speculative bubble of the 1980s burst due to a fatal combination of three factors: an economic recession, the war with Iraq leading to fewer American tourists, and a reduction in Japanese purchases of works of art. The price of Impressionist works and modern and contemporary art plummeted as a result, while Old Masters, drawings, silver, porcelain and furniture held their own. The speculation on Impressionist paintings can almost be seen as an allegory of Thatcherite economic policies. Services were made to fill in gaps left by the decline of manufacturing industry. Money was available for investment in speculative activities without considering the wider issue of market stability and long-term prospects. The Docklands project, that Mrs Thatcher was personally involved in, is a typical example of a speculative attitude that could only collapse when economic expansion was transformed into recession.

Before turning to the end of the 1980s and the bursting of the speculative bubble, it should be stressed that the whole of the Thatcher period is one of constant expansion in business terms and values too. This is not surprising as conservatism has a natural tendency to look towards the past and its sacred objects. Therefore, in the financial year 1989/90, Christie's and Sotheby's, the two biggest auction houses in London, sold over thirty individual works of art for more than $10 million and over, six hundred at $1 million or over.[1] The decline in values in 1990/1 affected auction house profits and these were obliged to lay off employees and cut back expansion plans. The value of trade fell by over 50 per cent. Dealers in antiques fared rather better than the big auction houses because they handled a wider range of goods and the average drop in business value was only 10 per cent for 1990/1. However, this average figure does not show the great divergences that exist within the category. Pictures and furniture held up remarkably well, while silver, ceramics and jewellery lost much more in value. The reduction in foreign visitors affected the south east of England the most, while the recession hit the whole of the United Kingdom.

The art trade is concentrated in England and London because export licences are very easily granted to foreign owned objects, to the benefit of the balance of payments. In 1990/1 the total value of works of art imported into the United Kingdom was £1512 million and that of exports £1766 million. This represented a £254 million benefit. An extraordinary progression of Japanese spending in this area occurred in this period. Japanese investors and collectors spent £24.7 million on British art and antiques in 1985. By 1990, the figure had risen to £400 million. Another even more surprising phenomenon was the increased investment from the European Community: £126.2 million in 1985, rising to £536.8 million in 1990. This was almost as much as the United States total for 1990. In 1985, the Americans dominated the market. In the space of five years they had become members of a group of three, and a fourth group formed by the Asian dragons was also emerging. Hong Kong, Taiwan and Korea come to mind as the main actors in this group. Unlike the cinema industry that became increasingly American dominated, the arts trade became more international in the space of five years.

Objects that have been in the United Kingdom for more than fifty years can be refused an export licence, but such cases are extremely rare. This policy of non-intervention has encouraged sales but caused worry to those concerned by the preservation of the national heritage. The 1952 Waverly System was set up to give the nation the possibility of purchasing national treasures before being sold abroad. This system set out three areas where export licences could be refused if:

1. The object is so closely connected with our history and national life that its departure would be a misfortune;
2. It is of outstanding aesthetic importance;
3. It is of outstanding significance for the study of some particular branch of art, learning or history.

In 1990, the Middleham Jewel that dates back to the War of the Roses was saved for the country after a public campaign and appeal to find £2.5 million. However, for every successful appeal there were many instances of national treasures leaving the country. For example the Badminton Cabinet went abroad in 1991.

The cases where the Department of Trade and Industry (DTI) refused to give export licences under the Waverly agreement show up the inefficiency of the system. In 1990/1, there were thirty-eight cases which were signalled to the Export Review Committee. Eight of these were judged not to come within the scope of the scheme, while eleven of the cases were withdrawn. The remaining nineteen were held up while monies were collected. Only six were in fact saved for the country at a cost of œ3 million. Six costing £23 million were sold overseas along with the remaining seven. Thus in 1990, the Waverly protection clause saved a pair of George III armchairs, the Middleham Jewel, two bronze fibulae, an enamel brooch, the papers of General Sir Eyre Coote and a drawing by Primateccio. The system quite obviously could not work without a significant increase in government funding at the national level. Mrs Thatcher did nothing to increase funds, considering this state of affairs as satisfactory. This was confirmed by the Reviewing Committee on the Export of Works of Art. The 1990/91 report stated: "These dismal figures show conclusively that the Waverly system of export control for major works of art has been, to all intents and purposes, killed off through lack of funds."[2]

There exists a private fund that depends on private legacies, donations and subscriptions and was set up in 1903 under the name of the National Art Collections Fund (NACF). Individual museums could also be helped in the buying of heritage objects by the National Heritage Memorial Fund (NHMF) which was set up in 1980, under the National Heritage Act, and was financed by the Department of the Environment (DOE) and the Office of Arts and Libraries (OAL). Yet another important way of preserving the national heritage was the Acceptance in Lieu Scheme which was also introduced in 1980. Since 1985, this scheme has been administered by the Museums and Galleries Commission. Capital Transfer Tax and Inheritance Tax could both be paid by selling works of art directly to the state. (Table 18.3 on page 492 shows the major items involved for the year 1990.) Although the amounts of money involved were not spectacularly large, they represented a real boon for those concerned. This added flexibility meant that parts of collections could be retained by individuals. These people could also count on a quicker response from the government agency rather than having to worry about private sales through auction houses. These were two significant measures to help preserve the national heritage.

Mrs Thatcher devoted two pages to the arts in her book The Downing Street Years.[3] One of these pages describes the tension that exists between those who promote art subsidy and those who believe in a free cultural market. She describes herself as somewhere in the middle. The other page gives an account of her great disappointment at losing the Thyssen Collection for the country. These paintings were valued by Sotheby's at $1.2 billion and they might have been secured for a sum in the region of £200 million. She concludes her description of the failed negotiations by remarking: "It was not only a great treasure but a good investment - in every sense". This would appear to be a rather restricted view of art and the arts. She devoted one page to the national glory model of limited state intervention and another to the failed purchase of expensive paintings at a cheap price. She referred to the cultural activities in the capital, but did not discuss the rest of the country, or the better quality of life that a pluralist point of view might entail.

Most significantly, the prime minister associated the arts with private objects and not communal activities. Paintings were seen as desirable objects, indeed described as treasures, to be acquired and representing safe investments. It is true that self-made businessmen and many others invested heavily throughout the 1980s in antiques and paintings. However, the notion of literally possessing cultural capital is closely linked to the idea of private cultural consumption. It is a private activity based on individual appreciation. One can measure here the difference that exists between this view and another conception of culture that is held by many other people who believe in communication and communal activity.

In this particular domain government action was very selective and there was little intervention as regards preserving national heritage in the interests of national identity throughout the 1980s. Neither was the market protected by state action. When values fell, they were allowed to go on a downward progression. The antiques market was made to find its own level and Mrs Thatcher maintained a strictly laissez-faire system, and as a consequence, many national treasures went abroad.

National heritage

This particular area of cultural policy is important in the construction of a national identity. The symbol of an elegant building, often set in fabulous gardens, is a potent one for British people and foreign visitors alike. In such a domain, the essence of Englishness and national identity are in evidence. Like other cultural activities, it attracts many tourists but represents a heavy investment as it is labour intensive. Mrs Thatcher tried to expand this area of cultural policy where the state can play a crucial role in saving unique buildings and parts of the countryside. One can refer to a heritage industry because it mobilises many thousands of craftsmen and gardeners and uses a lot of manpower. It is not, of course, a modern industry using mass production techniques.

Heritage, during the 1980s, was the responsibility of the Department of the Environment (DOE). The situation changed in 1992 with the creation of the Department of National Heritage. The 1980 National Heritage Act set up English Heritage or the Historic Buildings and Monuments Commission for England. In 1987, the Adam Smith Institute proposed the privatisation of this Commission along with the national museums.[4] This reflects the Victorian attitude of leaving to voluntary bodies as much as possible. Privatisation is now projected for the late 1990s. The Commission has 400 properties under its direct responsibility and the number of listed buildings rose by about twenty-five per cent from 1984 to 1988, from 313,500 to 413,000. This clearly shows the increasing public interest in historic buildings. Mrs Thatcher's policies in this respect reflected the prevailing trend. A parallel can be seen in environmental policy where small amounts of legislation gave Mrs Thatcher a lot of beneficial publicity. By being sensitive in this area, she gained a lot of political sympathy. The Department of the Environment (DOE) is also responsible for the Royal Parks and Palaces for which £30 million were spent in 1987/8.

The private sector of the heritage industry is in large part organised by the National Trust, a private voluntary association that was set up in 1895 to safeguard the treasures of the British heritage. English

Heritage largely copied the private model. In fact, throughout the 1980s, there was a dramatic rise in membership numbers of many voluntary groups. For example English Heritage membership increased five fold between 1985 and 1989. Other income, sponsorship, donations, membership fees, all increased in as spectacular a fashion as with the performing arts. Mrs Thatcher warmly encouraged this trend away from state financing which reflected a late Victorian minimalism in cultural policy .

The country of Wales has Cadw (Welsh Historic Monuments) that works very much like English Heritage but does not have the status of a quango. It is under the direct control of the Secretary of State for Wales. In Scotland, there is a Historic Buildings and Monuments Directorate (HDMB) that directly funds government buildings. There is also a Royal Commission on the Ancient Buildings and Historical Monuments of Scotland that is under the responsibility of the Scottish Office.

It should be noted that, over the Thatcher decade, there was a decline in the number of visitors to government-run properties such as the Tower of London or Hampton Court. This was probably due to the increased competition that existed. National Trust properties, on the other hand fared very well, at least those which do not charge admission. 1989 saw a surprisingly hot summer and this partly explains the increase in the number of visits to Trust gardens for that year. In 1989, the top eight gardens of this particular organisation had a fourteen per cent increase in the number of visitors. The Thatcher years saw a marked development of this sector, though one cannot say that government policy was directly responsible for it.

The work of various local authorities should not be forgotten. The English Tourist Board listed 1322 properties that were open to the public in 1979, the figure rising to 1783 in 1989. 774 of these were in private hands and 425 were under the responsibility of the local authorities. The latter, therefore, played a major role in the preservation of the national heritage despite the pressures of rate-capping and reduced grants.

National heritage mobilised many people and attracted numerous tourists. It was an area of cultural policy where Mrs Thatcher would have liked to continue the Victorian tradition of organising voluntary bodies. Surprisingly she created bodies that preserved many historic buildings and touched the heart and soul of the nation. This was in contradiction with her economic principles, but was appreciated by many citizens and strengthened a sense of national identity which was another of her priorities.

The National Trust

During the Thatcher years, the National Trust (NT, founded in 1895) significantly increased its membership and extended its responsibilities. It retained its political independence accepting volunteers of every hue and colour, true blue conservatives as well as socialists. It is this remarkably wide consensus constructed around the NT that can at first seem unusual, especially in a period of supposed conviction politics. In administrative terms, the NT keeps a centralised organisation that deals with national bodies. It also maintains a regional system that allows a high level of local interest and participation. Mrs Thatcher had a somewhat ambivalent attitude towards the National Trust. For instance, her free-market principles made her a firm defender of road building to the detriment of public transport although many road schemes threatened NT sites during the 1980s. At the same time she admired the enthusiasm and effectiveness of a voluntary association using committed members that were there to protect British houses, gardens and landscapes, the essence of an elitist past.

In the Thatcher decade, the National Trust took on many new projects such as Fountains Abbey (in 1983), Belton House, Lincolnshire (1984), Calke Abbey, Derbyshire (1985), Kedleston Hall, Derbyshire (1987), Stowe Landscape Gardens, Buckinghamshire (1990) and Kinder Scout in the Peak District (1990). These acquisitions would have been difficult to achieve had there not been the setting up of the National Heritage Memorial Fund (NHMF) in 1980. This was introduced by Mrs

Thatcher to avoid a repetition of the Mentmore fiasco of 1977. At the time, some of the contents of this house could have been bought at a very reasonable price for the nation. A lack of co-ordination on the part of certain Labour ministers had meant that the National Gallery and thus the nation, had to pay considerably higher prices than were at first asked for. A solution to such problems was the National Heritage Memorial Fund which, on the contrary, could get together sums of money for the preservation of British heritage in a very short space of time.

The policy of the National Trust can be characterised as one of saving stately homes whenever necessary, and also one of buying coastline and countryside of immense beauty. The National Trust acts as an effective co-ordinator between the various bodies that might be involved: the Countryside Commission, the National Heritage Memorial Fund (NHMF), the Historic Buildings Commission (HBC), the Landmark Trust and private benefactors. In the case of Canons Ashby in Northamptonshire, the NHMF and the HBC secured the house in 1980 with £1.5 million. The Landmark Trust put up £100,000 for the repair of the tower that was to be used to house visitors during the summer season. The Victoria and Albert museum helped in buying back certain pieces of furniture that had been sold previously to pay for death duty. This was completed in 1984. Simon Sainsbury made a private donation and a public appeal got local residents involved in the scheme. It is this patchwork of organisations all united in a community project that excited all the participants. The obvious success of the system certainly seemed to influence Mrs Thatcher, who tried to emulate it in the totally different area of the Docklands and inner-city policies.

Another successful example of conservation during the 1980s was the saving of Bridge Cottage and five miles of the Stour river that had inspired John Constable in paintings such as his famous Haywain. In the early 1980s, a local farmer was authorised to start an irrigation pond. Gravel was also extracted from the nearby land and the cottage foundations were severely tested. By the mid 1980s, the National Trust had bought Gibbonsgate Field, Bridge Cottage and stopped gravel excavation. In 1988, Flatford dry dock was restored and finally in 1991, the owner of the Flatford and Dedham meadows sold them to the National Trust. This can be seen as an example of saving a piece of England that is profoundly linked with the English identity because of Constable's pictures. However, a road scheme was also allowed to pass next to the site, showing that economic priorities still came before national cultural symbols and that contradictions existed in the prime minister's cultural policies.

A report in 1985, entitled Gifts of Time, stressed the fact that many of the volunteers who helped the National Trust were not in fact members of the organisation. This came as a surprise. Although there were 3,000 full time people working in 1990, there were also two million members. By 1992, which is just outside the time period, there were 26,456 volunteers giving 1.38 million hours of their time.[5] This value for money aspect must have impressed Mrs Thatcher the most: unpaid voluntary work organised by professionals to give very professional results.

Of course a number of conflicts inevitably developed between the National Trust, with its ideas of conservation at all costs, and the free-market Thatcher governments. As mentioned before, one of the sore points was over road building. The Stour river in Constable country had a motorway going along the side of it. It was therefore only half-saved. The Chairman, Lord Gibson (1977-1986), clashed with Nicholas Ridley who was then Transport Secretary. Some suggested that the building of the proposed M40 would ruin the view from Farnborough Hall. Ridley is supposed to have walked out of an interview between himself and Lord Gibson over the issue.[6] Another clash came over the Ministry of Defence's proposed building of an RAF underground bunker on the Bradenham estate, at High Wycome in Buckinghamshire. This was a reasonable challenge to the National Trust's duty to preserve an 'inalienable right' to the land. The regional and central structures of the National Trust agreed to the MOD's proposals but the public furore that was unleashed by this project quickly buried the plans. For mostly electoral reasons, Mrs Thatcher moved cautiously in a reactive manner.

Dame Jennifer Jenkins (wife of Roy Jenkins) took over as chair in 1986. She emphasised work on the countryside, despite her background in the Historic Buildings Council, and organised European conferences where experiences might be shared. She encouraged educational work by developing Sutton House in the East End of London. The Young National Trust Theatre made its headquarters there and organised productions on various historical or social themes. Acorn Camps, to help train youngsters in National Trust work, was also introduced by Roy Jenkins' wife. By 1993, there were 4000 children involved. Certain NT properties specialised in childrens' groups such as Home Farm, at Wimpole. What Mrs Thatcher thought of this work can be suggested in the fact that some of these projects were included in her 1988 National Curriculum.

One general trend through the 1980s was a major move away from stately homes to more mundane dwellings. Houses such as two semi-detached residences in Worksop are now open to the public. Number Seven, Blyth Grove is a house that has not changed since the 1930s. The two brothers who lived there did not modernise it in a desire to keep the house as it had been when their mother was alive. It is a very precious historical object. This can be seen as part of a trend to study how ordinary people lived as well as the elite. It also provides evidence of a bitter struggle between cultural elitists and cultural populists. Mrs Thatcher may be said to have played her part in this movement by appealing to the man in the street with her popular brand of capitalism.

During the 1980s, the National Trust became a mass voluntary organisation using modern marketing and administrative techniques. Like arts organisations, it went along with Thatcherite policies by developing commercial activities such as National Trust bookshops and coffee shops. The alliance between the National Trust, The Historic Buildings Commission and The National Heritage Memorial Fund functioned extremely well up until 1992. In fact the extent of NT success can be seen in the withdrawal of an Independent editorial suggesting that it be broken up. Public protest forced the withdrawal of the issue in 1990.[7] The National Trust also knew when to avoid becoming political in the case of the anti-hunting lobby. The policy that was adopted was to leave such moral issues to Parliament. In this way the Thatcher governments could not accuse the organisation of being 'politically correct'. With two million members the National Trust also commanded respect from a prime minister who could not ignore the vote-catching potential of such a typically middle-class organisation.

The administrative patchwork of responsibilities shows that each country England, Wales, Scotland and Northern Ireland, had its own way of dealing with its built heritage. Mrs Thatcher's fundamental policy in this area was to give the private sector as much as it could take. She thoroughly approved of the imaginative work of voluntary bodies such as the National Trust and even created new ones. Her policy here can be defined as encouraging a private sector-led heritage industry. The state tried to give a minimum amount of financial help. However, the prime minister also had a duty to preserve the major architectural jewels which have the additional advantage of attracting foreign tourists. In this case the state played a role similar to the one played in the elite arts, preserving an infrastructure that the private market could not afford. The justification for this state intervention was that of a national cultural identity that needed to be treasured up for future generations. Mrs Thatcher did play her role in this process even if it came in contradiction to some of her other declared intentions.

Mrs Thatcher had varied attitudes towards the various cultural industries that depended on particular factors such as historical tradition, pressure groups, and probable public reactions. The winners were the newspaper magnates, magazine producers, private television operators, the book publishers and the public library service, music and video distributors, the elite end of the film market, the private heritage protectors. The losers were the radical Press, the BBC, the major film producers and the university library service. It would seem that Mrs Thatcher did not follow a hard and fast rule. The main principle was that state help should never be large and wide-ranging. However, certain principles such as the public library service and the British Film Institute (BFI) were never put into question. The prime minister's official policy was to encourage the commercial part of this significant market and she certainly approved of the resulting private mode of cultural consumption. The project was a basically pragmatic one that evolved over time. Policies were diffuse and reactive, sometimes voluntarist, and could be highly interventionist as was seen in broadcasting and the ban on interviewing terrorist groups from Northern Ireland. Here again one comes up against an implementation gap which fluctuated according to the different media and their highly complex structures, but can be seen at its maximum in the very sensitive area of press freedom and especially concerning television.

Notes

1. *Cultural Trends* No 12, 55.
2. *Cultural Trends* No 12, 64.
3. Margaret Thatcher, *The Downing Street Years* 632-634.
4. Douglas Mason, *Expounding the Arts* (London: Adam Smith Institute, 1987).
5. Merlin Waterson, *The National Trust* (London: BCA, 1994) 212-214.
6. ibid., 228.
7. Exact details of this incident can be gained in Merlin Waterson, *The National Trust* 228.

Chapter 18
Mrs Thatcher and the Teachers: The National Curriculum

The transmission of social and cultural values is based on the family, civil society, particularly through the mass media, and of course, the education system. Pierre Bourdieu summed up this process of acculturation through his concept of cultural capital that covers the way one behaves as well as thinks and, according to him, is to a large extent structured by the education system. Mrs Thatcher wanted to transform the national attitude from what she perceived as a dependency culture into an entrepreneurial one. This inevitably had consequences on the education system as she found it. During her first two terms of office, the prime minister contented herself with cutting university expenditure. The schools were left to get on with their work. However, in the third term of office, the Education Reform Act of 1988 set out the most far-reaching reform of education since the 1944 Education Act. The changes that Mrs Thatcher proposed in this domain reflect the paradox that can also be seen in the arts, of two contradictory policy objectives: firstly, a need to centralise and aim for greater national efficiency; secondly, a desire to decentralise, taking power away from local education authorities and transferring it to individual schools. The prime minister tried to combine these two conflicting policy directions with contradictory policy results. The scapegoat that was chosen in this particular case was the supposedly left-wing local education authorities and 'loony left' teaching unions.

The financial problem

The characteristic of the period before 1988 is that of a great deal of policy fragmentation. In 1976, Jim Callaghan had announced in his Ruskin Speech that schools should prepare children better for their working lives. He urged greater participation and more direction from the Department of Education and Science (DES) and Her Majesty's Inspectorate (HMI). Various initiatives were taken to make education more practical. In 1980, at the beginning of the Thatcher decade, the General Certificate of Secondary Education (GCSE) was promoted in a vigorous fashion, thereby giving most pupils the possibility of some kind of qualification at age 16. The Manpower Services Commission (MSC) under Lord Young introduced a scheme requiring that all pupils of fourteen and over should have work experience of some sort. This was termed the Technical and Vocational Education Initiative (TVEI). The Department of Transport and Industry (DTI) for its part, tried to encourage an enterprise culture through various schemes. The DES also tried to make in-service training a priority, in order to avoid the left-wing bastions of the teacher training colleges. These examples show that the education system was moving away from one of broad and vague objectives towards a system of management by contract and specific objectives. The various departments involved also showed the administrative complexity of education. Administrative fragmentation during the 1980s was accompanied by a realisation that resources had become limited. During the 1980-1990 period, for example, spending on education went down from 5.6 per cent of GDP to 5 per cent.

About this time, various radical new proposals also came from the New Right of the United States of America. Declining standards were typically referred to as a justification for new solutions. In 1983, for example, the US National Commission for Excellence in Education produced a report that claimed that "the educational foundations of our society are presently being eroded by a rising tide of mediocrity that threatens our very future as a nation and a people".[1] In England and Wales the voucher scheme allowing parents to move their children to better schools was also much discussed. Keith Joseph decided against it because it was politically unacceptable and too radical. Right- wingers argued that the education system was a bottomless pit and that resources should be spent much more effectively. Left-wingers countered by claiming that inner-city schools had been under-resourced and under-financed, stressing the need for uniformity of provision and chances. Curiously enough, if both New Right and New Left agreed on the existence of an education problem, little research was conducted to back up the various assertions that often remained in the domain of dogma. Everyone agreed that the secondary school system in England and Wales was in a bad state, but there was no longer a consensus, if there had been one, on the necessary reforms.

Mrs Thatcher set about reasserting the authority of the state. Since the war and up until 1979, British governments had let education experts run their education system. It was they who decided what the priorities might be and they who organised the committees that brought changes to the implementation of the fundamental 1944 Education Act. Using monetarist justifications, Sir Keith Joseph punished the education profession by limiting pay awards in the early years of the decade as he considered teachers to have an anti-enterprise ethos. The pay freeze provoked a bitter and protracted pay dispute over salary levels during the 1984-1987 period. The designated villain of the piece was the National Union of Teachers (NUT) that was labelled Marxist and unpatriotic. Many teachers were discouraged and left the profession, to be replaced by sometimes unqualified supply teachers. Talk of market pressures and the new industrial needs of the market-place was designed to affect the morale of teachers and was very effective in that role. Mrs Thatcher would have liked to introduce private sector organisation and language into education. The conservatives therefore suggested that in education the consumers should be allowed to choose their childrens' schools. Teachers often saw this move as a way of encouraging good middle-class provision while allowing bad inner-city schools to lose their more able pupils. The unions reacted by claiming that this was a means of introducing a two-tier system.

It is against this background that Mrs Thatcher decided to decentralise and also centralise the secondary school system at one and the same time. The 1988 Education Reform Act was in fact prepared by the Policy Unit at Number Ten Downing Street. Open enrolment was introduced as well as per capita funding which allowed children to move from one school to another and transferred resources with them. In this way good schools would be rewarded and bad schools would be goaded into reacting or else be forced to close down. Standards and reputations had to improve if the schools were to attract enough pupils. The Local Management of Schools Initiative (LMSI) was also introduced, empowering schools to manage their own budgets. In grant maintained schools, governors would control their own budgets without LEA interference. Schools were strongly encouraged to set up trusts and cut themselves off from the LEA structure. Lastly, City Technology Colleges were introduced providing courses in practical skills that were required by industrial and commercial companies.

The national curriculum

Mrs Thatcher was all in favour of letting the consumer decide and freeing the market-place. However, the major problem with the decentralised and fragmented English and Welsh education system was that there was too much diversity with excellent independent or Public Schools and dreadful inner-city establishments with very poor standards. Certain minimum standards had to be clearly defined and Mrs Thatcher likewise believed that there had to be a return to basic principles in education. A basic grounding in the 3 Rs, that is to say reading, writing and arithmetic, was necessary and, if possible, to be achieved through traditional teaching methods. In her memoirs, the prime minister wrote about her aims in this particular field:

> It always seemed to me that a small committee of good teachers ought to be able to pool their experience and write a list of topics and sources to be covered without too much difficulty. There ought then to be plenty of scope left for the individual teacher to concentrate with children on the particular aspects of the subject in which he or she felt a special enthusiasm or interest. I had no wish to put good teachers in a strait jacket. As for testing, I always recognised that no snapshot of a child's, a class's or a school's performance on a particular day was

going to tell the whole truth. But tests did provide an independent outside check on what was happening.[2]

She also recognised the urgent need for greater accountability, schools needing to meet the requirements of industry as well as those of parents:

> Alongside the national curriculum should be a nationally recognised and reliably monitored system of testing at various stages of the child's school career, which would allow parents, teachers, local authorities and central government to know what was going right and wrong and take remedial action if necessary.[...] (There was a) healthy distrust of the state using central control of the syllabus as a means of propaganda. But that was hardly the risk now: the propaganda was coming from left-wing local authorities, teachers and pressure groups, not us.[3]

She had identified the chief culprit for declining standards. Intervention was needed because the profession had gone down the slippery slope of socialism. She also admitted the difficult nature of the job: "But it would be no easy matter to change for the better what happened in schools".[4]

So, with Kenneth Baker as Education Secretary, the third Thatcher government duly set up the National Curriculum Council (NCC) under the responsibility of Duncan Graham, a realistic and moderate teacher and administrator. The local education authorities were not to join in the consultation process, but the DES, HMI and the School Examinations and Assessment Council (SEAC) all had their word to say. Government guidelines were vague and the consultation period was to be limited to one year before producing reports, a significant speeding up of the process. The various subject working groups produced attainment targets that were cut back by the NCC and further modified by the DES before being accepted by the various Education Secretaries. Most of the problems that the NCC encountered came from a bad initial definition of functions and the fact that three ministers applied different rules and styles in the critical 1988-1991 period, when the national curriculum was being designed and introduced. The original three core subjects of Science, English and Maths were soon joined by other important subjects such as technology, modern languages, history and geography. The impact also varied with the different subjects in terms of their implications for the profession and for national culture.

Mathematics

The first aim of the national curriculum was to give priority treatment to the 3 Rs. Mathematics was one of these subjects and was naturally the first subject to be considered by the new NCC in its speeded-up consultation process. Mrs Thatcher wanted Britain's position in international comparative evaluations to be improved. These invariably showed German and Japanese children to be the best and it was supposed to be one of the reasons for these countries' economic superiority. In fact Great Britain did badly in these international league tables because of the decentralised nature of education and the consequent move to modern mathematics which had low status in these studies.

The first working group was set up and it was greatly influenced by the Cockcroft Committee that had taken four years (1978-1982) to come to recommendations as to new teaching techniques and an approach to mathematics from a practical, rather than a theoretical point of view. Most professionals agreed with this position, but it was exactly this kind of teaching that Mrs Thatcher wanted to reduce in secondary education. The only Thatcherite in the working group was Sig Prais, a member of the National Institute of Economic and Social Research. He resigned, much to Mrs Thatcher's anger, when the interim report had been finalised after six months of consultation. The chairman also resigned and Duncan Graham was brought in to pick up the pieces. In July 1988, the final paper was presented. Of the 354 attainment targets studied, fourteen were proposed and this was reduced to five by the NCC and the DES. The right-wingers in Parliament could not fault this rigorous report that proposed high standards using modern techniques. Mrs Thatcher reacted by asking for greater clarity, but the report was largely accepted.

Duncan Graham, the second chairman of the mathematics working group and Director of the NCC, later admitted that when he took over, the DES defined guidelines along which he had to work:

> This was the first evidence of a huge de facto power shift in the way education was controlled in England and Wales. The HMI were adjuncts and the inspectors on the working group were extremely helpful, but they were not the driving force. That was the civil servants. The national curriculum was their baby, the first major education reform in Britain that had not been created by the educational professionals.[5]

The arrival of the national curriculum coincided with a power shift from the teaching professionals to government that was to become increasingly obvious in England and Wales. (Scotland, of course, has its own distinctive education system.) Mrs Thatcher wanted to reassert the authority of the state against the monopoly of the teaching profession which of course was part of the cultural Establishment. In mathematics this change was little felt but it was to become apparent when the other subjects were considered.

Science

One of the main complaints levelled against the education system by the directors and managers of British industry was that the grounding in science was patchy and over-specialised because of the splitting up into three subjects, chemistry, physics and biology. In the case of science, the Public Schools exerted considerable pressure to retain GCSEs in these individual subjects although they had no obligation to stay within the system. This is a clear example of the tail wagging the dog, of a pressure group modifying the national curriculum to suit its interests. Public Schools were to keep the specialised subjects because they had a great number of specialist teachers who did not want to re-train. At the same time, in order to please industrialists, a double-subject GCSE was produced covering both physics and chemistry. The result was that specialist teachers in the state sector had to re-train in order to be able to cover the new course. Now pupils could no longer avoid science, and this was a desirable change.

Technology was given greater prominence too. Whereas previously girls would do domestic sciences and boys woodwork, technology was to offer much more, and even cover design. However, many science teachers complained about the watering down of their specialised subjects, talking about a decline in standards. This ties up with the arguments of the cultural elitists who justify their position in terms of an undefined golden age in the past. Duncan Graham perceptively points out the paradox of the government's action:

Mac Gregor also had to reassure Mrs Thatcher who had let it be known that any suggestion that mathematics and science were being downgraded would not be politically acceptable. Not for the first time, NCC was faced with the paradox of the government talking about a return to basics and the need to avoid over-complexity and over-prescription while at the same time being determined not to see mathematics and science reduced.[6]

In science, the debate over standards was to a large extent a red herring. The choice was between reducing and spreading or maintaining the specialised subjects which so displeased industrialists. This can be seen to tie up with the cultural debate between on the one hand cultural elitists, and on the other hand the cultural pluralists with their middlebrow products and their idea of gradual cultural progress. Mrs Thatcher was caught unpleasantly between the two conflicting movements. She understood the needs of industry but also used the declining standards argument as a stick to beat the teaching profession.

English

English was the most difficult core subject, because of the distance between the English teachers and Mrs Thatcher's hopes and desires. Mrs Thatcher had specific ideas in mind such as a return to basic reading techniques and memorising word lists or learning by heart. Duncan Graham refers to this as the 'chalk and talk' method of teaching and suggests that it cannot be used as a comprehensive method because of mixed ability groups and large class sizes. One major problem was that the working group under the chairmanship of Professor Brian Cox did not want to produce attainment targets. Among English teachers there was a remarkable consensus over the principles of the Kingman Committee (1988). These proposed grammar discussions when mistakes were produced rather than having formal grammar lessons. Kingman argued that less able children would have problems with the theoretical work, which is undoubtedly true.

The interim working group report in English proposed a list of books to be used in primary schools. Traditionalists immediately wondered why Biggles and Enid Blyton's Noddy were not included. The notion of a national curriculum authorised list was finally abandoned as finding a consensus on the subject was impossible. A list of examples was given instead to give guidance to teachers.

The proposals were then put before the NCC and these were modified by Kenneth Baker. He added poetry because of his personal liking of this literary form. Official encouragement of spelling lists and memorisation work was also included. However, this remained a pious wish and did not oblige teachers to have one part of their lesson devoted to this particular teaching activity: it illustrated the gap between Thatcherite hopes and professional practice.

In secondary education, a debate between traditionalists and modernists was conducted over the proportion the national curriculum would devote to classics and modern literature. Shakespeare was made compulsory. There was also a debate over what balance to achieve with regard to language and literature. In fact, there emerged a broad consensus on the need to have both.

The idea of having an official list of national authors is vital in dealing with Mrs Thatcher's cultural policy. As in the arts when the Royal Shakespeare Company (RSC) was subsidised and English theatre became associated with Shakespearian actors, so it was with a list of officially approved English writers. Whether Charles Dickens and V. S. Naipaul were included is of fundamental political importance, as was the case of Keats, Conrad, Ted Hughes or the Liverpool poets. It is significant that feminist protest led to the introduction of Jane Austen and the Brontes onto the suggestion list. Having an official list turned the works of these authors into sacred objects, thus defining the contents of cultural capital in an officially defined national culture.

History

This subject, along with English, caused grave problems. Mrs Thatcher believed that history teaching should be built around facts and that analysis should only come as an afterthought. The history teachers, on the other hand, believed that the two should go hand in hand, and some of the most innovative ones used techniques such as empathy, the imagined description of daily life in other time periods. The prime minister saw this as evidence of unclear thinking:

> It is impossible to make sense of such events without absorbing sufficient factual information and without being able to place matters in a clear chronological framework - which means knowing dates. No amount of imaginative sympathy for historical characters or situations can be a substitute for the initially tedious but ultimately rewarding business of memorising what actually happened.[7]

Kenneth Baker, likewise, stressed the need for a solid British history curriculum:

> The programmes of study should have at the core the history of Britain, the record of its past, and in particular, its political, constitutional and cultural heritage.[...] They should take account of Britain's evolution and its changing role as a European, Commonwealth and world power, influencing and being influenced by, ideas, movements and events elsewhere in the world. They should also recognise and develop an awareness of the impact of classical civilisations.[8]

The history working group set out its objectives in an interim report. Mrs Thatcher was horrified by what she read: "The guidance offered was not rigorous enough". When the final report came out she was appalled. "There was insufficient weight given to British history.[...] In particular, I wanted to see a clearly set out chronological framework for the whole history curriculum."[9] The final report went out of its way to explain that trying to set up a national curriculum around facts was an impossible task:

> Many people have expressed deep concern that school history will be used as propaganda; that governments of one political hue or another will try to subvert it for the purpose of indoctrination and social engineering. There will always be those who seek to impose a particular view of history through an interpretation of history.[...] Names, dates and places provide only the starting points for understanding. Without understanding, history is reduced to parrot learning and assessment to a parlour memory game.[10]

Having only facts is clearly a waste of time, as is pure analysis leading to vague generalisations. This seems to be but common sense, and recalls the criticisms levelled at the pluralists and the Marxists. In the final version, NCC history assessment gave twice as much to factual knowledge as to analysis. Duncan Graham admitted that it was no easy matter to gain acceptance for the history proposals: "By some inspired rearrangement we persuaded Mac Gregor that, while facts could not be included in the attainment targets, they were none the less an integral part of the course".[11] It is obviously easier to assess facts rather than make analytical constructions. When Kenneth Clarke came to Education, he did not want to have modern history as part of the syllabus. This might be because during the Second World War, Britain played the role of a major power, while the postwar years were marked by relative economic, political and military decline. His proposal of 1945 as the last year of the modern history period was not accepted and the year chosen was 1970. However, the Second World War was selected as a special category of national glory. The following list shows the outline of the final history curriculum:

> 5-7 years Myths and legends; 7-11 years Roman through to Stuart times; Ancient Greece; Exploration 1450-1550; either Britain in Victorian times or Britain since 1930; 11-14 years Roman Empire 1066 through to 1900; The Second World War; 14-16 years 20th century Britain; European history; World history.

The way history is treated and what proportions are given to local, national and international history, are obviously complex cultural and political questions. One can produce a strongly nationalistic version of English history that celebrates the Glorious Revolution, the constitutional changes in the 19th century and England's heroic role in the Second World War. As in the case of elitist culture and common culture, one can also discover, for example, the way peasants lived in the Middle Ages and not just learn the names of kings. How children understand history is vitally important in the study of cultural policy as national myths and sacred symbols are built around it. Mrs Thatcher influenced the final definition to a large degree. Facts were given priority in the assessment process and a factual history syllabus set out an officially approved version of British history. It came as a clear personal victory for the prime minister and strengthened a sense of British identity.

Other Subjects

Physical education (PE) became obligatory for all pupils up until fourteen. The NCC working group expressed the hope that PE would be presented in such a way as to encourage sporting practice in later life, thereby making the citizens of England and Wales more healthy. Everyone was to learn to swim by eleven, thus helping to avoid the many drowning accidents that occur around the British Isles every year. Dance was considered and it was decided to exclude it from the national curriculum. It should not be forgotten that sports was one of the main activities that was encouraged in the Public Schools. The idea of working as a team, of helping in a group effort, of giving up individualism in a collective effort to win, is of course socially desirable. However, during the 1980s there was a boom in individual sports such as tennis, squash and running, that seemed to mirror the individualistic ethos of Thatcherism. Nevertheless, cricket, football, rugby and athletics could still be regarded as national sports, and nationalism was and is increasingly expressed through international sports competitions. It should be noted that for minor sports the individual countries of the British Isles often combine under the name Great Britain or the United Kingdom, with the Republic of Ireland always separate. Sports teams organise imagined communities and identities that have little to do with such traditional forms of social stratification as class and culture.

Music and art are also areas of interest that concern cultural policy. Neither were made obligatory after fourteen. In these subjects a delicate balance had to be achieved between national and international content. In music, the right wing reacted by stating that not enough weight was given to classical and British music. The NCC recommended a suggestion list including, Bach, Beethoven, Schubert, Stravinsky, Britten and Tippet, Fats Waller and Duke Ellington, John Lennon and Paul Mc Cartney. Kenneth Clarke was delighted at the inclusion of jazz as he was an enthusiast. Yet, the learning of musical instruments did not come under the scope of the national curriculum because of the costs involved. This provoked an immediate outcry from classical conductors and musicians in general, and Simon Rattle in particular: they wanted more music making and less musical knowledge. In art, a suggestion list was drawn up including L. S. Lowry, Leonardo da Vinci, Henri Rousseau, George Stubbs and Elizabeth Frink. This reflected a more British outlook in art. Evaluation was to be based on facts rather than understanding or practice. This was pointed out by Duncan Graham:

> Art and music are the ultimate expressions of the government's determination to stress knowledge over understanding. Mac Gregor had made some concessions and Clarke had been forced to with history, but art and music allowed Clarke to reveal the pure streak that had existed in the beginning: knowledge was more important than skills. We live in an age where facts need more frequent updating than skills.[12]

Of course this reflects the debate over whether to promote a democratisation of culture or a true cultural democracy. The former produces what was put forward in the national curriculum, while the latter is interested in allowing everyone to participate according to their own particular skills and tastes.

The role of educational pressure groups

The decline of consensus politics and the reduced role of consultation meant that powerful pressure groups had more say on the subject of the national curriculum than smaller ones. The working groups for the NCC included teachers and administrators. The independent schools or Public Schools, through the Headmaster's Conference, had privileged and easy access to the Education Secretary. Duncan Graham suggests that their insistence blocked many of the innovative and radical proposals of the NCC. Other pressure groups were the NUT and the various teachers unions. Parents' Associations and governors of opted-out schools also wanted to express themselves. As the NCC reports started appearing, Mrs Thatcher realised that she was caught in an administrative mess. She herself admitted it in her memoirs: "By now I was thoroughly exasperated with the way in which the national curriculum proposals were being diverted from their original purpose".[13] However, the mess was partly of her own making. She had wanted to go fast without clearly setting out her policy means. She had maintained the complex administrative machinery of NCC, SEAC, HMI and the DES. At one moment in the later stages of Mac Gregor's short term of office, a flood of complaints came from disgruntled teachers claiming that they were confused by the various circulars and instructions sent to them. Mr Clarke responded by insisting that information should be given only on demand. The result was that good schools were well informed and bad schools did not even know that a specific request had to be made for information. This seems a curious example of communication in what was supposed to be a 'national' curriculum.

The LEAs represented another pressure group that was kept out of the educational debate. LEAs were to have a merely residual role in monitoring and assessing the national curriculum and its tests. These bodies had previously wielded a great deal of power by being the sole providers of public education. Mrs Thatcher and her Education Secretaries all refused any kind of dialogue with these local authority bodies:

> I believed NCC should have set up a regional network with the authorities, their education officers and advisory staff, who after all, are the people who have to implement the national curriculum. Every conceivable obstacle was put in the council's way because of the unremitting hostility to local authorities from all ministers including Baker.[14]

All these different pressure groups had their own particular priorities. The general public wanted to have good quality schools while the teachers would have liked school provision for all pupils and equal chances for all. In addition to that, the conservative politicians wanted to introduce consumer (parental) choice and the measurement of standards. The NCC had to try and find a middle way through these markedly different points of view. Given the problems, it did a remarkable job.

All in all, Mrs Thatcher was correct in identifying the problem of a need for a national curriculum. However, the means that she devoted were administratively inadequate:

> When justifying the introduction of the curriculum, ministers were keen to point out that it was the decentralised nature of the English education system and its consequent patchiness which led to uneven standards and incompatible lessons. These local variations, it was said, inhibited the mobility of labour and made it difficult to define standards. The national curriculum was designed to provide the right kind of uniformity. The reformers could have used the word entitlement had it not been politically suspect. What happened in effect was that a government which passionately believed in market forces prescribed a curriculum for state schools in unparalleled detail. Whatever the battles behind the scenes about a narrow 3 Rs prescription, Kenneth Baker and his civil servants triumphed with a broad ten-subject curriculum. They were correct in terms of the scale of change needed, but it is little wonder that the right wing were soon trying to cancel the contract.[15]

Because Mrs Thatcher had a pragmatic point of view, she did not insist on radically changing the curriculum to fit her own projects. She realised that she had a whole profession to face and that if the teachers had rejected her proposals there would have been a bitter political struggle with resistance from the teaching unions. As she had very few supporters among teachers, she wisely decided on a few realistic changes allowing a broad consensus on the new curriculum. Mrs Thatcher hoped for a 'cultural revolution' with a return to traditional teaching methods and a factually based 'national' curriculum. Owing to the complexity of the system involved and the limited means devoted, only modest change could be hoped for. An implementation gap separates an ambitious education project and very complicated and moderate policy applications.

Notes

1. US National Commission for Excellence in Education, *A Nation at Risk: The Imperative for Educational Reform*, 1983.
2. Margaret Thatcher, *The Downing Street Years* 593.
3. Margaret Thatcher, *The Downing Street Years* 590.
4. ibid., 590.
5. Duncan Graham, *A Lesson for Us All* (London: Routledge, 1993) 30.
6. Duncan Graham, *A Lesson for Us All* 100.
7. Margaret Thatcher, *The Downing Street Years* 595.
8. Duncan Graham, *A Lesson for Us All* 64.
9. Margaret Thatcher, *The Downing Street Years* 596.
10. Duncan Graham, *A Lesson for Us All* 67.
11. ibid., 68.
12. Duncan Graham, *A Lesson for Us All* 81.
13. Margaret Thatcher, *The Downing Street Years* 596.
14. Duncan Graham, *A Lesson for Us All* 107.
15. ibid., 117.

Chapter 19
Intellectuals and the Churches

Mrs Thatcher claimed that she wanted to change the way people thought, transforming Britain from a dependency culture into one of enterprise and initiative. The magnitude of the project makes it very difficult to measure the scale of the actual changes. Mrs Thatcher certainly modified British attitudes during the 1980s. But to what extent were these changes due to her or would they have happened anyhow? Were they superficial or profound? The results of this attempted 'cultural revolution' appear to be rather patchy especially when measured against the prime minister's ambitious plans.

After being elected leader of the opposition in 1975, Mrs Thatcher busied herself building up the group of intellectuals whose role was to give her new and radical ideas. For this purpose, she set up the Conservative Philosophy Group that included conservative politicians such as Jonathan Aitkin and Hugh Fraser. Intellectuals such as John Casey, Roger Scruton, the historian Hugh Thomas and the philosopher Anthony Quinton also attended regularly. Mrs Thatcher went to these meetings whenever she could to argue out the issues of the particular case with selected journalists and politicians. The prime minister also had economic advisers such as Alan Walters, Ralph Harris, who founded the Institute of Economic Affairs, John Sparrow, who later ran the Number Ten Policy Unit, and Gordon Pepper, one of the specialists on monetarism. She therefore managed to attract to her camp a number of keen brains that produced many innovative policy proposals. Of course, it was up to Mrs Thatcher to evaluate the probable electoral consequences of these various policy options.

New Right thought and monetarism would never have gained the prominence that they did in the 1980s, if the left had not been so divided. The postwar consensus had reached an impasse in the late 1970s when it seemed that pressure groups such as unions could effectively block government action. Economic conditions allowing both inflation and high unemployment, often termed stagflation, something that was unexplainable in classic Keynesian thinking, seemed to prove that radical new solutions, either to the left or to the right, were necessary. Political writers, grouped around the influential quarterly Marxism Today (that stopped being printed in 1993), such as the historian Eric Hobsbawm, were pessimistic about Labour's chances of gaining power due to sociological changes in British society. Others, such as Tony Benn, argued that Thatcherism was the last stage of capitalism, before the final triumph of socialism. This class politics thesis was made even more unlikely with the collapse of the Communist Block in 1989, at the end of the Thatcher decade. In this state of affairs, intellectuals limited their response to Thatcherite policies by generally resisting and obstructing whenever they could. What coherent alternatives to this innovative conservatism they proposed, were not given the necessary media coverage for a full public debate. However, despite the high media profile that was given to Thatcherite policies, these representing a break with traditional conservatism and its pragmatism and decentralisation, the ideas of the New Right neither dominated the Conservative Party, nor came to be adopted by the general public.

The prime minister was not an intellectual in the true sense of the term. She did not ask questions for the sake of having an argument. She was basically a problem solver, looking for immediate solutions. This can be seen in her own description of the way she thought. Her approach was very close to the scientist's: "You look at the facts and you deduce your conclusions". Secondly she was a lawyer: "You learn your law, so you learn your structures. [...] You judge the evidence, and then, when the laws are inadequate for present-day society, you create new laws".[1] She certainly disliked the idea of publicly financed ivory towers and wasting time and money on theoretical arguments. It is primarily for this reason that Mrs Thatcher challenged the intellectual Establishment and placed self-made meritocrats in quangos and government jobs that had previously been reserved for what can be termed the cultural Establishment. According to the prime minister this group of people was anti-business, anti-merit, internationalist and parasitic.

As a result, the universities were told to reduce their budgets by 18 per cent over three years after 1981. In 1982, a further 2 per cent was arbitrarily cut from the budget of higher education. The self-made men who surrounded Mrs Thatcher, such as Norman Tebbit, never missed an opportunity to revile the universities. The Green Paper Higher Education into the 1990s demanded that higher education serve industry more effectively. One may add that such a trend was international and also present in the French universities during the same period. Research organisations, such as the Social Science and Research Committee (SSRC), gave fewer grants. Salary costs were reduced by removing tenure and introducing fixed contracts for lecturers and professors. Anti-intellectualism was rife during the 1980s in Great Britain. Along with the loony left and the unions, intellectuals were turned into the scapegoats for Britain's relative industrial decline. Yet Martin Weiner, an American social historian, estimated that there has been a decline in the industrial spirit in Great Britain since the glory days of mid-Victorian society. Managerial incompetence or class conflict were not even considered by Mrs Thatcher's advisers.[2]

This cultural war was taken into the field of linguistics. Mrs Thatcher would not accept certain foreign words. In one interview she refused to accept the word 'bourgeois', saying: "Dear Peregrine, why does he talk about 'boojhwha'? Boojhwha? Why can't he find a plain English word for the plain people of England, Scotland and Wales? The boojhwha live in France."[3] Significantly, she left out Northern Ireland. This desire to speak in plain English shows us a Little England attitude and was a reaction against the internationalism of the intellectuals, artists or even businessmen. She wanted to use a populist discourse. For the same reason she rejected 'consensus', preferring the term 'leadership'. This reduction of terms inevitably led to a poorer 'universe of discourse', although it had the advantage of making populist messages easy to transmit into the Press and the mass media. Clearly, she appeared to be siding with the people against the intellectuals in their 'ivory towers'. Even when attending meetings of the Conservative Philosophical Group, she was always on the look-out for plain English catch-phrases to feed the media with.

The reaction of the intellectuals was predictable. The cultural elite had been challenged and it hated the prime minister's style, her populist discourse, her materialistic petit bourgeois mentality. In 1985, the University of Oxford refused to give Mrs Thatcher an honorary degree, although it had been the custom for prime ministers to receive one. In 1987, Roy Jenkins, who in many ways represented the opposite of what Mrs Thatcher stood for, was elected as Chancellor. He was a consensualist, a staunch European, tolerant and extremely cultivated. Academics criticised her, among whom can be found Malcolm Bradbury who even wrote a book under the title Cuts, (a pun on the title of the musical Cats) in which the trendy university organises more practical courses such as billiard studies. Melvyn Bragg, a cultural critic, admitted to being revolted by the "gloating incantations from a woman dangerously in love with her own publicity". Dr. Jonathan Miller, a theatre director, suggested that the prime minister was "loathsome, repulsive in almost every way, her odious suburban gentility and sentimental saccharine patriotism, catering to the worst elements of commuter idiocy"[4]. This recalls the quotation in Chapter 5 on railway idiocy and lowbrow books. It has already been noted that Lady Warnock loathed Mrs Thatcher's manner. The conservative 'wets' such as Ian Gilmour and St John Stevas, were likewise enraged by the prime minister's direct and populistic style. Through her own explicit style, Mrs Thatcher provoked an unusually direct reaction from the cultural Establishment.

What is surprising is that Mrs Thatcher did not fill the universities with her followers. One of the reasons was that there were very few Thatcherite academics. On top of this, reduced university budgets meant that there was little mobility among the lecturers and hardly any new posts were created. Thus old professors stayed on when they should have retired. One can also argue that conservatism and even modern Thatcherism is more of a reaction to change than an ideological construct, and avoids theoretical discussions. With this reactive rather than theoretical position, Mrs Thatcher's pragmatism and practicality reflected the policies of many conservative prime ministers before her. It is an added reason why so few academics were attracted to the Thatcher camp.

The Churches

The intellectuals were not the only targets to be aimed at in the expected 'cultural revolution'. Most of the clergy of the Catholic Church, the dissenters and especially the hierarchy of the Church of England, all criticised the individualist elements of Mrs Thatcher's enterprise ethos. Her kind of Methodism stressed the notion of personal responsibility, self-help, prudence and discipline. The new Tories wanted the Americanisation of cultural life and its values. They did not have any respect for the Establishment and their dream of a carefully nurtured national community. Therefore, many of the institutions of civil society still believed in the social democratic postwar consensus, and it is in this category that the churches can definitely be placed.

The clergy of all the major Christian church groups in Britain had been educated in the liberal tradition, believing in open-minded education and disliking the brusque and brash enterprise ethos. Sociologically, the clergy belonged to the upper middle-class Establishment, just like the teachers and members of the professions. The new values of Thatcherism were such a challenge to their most deeply held and felt beliefs that the clergymen quickly produced counter-arguments that contradicted the emphasis given to individual responsibility.

Various incidents can be listed. Firstly, came the service of reconciliation with Argentina after the Falklands war on 26th July 1982. Just as in the case of the BBC, the Archbishop of Canterbury, Dr. Runcie, was not patriotic enough according to Thatcherite back-benchers. Secondly, Dr. Runcie had an interview printed in The Times in 1984 in which he complained about the disappearance of consensus politics and openly criticised Mrs Thatcher's divisive policies. A third incident came with the publishing of a major report entitled Faith in the Cities (1985) that laid the blame for inner-city deprivation on government policies and actions. Many back-benchers claimed that the report must have been written by Marxists. The Queen was even criticised by the New Right when she seemed to suggest that Mrs Thatcher's policies showed an uncaring attitude towards the poor and tended to exacerbate divisions in British society.

Many bishops attacked the basic values of Thatcherism. The Bishop of Sheffield stressed the dangers of having a North/South divide. The Bishop of Birmingham, Mark Santer, attacked defence spending, as did J. Austin Baker, Bishop of Salisbury. David Sheppard, the Bishop of Liverpool, defended community values against individualism in his Dimbleby lecture. There were in fact very few clerics who supported Mrs Thatcher's views. The exceptions were the Bishops of London, Peterborough and Oxford. The latter was resolutely anti- Campaign for Nuclear Disarmament (CND). One can see evidence of this social democratic domination in that half the clergy of the major denominations supported the Liberal and Social Democratic Alliance in the mid-1980s at a time when only one quarter of the electorate did.[5]

Mrs Thatcher never really counter-attacked. She was certainly shocked by the contents of Faith in the Cities but her public reactions were rather muted. In 1987, she commented:

> Churches are your great institutions, as are your great voluntary associations. And you are entitled to look to them and say "Look, there are certain standards and if you undermine fundamentally these standards, you'll be changing our way of life." When the authority of these institutions is undermined because they haven't been forthright, it is then that people turn too much to the state.[6]

At the Church of Scotland General Assembly in 1988, Mrs Thatcher pleaded for individual responsibility, making numerous biblical references: "How can we invest for the future, or support the wonderful artists and craftsmen whose work glorifies God, unless we have first worked hard and used our talents to create the necessary wealth".[7] One should stress Mrs Thatcher's work ethic, her use of the term investment to describe the arts and also the idea of creating wealth before moving on to glorify God. However, in general, she kept a low profile in her dealings with the churches. She left fierce criticism of the church hierarchy to politicians such as John Gummer, Norman Tebbit and Thatcherite back-benchers. Dr. Runcie was a popular target because of his complex analyses of morality and his moderate positions. Another surprising element in her relations with the Anglican Church was that she rarely used her powers of appointment. She did so only twice, in the case of the Bishop of London in 1981 and the Bishop of Birmingham in 1987, the latter turning out to be a nuclear disarmer.

British social attitudes certainly changed during the Thatcher decade. Added to this, by attacking what she called the 'British guilt complex',[8] Mrs Thatcher also launched an attack on the cultural Establishment of the land: the BBC, the universities, the churches. Her explicit message of self-help and individual responsibility was in large part rejected by these primarily middle-class institutions that remained loyal to the social-democratic ethos. However, her populism meant that she was more successful with the lower-middle classes and the upwardly mobile lower classes. As a result of this popular support, the unions' strength was impaired and the state was able to reassert its authority. Globally, the prime minister's message of a radical change in attitudes was unevenly received by the different strata of British society. Perhaps this is where the Thatcher project was the most ambitious and therefore failed in the most spectacular fashion. In the same manner as Gramsci's concept of hegemony requiring an active participation in the capitalist system, so Mrs Thatcher needed to have widespread support throughout the country. This is what the term consensus is all about. Her apparent disregard of the views of the general public as expressed in opinion polls meant that she could not succeed. However, one has to qualify the previous statement as the prime minister also knew when to bend to electoral pressure. This can explain the uneven and fragmented results she achieved in this domain. Mrs Thatcher tried to revolutionise attitudes in British society. She did not quite succeed, but the ambitious project may well have long-term effects through into the next century.

It will be up to historians in the future to measure the impact of her actions in this particular area. For us contemporaries, we are still too close and perhaps too partisan to pass a definite judgement on it.

Notes

1. Hugo Young, *One of Us* 407-408.
2. For a rather controversial discussion of the decline of the industrial spirit, read Martin Weiner, *English Culture and the Decline of the Industrial Spirit* (Cambridge: Cambridge University Press, 1981).
3. *The Sunday Telegraph* 28 June 1987.
4. Dennis Kavanagh and Anthony Seldon (eds), *The Thatcher Effect* 336.
5. Dennis Kavanagh and Anthony Seldon (eds), *The Thatcher Effect* 336.
6. Hugo Young, *One of Us* 421.
7. ibid., 426.
8. Hugo Young, *One of Us* 420.

Chapter 20
Film Directors and Producers in the 1980s

British film production when Mrs Thatcher came to power in 1979, was already in a poor state. Hollywood held an almost monopolistic position with regard to the international film market, and the various European national industries were all propped up to varying degrees by state subsidies. The measures taken in Great Britain were limited financially, and rather ineffective, compared, for example, with the policies of the French Socialists who poured money into the then commercially failing but prestigious French film business in the 1980s. In 1985, Mrs Thatcher removed the limited government help that was available and Britain's creative energy as a result turned away from feature film production to television films which were much cheaper. During the 1980s, a new type of television financed film emerged and many commentators speak of a mini film revival to describe the Thatcher years. Mrs Thatcher's freeing of the film market provoked an unexpected reaction which formed the basis of a film Renaissance in which a string of imaginative, oppositional and visually oriented, modernist films were created. Another consequence of this withdrawal of state subsidy was that the explicit political message of Thatcherism was openly challenged by many film producers. As Mrs Thatcher proposed an ideological agenda of change in favour of the self-made entrepreneur, film-makers responded by criticising the nature and the consequences of Thatcherite policies in general, and occasionally film policies in particular. What follows is an analysis of the most oppositional British films of the 1980s.

The influence of Channel 4

In the 1981-1990 period, Channel 4 helped in the financing of 170 films produced by independent film companies. About the middle of the decade, the policy of sole funding was dropped in favour of co-funding with other companies such as Goldcrest and the National Film Finance Corporation (NFFC), the latter having been privatised in 1985. The so-called Channel 4 films were shown at first on cinema screens and then on Film on Four and Film International. A certain Channel 4 aesthetic emerged during the decade, this referring to the placing of unusual subjects in mundane settings. By its very nature, television produces sitcoms that celebrate the everyday, the ordinary repetitive activities. Channel 4 injected tension into this reassuring context, by presenting images of rigid moral codes, intolerance, brutality, racism and greed. The typical message, however, is a conservative one with an orderly beginning, followed by a threatening middle section and a return to apparent order at the end. Very often the films are critical of Mrs Thatcher's policies and their values, but surprisingly, they rarely propose radical alternative solutions. They limit their role to highlighting the problem.

The typical Channel 4 film has to work within the limitations of television production. Certain film critics have argued that in contrast to television films, a feature film can focus on one or two characters and this gives the product a strong narrative line. An international audience means that visual effects are often used to produce a spectacular display in cinema films. Dramatic effects are encouraged by this framework and a lot of close-up work can be integrated. Television films, by contrast, concentrate on groups of people and give the viewer an atmosphere. Many medium range shots are used to convey a sense of the ordinary based on everyday events. In addition, British television films are strongly influenced by the documentary film tradition, thereby giving them a sense of realism. This tradition comes from 'docudramas' and what was termed 'faction' in the 1970s and 1980s. One can also stress the influence of the theatre and theatrical actors on British television films. (Diana Rigg was also a Shakespearian actress before making the Avengers series in the 1960s, and the example of Kenneth Branagh can be cited in the 1980s and 1990s.) Mrs Thatcher's policy of freeing the cultural market-place had the effect of shifting production to the television end of the audio-visual business, Hollywood being allowed to dominate feature film production. However, this move was not necessarily a bad one, as the costs involved were much more reasonable. Often expenses are ten to twenty times higher in the case of full feature films. What has to be remembered is that television films have to be judged on their own particular merits, and cannot be compared with feature films that constitute a different genre.

Cultural elitists often argue that cinema films are the true representatives of highbrow art. These are claimed to be unique creative expressions that reflect the individual genius of the producer. Mamoun Hassan, managing director of the British Film Finance Corporation in 1984, suggested that there was a crucial difference in quality between the two genres:

> Television films and programmes have to be topical; cinema films have to be more universal than timely.[...] Television is at its best dealing with concepts, explaining and describing (it is no accident that the drama documentary is the preferred form of television drama); cinema is at its best when it concerns itself with the ineffable, with that which cannot be expressed.[1]

This is very close to the position of the cultural elitists and also that of the Frankfurt School with its ideas of a unique 'aura' and timeless cultural products. Certain film directors such as Derek Jarman, Chris Petit, Alan Parker, Lindsay Anderson, denounced Channel 4 as a safety-valve allowing the status-quo to continue its existence. Derek Jarman termed it the television of 'Little England', while Chris Petit saw it as 'television hardback', implying that it was stuffy and elitist. In an interview in 1989, Lindsay Anderson also expressed his personal opinion on the subject:

> I think the real difference is the kind of subject liable to be financed by Channel 4, which leads to some of the new British films being a bit lacking in ambition or idea, rather than the feeling that if you make a film financed by television you have to restrict in terms of technique and style.[2]

At the other end of the critical spectrum, some commentators such as Norman Stone, expressed outrage and shock at the kind of film Channel 4 was producing. Stone wrote about "sick scenes from English life" in a Sunday Times article on 10 January 1989. Many conservative back-benchers claimed that Channel 4 was "letting the loonies on the air". Norman Tebbit, a cabinet minister in 1984, informed Jeremy Isaacs, the first Channel 4 Controller, that the minority interests he had in mind were golf, sailing and fishing. He claimed that the new channel was being used by "homosexuals and such". Despite this cabinet criticism, Mrs Thatcher, surprisingly, took the view that the new channel could be used as an effective escape valve for much-criticised intellectuals, showing that she knew how to be pragmatic as well as dogmatic. The typical sub-contracting system used by Channel 4, was also a useful way of introducing more commercial work practices that weakened the power of the unions.

David Puttnam

David Puttnam and Richard Attenborough were the two British film directors who had the greatest commercial success during this period. The former produced the oscar winning Chariots of Fire (1981). At the award ceremony Colin Welland, another film producer, made the claim that the "British are coming". This comment was supposed to mean that British film directors and producers were about to be snatched up by the various Hollywood studios. This trend seemed to be confirmed when Attenborough's Gandhi similarly won oscars in 1982. Puttnam went off to Columbia Pictures to work in the United States, although he was not particularly successful there. In 1985, neither Puttnam nor Attenborough succeeded in convincing Mrs Thatcher that film production should be regarded as a cultural exception to the law of the free market. After all, they argued that Rover Cars and Westland Helicopters had been bailed out by Thatcher governments. It would appear that Mrs Thatcher did not consider the enormous economic power of the Hollywood film industry as a threat to the healthy working of the market. Perhaps she considered the risks involved, in putting up considerable amounts of capital and often making no profit at all, as simply too great.

Even David Puttnam, with his commercial grounding and success, was in some ways an anti-Thatcherite. Chariots of Fire showed a certain amount of national pride and Ronald Reagan claimed that it was one of his favourite films. Yet it cannot be considered as a pro-Thatcher film. The various heroes come from different ethnic backgrounds and are all basically anti-Establishment. Harold Abrahams (Ben Cross) is the son of a Jewish immigrant, and he hires an Italian-Arab, Sam Massabini (Ian Holm) to train him in running. This self-made ethos does not go down well at traditional, conservative Cambridge, which represents the cultural Establishment. Abrahams wins the 100 yard dash in the Olympics and ultimately joins the social mainstream, being later buried in an Anglican church. In the end, he is incorporated into the cultural Establishment. However, the film criticises the rigid class structure in Great Britain and promotes meritocratic ideas. Mrs Thatcher certainly shared many of the values that were portrayed in this film.

Puttnam was a free marketeer, hoping that the British film industry would successfully compete on the world market:

> Our job in the UK is to set about defining "British" pictures in the broadest possible terms. Our cinema can and must reflect a genuine creative perspective. It must reflect the desire to see Britain and the world through British eyes and attitudes, and to communicate what we see in an entertaining and comprehensive manner to our audiences around the world.[3]

Despite this very commercial and British attitude, Puttnam could do nothing to halt the decline of the feature film during the 1980s. The business was simply too risky for Mrs Thatcher, and she refused to make British films a cultural exception. This seems all the more curious as the subsidised sector in the theatre business continued to receive state subsidy. In retrospect, the two most successful films Chariots of Fire and Gandhi form a bubble which burst in the latter half of the

1980s as feature films were transformed into cheaper, television films, due to the abolition of the Eady Levy.

Peter Greenaway

This film producer belongs to the modern art movement, which as an artistic wave of expression was not political in its outlook, and it is therefore surprising to see that Greenaway's film production during the 1980s becomes more political and more anti-Thatcher. In the 1970s, his films were rather avant-garde and non-commercial experiments in style. In the 1980s, though still remaining very personal, some of them attracted international success while becoming increasingly political.

Peter Greenaway received funding from the British Film Institute (BFI) and the Arts Council for his early experimental films in the 1970s. Channel 4 became interested in his work in the early 1980s, and in the latter half of the decade, he signed up deals with European companies such as the Dutch group Kees Kasander. This progression away from state subsidy to private and European financing was what Mrs Thatcher had in mind for all arts and cultural enterprises. Despite this movement to the commercial side of the market, Greenaway became extremely critical of Mrs Thatcher's policies as they began to show results. His Draughtman's Contract (1982) was a formal exercise on power and all the symbols that accompany it. The film did not deal with contemporary politics. Neither did The Belly of an Architect (1985), nor his Drowning by Numbers (1988).

It was left to The Cook, The Thief, His Wife and Her Lover (1990) for Greenaway to openly challenge Thatcherite policies. In this controversial film, Spica (could this be an aspic and thus a viper?) is the greedy authoritarian owner of an extravagant restaurant. Spica is the supposed result of ten years of Thatcherism. The restaurant is a symbol of the conspicuous consumption of the 1980s. Greenaway shows Spica to be a vulgar Philistine who is obsessed with power and its abuse. This is clearly a criticism of the self-made man ethos. In 1990, Greenaway spoke of his "anger and passion about the current British political situation".[4] It had taken ten years of Mrs Thatcher's explicit messages for the artist to react in a similarly explicit manner. Vomiting scenes in the film shocked some audiences, but it is rather the harshness of the film that surprises the viewer. Spica has no saving graces. He is utterly bad: sadistic, nagging, crude, loud, anti-semitic, racist, misogynous, homophobic and drunken. In the restaurant, the rich play degenerate games which in no way can help the homeless poor. Spica is filmed at the centre of the banquet table, spoiling specially prepared dishes, charging off to the kitchen and bathroom. Bodily functions become an obsession in the film, with Spica as the lord of the orifices. He prevents people from smoking and proclaims that someone will "shit through your dick". The lovers cower in the shadow of Spica's authoritarianism and are forced to meet in larders, freezers and toilet stalls. One of the shortcomings of the film is the total domination of Spica. This is a grotesque exaggeration of Mrs Thatcher as an individual. She certainly did have a strong personality and this was necessary to combat the considerable amount of resistance she encountered, but she was merely one individual, albeit a dominant one, within the Conservative party.

Richard Eyre

Richard Eyre's *The Ploughman's Lunch* (1983) is a damning condemnation of the whole marketing strategy of Mrs Thatcher's brand of conservatism. This is a critique of the way myths are invented in order to rewrite history. A BBC news editor, James Penfield (Jonathan Pryce) is socially and professionally upwardly mobile. This is another example of a self-made man, but he will trample on truth, on honesty and personal integrity to reach his goal of professional betterment and a higher social status. He also chases a woman called Susi (Charlie Dare). James is extremely individualistic and so thick- skinned that he shows no emotion when his mother dies. His political views vary according to the circumstances. At one point, he is a supporter of the British Suez invasion when speaking with a publisher. At another point, he criticises the very same invasion when in the presence of a left-wing historian. In the end, Penfield rewrites history by claiming that the glorious Suez campaign was a precursor of the similarly impressive Falklands victory. The implication is that myths are invented to justify the present.

Everyone is criticised in this film. It shows public people to be creators of myths and images that are plain distortions of the truth. To make sure that the viewers make the link between film and reality, footage of the 1982 Tory Party conference was used where Mrs Thatcher enthused about British renewal in what was a carefully orchestrated event. The very title of the film is a reference to the myth of 1960s marketing people who invented the Ploughman's Lunch (that is to say, a roll of bread, cheese and some pickle) for mass consumption. Nor does Eyre think that the left-wing opposition can offer a coherent alternative. The socialist historian is seen to live in a comfortable ivory tower in the country, her lifestyle at considerable odds with her political ideas. Even the Greenham Common protesters are shown as idealistic and lacking in realism. Eyre demonstratively lays bare the negative sides of Mrs Thatcher's cultural policy: the intensified use of image making, the construction of myths and the rewriting of history, the gap between official discourse and policy realisations, and the effect of these tendencies on the quality of the resulting political debate. Above all, Eyre is critical of the omnipresent market that measures everything in monetary terms and does not consider the quality of human relationships, or the environment, or the community.

Mike Leigh

High Hopes (1988) is another example of an anti-Thatcher film, but this time, a solution is proposed in fighting the laws of the market. In this film, three couples and an ageing mother highlight the tensions of 1980s London. The heroes are Cyril (Philip Davies) and the buck-toothed Shirley (Ruth Sheen), a former motorcycle messenger, who smokes marijuana and reads Lenin for Beginners. They both have left-wing sympathies, but cannot formulate an alternative agenda to Mrs Thatcher's market economy. In their flat they have a prickly cactus called Thatcher. These anti-heroes are examples of the invisible people of the 1980s who offered resistance but could not propose radical alternatives. They are sympathetic because of their bohemian lifestyles and their sensitivity towards each other.

The typically visible people of the 1980s are the other two couples. There is a snobbish one, which lives next door to Cyril's ageing mother. Laetitia (Leslie Manville) is aggressive and upwardly mobile. She tells Cyril's mother, Mrs Bender (is she going round the bend?) to buy her flat and then sell it, thus making a handsome profit. This seems a direct rendering of the speculation fever that was rampant throughout southern England during the late 1980s. Laetitia makes malapropisms ('tip top' or 'post haste' are badly used) this fact tying up with Bourdieu's definition of cultural capital. The upwardly mobile do not have a 'natural' feeling for cultural capital and have to learn the hard way by making mistakes. They do not naturally possess distinction. Laetitia has a poor working class granny living in the flat next to her and Mrs Bender can only lower the property value of the area. Everything is reduced to market value. The other visible couple is seen in Cyril's sister who is a vulgar example of the nouveau riche class of people. She gets ideas on dress and style from Laetita but she in fact has no style at all. She lives in a garish suburban house and her husband is a lout of a secondhand car dealer. He is lecherous and uncaring, the implied result of Thatcherite individualism.

The film suggests that the only way to avoid the pressures of the market is to create a private cocoon to protect you and your family from the harsh outside world. Cyril and Shirley try to live a humane and caring life with each other and Cyril's mother. These two people come over as genuine and sincere, standing in sharp contrast to the uncaring, harsh market.

Steven Frears

One of the most ardent critics of Thatcherite values was Steven Frears who produced three remarkable films during the 1980s: My

Beautiful Laundrette (1985), Prick up Your Ears (1987) and Sammy and Rosie Get Laid (1988). The first and third are based on books by Hanif Kureishi, an English writer with a Pakistani background, while the middle one was written by Alan Bennett, one of the most successful British playwrights of the 1980s. These films offer an increasingly explicit criticism of Thatcherite policies which Frears openly admitted in 1988: "Thatcher has divided the country between North and South, between the employed and the unemployed, between the rich and the poor, between the people who've got and the people who haven't".[5]

The first of these films deals with racism, showing that personal relationships and loyalty that cross over ethnic boundaries are still possible in an increasingly competitive world. The Pakistani community is shown to be doing well out of the new free-market philosophy. The entrepreneurial spirit among Pakistani businessmen is pushed onto the other side of the legal limit, some of them trafficking in drugs. Here can be detected a direct criticism of the profit motive and individualism. Omar, a young Pakistani, opens a brand new laundrette that is an instant success. He hires a former schoolfriend, Johnny, to do odd jobs at the laundrette. They fall in love and their relationship survives despite disapproval from both the white and the Pakistani communities. There is racial violence, and the launderette is burned down by a gang of lumpen whites, but despite this, there is hope for the future when a whole new chain of laundrettes will open.

This mildly positive version of enterprise culture is transformed in Sammy and Rosie get Laid. Here, London is transformed into a kind of Beirut, with racial rioting on every street corner. The individualistic and selfish young Pakistani, Sammy, is looking for a mother figure while at the same time trying to ignore the social problems on his street. Rosie, his wife and a social worker, gives him a certain amount of support but has to help many other people in her work. This is seen as a direct result of Thatcherite policies that have caused unemployment and homelessness on a massive scale. Families and family values are just impossible in such a social and economic environment. The police are depicted as brutal and inhuman, accidentally murdering the mother of a young black suspect. Rafi, Sammy's father, is a rich Pakistani politician, with blood and guilt on his hands. He tries to rediscover the quiet suburban London that he had known thirty years previously by visiting his former lover Alice. Even these normal people with establishment values find love impossible. Rafi is shown to be racist and sexist and Alice cannot put up with his paternalism. Normal heterosexual relationships now appear to be highly difficult because of social and economic pressures. Ethnic and class barriers are almost impossible to cross.

The only positive characters in the film are Rosie and her girlfriends. Rosie is a compassionate mother figure trying to combat the business ethic. Her friends are fighting against racism and sexism, while speaking to Alice about Rafi. At the end of the film, communities are shown to be destroyed by greedy businessmen and urban developers. This is a fiercely critical vision of Mrs Thatcher's Britain.

The third significant film of the 1980s is Prick up Your Ears. This is a description of Joe Orton's life. Frears wanted to shock the Establishment by showing a sexually repressed and homophobic 1950s and 1960s Britain. This is in fact an analogy of 1980s Britain. The relationship between the working class Orton and the middle-class Halliwell does not survive. Orton achieves financial success and an international reputation, while his lover gains neither. Halliwell disapproves of his lover picking up men in public lavatories and finally murders him. This depiction of a throwaway society can be seen as a critique of a mass society, with its mass production and lack of fundamental human values. Furthermore, it should not be forgotten that Mrs Thatcher introduced legislation in the form of Clause 28, preventing local authorities from presenting homosexuality as a viable family alternative. Frears clearly wanted to parallel the homophobia of the 1950s with that of the 1980s.

David Hare

Another film set in the 1950s is Wetherby (1985) which compares life as it was then with that of today. It starts off by showing a sequence in which Richard Nixon asks: "Do you remember?" "It wasn't so long ago." "Only ten years." "It's funny how people forget." A direct link can be made between these phrases and Mrs Thatcher's LBC interview: "You don't hear so much about these things these days [...]", (see page 11). Both these politicians conjure up mythical golden ages in the past. Wetherby shows the 1950s to be years of apparently happy family tea parties which, in fact, hide enormous sexual insecurity. A repressive society is portrayed and this is put up against the supposedly similarly repressive 1980s. In this film, memory is vague, decoding and reordering past events become crucial in defining the present. Myth making, as in many of the other films, is ever present.

The heritage films of the 1980s

One area of film-making that was very successful and can be considered as an epi-phenomenon is the heritage film. A specific case must be made for them. While not directly critical, they seem to embody much of the compensatory dreams that developed in the Thatcher years. Quality costume dramas were specially made to present a certain image of Britishness and more particularly Englishness, on the international market. The most popular of the genre were; Chariots of Fire (1981), Another Country (1984), A Passage to India (1985), A Room with a View (1986), A Handful of Dust (1987), Maurice (1987), Little Dorrit (1987), The Fool (1990). Although these films all have elements of social criticism in them, the original literary texts are often transformed into nostalgic and quaint tales set in beautiful surroundings. These films are all placed in a pastoral past where the threats of unemployment and multiculturalism do not exist and where British identity is strong, both physically and economically. A cultural golden age is presented, reminding one of the cultural elitists and their ideas. The tension in these films comes from the contrast between the visual splendour and the narrative progression.

The kind of audience these films attracted were rather older and more middle-class than those for Hollywood productions. Heritage films are often constructed around literary novels and appeal to a literature-based culture. So this type of film refers us to a cultural mode of production, while Hollywood productions, on the other hand, rely on the industrial mode of production. Such films concentrate on historical details and immerse the viewer in an epic past. The modern day tourist or historian proceeds through a historical spectacle giving an impression of timelessness. In this way, Little Dorrit is no longer set in the terrible slums of Victorian London, but in quaint and picturesque poverty. Charles Dickens' social criticism is transformed into a positive image of lower class life. As for the other films they often use a huge country mansion as a setting, in the middle of rolling English countryside and woods. This is the typical kind of house that the National Trust buys up. In A Handful of Dust, Evelyn Waugh writes that the house is expensive and difficult to maintain. In the film version the country pile (Hetton Hall) is transformed into one of the principal actors because of its visual glory.

These heritage films, not surprisingly, attracted theatrical actors such as Judi Dench (A Handful of Dust, A Room with a View). Maggie Smith (A Room with a View), Simon Callow (A Room with a View , Maurice). These actors are used to conditions that privilege settings and atmosphere without the modern techniques of close-ups and special effects. Often secondary characters are used as background decoration, a technique that is common in the theatre. There are few action sequences. Atmosphere, milieu and setting are given precedence. In Maurice, Cambridge is used as an introduction to subsequent events. The town plays a minor role afterwards. However, it has set the scene and may attract potential tourists. All these films exaggerate the visual splendour of things, concentrating on surfaces and never going deep down into the 'universe of discourse'.

These reassuring settings show the economic and symbolic power that exists in a typically English setting while the tension is organised over a social problem. Inter-class relationships is the theme of A Room with a View. Maurice and Another Country deal with homosexuality in a rigid moralistic society. The Raj of A Passage to India shows British power, not Indian resistance to the colonial power.

Here, national identity is pure and it is only later in the film that corruption is uncovered. In all these films the viewer remembers the visually marvellous and not the irony or social criticism of the original literary text. The ends of the films suggest consensual and conventional solutions to the social problems. A similar line of costume dramas emerged in the second half of the 1980s centred around the lives of ordinary people. This move towards mass society and a common culture can be seen in Dance With a Stranger (1985), Wish You were Here (1987), Hope and Glory (1988). This shift away from the elite towards the ordinary people coincided with an emphasis on more middlebrow content.

Heritage films of the 1980s served as a refuge from the newly competitive and aggressive Thatcher world. The prime-minister encouraged market-led identities rather than class based ones and these destabilising changes made some people turn to the heritage films for compensation. These productions do not actually laud Thatcher virtues, nor do they depict self-made successes. These films rather criticise the upper classes while at the same time showing their possessions as worth having. They all stress culture as represented by objects and not culture as an intimate part of the individual. All were commercial successes and all were strongly influenced by television. While not exactly encouraging the Thatcher ethos, they did not propose radical alternatives and can therefore be considered as mildly consensualist.

One can see the move of English film producers to Hollywood as a sign of the 1980s. David Puttnam or Alan Parker went over to Hollywood in order to make more commercial films. In many ways, the American film industry became an international film machine and lost its specifically American identity during these years. Hollywood was influenced by these British directors. The same can be said for many German and French film directors. Wim Wenders shot Paris, Texas and Louis Malle Atlantic City, developing new and interesting cultural hybrids.

Although Mrs Thatcher hoped to free the British film industry, there was in fact, very little state subsidy that could be cut. The small sums that were removed alienated the film-makers, who replied to Mrs

Thatcher's explicit language. They, in turn, made explicitly critical films. A remarkable anti-Thatcher consensus built up among British film-makers during the 1980s. The same can be said for playwrights and theatre directors. The opinions of these producers can in no way be regarded as a true reflection of the general public. However, the issues that were dealt with concerned everyone in Britain. Their work is symptomatic of the times. The quality of the production was of a high standard and one can say that there was a film Renaissance in Britain over the period. This is all the more remarkable as Hollywood became increasingly dominant during the same years. In the meantime, Mrs Thatcher allowed the Channel 4 subcontracting system to come into existence while also providing, in spite of herself, the motivation for a lot of the production.

One is struck by the failure of these film directors in proposing a positive alternative to Thatcherite policies and values. They limited their role to criticism, without offering anything better. Paradoxically, Mrs Thatcher's reactive policies had a significance far in excess of their real value. At the same time, she deregulated and shifted production over to the cheaper television companies. In so doing she provoked a success story that can be compared with the glory days of the 1940s Ealing productions.

Notes

1. "Life before Death on Television", *Sight and Sound No 53*, 115-122.
2. " 35 Days in Toronto", *Sight and Sound No 58*, 95.
3. M. Auty, N. Roddick (eds), *British Cinema Now* (London: BFI, 1985) 49.
4. Gavin Smith, "Food for Thought" *Film Comment 26/3*, 55.
5. Robert Lindsay, "The dangerous leap of Stephen Frears", the *New York Times*, 18 December 1988.

Chapter 21
Ethnic Minorities and Cultural Policy

What exactly were the effects of Mrs Thatcher's cultural policies on the various ethnic minorities that live together in Great Britain today? Mrs Thatcher proposed that all of them should find satisfaction in a free and commercial cultural market-place. But all could not be treated equally, their status depending on their market potential and the time period when they came to Britain. The problem is a general one: those minority cultural practices that have commercial value can be integrated into mainstream white culture, while those that represent a small and isolated group will tend to be excluded from the market. Also, the longer the minority has been living in Great Britain the stronger the claim to official government backing. The difference in treatment is clearly seen in a few cases that have been selected as the most interesting during the 1980s. The first is black British music that was to varying degrees integrated into mainstream white pop music. The second is Hindi films that are distributed in Britain because of the enormous market that already exists in India and worldwide. The third is the Welsh language that has little support from the young but represents a culture that has developed in the British Isles for over four millennia and therefore has a fundamental right to government subsidy.

Black Music in 1980s Britain

The relative integration of black music into pop music may perhaps be explained by the long tradition in this domain dating back to the Elisabethans. The first written reference to black musicians occurred in the 16th century. During the reign of Queen Elizabeth 1, a group of ten musicians and dancers was kept at her court. They were probably a mixed number of what was termed 'tawny' people and 'Moors', that is to say native Americans (red Indians) and black Africans. The term 'tawny' was equally used for Asians at the time.

In the late 19th century, American minstrels started touring the country. Black musicians were given a good reception because of the nonconformist support of the anti-slavery movement. Queen Victoria herself reacted favourably to the Fisk Jubilee Singers by saying: "tell them we are delighted with their songs".[1] In 1872, the 'Foreigner's Fete' was held in Streatham and was held regularly until the mid 1880s. It brought together: "Asiatics and many tribes from central Africa[...] Turks, Arabs, Gujeratis, Bengalese and a few unusual localities".[2]

International exhibitions during the 1870s and 1880s brought different musicians such as "Zulus, Maoris, Japs, Chinese, even American Indians and Dahomian Amazons".[3] The fundamental idea was to show the great cultural diversity of the British Empire that covered a quarter of the world at the time.

All these examples are of imported cultures. At the end of the Second World War and especially during the 1950s and 1960s, immigrant communities started to become sufficiently large to be able to make their own collective music. As a result, during the 1980s, some of these cultural forms such as West Indian reggae and South Asian Bhangra came to be integrated into the white cultural mainstream. Mrs Thatcher's brand of commercial and middlebrow culture certainly intensified this particular trend and helped the move towards cultural democracy.

The term black is a deliberately vague one. The Elizabethan term 'Moor' was transformed into 'Blackamoor', 'Ethiopian' and later in the mid-19th century into negro. By the 1970s, the term negro had been replaced by coloured or black. 'Black' applies to all communities that are not white. The term black music is used in contrast with the commercial white music industry. According to this definition, any folk-type music based on the oral tradition and executed by non-white musicians is regarded as authentic black music. But what happens when black musicians join the commercial music machine? Is their music no longer authentic? What about white musicians who integrate another musical style and produce black music? Some purists argue that this is a watered down and commercial culture and therefore cannot be termed black music. One can argue the opposite. Black music is in fact 'black musics' and there are a multitude of different forms. Diversity and fusion is what culture is all about. During the 1980s, there was a definite blurring of the boundaries between authentic black and commercial white music in Britain.

Two geographical areas can be taken as examples: South East Asia with Qawwali and the more commercial Bhangra and the West Indies with steel bands and reggae. Why did this happen in the 1980s? Because black musical forms became visible and began to join the white cultural mainstream, although as shall be seen, to varying degrees. Also, the second generation of British blacks, while not rejecting their cultural roots, started producing their own fusion of traditional and modern styles. This was a radical break with the 1960s and 1970s tradition of importing records from the countries of origin. All the black musicians of the 1980s felt a terrible tension in their lives in which they were torn between a desire to serve their individual communities and the temptation of commercialisation and professionalisation. Mrs Thatcher, through her commercial definition of culture empowered these various immigrant communities. Her policies made the technology available, permitting a move to professionalism that led to a multicultural mainstream culture. In the process, the cultural mainstream was profoundly modified.

Qawwali music

Qawwali is a traditional type of Muslim religious music that originated in the Indian subcontinent. It is often considered as a light form of Hindustani music (Indian classical). The typical course of a Qawwali gathering is devotional poetry, group singing and playing, and hand clapping. It is exhilarating and can lead to religious ecstasy.

Usually the music is performed at sacred Sufi shrines that are all located on the Indian subcontinent such as Nisamuddin Auliya in New Delhi. There are no shrines in Britain. There is no fixed form as the religious hierarchy directs but the musicians also respond to the desires of the audience. Audience reactions influence the direction of the Qawwali celebration. Offerings are made only if the musicians manage to take the listeners into a state of religious ecstasy.

There is also a more profane side to Qawwali playing. Certain talented artists such as Nusrat Fateh Ali Khan tour the world playing to all kinds of audiences. He is a professional musician and performed throughout the 1980s. There is also Qawwali playing and singing in the very prolific Indian film industry. This music, however, is often sung by women, something that is unimaginable in the religious setting. The subjects of the films are not so spiritual: love, family life or intrigues. Music, however, is a considerable component of these films.

Another factor that needs stressing is that Islam makes a distinction between singing religious songs and playing musical instruments. The call to prayer is sung and therefore is not considered as music, while playing musical instruments is sinful. Musicians are often associated with drinking alcohol, prostitution and all kinds of vice. It is for this reason that music playing in the Indian subcontinent was performed by a low Mirasi caste. Because music plays such an important role in Hinduism, the Muslims in the area found it difficult to impose a total ban and thus religious music was accepted at weddings and celebrations.

What happened when the Sufi Muslims of the Mirpur area of Kashmir moved to the Bradford area? There are currently 60,000 south Asians in this northern English city of about 350,000. Roughly 85 per cent are Muslim Asians and about 35,000 of these are Mirpuris.[4] First generation men came to work in the textile mills in the 1950s and at the time kept a low cultural profile because they considered the work as temporary. Their families came in the 1970s and 1980s, encouraging the building of mosques and the expression to their cultural traditions. The Mirpuris are orthodox Muslims and many of the women maintain purdah (the veiling of women). For this reason the community believes in single sex schools. The ancient Mirpuri musicians of the Mirasi caste lost their old identities in the journey to Great Britain and conveniently forgot about their modest origins. As a consequence, the Mirpuri population has little traditional music either at home or at school and the only source is in Indian films. This also caused problems over music teaching when the national curriculum was introduced by Mrs Thatcher in 1988:

> The children appear to be protected from live music situations. Very few of them play an instrument or have an instrumentalist in their family, very few of them learned any songs as small children, had any songs sung to them, or experienced any singing at home; very few of them are allowed to attend school discos. On the other hand, all the children listen to a considerable amount of music at home of various descriptions and watch films, as well as television programmes, which include dance.[5]

This void was filled by certain musicians in Bradford who belong to the small Khalifa community, which moved from India to east Africa and then on to Britain in the 1970s. The Mirasis were simply replaced by the Khalifas.

Gulam Masa (one of the few Mirasis to continue) is the leader of Saz aur Awaz and this group specialises in religious music at weddings. They are unpaid amateurs who play for their friends and the larger community. The musicians of the group like classical poetry and rehearse at home. Typically, they use a naghma instrumental to warm up followed by several Qawwalis, and finishing with Most Qalandar. Occasionally ghazals are sung along with older film music. In 1994, the younger singer Shaukat had plans to dance on stage and to use electric sound equipment, partly financed by the local authority, in order to reach bigger audiences. This was despite his declared dislike of dancing in general. There can be no doubt about the pressure of professionalisation that this group experienced during the 1980s. This was part of the move away from hereditary low-status musicians to a more commercial musical set-up.

The second group in Bradford that is of interest is Naya Saz (New Music) and these musicians are more profane than those of Saz aur Awaz. Half of them come from the Khalifa community. They play mostly Bhangra and film music for people to dance to. However, despite the commercial success of such Bhangra groups as Aleep and Heera, Naya Saz does not have a large enough following to become professional and the members have full-time jobs and play during their free time.

All in all, the music scene in Bradford is not as subdued as might be expected due to the concentration of orthodox Muslim Mirpuris. One should also stress that music is vital for the immigrant community in defining its roots and cultural traditions with regard to the surrounding white community.

Bhangra

There was a Bhangra explosion in the 1984-1988 period in Britain. It concerned the second generation south Asians who adopted this musical form for dancing to. Groups such as Aleep, Heera and Holle Holle regularly sold 50,000 official records and cassettes. Bhangra is a mixture of rural Punjabi dance, pop and disco. Punjabi communities use this music for discotheques, parties and weddings.

The second generation Punjabis do not reject their Indian roots and are proud of their specific backgrounds. Most south Asians are Sylhettis, Bangladeshis, Gujaratis, Bengalis, Tamils, and east Africans. Bhangra can cater for all these groups. It is usually associated with harvest and the new Year (Vaisakhi). The leader of the group is the drummer of the dholak (drum with stick) and the lead singer is the deputy-leader. In the mid-1980s, large and flamboyant crowds of young Asians were seen going to Bhangra concerts at various venues such as the Hammersmith Palais (1986) or the Empire Ballroom on Leicester Square (1987). Asian culture came out of the immediate community and became visible. Without the existence of the Indian film industry, Bhangra would certainly have been less popular, as the films acted as free advertisements for the music. Film music is often a mixture of Indian folk and light European music. Bhangra could easily be used for this purpose and it also benefited from the industrial distribution of the cinema business. Bhangra therefore satisfied a mass demand and spread to the United States, Australia and East Africa. Mrs Thatcher's commercial definition of culture empowered the various south Asian communities, and helped them to become more visible.

Before the 1980s, there were several 'natural' brakes to the professionalisation of Bhangra music. These brakes were loosened up during the decade. In 1980, most south Asian music was distributed through grocery chains and specialised shops. Sometimes producers would ask distributors for a certain sum before allowing them to pirate the music. In these deals the musician would get practically nothing from sales. It should be stressed that pirating is rife in India and it has been estimated that 95 per cent of the cassettes sold in markets are illegal versions.[6] This is one element that clearly shows cultural production to be a risky business with no one guaranteed a hit, while cultural reproduction is extremely lucrative as it removes sales taxes, royalties and production costs. The structural brake to professionalisation in the Asian music business was the lack of infrastructure and the resulting problem of pirated tapes.

By the mid 1980s, there were ten to fifteen major all-male groups wearing white flared trousers and sequined shirts. Distribution moved from the direct sale grocery stores to professional companies such as Arishma, Savera/Multitone, the Gramaphone Company (EMI). Before this change, musicians made money mostly out of live performances. Pirating was attacked by musicians joining the Performing Rights Society (PRS) and the Mechanical Copyright Protection Society (MCPS). Also a campaign was conducted in India in 1987, to prosecute cassette piracy in both civil and criminal proceedings. Consequently, the situation was greatly clarified during the 1980s.

Another brake on Bhangra sales and professionalisation was the fact that no Indian music shop was represented in the Top 50 selection. The 700 Gallup chart shops quite simply did not sell Bhangra records. Producers were criticised for not advertising enough and for keeping too low a profile. Now, in the 1980s, some of the Top 50 shops stock Asian products. Some groups such as Culture Shock want only mainstream distribution: "we are not supplying house Bhangra to any

Asian record shops because we don't want to be put into a category as another Punjabi group, although we are proud of our Punjabi roots and will draw upon it for the future prospects we have planned."[7] In 1988, Alaap took on the professional manager Freddie Anne. Some white producers also helped, such as Andy Cox and John Mosstyn of Fine Young Cannibals, who gave advice to Sarbani Mukerjee's Ishka deh Marmaleh. A sign of the times was the way Manjit Kondal, lead singer of Holle Holle gave up his engineering job.[8] However, despite this move towards professionalisation, these groups still performed free at weddings and remained very much rooted in their communities. Thus despite the existence of a mass market, many Bhangra musicians would not and still will not give up their amateur status. The prime minister's preference for commercial culture was not sufficient to turn these ethnic musicians into pure professionals. However, it was during the 1980s that they did move from an amateur status to a semi-professional one.

Steel Bands

The origins of steel bands can be found in Trinidad and Antigua. In 1884, the colonial administration banned the use of African drums in order to prevent wild revelry in the streets. This recalls the struggle of local authorities in Great Britain to remove all roughness from popular culture during the 19th century. The locals found a rhythm substitute in the spoon and bottle and in the 1930s oil drums started being used. The 1950s and 1960s were the golden years of immigration to Britain and many West Indians came over to supply the unqualified labour that was needed at the time. Steel bands came over with these British Commonwealth immigrants.

Steel bands are very complex organisations. A leader directs the numerous players who do not need to be able to read music. Everything is learnt by heart and it thus belongs to the authentic folk tradition. A corporate structure is used and bands can perform in almost any setting: street, concert hall, square, church, school. As an art form, it can be used for both background and foreground music. It is a purely instrumental musical form and an essentially amateur activity in Britain. There are many public performances and very few recordings, although this should change with the development of new and cheaper technology.

Various points emerge from this description. Steel bands have a very obvious pedagogical value. Players do not need to know how to read music and so school children are encouraged to play. Bands often get free rehearsal space from the local authorities that also often help in the purchasing of instruments. The number of people playing can vary according to the size needed. Large numbers of amateurs results in many members of the community getting involved. It is a very community-centred activity. Terry Noel of the Steel Band Advisory Service claimed that by the end of the 1980s, there were more white participants than black musicians playing this music.[9]

Another point that needs stressing is the amateur nature of British Steel bands. In Trinidad, there are professional groups because this is part of their national culture. In Britain, there is limited demand and the market is not sufficiently commercial. However, commercial sponsorship helps pay for instruments. During the 1980s, bands such as the Heineken Pan Vibes, the Amoco Renegades, or the Guinness Cavaliers did well. The City of London Carnival, that occurs every August, and a 'Panorama' competition can be considered as the main British event where players can compare sounds. Some of the more popular ones are Phase One Steel Orchestra from Coventry and the City of London All Stars. This kind of sponsorship was exactly what Mrs Thatcher's cultural policy tried to promote.

All in all, the steel band sound is acceptable to western ears. It is a melodic and harmonious sound that most British people have encountered in one form or another. Despite this popularity, the move to professionalisation has not materialised and the musical style has remained an authentic folk art. The latest threat to this state of affairs is a shift towards classical and even symphonic music. But even with this new trend it seems unlikely that there will be any professionalisation. In this case, as well as with Bhangra, the commercialism that Mrs

Thatcher proposed was not sufficient to transform steel bands from amateur groups into professional ones. However, as these amateurs did not cost anything to the community, except for the use of local authority halls, this kind of culture had the prime minister's entire blessing.

Reggae

The roots of reggae can be observed in ska, blue-beat and rock-steady. Ska was very popular in Jamaica in the 1960s. Imported records from Jamaica were listened to by white youths and Prince Buster's Madness (1964) was a particular favourite of the white mods. The next phenomenon was the rude boy working-class movement in which Skinhead style was adopted in reaction to middle-class hippy fashion. Ska and rock-steady were appropriated by the Skinheads who were violent but turned to racism only in the 1970s. Due to media coverage the music remained unpopular because it became associated with urban violence.

During the 1970s, there was a definite professionalisation of West Indian music. The Trojan and Island record labels sprang up and the latter started marketing reggae products for middle-class hippy audiences. Artists such as Jimmy Cliff and Bob Marley became integrated into mainstream culture with all the trappings of the professional: managers, producers, record companies, commercial tours, mass record sales.

Like the skinheads, the punks at the end of the 1970s also adopted reggae. Both Capital Radio and BBC Radio London started reggae programmes with David Rodigan and Steve Barnard in 1979 and reggae music was placed in the charts. The Rock against Racism movement propelled such groups as Misty, Matumbi, Steel Pulse, Aswad, Black Uhuru and Third World. In 1981, the priest of reggae, Bob Marley died, and in the mid-1980s the other major popular black music, hip-hop, replaced it. However, pirate radio stations such as Dread Broadcasting Corporation (a pun on the BBC) continued to

function as did the black sound systems, an independent and unofficial black entertainments industry. In the late 1980s, reggae again became popular in the commercial music market with Aswad, Smiley Culture and Tippa Irie. This can be seen as yet another case of commercial culture empowering small ethnic minorities in a truly democratic trend.
One can see that reggae is a good example of cultural assimilation or incorporation. This typically Jamaican sound was reproduced in Britain and adopted by white groups such as Police. Rastafarian hard-liners preferred purer reggae versions, while commercial artists produced watered down or 'sweet' reggae for the mass white audience. Second generation British citizens of West Indian origin have, therefore, been successfully integrated into commercial and mainstream British culture. Mrs Thatcher assisted in this process of incorporation through her cultural policies in this domain.

Sound Systems

At the end of the 1970s period, a split occurred between reggae and soul. The former was easily assimilated while the latter became more specifically black. Bob Marley's records started to sell by the million, and at the same time he popularised Rastafarian ideas. Some white bands like Bad Manners and Madness simply assimilated the musical styles and reproduced the sounds. Others like the Beat and the Specials reinterpreted the sounds by producing their own styles. This sudden prominence of Caribbean music as an influence on commercial pop music started off with airplay on the radios and the development of specialised record labels that were eventually bought up by major record companies such as Island or Rough Trade. Thus did reggae enter into mainstream commercial pop music.

The same phenomenon of assimilation occurred with hip hop, rap and to a lesser extent sound systems. White groups used hip hop and rap in their own styles by making them more commercial. This was rather strange as one of the original ideas of hip hop was to tear off the record labels and to dance to anonymous music. The Mike Chanter

(MC) was supposed to concentrate on creating a certain non-commercial ambiance that could never be recreated. Hip hop originally had a professed anti-commercial streak. The white groups that integrated hip hop and rap into their own music deradicalised both musical styles and moved them into mainstream pop culture, in a process that is by now familiar. The subculture was assimilated, but the mainstream had also changed in the process. Sound systems were not so easily integrated because based on alcohol-free venues and catering specifically for young black people.[10] This particular cultural expression is organised around unemployed or badly paid young blacks who are excluded from the market place due to low consumer potential. The commercial market integrated certain forms of Caribbean music because they had a large market potential. Without this strategic position, reggae would have been ignored. Once again, Mrs Thatcher could only applaud this commercial evolution, despite the 'alternative' and subversive nature of sound systems.

Hindi Films

Indian films have a special significance for the Indian sub-continent and for Indians who live all around the world. In the areas in Britain where Indians concentrate, there was a 1970s phenomenon of local cinemas showing Hindi films. In the 1980s, the cinemas were replaced by the use of video machines (VCRs). There was an easy supply of films available from India. It should not be forgotten that India is currently the biggest producer of films in the world. Consequently, the viewing of Indian films became less of a community-based activity but more of a private family activity as the number of VCRs increased. This move from the centralised cinema to the decentralised home was a direct consequence of Mrs Thatcher's cultural policy.

Marie Gillespie conducted a piece of research in the Southall area on youth attitudes to video viewing.[11] This area has all kinds of nationalities but an especially high proportion of Sikh families. It was found that in 1989 approximately 80 per cent of households had a video recording machine, this representing almost double the national average. This is a good example of Mrs Thatcher's cultural policy empowering certain large subgroups in Great Britain during the 1980s. Most of the films that were offered in the local video shops were either Hindi or Bombay films. Young south Asians were not always happy about this state of affairs as these films strengthen ties with the mother country, which is in the interest of parents and grandparents, who are looking for nostalgia, but does not help young people, because the different value systems cannot be applied to modern Britain. It was found that weekend viewing of Bombay films was a family ritual and often an occasion to chat. Usually, it was the father who decided when to watch and the mother who decided what film was to be viewed. Girls tended to stress the moral aspects, while boys disliked the backwardness and the negative views of Indian life. The whole genre was found to be based on an 'ideal moral universe' that pervades all Hindi films. The films are often not linear but fantastic, circular and unrealistic as symbolism plays a major role.

The older generations were glad to hear the Hindi language and to see representations of Indian life. They hoped that some of the values expressed in the films would rub off onto their offspring. Religious themes are sometimes presented in these films. For the younger generations, it was a chance to hear the mother tongue. Young people rarely write the language, but they can often speak it. Social constructs such as the caste system or arranged marriages were sometimes hotly debated after viewing.

What can this tell us about Mrs Thatcher's cultural policy? Actual facts in this domain clearly show that the south Asian community in west London was not satisfied with the national broadcasting system and therefore moved to foreign production and private consumption. VCRs are in this case discovered to be democratic cultural instruments encouraging choice, flexibility and empowering certain racial minorities that would otherwise have been excluded. Mrs Thatcher's cultural policy played a significant role in this process. However, the national broadcasting system did not satisfy the needs of these communities, which is paradoxical as they had to pay the television licence just like everyone else. What is certain is that the existence of a thriving film industry in India gave Indian families in Southall a large choice of films. However, this would not have been possible without a commercial Indian sector. It is also noticeable that Hindi films have not been integrated into film production in Britain or the United States. The film styles have retained their different characters and have not mixed. Thus Mrs Thatcher's policies played a crucial role in empowering certain ethnic groups in a private mode of cultural consumption, but obviously only insofar as the cultural material could be integrated into mainstream culture.

The Case of the Welsh language

Newly arrived ethnic groups were and are allowed to express themselves in the commercial market with practically no official recognition. However, traditional ethnic British groups were given a totally different treatment. A good example is the Welsh language, which is a Celtic one and has common roots with Breton and Gaelic. The Welsh cultural heritage is extremely rich in terms of architecture, history, literature, music and art.

The Secretary of State for Wales spends a certain proportion of his budget on subsidising the Welsh language. Table 22.1 on page 494 shows the monies spent during the Thatcher decade by the Welsh Office (WO) on the various Welsh museums, the Welsh Books Council and the Royal National Eisteddfod, that is to say, the cultural high point in Wales. Although the information is patchy, one can note an expansion in the spending on museums. This is implicitly justified by their potential to attract tourists. Between 1978/9 and 1987/8, central government spending on museums and the arts almost quintupled for Scotland and quadrupled for Wales. The ancient Welsh identity was therefore given official approval, in marked contrast with the more recent ethnic minorities.

It is well known that the Welsh enjoy communal singing that might be compared with the Basque or Zulu popular singing traditions.

It is, therefore, surprising to discover that highbrow music got the lion's share of the subsidies. The Welsh National Opera received œ1.39 million in 1983/4 that rose to œ1.68 million in 1987/8. For the same years, œ513,000 rising to œ609,000 respectively were spent on various musical activities by the Welsh Arts Council, mostly on the BBC Welsh Symphony Orchestra. This was an important strategic decision. The Welsh Arts Council did not spend money on middlebrow folk choirs or even lowbrow Welsh rap groups. Highbrow music was given precedence by official bodies.

What of literature? The Welsh Books Council increased its spending from œ300,000 to œ400,000 between 1984/5 and 1988/9. The commercial book market effectively excludes minority interests because of the relatively high costs of small print runs. It is for this reason that resources were poured into an uneconomic sector of the book market. The main aim of the Welsh Books Council, that was set up in 1961, was "to ensure a supply of popular literature in Welsh for readers of every type and age group".[12] Different policies were implemented, such as grants to publishers, support for literary magazines and organisations, and various awards and grants. Over the 1980s, there was a noticeable change in emphasis away from awards to helping publishers, due to the economic squeeze that publishers experienced throughout the period. In the name of cultural heritage, Welsh language publishing was wholly government financed. This is a rare example of total government control. It can seem strange that a community of perhaps 5 million people, only 20 per cent of which speak the language, should get this government support, when those who speak Urdu or Punjabi do not. The fact that Mrs Thatcher wanted to keep subsidy to a strict minimum may explain the difference, but not in a satisfactory way. A two-tier policy was implemented in this particular area.

A survey conducted by the Welsh Studies Department of the College of Librarianship, Wales was published in 1988.[13] It identified 19 per cent of Welsh speakers in the Principality and found that 42 per cent had read only English books in the previous year; 5 per cent had read only Welsh books and 32 per cent had read at least one of each. Not surprisingly, due to the wider selection of English books available, on average, Welsh speaking readers read five times as many English books as Welsh ones. This clearly shows how the commercial market, by its very nature, excludes minority sectors and cultures and hence the importance of a subsidy policy that for once contradicts the market laws supported by Mrs Thatcher.

One possible reason for the subsidy of the Welsh language was that there might be wider commercial interests such as tourism to take into account. Welsh culture can act as a magnet for the Welsh tourist industry. The justification for this type of argument is similar to that of national pride and an international reputation. In this case, one can talk in terms of local (national and Welsh) pride. Many tourists come from Birmingham, Manchester and London to spend weekends in North Wales, and some of them try to learn the language on television. Most of the Welsh-speaking population is concentrated in the northern part of the Principality. During the 1980s, there was also a phenomenon of resistance against the English 'holiday home invasion'. Holiday homes for affluent Londoners were considered by many as unacceptable when many young people could not afford to buy a main residence. Many of these houses were burned down by Welsh extremists.

Broadcasting was used to promote the Welsh language in the 1970s with BBC 2. In 1982, Channel 4 took over. The Welsh Fourth Channel Authority controls the output of the Welsh Fourth Channel (S4C) and in 1987/8, 26 per cent of production was in Welsh, especially during peak evening hours. S4C received œ400,000 in net advertising revenue in 1988/9. There is also Harlech TV (HTV) which is one of the fifteen independent ITV companies that produce programmes for the ITV networks. Officially approved Welsh culture could be seen in the broadcasting industry. This was certainly not the case for the Indian, Pakistani or Caribbean communities.

There was less of a demand for Welsh language video films than for Bombay films. This can partly be explained by the rural character of the Welsh speaking population that occupies a mostly northern, less urbanised part of Wales. Urban concentrations mean easy distribution for cultural products as in the case of Southall in west London. Another part of the explanation is that all Welsh people are bilingual and can cope with British films. This is not always the case with the older generation of Asian immigrants who prefer national film content. Also, as Welsh broadcasting exists, demand is catered for in this way rather than through rented videos. The broadcasting industry therefore meets the demand for Welsh television programmes. The same reasoning applies to new technology. The markets are not large enough for a private Welsh satellite channel. By contrast, in Europe for example, there is a Turkish satellite channel for Turks living in Germany, France, Belgium and Holland.

One clearly sees that distinct categories and different treatments can be discerned among ethnic minorities. Their situation, during the 1980s, varied according to their rank as regards total market potential. As the cultural market was increasingly a world market, the larger the group on an international basis, the greater the strategic power. Content must also be considered, and the integration potential of particular ethnic cultural practices. Some were slowly being assimilated into mainstream white culture, while others were kept firmly away. Finally, national British pride could justify pure interventionism as in the case of the Welsh language, yet this was never a thought-out or explicit project. Despite the many issues raised by this supposedly commercial market, it was never fully debated by the Conservatives although there was an officially declared policy of freeing the cultural market-place. These various examples of ethnic cultural practices illustrate a general point. Mrs Thatcher's definition of commercial culture empowered certain ethnic groups in a truly democratic movement. It also encouraged the private mode of cultural consumption and strengthened traditional identities and communities. Those groups which had few members or were dispersed geographically did proportionally less well than the bigger ones.

Notes

1. Paul Oliver (ed), *Black Music in Britain* (Buckingham: Open University Press, 1990) 31.

2. ibid., 11.

3. J. Slater, *The East in the West* (London:S. W. Partridge and Co, 1895) 62-65, 131-133.

4. Paul Oliver (ed), *Black Music in Britain* 156.

5. P. D. Jones, *An Investigation into Curriculum Music in Middle Schools* (B. Ed. diss. Bradford College, 1984) 70.

6. J. Dubashi, "Cassette piracy: high stakes", *India Today* 31 March 1986, 112.

7. V. Dewan, "Culture shock" in *Ghazal and Beat* No 6, 4.

8. Paul Oliver (ed) *Black Music in Britain* 150-151.

9. Paul Oliver (ed), *Black Music in Britain* 133.

10. For a fuller account see Paul Gilroy, *There Ain't No Black in the Union Jack* (London: Hutchinson, 1987).

11. Marie Gillespie, "Technology and Tradition: Audio-visual Culture among South Asian Families in West London", *Cultural Studies*, Vol 3, No 2, (London: Methuen, 1989).

12. *Cultural Trends* No 2 1989, 15.

13. *Welsh Studies Department of the College of Librarianship*, Wales, "The Book Trade in Wales" (Wales: Welsh Arts Council, 1988).

Chapter 22
Common Culture

Culture can be considered as a continuous spectrum. As suggested in an earlier chapter, it would be a grave mistake to concentrate exclusively on the arts and highbrow cultural expression. All highbrow arts have a middlebrow and lowbrow equivalent and all are fighting for symbolic domination as explained by Pierre Bourdieu. Therefore, if classical ballet is taken as an example, the middlebrow equivalent is ball-room dancing, while there are many forms of lowbrow dancing such as hip hop, rock 'n' roll or disco. In music, one can consider the case of symphonic music, with easy listening in the middle and the lowbrow equivalent in rock, punk or reggae. However, the term lowbrow has pejorative connotations as it is situated at the bottom of the cultural hierarchy and the term 'common culture' is more appropriate because more descriptive. Although 'common' also has a vulgar meaning, it has the advantage of being accessible to everyone. Moreover, it corresponds to an altogether different approach. What follows will examine in detail what happened to common culture as seen in everyday lifestyles in the 1980s, what exactly Mrs Thatcher did to influence its evolution and how it reacted to such policies, both positively and negatively.

Raymond Williams was one of the first literary theorists to suggest that culture was, in fact, everyday life as well as the arts. With E. P. Thompson, Stuart Hall, Richard Hoggart, he started the momentum for what is now the cultural studies movement that examines all forms of common culture. Everyday actions, that were previously considered to be of no particular relevance, are now seen as having great symbolic value. The way one dresses, eats, drinks, in what circumstances, the way one speaks, what one does during leisure periods, are all considered valid areas of study. They express a person's identity within a local, national and now increasingly international community. As with the cultural industries, these expressions of symbolic creativity can be set out as a series of subtle fluxes that move upwards as well as downwards. They are definitely not one-way movements from the sender to the receiver. In common culture the difference between production and consumption has become increasingly blurred due to its flexibility in terms of technological and social changes.

Another characteristic of common culture is that many ordinary people are much more creative than was previously thought:
The cultural world is much more varied than the mass culture theorists ever dreamt of. Individuals and groups respond differently and creatively and with their own grounded aesthetics to a whole range of mass inputs, from music to style and fashion, from advertisements to film and television.[1]

Fashion

The period under consideration saw a marked change in these domains. Theoreticians and people in general became more conscious of these realities. The top end of the market is catered for by exclusive designer shops. These products are considered to be unique creations that can be either in the avant- garde of creation or else more in the classical line. The exclusive nature and the price of these garments make them inaccessible to most. During the 1980s, exclusive furs became unfashionable due to pressure and clever advertising by ecologists, but designer clothes did rather well, while at the end of the decade, as money became more difficult to borrow, demand slackened off. The self-made ethos, of course, enjoys the ostentatious showing off of worldly success and this is reflected in the clothes one wears.

Mrs Thatcher was more interested in middlebrow and commercial cultural expressions than in this type of brashness.

Anecdotally, it was reflected in her personal taste for middle-class clothing. Although Hugo Young wrote of Barbara Castle's jealousy of the fine clothing that Mrs Thatcher had in the House of Commons,[2] one can say that she preferred reasonable and discreet clothes. She claimed that she bought her underwear at Marks and Spencers. This is the example of the sensible clothes store where good quality is sold at a reasonable price. Certainly clothes shops in this category such as Burtons, Next, Aquascutum and Principles, did remarkably well during the 1980s. All of them offered designer-style clothes to the mass market.

What one wears has great social significance. It can give information to others about many aspects of one's social identity: economic position, leisure tastes, relationship to time, cultural capital, imagination, originality, political sympathies. Those who have little money available try to shop around for the best price. Second hand shops can allow someone with reduced income to have access to cheap and at the same time stylish clothes. One should stress that high unemployment was one of the inevitable consequences of Mrs Thatcher's economic strategy at the start of the 1980s. Thus economic policy had significant effects on cultural consumption. Certainly, charity shops grew in number during the 1980s.

Common culture can challenge the dominant highbrow/middlebrow cultural consensus by putting together different styles in a surprising manner. For example punks dressed in strange combinations of clothing adorning trousers and jackets with non-functional zips. Mass produced and cheap safety pins would be used as decoration. The 1980s were very creative in this domain: after the initial shock of the contrasting styles, punk fashion was gradually assimilated into the mainstream and was eventually used by the designers. Punk fashion could then be mass produced for mass consumption. At this point it came to be incorporated into mainstream fashion. This example shows the reverse movement of fashion that is a flux working from top to bottom. It can equally function from bottom to top. In this case the original style was invented by creative individuals who used cheap materials at the 'common' end of the market. Then, designers such as

Malcolm McLaren and Vivienne Westwood sold such clothes on the King's Road in London during the late 1970s and 1980s. They acted just like the high fashion designers but on the basis of and in reference to common culture. By the end of the period such fashions had worked their way up, their development having been partly fostered by the spirit of the age but also made possible, as in other domains, by the individualistic and entrepreneurial ethos prevalent in the Thatcher years. A movement that in itself was one of protest and nonconformity, had been integrated into the general flux of ideas and practices of the period.

Music

Music is the cultural form where common culture is most clearly visible. As in the case of clothing, common or popular (pop) music should be considered as a series of fluxes. Young people listen to certain songs and then try to imitate them. After a few years of copying, the amateur group can start producing its own original songs. During the copying stage, these pop groups also act creatively as they interpret in their own fashion. As in the case of clothing, second hand shops play an important role. Young people discover old records and old pop trends and styles, just as clothes manufacturers will return to past fashions. To give an example, hippy music was marketed once again in the late 1980s and records of artists and groups such as Jimi Hendrix, the Doors, the Velvet Underground were re-issued. Bell bottom trousers and flowery shirts come to mind in the fashion world around the same period. These suddenly reappeared too. One does not need much money to participate in the pop world. All one needs is a radio cassette recorder, some blank tapes and one can start recording for oneself or for others. In fact, taste-leaders can give advice on various musical trends, often playing an important role in defining group tastes. Symbolic creativity, power and economics, are obviously linked and counteracting in these processes.

Pop music often challenges official culture. In the 1980s, there were many examples of common cultural movements that, if only briefly, challenged the status quo of the cultural Establishment. One only has to consider punks, hip hop, rap, house music and acid house raves, to see that these movements, though transient, are indeed significant. All these musical forms were heavily influenced by the music of the various black communities. There was the Indian community with its fusion of pop and traditional music known as Bhangra. The Caribbean community had ska and reggae. During the 1980s, as in film-making, there was also a certain politicisation of pop music. There were the Rock against Racism and Rock against Thatcher movements and many groups such as Gang of Four or Crass expressed direct political messages.[3] One should not underestimate the political significance of songs that were repeated many times on radios which became increasingly independent.

Another significant trend of the Thatcher decade was the development of dance clubs. These were often situated in the city centres and catered for particular groups with alternately soul, funk, hip hop, reggae, hippy, or punk. Entrance charges were reasonable and some clubs did not charge those on social security possessing UB40 cards. This was one way of re-integrating people who had been excluded by Mrs Thatcher's economic policies. Licences for the sale of alcoholic drinks were not necessarily the rule and all-day dance sessions became popular. Pop groups often played in pubs and one should not ignore the significance of these musical groups. One study found 1000 bands in the Merseyside area alone.[4] These groups act as flexible social units for the young. You find members from all social classes in a common and truly democratic culture. In this area again, though Mrs Thatcher disliked popular music, the general conditions made it possible for all these dissident, fringe and anticonformist tendencies to become partly integrated.

The Music of the Black Communities

As for themselves, the various black communities that live in Great Britain were almost totally excluded from the highbrow or elite end of the cultural market-place during the Thatcher decade. The large majority of them find cultural expression in the pop music market. That is not to say that the middlebrow sector ignores them altogether. If the commercial gains are sufficient, black pop groups can gain national prominence. The British black communities have produced local equivalents of gospel music, ska, reggae, soul, funk. However, the commercial side of the pop music market did not at first provide for these specialised tastes. Also, in the 1960s and 1970s, the cultural meeting places for blacks and especially young blacks were subjected to official disapproval. The police would try and disband groups that congregated around these clubs using special laws such as SUS.[5] These laws allowed the police to take people that they suspected were about to commit a crime back to the police station. 95 per cent of the cases of SUS applied to black youngsters. Such a situation encouraged the formation of an alternative black music network of production and distribution that became visible in the 1980s.

During the Thatcher years, a black local entertainment industry came to maturity. There developed a whole chain of alternative recording studios, record companies, night clubs, discos, record shops, shops and pirate radio stations that were closely associated with the black communities. Cultural phenomena such as roasting and rapping and recitals of black poetry developed. Sound systems, that is to say mobile discos that use mike chanters (MCs) rather than disc jockeys (DJs), were used to liven up evening dances. Different patois were developed to exclude outsiders and also to strengthen the sense of group identity. Technically, these MCs mix sometimes two or even three records, sometimes talking on top of the music, to create sounds and atmospheres that are unique experiences. Carl Cox, for example, started as a scaffolder in the early 1980s earning œ75 a night for his DJ work. By 1993, just after the end of the Thatcher period, he had gained such a reputation as to earn at least £100,000 a year.[6]

This example shows that there was a certain commercialisation of black music in Britain during the 1980s. Mainstream culture certainly integrated reggae, soul, funk, and after 1985, hip hop and rap. Many members of the black communities tried to resist this commercial trend and a movement to incorporation:

> I think they're spoiling it, really squeezing everything out of it. We're trying to keep away from all that. We've got our own nations and we're having our own thing. It's our world, our hip-hop world and I'm not going to let them destroy it like they did everything else.[7]

This desire to keep a culture pure and exclude commercialism was also apparent among punks, skinheads and other subcultural movements. Rastafarians, for example, described free-market capitalism as Babylon. The problems encountered in modern society were called Dread. For these people black cultural identity as represented in the Emperor Haile Selassie, Africa and a special interpretation of the Bible were sacred and came before economic success.

Thus resistance to the free cultural market-place that was favoured by Mrs Thatcher, expressed itself in unauthorised and unofficial forms that satisfied the needs of the local community better than the commercial market. Many young black people started making their own music and did not pass through the officially approved commercial record shops. They listened to pirate radio stations, bought independent records and danced in independent black clubs. In this way the black communities resisted Mrs Thatcher's commercial culture and young people felt as if they belonged to a specific youth culture.

Subculture

Common culture is, therefore, the general term to describe part of the cultural spectrum that Mrs Thatcher disapproved of from a content point of view. Her reaction, however, was ambiguous because common culture is split between the officially approved commercial market and the unofficial black economy. It is certainly commercial and once demand is sufficient, record companies sign up artists, clothes producers start mass producing, thus integrating into mainstream culture the previously excluded style. But it is also subversive as it can challenge the economic system by using techniques that bypass the officially approved channels of production and distribution. In this way excorporation challenges the status quo.

One subsection of common culture that had Mrs Thatcher's complete disapproval is subculture. This is a style of communication that is based on disorder and the emphatic, expressive mode that Roland Barthes noticed in certain advertisements.[8] Subculture uses this emphatic mode to challenge the 'natural' order of the status quo. Expressive clothes, outrageous music and a special patois, distinguish this group from mainstream culture. Subcultural forms all pose a threat to the established order. Typically, they take up an oppositional stance to official culture that is then defused through familiarity over time. They offer resistance to start off with and then are slowly incorporated into mainstream culture. To understand this movement from rejection of establishment culture and also Mrs Thatcher's commercial cultural policies, to relative and partial integration, one has to go back to the various historical forms that preceded it and made it possible.

In the 1950s, a new commercial culture for the young seemed to confirm the emergence of the classless society that had been predicted by the pluralists. Adolescents in industrial societies found jobs easily and became relatively affluent, thereby being able to develop their own youth styles in terms of clothes, music and leisure activities. In the 1960s, Peter Willmott challenged the classless thesis and proposed that youth culture was merely a reflection of class society. Various subcultures could be observed. For Phil Cohen, subculture was a "compromise solution between two contradictory needs: the need to create and express autonomy and difference from parents [...] and the need to maintain the parental identifications".[9]

Various subcultural adolescent groups could be identified during the 1960s by their clothing. Teddy boys were young working-class males who were nostalgic about an Edwardian golden age and therefore dressed elegantly, also using Brylcream to hold their quiffs in place. Their sacred symbols were various rock 'n' roll stars and film stars and they believed in traditional values. Theirs was an alienated violence reflecting their boring family life, their dull work and their general dissatisfaction. Another group, the skinheads, wore model worker clothes such as drainpipe trousers and braces, clean shirts and bovver boots (bovver means trouble in skinhead patois). Their particular sign was the close-cropped hair that gave them the symbolic power of elite squad soldiers. They too believed in social order and were nostalgic about a past when national identity was strong within an Empire. They had a reputation for being violent towards immigrants especially in the 1970s and 1980s. Greasers or rockers were motorcycle riders who wore leather jackets and listened to progressive rock music. Mods were more subversive because they preferred more reasonable clothing. They chose smart clean clothes as they often had office jobs, modern trousers, Parka coats and scooters as a means of transport. These were the outside signs of the mods. They also had a reputation for taking amphetamines in order to make their leisure hours last longer. These groups developed over the Thatcher period.

The Punks

Towards the end of the 1970s, amid media pronouncements about the imminent collapse of British society, arrived the punk movement. The term 'punk' means rotten and worthless and was originally used in the United States during the 1960s. In Britain, punks were satirists who challenged the traditional sense of community and family values. They threatened the very essence of Thatcherite politics. Punks appropriated for themselves the term crisis and then made fun of it. (A good example of this is the lyrics of God Save the Queen and Anarchy in the UK by the Sex Pistols.) In response to Mrs Thatcher's explicit language, they used crude direct language that was full of expletives. They desacralised sacred national symbols such as the Queen or the Union Jack. The Sex Pistols, for example, cut up a photograph of the Queen for the album cover of their first long player (LP) Never Mind the Bollocks. Their very names parodied the dominant values in such a competitive society of the 1970s and especially the1980s: the Unwanted, the Damned, the Rejects, the Clash, the Worst. Typically punks would challenge the meaning of any sacred object. They would wear the Swastika not because they subscribed to Nazi ideas, but because they wanted to render this negative symbol worthless. The aim was purely to shock and certainly not to encourage racist ideas. In fact, in political terms, many had rather left-wing sympathies. All symbols were there to be criticised and devalued. According to Umberto Eco they acted as "semiotic guerrillas".[10] If Mrs Thatcher believed in timeless paintings of old masters, then punks believed in a state of permanent change and flux. Of all the subcultural groups, the punks seemed the most dangerous because they criticised all forms of authority as seen in the state, the family and all social institutions.

This movement was very present in the first half of the Thatcher decade. They used ordinary objects out of context to produce 'unfashion', in order to shock: toilet chains, plastic bin liners, tee shirts with swear words, clothes pegs, tampons or razor blades were used. The cheapness of the materials meant that it was a democratic trend. Racial and gender stereotypes were systematically challenged. Reggae music was integrated into the punk style. Make-up was used for both boys and girls and bright and garish colours were mixed up to challenge classical aesthetics. School uniforms were defiled, while sexual fetishist clothes were worn in everyday life. Every normal discourse was to be undermined and challenged in all possible ways. Punk dancing was anti-dancing in the form of the minimalist pogo or the alienated and dehumanised robot style. In fact, the punk movement was the most expressive and visible form of resistance and reaction to official culture during the Thatcher period. It challenged both elitist establishment values and middlebrow culture.

As with the case of the black communities, record companies and clubs at first did not want to take the risk of signing up punk groups. EMI for instance broke off its contract with the Sex Pistols and W. H. Smith refused to distribute the first album Never Mind the Bollocks. The punk groups carefully manipulated the media by stage-managing shocking events such as vomiting at Heathrow Airport or on stage. Because of the bad publicity, new and independent record companies specialising in punk music took over when the major companies decided to cancel a contract,[11] for instance Rough Trade Records. Distribution was done often on a local basis without going through the advertising agencies. Punk groups often produced singles that were cheaper than LPs. Some groups such as Crass sold over 50,000 LPs without any commercial advertising and just using graffiti on walls. This trend posed a temporary but significant challenge to the commercial cultural system of record companies, advertisers and distributors.

Skinheads and the Right

The skinhead phenomenon continued its slow but gradual progression during the 1980s. This was a proletarian reaction to modern, multicultural Britain. Like the teddy boys, they had an ideal view of society that is rooted in the past with its belief in the British Empire and a rigid but stable social organisation. They referred to a golden age and as with the creation of most myths, there were scapegoats. In this case it was immigrant workers who were supposed to take jobs away from the traditional working class. Punks and other parasites were also blamed for a decline in moral standards and an attack on the work ethic. This echoes the debate between the New Right and the proponents of a permissive society. Their uniform was that of a perfect worker whose Doc Marten boots were used to kick any opponents found on their territory. 'Aggro' was their term for aggression that was handed out when 'Paki-bashing' (beating up Pakistanis).

Skinheads would listen to loud, raucous music such as Slade or Status Quo, but also black reggae, as they could empathise with the problems of the black communities. Their sacred symbols were the Empire, the Monarchy, the Union Jack and all symbols of national pride. Football teams also often became objects of local pride. Skinheads shared these symbols with supporters of the National Front (NF), who argued that the traditional way of life was being swamped by alien cultures and Europeanisation. Here can be seen the 'Little England' tradition which Mrs Thatcher used for her own ends too. When race riots erupted in such English cities as London, Birmingham, Liverpool and Bristol in the first half of the Thatcher decade, they were taken to be evidence of a total breakdown of law and order. The underlying social and economic conditions were ignored. However, one should also add that the prime minister invested heavily in the police forces of Great Britain and that changes in procedures in difficult areas resulted in better police relations and a decline in disorder. What is surprising is that skinheads and supporters of the National Front (NF) managed to appropriate for themselves the sacred national symbols. This is one among many reasons for the decline in popularity of the Royal family that occurred during the 1980s.

Mrs Thatcher had little sympathy for these lumpen proletarian groups as evidenced by her failed attempt to introduce an identity card scheme for football supporters. Her cultural project was to encourage commercial culture which neither the skinheads nor the National Front believed in. These groups called for a return to a visible community using sacred national symbols. For them community came first, which was not the commercialism that Mrs Thatcher wished for. In this case one can observe a fundamental conflict between commercial and community values. This observation is vital in understanding the paradoxes underlying the prime minister's cultural policies. Mrs Thatcher apparently wanted both and yet commercialism inevitably undermined the sense of community.

All these subcultural groups follow the same pattern of subversion, challenge and excorporation, followed by a gradual integration or incorporation into mainstream culture. The same cultural phenomenon occurred with the Impressionists in the 19th century and the Surrealists in the 20th century, being true of all cultural expressions that originate in a subversive challenge of the existing system. The process is clearly observable in press reactions. At first, there came righteous indignation as punks, for example, were seen as violent or dangerous. Once the initial shock had worn off, the Press started printing stories about happy little punk families.[12] Thus the subversive side of subculture eventually declined as it became integrated into mainstream culture. Mrs Thatcher nevertheless, was greatly irritated by these very visible phenomena of resistance to her conception of collective culture.[13] It would also seem that common culture often starts off as a challenge to commercialism and in the case of the 1980s, to Mrs Thatcher's 'traditional' values. The movements that were produced cannot be disregarded as they all represented threats to the authority of the state. It is for this reason that the prime minister felt so strongly about them and wanted to show clear leadership in this domain. However, the democratic British state could in fact do very little to counteract these organic social movements as was demonstrated throughout the 1980s.

Notes

1. Paul Willis, *Common Culture* (Buckingham: Open University Press, 1990) 131.
2. Hugo Young, *One of Us* 307.
3. New Musical Express, *The Rock 'n' Roll Years* (London: BCA, 1994) 357, 373.
4. Ruth Finnigan, *The Practice of Music* (Cambridge: Cambridge University Press, 1989).
5. Paul Gilroy, *There Ain't No Black in the Union Jack* .
6. *The Observer* colour supplement, 2 January 1994.
7. Paul Willis, *Common Culture* 76.
8. Roland Barthes, *Mythologies* (London: Paladin, 1973).
9. Phil Cohen, *Sub-cultural Conflict and Working Class Community* (W.P.C.S.2, University of Birmingham, 1972).
10. Umberto Eco, *Towards a Semiotic Enquiry into the Television Message* (W. P. C. S. 3, University of Birmingham, 1972).
11. One can usefully consult the New Musical Express, *Rock 'n' Roll Years* (London: BCA, 1994) 292-319.
12. See "Victim of a Punk Punch-up" in the *Daily Mirror*, 1 Aug 1977, and "Punks and Mothers" in *Woman's Own*, 15 October 1977.
13. For more information about punks see Dick Hebdige: *Subculture* (London: New Accents, 198⁴⁾

Chapter 23
Local Authority Resistance

Probably the strongest challenge that was presented to the commercial side of Mrs Thatcher's cultural policies was that of certain local authorities. Although rate-capping started being applied to certain Labour-controlled councils after 1986, most decided to pass off increased costs through the local rates. These councils sometimes had ambitious projects in the area of cultural democracy. It was argued that every citizen had a right of expression in the various cultural industries that were otherwise reserved for private companies. The main justification for this policy was that the free market could only give access to major social groups, thereby excluding certain minorities and minority tastes. To overcome the problem one had to subsidise various cultural infrastructures so that interested citizens might come and express themselves. A recording studio might be used by local pop groups or a video workshop might be made available to local people to make non-commercial videos. Public money was to be made use of in the name of cultural democracy. Mrs Thatcher and the conservatives in general disagreed with these ideas as it was mostly middle and higher income families that paid for the rates and critically-minded citizens who expressed themselves.

Throughout the 1980s, Sheffield developed its own local authority strategy by organising various projects around the Tudor Square scheme. In 1982, the Leadmill was started up and was used as a rehearsal area for rock groups. It was then transformed into a local authority cultural centre offering photography, video production and music recording studios. This can be seen as the equivalent of community arts but on a city-wide scale. The Tudor Square

Development also integrated two theatres, The Crucible and the Lyceum and the Ruskin Art Gallery. Hotels were built next to these cultural facilities and a pleasant environment was thereby created. One can also notice that different cultural levels of expression were catered for in this project and not just elitist culture. It was imaginative and forward-looking and organised by a solid Labour council.

Bradford also had some ambitious schemes that were this time approved of by both Labour and Conservative councils. The West End area of the city was totally rebuilt and re-organised. The centre-piece of the project was the restoration of the Alhambra Theatre, next to which was built St George's Hall and a Film and Photography Museum. This project did not propose cultural democracy and was much more commercial than the Sheffield one, but the museum did not charge admission. The West End scheme was aimed at the highbrow end of the market. However there was also the idea of building a market that was supposed to get the local Pakistani population involved in the scheme. Thus lip-service was paid to the local ethnic community.

The Burnley Blues Festival and the Great British Rhythm and Blues Festival in Colne and Burnley are both examples of local government-led initiatives that attracted both excitement and tourists to otherwise unattractive northern areas of England. Gary Hood, a local government entertainments officer started the blues festival in 1988, when the Burnley Mechanics Institute invited the Spencer Davies Group, the Climax Blues Band and some local musicians. During Easter 1989 the first of the National Blues Festivals booked some American artists. The total budget was a mere £9,000 to cover five days and nights of music and workshops at the 400 seat Mechanics' Hall. It proved to be a sellout and local accommodation was booked out. Other blues festivals were organised in other cities such as Redcar, Portsmouth, Gloucester, Barnsley, with equal success.[1] This is another example of tourism being stimulated by a cultural activity.

Gary Hood was offered a job at nearby Pendle Council where he organised a Great British Rhythm 'n' Blues Festival for the towns of Colne and Burnley. The first event took place in August 1990, with mostly British acts. It proved to be another success. And so the summer season came to have another East Lancashire blues festival. The result was that local accommodation was booked over Easter and summer too. Both festivals now attract around 5,000 people coming from all over Europe and America. Their success can be seen in the late Albert Collins' desire to return in 1994, despite his difficult temperament. The mayor of Nashville Tennessee even sought advice from Burnley Council on how to organise blues festivals. This shows that local authorities could generate cultural excitement with very limited resources. It also showed that the lack of central government enthusiasm and backing could in part be compensated by local authority initiatives in this area.

The most imaginative metropolitan authority was the Greater London Council (GLC) that used cultural policy as one of the main issues in the fight against Mrs Thatcher's proposal to abolish it. In 1984, the GLC issued a very clear and lucid document Recreations in Ruins, that outlined the administrative chaos that would result from the abolition of the metropolitan areas with regard to parks, sport and culture. The GLC had its own Greater London Arts Association (GLAA) which tried to help minority expression that was not catered for by the Arts Council or the commercial sector. The Labour MP, Tony Banks, gained media coverage for cultural events sponsored by the GLC. Just as sponsors could give small amounts and get mentioned in the advertising, the GLC demanded a mention but for much larger sums of money. However, the GLC was abolished in 1986, in spite of this use of cultural policy as a high-profile argument to defend the metropolitan authority.

Two illustrations of the type of non-commercial culture that some local authorities encouraged can be observed in the black British film collectives and the women's workshops that flourished during the 1980s and especially after the 1982 Workshop Declaration of the Association of Cinematic and Television Technicians (ACTT). The declaration was "formulated to acknowledge the specific and exceptional conditions prevailing in the cultural and grant-aided sector and [was] designed to encourage the development and growth of stability and permanent employment in this sector".[2] By 1983, there were ten workshops all over the country, and by 1985, there were eighteen which had franchises. Money was put forward by Channel 4, the British Film Institute and local authorities. In 1990, the Declaration became obsolete as both Channel 4 and the BFI pulled out of the scheme.

Black British film collectives

Mrs Thatcher's encouragement of commercial culture meant that there was a certain democratisation of previously inaccessible art forms. One of the areas in question was video production. The technology, mostly from the Far East, became increasingly cheaper during the 1980s, thereby making production less costly. Many black film collectives were created whose aim was to give alternative versions of black identity.

Up until the arrival of these black collectives, the only black representations were the stereotypes as seen in, for example, the BBC's Love Thy Neighbour situation comedy. The typical stereotype was a shiftless, lazy and criminal black male. In 1982, the GLC organised a conference to assess black media production. Both the so-called free and controlled sectors of the market were shown to exclude black production. Even Channel 4, that was supposed to cater for minority interests, used white producers when dealing with black problems as in the cases of Black in Black, Ebony and Eastern Eye. However, to do Channel 4 credit, their situation comedy No Problem depicted black people as hard-working and responsible citizens.

Unions also restricted access to black film production: the Association of Cinematographic and Allied Technicians (ACTT) "traditionally [was] a highly protective union - indeed, it [was] a closed shop and reputedly one of the most difficult unions to get into. For those on the outside, the problem [was] that without a union card it [was] practically impossible to get employment in the industry."[3] Would-be black film producers were simply denied access to film making in the industry. Jim Pines wrote of his reaction to this exclusion:

programmes like Black in Black and Eastern Eye should be more propagandist in their orientation. In other words, given the dynamics of race politics in Britain at the moment, you should be concerned with putting across black political and cultural views which are explicitly in opposition to the white mainstream.[4]

The consequence of this structural and union exclusion was a very high level of militancy among potential black film producers. This black awareness expressed itself in the film collectives such as Ceddo, Sankofa and Black Audio. These were at first financed by the GLC's Greater London Arts Association (GLAA) and later, after abolition, by Channel 4 and the BFI. After 1986, it was the turn of individual boroughs to give their minorities access to production. John Akomfrah of Black Audio Film/Video Collective set out his group's aims:

(1)   To look at racism in the cinema;
(2)   To examine the politics of representation and not merely propose positive black images;
(3)   To make films through collectives rather than by using individuals.

John Akomfrah stated that he wanted "to look critically at how racist ideas and images of black people are structured and presented as self-evident truths in cinema. What we are interested in here is how these self-evident truths become the conventional pattern through which the black presence in cinema is secured."[5] He also commented on the collective stance:

> The strategy was to encourage and emphasize collective practice as a means of extending the boundaries of black film culture. This would mean attempting to demystify in our film practice the process of film production; it would also involve collapsing the distinction between 'audience' and 'producer'. In this ethereal world film-maker equals active agent and audience usually equals passive consumers of a predetermined product. We have decided to reject such a view in our practice.[6]

This brings up many of the points relevant to the debate on common culture and also proposes a collective practice which contrasts with the decidedly more individualistic and private concept of commercial culture that was encouraged by Mrs Thatcher.

Black Audio produced a film called Handsworth Songs that showed a riot from the rioters point of view and not that of the police. The film used an extract from one of Mrs Thatcher's television addresses:

> I think it means that people are really rather afraid that this country might be swamped by people of a different culture. The British character has done so much for democracy, for law, and done so much throughout the world that if there is any fear that it might be swamped, then people are going to be rather hostile to those coming in. We are a British nation with British characteristics. Every country can take some minorities, and in many ways they add to the richness and variety of that country. But the moment the minority threatens to become a big one, people get frightened.

As in the LBC interview (on page 11), there is a clever mixture of the first person singular and the first person plural, mixing the British people with the prime minister. The emotive term 'swamp' is used, hinting that immigrants come from swampy or at least uncivilised areas full of mosquitoes and diseases. This is brought out by the contrast with British civilisation. The message is certainly that Mrs Thatcher speaks in the name of white Britain.

Sankofa Film Collective is another black film collective that sprung up in the 1980s. According to Martina Attille, one of its members, it was set up primarily to examine policing in Britain with regard to the black communities. This film collective wanted to find out why "images of black people are defined in very narrow terms and contained as problematic, policing being a predictable arena".[7] She wanted to question mainstream media stereotypes and attract a new audience through a pleasurable cinema rather than through a militant presentation:

> We wanted the film to appeal to young people, the politically aware and those who could become politically aware, a film for Europe about being young and black in Britain at a time of uncertainty. We also wanted the film to retain its original integrity - e.g. the realities of policing in its broadest sense - and to assert the politics of being a black woman.[8]

There was also an interest in gender and sexuality: "Sankofa's particular character in terms of race, gender and sexuality meant that the unfinished business of the 1960s/70s (black, gay and feminist movements) was something that we felt needed prioritising in the present, particularly in relation to those three areas of experience".[9] This can be considered as a triple handicap in commercial terms, dealing with black, women and homosexual subjects.

Sankofa produced Territories and Passion of Remembrance. In the first film two gay men dance on a Union Jack looked on by suspicious policemen. National culture here is being contested and yet somehow appropriated by minority groups. There is another scene that challenges the dominant mainstream stereotype of black males being muggers. An elderly woman crosses the street that is full of young black males. When she gets to the end of the street the tension is removed by playing the whole sequence backwards. Territories is meant to make the spectator think about stereotypes and try and construct more positive racial attitudes.

The third black film collective was the most militant one and was called Ceddo Film/ Video Workshop. This group produced The People's Account that was made in 1986 and is a documentary on the 1985 Tottenham riot at Broadwater Farm. It was hoped at the time that it would counterbalance the police and media versions of the events. The IBA censored the film because of the comparison made between the apartheid and the British system. The film accuses the police of "terrorist raids against black communities". The term 'uprising' is used in contrast with the white term 'riot'. Ceddo considered films, just like music, to be weapons in the struggle for black liberation. Thus Ceddo film units were present at many of the 1980s 'uprisings' and many extracts of the footage were used in black films. Ceddo Film/Video also considered the subject of women in the supposedly macho Rastafarian organisation. The usual white stereotype of a conservative and sexist organisation was challenged and interviews were shown both in Britain and in Jamaica. The women are shown to be articulate and not submissive. In fact they fully participated in the movement, contrary to the usual stereotypes.

All these films try and answer a few of the questions posed by black identity. First and second generational attitudes are a major theme. Dress, links with Africa, the Caribbean, Europe, America, are all dealt with. Much of this work was made possible through a mixture of local authority, Channel 4 and BFI financing. In 1990, both Channel 4 and the BFI withdrew from the Workshop Declaration. Financing for the 1990s is very uncertain, as the change of policy towards funding individual production makes it impossible any longer to support film collectives. Individual directors such as Julien, Akomfrah and Shabazz now have to work on a more individualistic basis.

What remains curious about the whole black collective enterprise is that it occurred in the 1980s and that it was supported by state money, when Mrs Thatcher hoped that commercial culture would dominate the market-place. The prime minister's support of commercial and middlebrow culture also empowered black video producers. She increased funds to the BFI which then subsidised these workshops. Thus Mrs Thatcher's policies were seen to play an indirect but neverthless vital role in developing the means for these minorities to express themselves.

Women's independent cinema

The independent circuit in the 1980s became increasingly squeezed both in terms of production and distribution. Production costs increased and government policy liberated the market, thereby removing any financial advantages that had existed. (Refer to an earlier chapter for a fuller account.) On the distribution side, independent cinemas found it difficult to make the necessary changes and investments for multi-screen facilities.

The 1982 Workshop Declaration was supposed to help the independent sector, giving funding guarantees. Thus for a period of ten years (1982-1992), various workshops had a regular source of income. Certain feminist film collectives were set up: 20th century Vixen, Red Flannel, Sheffield Film co-op. Another striking example is the Leeds

Animation Workshop (LAW) that started in 1978 in Leeds. It was the least subsidised workshop, earning a high level of revenue from renting out films and sales. It was therefore very good value for money, proposed original and anti-commercial material, and like the black film collectives, believed in the collective formula. The ten LAW films that were produced during the 1978-1991 period, that is to say slightly overlapping the Thatcher years, dealt with important subjects: privatisation, nuclear proliferation, the environment, domestic violence, sexism, Third World famine and debt, child-care, housing and worker safety. This workshop specialised in short animated films of 10 to 15 minutes, due to low costs.

LAW always remained close to its local roots. The members of the workshop consulted teachers, local pressure groups and various interested persons. In this case too, one can notice a definite blurring of the traditional producer/consumer divide. Borrowers of films were termed 'users' and not 'consumers'. Films were there as a tool in a wider discussion on the various topical subjects. Commercial success was not the primary purpose and a whole alternative distribution service was set up around the Leeds area. The ten films all used animated sequences that were to bring the subject matter to the fore in contrast with the realism of the 1970s avant-garde. Animation had the advantage of not being elitist and could be understood by most age groups and most cultures. The points of view put forward in the films were uncommercial and unconventional. LAW's definition of culture was based on the involvement of people in the process of making a film as well as showing a final product. Culture was people-oriented and not based on sacred objects. Local accents and locations were used, thereby making them closer to the local community and not producing a standardised international product which is what the commercial market-place demands.

All these films have a definite political point of view. Pretend You'll Survive and Council Matters are both very committed statements. In the first film, the aim was to help the 1981 Greenham Common women's protest movement in its struggle against the installation of cruise missiles in Great Britain. In Council Matters the local authority, while not a perfect instrument, is portrayed as a tool of local democracy and empowerment. Central government is shown to be distant and merely interested in spending on arms. Another film deals with gender roles. Give us a Smile looks at the way women are treated in general, dealing with sexual harassment and rape, in particular. It should not be forgotten that for several years before his arrest in 1981, the Yorkshire Ripper had terrorised the north of England. Women's groups proposed a curfew on men at night and also the banning of sex shops. Several sex shops were in fact burned down in Leeds. Give us a Smile ends with an animated burning of a porn shop. Home and Dry considers the consequences of Mrs Thatcher's policy of selling off council homes. Various women are shown to stay in unsatisfactory relationships because of the housing problem.

In 1991, LAW reduced its staff from 6 to 5 due to the withdrawal of the Workshop Declaration. Alternative funding was sought, especially as a sign of the times could be seen in the members of the Sheffield Film Co-operative having to sign for unemployment benefits in 1991. European financial help was found for a film on occupational hazards, but the future outlook is rather bleak. Local authority help, while having played a vital role in the 1980s is not sufficient to keep these organisations going in the even more competitive 1990s. While middlebrow cultural policies allowed these film co-ops to spring up, the effects of Mrs Thatcher's long term commercial policies are seen here in their negative consequences, but these came out only in the 1990s.

Community arts

This area of study brings out some of the most characteristic ambiguities of Mrs Thatcher's cultural policy. Community arts is a movement for cultural democracy that wants everyone to express themselves in their own particular way as a right. This is totally opposed to Mrs Thatcher's idea of a commercial culture that produces cultural forms only if they are economically viable.

What exactly comes under the heading community arts is difficult to measure. The 1976 Arts Council of Great Britain Directory of Arts Centres set out four criteria:

a. There is a programme and a policy for more than one art form;
b. More than one space is used for arts activities;
c. There is some professional input;
d. There is a substantial usage which is not part of formal education for adult education provision.[10]

Community arts also spans the cultural spectrum of providing jobs for unemployed youths and adult education for rich middle-class citizens. No figures are available for Wales as they are placed in a more general category. There is also great diversity as to content. Some projects are annual festivals, while others are groups that function as a fully paid team over many years. Both types are included in this study. Official figures show a reduction in the total number of community arts projects and this reflects closures in the Merseyside, North West and South West areas. In all the other areas, projects were maintained if not expanded. Some of the reduction can be explained for technical reasons. However, some of the schemes could not continue in the face of government disapproval and also the North West area was overprovided in 1982 and found a more 'natural' level in 1985.

In money terms, there was a slight increase in community arts spending as RAAs distributed £1.5 million in 1981/2 that rose to £1.75 million in 1983/4. (The different activities are shown in Table 24.2 on page 496.) Drama, photography, music, murals, dance and video were the top community activities during the 1980s. Only drama, murals and dance can be considered as intrinsically community bound, because done by many individuals at a given time and place. Music playing also often involves communal activity, but it can involve solo instrumental music making. Photography and video can be considered as basically individual arts activities that can equally be done at home and they represented types of cultural activity that Mrs Thatcher wanted to encourage. These categories fitted in well with her definition of commercial, middlebrow and privatised culture. They all developed considerably as costs came down throughout the 1980s. The other community based activities needed little investment but involved a common purpose. Yet this kind of consciousness was often found to be lacking in deprived inner-city areas.

Almost all such arts centres can be considered as community arts centres that are supposed to be close to the community. Local authorities contribute greatly to arts centre funding. In 1983/4, more than œ50 million were spent on over 300 arts centres in Britain. The numbers employed at arts centres were considerable in 1983/4. There were 5100 full and part-time staff with 760 Manpower Services Commission workers. On top of these, 5,600 volunteers also worked at these centres. The total œ50 million expenditure was undoubtedly a considerable sum in proportion to total arts spending. This represented a local authority responsibility that was not specifically singled out for cutting and one can deduce that Mrs Thatcher basically approved of much of the enterprising work that was carried out in these centres. The voluntary work was particularly appreciated. However, there were also a few reservations about the more political and ideological aspects of community arts work. Mrs Thatcher disliked the principles behind cultural democracy and cultural rights. Many arts centres were, therefore, involved in various schemes organised by the Manpower Services Commission (MSC, now called the Training Commission) aiming at finding work for high risk groups. Young inner-city black males were particularly targeted by the MSC schemes. This was due to the urban riots that had marked the first half of the 1980s. Funding for the MSC Community Programme grew from œ117 million in 1980 to œ1080 million in 1988, when it was removed. The scheme provided 6751 jobs at a cost of œ24 million in 1986/7. Community arts jobs needed little investment providing non-commercial work that could absorb indefinite amounts of time and kept young people off the streets. They could also inspire them to engage in various commercial artistic activities such as tee-shirt printing, photography or crafts. The pragmatic Mrs Thatcher saw this as a cheaper means of making the streets safe than policing.

The anti-conservative, anti-enterprise ethos that surrounds community arts did not go down well with the prime minister. Many artists did their work conscientiously. But a vociferous minority with extreme left-wing opinions monopolised attention. To many conservatives, it seemed that community artists were biting the hand that fed them. As the threat of urban rioting seemed to disappear during the late 1980s, the excesses of this minority were used as a justification for cutting back resource levels. The MSC schemes were reduced and expansion is unlikely in the future.

Local authority resistance to the pressures of conservative government cultural policy was mostly financed by increasing the rates. In view of the emphasis on commercial culture, the 1980s saw the surprising growth of phenomena such as workshops, collectives, and community arts that allowed minority views to be expressed. Part of the explanation for this phenomenon is the commercial market providing cheap new technology that empowered the grass roots of society in a truly democratic process.

Mrs Thatcher's support of commercial culture had various consequences. Firstly, on the production side, it empowered certain minority groups that had previously been excluded from official establishment culture and the mainstream market. Cheaper new technology meant that many more could produce in a genuinely democratic movement. Mrs Thatcher only partly approved of the consequences. It fostered middlebrow cultural content as opposed to highbrow culture. Secondly, it also allowed the expression of critical ideas by minority groups which had previously been excluded: ethnic groups, feminists, homosexuals. Thirdly, this radically transformed the cultural mainstream. Mrs Thatcher's reactive policies had unforeseen consequences. Commercial culture symbolically challenged the arts Establishment. At the same time it opened the Pandora's box of the subversive side of popular culture. Its very existence actually encouraged the resistance that was offered by both the cultural Establishment and the subversive elements of popular culture.

Notes

1. See the Observer, Sunday 11 April 1993, 24.
2. ACTT, The Workshop Declaration (London: ACTT, 1984) 10.
3. Jim Pines, "Channel 4: A Pandora's Box for Blacks?", Artrage _ 1983, 2-5.
4. Jim Pines, "Channel 4: A Pandora's Box for Blacks?" 20.
5. John Akomfrah, "Black Independent Film-making: A Statement by the Black Audio/
Film Collective", Artrage _, 29.
6. ibid., 29.
7. Martina Attille, "The Passion of Remembrance: Background, in Black Film, British
Cinema", ICA Documents No 7 (London, 1988) 53-54.
8. Martina Attille, "The Passion of Remembrance" 53.
9. ibid., 54.
10. John Myerscough, Facts About the Arts 2 225.

Chapter 24
A National Identity Under Threat

In the 1980s, the national British or rather English identity appeared to be threatened by various influences. An increasingly European-scale and world-scale economy meant that national institutions, the Bank of England, the British Parliament or the Monarchy lost a degree of power and prestige. The most clearly visible threats, and those that got the most media coverage, were of course immigration and also several other subcultural phenomena. The resulting multicultural and subcultural expressions were seen by certain sections of British society as a challenge to traditional law and order. The police force, likewise, felt threatened by the behaviour of some second generation ethnic youngsters. They were the ones involved in the urban riots of the first half of the 1980s. Extremists of the National Front were quick to seize on this particular point as proof that the new groups could not be assimilated into British society. Mrs Thatcher, while not agreeing with these extremists, had some sympathy for the popular notion that British or English culture was being watered down and that this was inherently bad.

Immigration

There had been tensions within the Conservative Party since the 1950s over this particular issue. During the 1960s, cheap and unqualified labour was needed to perform lower paid jobs such as driving buses or collecting tickets on the London Underground. The immigration issue involved potent national symbols such as the notion of

British citizenship, the British Empire and the Commonwealth. Much nostalgia could be detected in the way these very British symbols were used to fuel the debate. Enoch Powell became the spokesman of those who feared that British culture was being swamped by alien ways of living. Mrs Thatcher took up many of these fears and argued for a tough stand on immigration. This comes out clearly in the following extract that makes a strange and intentional amalgam of various negative and foreign influences:

> I was not prepared to give up our powers to control immigration (from non-European Community countries), to combat terrorism, crime, and drug trafficking and to take measures on human, animal, and plant health, keeping out carriers of dangerous diseases - all of which required proper frontier controls. There was, I felt, a perfectly practical argument to this: as an island - and one quite unused to the more authoritarian continental systems of identity cards and policing - it was natural that we should apply the necessary controls at our ports and airports rather than internally. Again this was an essential matter of national sovereignty, for which a government must answer to its own Parliament and people.[1]

She believed that the first generation immigrants were hard working. Indeed she felt quite at ease with them as they often shared her own values. After the Brixton riots she "talked with the West Indian ladies in the canteen. They had gone into work throughout the disturbances, determined that the police should be supported with proper canteen facilities whenever they needed them at any hour of the day or night. They were clearly as disgusted as (she) was with those who were causing the trouble."[2] According to the prime minister immigrants often concentrated in inner-city areas where the wrong kind of values were picked up by the second generation in a sort of process of cultural contamination. Here lay the root of the problem:

> On Monday 13 July I made a similar visit to Liverpool. Driving through Toxteth, the scene of the disturbances, I observed that for all that was said about deprivation, the housing there was by no means the worst in the city. I had been told that some of the young people involved got into trouble through boredom and not having enough to do. But you had only to look at the grounds around those houses with the grass untended, some of it almost waist high and the litter, to see that this was a false analysis. They had plenty of constructive things to do

if they wanted. Instead, I asked myself how people could live in such circumstances without trying to clear up the mess and improve their surroundings. What was clearly lacking was a sense of pride and personal responsibility - something which the state can easily remove but almost never give back.[3]

She talked with some of the young people: "I reminded them that resources had been poured into Liverpool. I told them that I was very concerned by what they had said about the police and that while the colour of a person's skin did not matter to me at all, crime did. I urged them not to resort to violence or to try to live in separate communities from the rest of us."[4] This breakdown could not be said to be due to acculturation, the destabilisation caused by the passing from one culture to another with all the consequences it entails. The surprise it caused was all the greater as immigrant communities in Britain are very close and cohesive, often believing in self-help. According to Mrs Thatcher, the root cause of the riots was a breakdown of a general sense of community:

> The rioters were invariably young men, whose high animal spirits, usually kept in check by a whole range of social constraints, had on these occasions been unleashed to wreak havoc. What had become of the constraints? A sense of community - including the watchful disapproval of neighbours - is the strongest such barrier. But this sense had been lost in the inner cities for a variety of reasons. Often those neighbourhoods were the artificial creation of local authorities which had uprooted people from genuine communities and decanted them into badly designed and ill-maintained estates where they did not know their neighbours. Some of these new 'neighbourhoods', because of large-scale immigration were ethnically mixed; on top of the tensions which might initially arise in any event, even immigrant families with a strong sense of traditional values found those values undermined in their own children by messages from the surrounding culture. In particular, welfare arrangements encouraged dependency and discouraged a sense of responsibility, and television undermined common moral values that would once have united working-class communities. The results were a steadily increasing rise in crime (among young men) and illegitimacy (among young women).[5]

There is much that needs commenting on in these extracts. The first thing to be stressed is the term 'animal'. The prime minister uses it in the sense of uncivilised, uncontrolled and instinctive violence. There is the underlying connotation of the wild animals of Africa, such as lions, tigers and elephants which hunt and defend their territories, but can also sometimes go on wild rampages of apparently meaningless violence. However, if one turns to the targets of the urban rioting that took place during the 1980s, most of it was directed against symbols of authority such as police stations, community centres or local authority buildings. Therefore, most of the violence was not wild but in fact calculated. There was a certain logic to it.

A second aspect that needs commenting on is the notion of a scapegoat in the form of the local authorities. They had supposedly created 'artificial' communities that could never function properly because full of irresponsible and unmotivated people. This was clearly part of Mrs Thatcher's strategy to strengthen the state. Another culprit is television. It is represented here as the servant of the permissive society, giving its consumers dangerous ideas. The implication is that television's obsession with violence, sex and crime could only lead to breaking the law and causing unwanted pregnancies.

This appears to be a rather simplistic point of view. Urban rioting is a world phenomenon and occurs in communities that feel excluded from the mainstream. Young people think that they have nothing to lose and therefore act in a lawless manner. However, Mrs Thatcher was right in identifying the problem as a lack of constraints. Getting these youngsters to participate in their communities seems to be the obvious and simple answer. Many different ways of creating this participation come to mind but no consensus developed during the 1980s.

Another popular association that gained currency during the Thatcher years was that made between the immigrant communities and the increasingly widespread use of drugs. Heroin comes mostly from Asia, while cocaine comes via the West Indies. Because of this the media, in the latter half of the 1980s, focused their attention on Jamaican drugs gangs such as the Yardies who used particularly violent methods. In this case the foreigners were given the villain's role, while the white bobbies were presented as the guardian angels or custodians of the traditional British way of life.

A seemingly comic example of the immigration 'problem' can be observed in the British attitude to garlic. This is not only a recent difficulty. In the 1950s, C. S. Lewis gave a very Eurocentric description of Mediterranean-type Calormenes in his Chronicles of Narnia: "Then the dark men came round them in a thick crowd, smelling of garlic and onions, their white eyes flashing dreadfully in their brown faces."[6] This vegetable is very beneficial to health, helping blood circulation and acting as a disinfectant and thus could be said to help save money for the National Health Service. It is very much part of Asian cooking and was used by those who adopted Mediterranean food, that is to say those who travel and are pro-European. During the 1980s, a debate took place in the newspapers and on BBC Radio 4, over whether garlic could be acceptable. Were garlic eaters social pariahs like those who smoked in public places? The discussion seemed to touch the very centre of Britishness. English blandness was being challenged by spicy garlic. The English way of doing things was discreet, while garlic was the very opposite, attracting unwanted attention. Whatever the pros and cons of the argument, the fact that it occurred reflected a growing challenge to multicultural Britain.

Mrs Thatcher, in her public statements and speeches, sometimes reflected this fear of multiculturalism. (The previous quotation stresses the fact that multiculturalism and a dependency culture can make an explosive mix.) The way to defuse a dangerous situation, according to the prime minister, was to avoid ethnic concentrations in dilapidated local authority estates, and also to attack the ideology of this dependency culture. The Scarman Report, that looked into the causes of the Brixton riots, suggested that there were deep structural reasons for these violent incidents, such as unemployment, racism, or an adverse physical environment. Mrs Thatcher did not openly accept many of the recommendations. However, by using the Manpower Services Commission (MSC) up until 1988 to target specific inner-city groups, she implicitly accepted the logic of Scarman. Yet again, while claiming that left-wing extremists were trying to destabilise the country, the prime minister's policies were aimed all the same at defusing the explosive atmosphere of certain inner-city areas.

Hooliganism

The visible breakdown of law and order, in this case due to ethnic tensions, could also be observed in 'football hooligans' and 'lager louts'. These were just two more examples of what many considered was a general onslaught against traditional social values. It was argued that the British way of life was being undermined by irresponsible and lawless elements in society such as joyriders, car thieves and burglars that were left unpunished. Many of the riots occurred in black areas, such as Brixton, and were primarily due to friction that existed between young blacks and the police. This was quite simply a breakdown in communication between the youngsters and the police as figures of authority. In Moss Side, by contrast, there was no confrontation with the police force. Instead hooligans merely looted and pillaged shops and houses. In Brixton the violence could be justified as an act of frustration. In Moss Side there was general lawlessness based on criminal greed.

As for football hooligans they cannot be said to have been motivated by economic reasons. They came from all cross-sections of society and merely wanted gratuitous, random violence. They and the lager louts became the prime minister's bête noire. The football stadium catastrophe in 1985 at the Heysel in Belgium, caused by English football hooligans, marked a low point for national pride. This represented the exact opposite of what Mrs Thatcher thought the nation's reputation should be. She tried to introduce legislation with football identity cards, but there was such a vigorous reaction from civil liberty groups that the proposed legal changes were put aside. Ultimately, discreet and effective police work on identifying trouble-makers through information units, and simple measures such as the banning of alcohol from football stadiums and having all seat stadiums, considerably reduced the number of incidents in the grounds. However, the European dimension meant that many of the violent football supporters who went abroad to do their dirty work could be neither prosecuted in the continental countries nor charged in England after deportation.

Concerning police conditions, Mrs Thatcher made police pay a priority. She also emphasised the need to have bobbies back on the beat and visible within the community. The prime minister expressed repugnance at the extent of violence that existed in 1980s Britain and that the police had to face: "It was something of a shock to contemplate the kind of equipment the British police now required, which included a greater variety of riot shields, more vehicles, longer truncheons, and sufficient stocks of rubber bullets and water cannon".[7] This mounting violence in society was often blamed on drug-related lawlessness. The media used the violence of West Indian drugs gangs to launch a campaign to arm the police. During the 1980s, the police force became increasingly armed, although the majority of police officers did not want guns. This process is similar to the one that Stuart Hall described in his 'moral panics', designed to introduce authoritarian measures in order to strengthen the legal powers of the state.[8]

Globalisation

The increasingly globalised world economy of the 1980s led to standardised products and an integrated global strategy, in terms of production, distribution and consumption. This inevitably meant that national symbols and representations were weakened as they offered potential competition to the full global market potential of a cultural product. The private mode of consuming commercial culture also meant that there was less of a community spirit. Consumption was carried out on an individual basis and not within a community with common tastes. This trend benefited the American companies specialising in entertainment and information. Mrs Thatcher was left unworried by this concentration of strategic power and the growing Americanisation of the British way of life.

The film industry is a good example of a global cultural industry. The world market is dominated by Hollywood companies such as Paramount or MGM. These have to take significant risks in producing costly films. Certain films such as Crocodile Dundee did very well during the 1980s with an Australian subject and American financing. Once the film has experienced global success it can then move into other directions. Books and video versions are marketed and sold. Special products are produced to be distributed in supermarkets, using the free advertising provided by the film's popularity. Here can concretely be seen how the economic logic of this process leads to a more private home-based mode of cultural consumption and this to the detriment of a community spirit. Put very simply, the 'public sphere' and the sense of belonging to a specific community are greatly reduced by commercialisation. During the 1980s, Mrs Thatcher greatly encouraged private cultural consumption while at the same time, in a contradictory move, she tried her best to strengthen a national identity in other domains - for instance in her fight against European Community regulations. Such was the Thatcher paradox in this area.

The European dimension

This world economic vision existed at the European level too. Both businessmen and investors were keen on speeding up the process of European integration. Mrs Thatcher was likewise intent on reaping the benefits of a single integrated market. However, in the interests of a strong national identity, she used Europe and the Brussels bureaucracy as a scapegoat. This is very obvious in the following extract from Mrs Thatcher's commentary on her famous Bruges Speech:

> Not the least of these opponents was Jacques Delors. By the summer of 1988 he had altogether slipped his leash as a fonctionnaire and become a fully fledged political spokesman for federalism. The blurring of the roles of civil servants and elected representatives was more in the continental tradition than in ours. It proceeded from the widespread distrust which their voters had for politicians in countries like France and Italy. That same distrust also fuelled the federalist express. If you have no real confidence in the political system or political leaders of your own country you are bound to be more tolerant of foreigners of manifest intelligence, ability and integrity like Mr Delors telling you how to run your affairs. Or to put it more bluntly, if I were an Italian I might prefer rule from Brussels too. But the mood in Britain was different. I sensed it. More than that, I shared it and decided that the time had come to strike out against what I

saw as the erosion of democracy by centralisation and bureaucracy, and to set out an alternative view of Europe's future.[9]

Mrs Thatcher clearly saw Europe as a fundamental threat to the British way of life. Europe was somehow associated with tyranny and said to promote undemocratic, un-British procedures. And yet Mrs Thatcher's policies often went in the direction of centralisation and reduced democracy through the setting up of bureaucratic organisations. However, the prime minister singled out all the sacred symbols of British life that were supposed to be challenged by European Community bureaucrats. The very British pint was to be replaced by a half litre (which in fact did not happen). Pints of pasteurised milk in glass bottles and delivered to the doorstep were to be transformed into a cheap long-life supermarket product. In actual fact, in that particular case, many people preferred the cheaper foreign milk and its convenient supermarket distribution. Even the British pound was threatened by a new European ecu and the possible Economic and Monetary Union (EMU). Worse still, the very heart of the British identity was being threatened:

> The more I considered all this, the greater my frustration and the deeper my anger became. Were British democracy, parliamentary sovereignty, the common law, our traditional sense of fairness, our ability to run our own affairs in our own way to be subordinated to the demands of a remote European bureaucracy, resting on very different traditions? I had by now heard about as much of the European 'ideal' as I could take; I suspected that many others had too. In the name of this ideal, waste, corruption and abuse of power were reaching levels which no one who supported, as I had done, entry to the European Economic Community could have foreseen. Because Britain was the most stable and developed democracy in Europe we had perhaps most to lose from these developments.[10]

Of course she was not alone in the fight. At another level and concerning the relations between Europe and America, many intellectuals later argued that there existed a cultural exception that was officially recognised with the signing of the GATT agreement in 1993. Alan Bennett argued convincingly in this direction:

> With a limited number of channels, television is a topic of discussion - a play or a documentary is talked about the next morning. But the more channels there are, the less this is going to be the case. [...] The very same people who fuss about the nation losing its identity in Europe are quite happy to see national television lose its identity and go the European way so that we end up with pap and crap. One wants to ask such people: what is it that helps to hold the nation together? A shared interest in the novels of Lord Archer?[11]

In this extract, Bennett refers to the significant privatisations of television channels that had occurred in France and Italy during the 1980s. Bennett judges this trend harshly by claiming that it produces 'pap and crap'. Here, he clearly defends the BBC public service model that insists on education and quality rather than maximum profits. To a large extent Mrs Thatcher sided with such an approach by maintaining the duopoly system, thereby keeping the BBC as a major tool for creating a national identity and making such a defence possible. The new satellite world has empowered significant European and international groups. This new market is a reality and constantly weakens purely national identities. Though Mrs Thatcher stood for the special relationship with the United States, she at the same time defended Great Britain from all kinds of outside influences, in particular Europe and what was felt to be a creeping bureaucracy. Foreign cultures, Europe and disrespect of the law, were all seen as influences that eroded the authority of the British state.

Local Identities

Along with global and European economic trends, the rise of very local or regional identities could be observed. Devolved and decentralised policies empowered local rather than national identities and movements. This certainly was felt in the arts, where Regional Arts Boards (previously Regional Arts Associations) were given a much more prominent role after 1992, which came just after the Thatcher time period. The international pressures of commercialism forced people to think locally. Globalised consumption weakened national identities while at the same time creating a reaction that reinforced local identities.

Mrs Thatcher certainly wanted to encourage individuals and small local groups to look after themselves.

In cultural terms, the increasingly decentralised new technology of the private mode of cultural consumption allowed minorities to express themselves. During the 1980s, local communities could make video films and project them in community centres whereas this had not been possible previously. Similarly, recording your own music could be done with a simple cassette recorder rather than having to go through a recording studio. The whole logic of Mrs Thatcher's commercial definition of culture led to an encouragement of private and individual identities. This inevitably led to the undermining of a more national sense of community. The result was that specialist audiences had to be catered for. Ethnic groups tended to congregate in certain areas thus creating a visible local group identity. Roy Strong, ex-Director of the Victoria and Albert Museum, stressed this aspect:

> I didn't find anybody who had a bash into the Big Three (the RSC, the ROH and the National Theatre); everybody thinks we should have these centres of excellence, but the tide is not going to go the way of these old war-horses. They will be maintained, but the excitement, the push, the drive will be with the wider cultural spread throughout the country.[12]

This 'wider cultural spread' was the essence of Mrs Thatcher's cultural policy in her encouragement of commercial culture. Moreover, the local centres of excellence gave English culture an international reputation and therefore strengthened national identity. This is the reason why Mrs Thatcher had highly paradoxical reactions towards, for example, the cultural policy of Birmingham. In that case, she had very little to do with renewed interest in local action. Here a Labour council encouraged an adventurous multi-cultural programme all over the city. By 1990, £25 million were being spent on the arts alone and councillor Bryan Bird was proud of his council's work in sports and the arts:

> I remember many lads on the railways and shop floor had amazing talents, as artists and so forth. But somehow the arts weren't for us. You got your one school visit to the art gallery as a kid and that was about it. What we want is for the arts to be a normal part of Birmingham people's lives. For the galleries, I'm a

firm believer in free and equal access for all. It's our job to make the provision where people need it. Elsewhere, I believe everyone should have ample opportunity at a price they can afford, of enjoying themselves.[13]

This is a particularly clear example of the democratisation of culture justification. Roy Strong also noticed this trend away from metropolitan excellence to provincial enthusiasm in various cities such as Glasgow, Sheffield, Bradford, Manchester, Liverpool and Birmingham: "You could not go to a place like Birmingham 10 years ago and interview their chief executive about cultural policy. It's a complete revolution."[14] And it would seem that this revolution occurred despite Thatcherite policies, rate-capping and the rest. Mrs Thatcher certainly wanted middlebrow culture to expand, but given the choice between highbrow and popular culture, she preferred the former. She believed in spreading as well as raising the general cultural level. In Birmingham, unique local conditions created by a Labour council along with some talented musicians and artists led to an explosion of artistic activity. However, the prime minister refused to have this paid only by the rate-payer. She believed that artists had to 'hustle' or fish for a mixture of funds.

Englishness and the development of national character

When discussing such a wide embracing and yet influential concept as national character, one inevitably is led to make generalisations that, if taken out of context, might appear rather odd. Whatever the difficulties in defining such a notion, the idea of an English character certainly did exist in the late 19th century, and exists in a less visible or more diffuse form today. The most useful way of considering the concept is to use a model based on the idea of a core and a periphery. There exists a core national identity with local and regional cultural expressions placed on the periphery.

At the end of the 19th century, there was a strong English identity that was fostered by and around Public Schools, Oxbridge, the army, the Empire, the monarchy and the Church of England. Certain cultural institutions served a national need: the British Museum, the Royal

Academy or the Albert Hall. These national symbols were expressions of metropolitan values. Other major institutions appropriated this sense of Englishness: Parliament, the Church of England, the legal profession. In all these bodies one had to learn to speak Queen's English and use received pronunciation. The recruitment excluded all those who did not one way or another master the language in its received forms: many women (for lack of an appropriate education), the lower classes, and on the periphery, the Welsh, the Scottish and the Irish.

During the 20th century, this core of language based and normative Englishness became more loosely defined and more diffuse. The suffragettes fought for the vote through civil disobedience in the early 20th century. They were finally allowed to vote in 1918 for those over thirty and in 1928 for those over twenty-one. Strikes led to social legislation that gave certain rights to factory workers. The Welsh language began to be taught at the Trades Unions college in Oxford in the interwar period.[15] These excluded categories were gradually integrated into the English core and it was only the ethnic and social minorities that remained on the periphery. Some of them, such as the Jewish communities from Eastern Europe were assimilated rather quickly and had an unprecedented influence on cultural production. Others encountered more difficulty. This process of official recognition by the English system through a combination of violence, threatening or intimidating behaviour and obstruction was in fact repeated during the Thatcher period when urban and racial riots occurred.

The result was that certain inner-city policies were designed specifically around young black groups so that explosive situations might be defused. The opinions of old people or isolated mothers were, on the other hand, not taken into account because they did not pose a direct and visible threat to the status quo. Conversely, young black children were often given resources to organise sports groups and small workshops in order to encourage integration. Football is undeniably an international sport, but is also particularly important in English cultural history. It is a collective sport that channels individual energy in a communal effort. Workshops set up to create tee-shirts of African designs could also be part of this process of integration. Inner-city youths had to cater for specific tastes but also for wider English tastes if they were to become successful. In this way among others, during the 1980s, many of the peripheral groups were slowly integrated into the cultural core which was consequently profoundly modified.

What was the global effect of this evolution on the core English culture? One can certainly argue that the great beneficiaries of Mrs Thatcher's economic policies were those who lived in the home counties. Most of the new service jobs were created in or around London. As a result, all the south of England, except for certain parts of London, voted solidly conservative. Moreover, the idea of the union between England, Wales, Scotland and Northern Ireland no longer attracted much support and enthusiasm. In fact, the sacred symbols of unionism, that is the monarchy, the Union Jack and the national anthem, might have been somewhat devalued because of their appropriation by extreme nationalists. This is particularly true of the National Front and its excessive use of the Union Jack.

As concerns Northern Ireland, Mrs Thatcher tried to encourage a political solution by signing the Anglo-Irish Agreement in 1985, while insisting at the same time on the right of the majority to self-determination. She also stood firm as regards paramilitary terrorism. This was particularly important as IRA groups were operating on the mainland during the 1980s, and even tried to kill the prime minister herself in the 1984 Brighton bombing. Like football hooligans, terrorists came high on the premier's list of priorities. One may say that most of the frictions that emerged between the media and Mrs Thatcher arose from the subject of Northern Ireland. The message given by the media was that there seemed to be no solution to the troubles. It was also seen to be expensive to use troops to police the province. For these reasons many people on the mainland had little sympathy for those in Northern Ireland. The implicit message of the media was clear. The traditional English way of life was under threat from Irish violence, often aided by foreign powers such as Libya and Iran.

These same issues, but with totally different results, were seen in the Falklands when the Argentine junta decided to invade these sparsely populated islands in 1982. The sacred English symbol of democracy had to be defended against despotism. A moral crusade united the nation in a way that had not occurred since the Second World War. 'Our boys' became Mrs Thatcher's boys, and were seen as the clear heroes in a fight between good and evil. The armed forces proved their usefulness and efficiency and the authority of the state was thus strengthened. Mrs Thatcher appropriated for herself and the whole enterprise she had launched this feeling of national pride and national action as shown quite blatantly in the following statement:

> We have ceased to be a nation in retreat. We have instead a newfound confidence - born in the economic battles at home and tested and found true 8000 miles away.[...] And so today we can rejoice at our success in the Falklands and take pride in the achievement of the men and women of our task force. But we do so, not as at some flickering of a flame which must soon be dead. No - we rejoice that Britain has rekindled that spirit which has fired her for generations past and which today has begun to burn as brightly as before. Britain found herself again in the South Atlantic and will not look back from the victory she has won.[16]

The whole extract recalls former Second World War days when Winston Churchill defended Britain from the Nazi oppressor. The symbolic vision of islands defended by ships went deep into the heart of the British people. During the Second World War, the convoy system had kept Britain fed and armed despite the menace of German U-boats. With the Falklands the very same situation was repeated when the Royal Navy was seen to defend innocent islanders from foreign dictatorship.
More generally, R. W. Johnson has suggested that the national culture is basically a Tory one. This involves a sense of racial and national superiority, deferential attitudes towards authority, an anti-egalitarian ethos and a well defined status hierarchy. The author also proposed that the practice of high politics was surrounded by secrecy.[17] These ideas certainly tie up with the class ridden reality of today's Great Britain. However, the English component was on the wane during the 1980s.

Likewise, the monarchy and the Church of England are fundamental and central English symbols. Mrs Thatcher's attitude to these particular national representations was somewhat ambiguous. She supported the traditional conservative symbol of national unity, the

Queen, who embodied the idea of national dignity but also represented a stable and safe society. But the prime minister also wanted radical change and therefore supported newcomers such as Rupert Murdoch with his media plans, even though his popular press often criticised the monarchy. This may have been partly due to the tycoon's republican sympathies. In the meantime, the young royals developed what seemed to her a rather strange taste for ostentation that could either be considered as 'nouveau riche' or aristocratic. They drove sports cars, bought country houses, played polo and went grouse shooting. This did not go down well with the voters who had to face many years of austerity.

As to the Church, its leaders were often criticised by conservative back-benchers. Mrs Thatcher never openly criticised the Anglican Church although she was shocked by the report Faith in the Cities (1985). She dearly wanted to maintain a traditional sense of community as seen in received religious forms. But not at any cost. She also wanted to encourage a meritocracy in which people were rewarded according to their enterprise. A sizeable majority of the Church of England did not agree with this system that implicitly accepted a certain social inequality. Throughout the 1980s, its leaders argued that individuals had a right to basic human dignity and that increasing homelessness and poverty at the end of the decade was a national scandal. Mrs Thatcher must have felt in some agreement with Roy Strong when he wrote a few years after she left office: "neither the monarchy nor the Church is holding our society together any longer."[18]

The Little England alternative

In despair at seeing the old symbols of national unity lose their appeal, Mrs Thatcher seemed to encourage a Little England attitude. The typical example of this kind of thinking might be found in Selsdon Man, the term coined by Harold Wilson to describe a right-wing move in the Tory party. Anti-European and very insular, often having a siege mentality, the stance consists in defending the sacred symbols of the

English everyday life like the local pub or the traditional fish and chip shop. English food also had to be protected from all the foreign imports: bangers (sausages), the English breakfast, tea and beer, as opposed to French pat,, coffee and wine or German lager. In this sense a cultural war, based on national products, identity and preference was waged during the 1980s. Little England played rugby, football and especially cricket and bowls. The latter categories conveniently excluded the rest of the world except the Commonwealth. The Little England mentality believed in traditional English gardening, country cottages and villages. Grandiose and costly metropolitan projects were thought to be a waste of time and money. The archetypal little Englander could be seen in Essex man (a caricature often encountered in the Press), a firm patriot who despised all foreign influences. In fact, anything that symbolised the 'essence' of Englishness was considered to be inherently superior to any foreign equivalent, including Scottish and Welsh ones. This was of course a patent untruth and a compensatory construction, yet Mrs Thatcher was often seen to adopt attitudes which came very close to this narrow approach to life.

The specifically English identities, be they highbrow, middlebrow or lowbrow, found it more difficult to compete in the commercially competitive and increasingly internationalised world of the 1980s. Although Mrs Thatcher in theory believed in powerful British symbols of national unity, she thought that the rather small amounts of money spent on them were, even so, too great and represented a poor investment. She considered that the resources of the state could be better spent in making it possible for individuals to increase their private consumption. This illustrated the clash that occurred between the ideas of the cultural Establishment with its elitist values and support of national institutions, and the Thatcherites who believed in commercial efficiency. In the long-term, this process of proportionally less state subsidy for such national institutions inevitably meant a weakening of the British state identity which comes as a consequence of the prime minister's paradoxical positioning. Her policies could not satisfy all the contrary aims that she had defined.

Notes

1. Margaret Thatcher, *The Downing Street Years* 553.
2. ibid., 145.
3. Margaret Thatcher, *The Downing Street Years* 145.
4. ibid., 146.
5. ibid., 146.
6. C. S. Lewis, *The Last Battle* (London: Lions, 1992) 29-30.
7. Margaret Thatcher, *The Downing Street Years* 145.
8. Stuart Hall, *Policing the Crisis: Mugging, the State, and Law and Order* (London: Macmillan, 1978).
9. Margaret Thatcher, *The Downing Street Years* 742.
10. ibid., 743.
11. Alan Bennett, *A Night with Alan Bennett*, BBC 2, 5 July 1992.
12. Roy Strong, "A torrent of Strong language", *The Observer*, 6 September 1992, 60.
13. "Second city firsts", *New Society*, 19 April 1991.
14. Roy Strong, "A torrent of Strong language" 60.
15. See Philip Dodd, *Englishness and National Culture* (London: Routledge, 1980) 13.
16. Margaret Thatcher, *The Downing Street Years* 235.
17. R. W. Johnson, *The Politics of Recession* (London: Macmillan, 1985) 224-255.
18. Roy Strong, "A torrent of Strong language" 60.

Chapter 25
A 'Cultural Revolution'?

It is on the question of attitudes that the best case can be made for a 'cultural revolution'. Of course, British society reacted in a dramatic fashion to Mrs Thatcher's policy realisations, but these do not represent such a profound break with the past as some critics have claimed. Apart from the privatisations, the basic British economic and political system was not greatly modified during the Thatcher years. It is for this reason that it would be better to talk in terms of a so-called 'cultural revolution' using inverted commas to qualify the unfinished process.

Various points need to be stressed. Firstly, the prime minister transformed the relationship between unions, employers and the state. She likewise brought a more positive meaning to previously politically incorrect words such as 'enterprise' and 'profit'. Secondly, she strengthened the authority of the state, by successfully winning the Falklands war in 1981, by resisting the miners in 1984-1985 and by standing firm against the threat of terrorism. She displayed clear and yet flexible leadership qualities throughout the decade, waiting patiently for five years before challenging the National Union of Mineworkers (NUM) or nine years before introducing her national curriculum. Thirdly, Mrs Thatcher extended private ownership into many domains. The privatisations of British Aerospace (1981), Associated British Ports (1983,1985), British Telecom (1984 until 1991), British Gas (1986), British Airways (1987) and British Steel (1988) now seem irreversible. It would simply cost too much to restart a massive renationalisation programme. Fourthly, and by extension, the prime minister introduced a number of commercial private sector practices into all central and local government procedures. This can be seen in the generalisation of compulsory private tendering and the use of consultants to look at ways of reducing everyday running costs. The fifth aspect of this 'cultural revolution' is a consideration of those who actively supported Mrs Thatcher's views. Who changed sides and for what reasons? Who supported her, despite the ruthless image that she presented of herself? Lastly, one needs to wonder to what extent these trends were inevitable and might have occurred under a Labour government too. The monetarist road was begun in 1977 with Mr Callaghan as prime minister. In a way, Thatcherite policies might be considered as a logical response to global pressures such as the oil price rise in 1973 and a more competitive global market that made a policy of reduced state spending inevitable.

Trade union relations

When Mrs Thatcher came to office in 1979 the Trade Unions Congress (TUC) and its leaders could both directly and indirectly influence government policy. Before Mrs Thatcher's premiership, one remarkable example of direct intervention could be seen in the miners' strike of 1974 which precipitated the February general elections. Another example that brought the leader of the Opposition her first election victory was the Winter of Discontent which showed that voluntary incomes policies were impossible to apply because of union resistance and division. What Mrs Thatcher achieved in this domain is her greatest contribution to the 'cultural revolution' that she triggered off.

The prime minister refused to consult the secretary generals of the TUC, Len Murray up until 1984 and after that date Norman Willis. Previous governments had all consulted these top union leaders, paying lip service to them. Mrs Thatcher clearly defined her role as head of a democratically elected government that fully intended to make decisions for the good of the nation, without having to consult unions, that were henceforth considered as just one among many pressure groups. The successive union legislation in 1980, 1982, 1984 and 1988, redefined the role of trade unions. Secondary picketing was made illegal, as was the right to organise a closed shop. Everyone was given the right not to join a union. This was a truly radical change in Britain's economic climate and brought the country more in line with other European countries which have lower unionisation levels.[1]

As a direct result foreign money was invested into Great Britain. Nissan started its production in 1984 in Sunderland and was quickly followed by Toyota in Derby, while Honda worked with Rover cars. These Japanese car companies brought with them their own work practices and production rates, thereby introducing a Japanese work ethic or culture. This, likewise, weakened union influence. Privatisation also reduced union militancy and had the added advantage of temporarily financing the spending of the state. As a result, from 13 million union members in 1978, this representing 53 per cent of the work force, the figure had dropped to 10.2 million by 1988, that is to say, only 38 per cent of the working population.[2] Structural changes, such as jobs being created in the service industries rather than in manufacturing or heavy industry, influenced this tendency. Services attracted many part-time and full-time women workers, while in manufacturing foreign competition meant less union militancy.

Certain employers such as Rupert Murdoch demanded no strike clauses in their work contracts, although this did not become the general rule. However, there was a dramatic reduction in the number of days lost in strike action. 29.5 million days were lost in 1979 and this had dropped to 1.9 million in 1990. Britain became one of the most work conscious countries in Europe.[3] Yet this might have happened anyway because of increases in unemployment which acted as a natural break to union militancy. Productivity levels also rose in a regular fashion throughout the Thatcher decade. The price that had to be paid for this slimmer and more efficient industrial base concentrating on services was occasional high levels of unemployment. Unions of course saw these structural changes but did not directly challenge Thatcherite policies after 1985 in what was termed a spirit of 'new realism'.

Mrs Thatcher and a strong state

Along with this change of attitudes among both unions and the general working population, Mrs Thatcher reasserted the authority of the state. The prime minister presented a strong image of her premiership that contrasted sharply with the previous Labour government. All around the world the 'Iron Lady' was viewed with a mixture of amazement, admiration and disdain. Mrs Thatcher proved that she could be an effective leader by reclaiming the Falkland Islands in 1982. In this difficult military operation, she displayed qualities that are more often associated with men. The Argentine junta was shown to be inefficient and incompetent. On top of that, she also proved that terrorism could not make her change her mind.

This clear message of firmness helped her in attracting foreign investors to the British Isles. With such a determined leader one could hope for long-term stability. Thus in 1989, 41 per cent of American investment and 38 per cent of Japanese investment in Europe came to Great Britain. This appeared a major turnaround after the ignominy of the 1976 International Monetary Fund (IMF) loan, that had been granted only after very strict conditions had been met .

In her attempt to strengthen the British state, Mrs Thatcher invested resources into both the police force and the army. The police force proved to be vitally important during the miners' strike in 1984 and 1985. Between 1979 and 1991, there was a 41 per cent increase in real terms in police pay. The bobby on the beat also reappeared during the period in an attempt to reassure citizens that there was no crime explosion. True to Conservative principles, Mrs Thatcher also defined the limits of state responsibilities and encouraged people to empower themselves in moves such as Neighbourhood Watch and Crime Concern. The former started in 1982 and was designed as a means of fighting burglary. The latter was started in 1988 and was more business oriented. Thus, the better paid police force acted in a limited area while citizens organised their own private actions to complete minimum but visible services.

Privatisations

Hand in hand with reducing the power of the unions came privatisation. This is now a world trend that Mrs Thatcher seemed to initiate. She showed that it was possible and could be done on a massive scale. The result has been a profound change in economic attitudes in Great Britain. Privatisation provided instant cash for the state and it appeared popular because sufficient numbers of people were involved in the process. By 1991, 11 million individuals had shares of one form or another. The prime minister introduced popular capitalism to Britain and it was a great success. While privatisations had a significant effect on union levels, it is far from certain that private monopolies such as British Telecom (1984-1991) are necessarily more efficient from the consumer prices point of view. The various regulators that have been appointed to Ofgas or Oftel, the organisations that calculate what market prices should be, have all been surprised by the unjustifiably high profits made by privatised British Gas and British Telecom due primarily to lack of competition. As in the case of the cultural industries, strategic power can play a crucially important role.

All areas of British industry were affected by the privatisation campaign. The main areas of resistance came over water (1989) and later, after Mrs Thatcher's period, in British Rail (1995). Education and National Health Service reforms also proved to be practically impossible. However, the vast majority of people in Britain accepted the need for privatising all the other sectors of the national economy in a bid to reduce state expenditure. Education and health appear to be the last bastions of the welfare state, that is to say comprehensive social services for the good of all the population. One may assert that the free market will, in future, find it difficult to reduce the influence of the state in these areas.

What did Mrs Thatcher do in higher education? She punished the universities for not being in contact with the realities of the market and therefore encouraged the polytechnics that provided more practical courses. Private student loans were introduced as a way of expanding student numbers without having to increase state spending. Student numbers in both polytechnics and, to a lesser extent, universities went up during the 1980s. In 1979, there were 500,000 students and by 1990, well over 600,000. As for secondary schools there was a limited movement away from state provision with 40,000 pupils opting out in favour of direct grant schools out of a total of 9 million pupils. This can only be seen as a failure. This case shows that education cannot be provided on a two-tier basis for the moment. For that matter, Mrs Thatcher wisely did not interfere in too much detail with the pedagogical aspects of teaching as seen in the question of the national curriculum.

Another area that appeared untouchable and that Mrs Thatcher left for her third term of office was the National Health Service. The NHS had widespread popular support and Mrs Thatcher tried to put a break on spending without modifying the founding principles. In this domain, the Thatcher decade can be split up into three main periods. Between 1979 and 1982, a certain amount of decentralisation occurred. Then, in 1982-1989, managerialism was used to try and make administrative savings. The last period (1989-1991) was when medical decisions were considered according to efficiency criteria. This search for the best value for money produced very mixed results as it was a politically explosive issue. While private health care schemes such as BUPA now abound, the basic principles of a minimum health service for all have survived through the Thatcher years. Here one encounters the limits of Mrs Thatcher's so-called 'cultural revolution'.

Another area where there was very limited action was social security. This is, likewise, a stunning example of Mrs Thatcher's pragmatism as opposed to what her critics termed her ideological outlook. The New Right wanted to make economies in this area either by reducing the services offered or removing certain of the 28 benefits that existed at the time. Demographic and economic trends meant that the real amounts spent on social security went up from £14 billion in 1979 to œ52.6 billion in 1989-1990. To give an order of size, in 1989, £20 billion were spent on health, £20.3 billion on defence and £5.7 billion on education.[4] Mrs Thatcher could not subsidise unproductive jobs because of free market principles and high unemployment was the price to pay for a leaner and more efficient economy. Thus, the unemployed received unemployment benefit for one year, after which they received income support. The number of pensioners also rose from 8.9 million in 1980 to 9.9 million in 1990. The number of people receiving disability benefits nearly doubled from 1980 to 1990 to 1.2 million. This can be explained by a high incidence of depression in areas of unemployment. Doctors gave out long-term sick leave certificates. This was one way of getting improved conditions within the social security system.

Although targeting specific groups of people through means testing was extended, the social security system in 1990 could be placed somewhere between the American residual model and the highly structured means tested Australian model that was introduced by a Labour government. The changes in Australian can be regarded as another instance of political pragmatism. The fact that the social security system was retained, although not for young people between 16 and 19, shows the extent of Mrs Thatcher's political pragmatism. A true ideologue would have dismantled large areas of the British benefits system.

Commercial procedures

One area that was the direct responsibility of the government and where considerable savings could be made was in central government. There was also an attempt to control local authority spending. From the early 1980s, the Civil Service was scrutinised by Derek Rayner (of Marks and Spencer's) and the Efficiency Unit. Practical suggestions were made to simplify the number of forms and reduce the number of personnel and this resulted in considerable savings. By 1990, there were 555,000 civil servants, whereas there had been 732,000 in 1979.[5] Other areas of the public service such as the Royal Mint and HMSO had to adopt more commercial practices.

In local government, compulsory private tendering was made the rule. Although this sometimes resulted in private monopolies, the principle has been widely accepted and it is justified for services that have no social content. Refuse collection and canteen meals benefit from private competition. The local authority does not need to run these services directly and can subcontract them out. The London borough of Wandsworth was the most enthusiastic Conservative council that had one of the lowest community charge and council tax levels in the early 1990s. Without a shadow of doubt, considerable savings have been made in this area.

Changing public opinion

In January 1988, Mrs Thatcher made a speech at the Institute of Directors annual lecture:

> We believe that dependence in the long run decreases human happiness and reduces human freedom [...]. Therefore the next step forward in the long evolutionary march of the welfare state in Britain is away from dependence towards independence [...]. Everyone knows the sullen apathy of dependence and can compare it with the sheer delight of personal achievement [...]. Two things need to be done. The first is the most important. It is to change the climate of opinion.

To what extent was the climate of opinion changed? Enterprise culture was certainly rehabilitated. Council house owning workers turned out to be just as proud as the Porsche owning golden boys. Both supported Thatcherite principles. However, these symbols of the Thatcher decade are not the only ones and can become stereotypes. The 'cultural revolution' was intended for everyone. It would seem that Mrs Thatcher won the votes of a considerable part of the 'new working class' that is to say the home owning, non-unionised, southern manual workers. Even the poor, those who gained the least from Mrs Thatcher's policies, often voted for her because of her strong views on hanging, law and order, clear nationalism and traditional values. The basic values that the prime minister believed in were hard work, deferred gratification and a meritocracy of self-made individuals. The Labour Party and socialism could be easily contrasted with this economic vision:

> Our struggle with the Labour Party has never been a matter just of economics. It concerns the way of life we believe is right for Britain now and in the future. It concerns the values by which we live. Socialism is a creed of the state. It regards ordinary human beings as the raw material for its schemes of social change. But we put our faith in people - in millions of people who spend what they earn, not what other people earn. Who make sacrifices for their young family or their elderly parents. Who help their neighbours and take care of their neighbourhoods. The sort of people I grew up with.[6]

The election results testify that there were enough people who supported these views and the changes that Mrs Thatcher proposed. However, in her last term of office she turned her attention to the sacred symbols of education and the NHS and this is where she was not followed by the majority of British people. Moreover, her attempt at reforming local authority finances ultimately brought her down. It is only within these limits that one may talk in terms of a Thatcher 'cultural revolution'.

Professional people were the most passionate critics of the Thatcher ethos. Her simple prescriptions and her moralising tone did not go down well with them. Resistance gradually built up over the 1980s. In 1977, a Gallup poll showed 35 per cent thought that poverty was due to laziness. This figure had dropped to 13 per cent by 1987. Whereas 30 per cent wanted to curb union power in 1979, the figure had dropped to 19 per cent in 1987-1988. By the end of the decade there was a 6 to 1 majority in favour of increased government spending.[7] Thus, the Thatcher 'cultural revolution' rehabilitated enterprise, attacked the dependency culture and privatised large areas of national industry. In fact, by the end of the 1980s, most people agreed with her practical ways of problem solving. However, the scheme had gone as far as was politically possible. The term 'Mrs Thatcher's Britain' was considered a term of abuse by the end of the 1980s and it was only because the conservative Members of Parliament changed their leader in November 1990, that the party avoided an election defeat.[8]

The economic dividends of the Thatcher 'revolution' were spread out in an uneven fashion. The standard of living of those living in the south of England improved significantly throughout the 1980s. Those who found themselves unemployed and over the borders did not do so well. Using a base of 100 for GDP per head between 1979 and 1986, one arrives at a figure of 107 for East Anglia and 103 for the South-West. Wales and Scotland both got 98 and the West Midlands got 96, because of the steep decline in manufacturing industry.[9] This uneven regional distribution of the fruits of economic growth can clearly be traced in the voting patterns, with the majority of conservative Members of Parliament coming from the south of England and the home counties, and the bulk of Labour MPs coming from the regions. On the one hand, the Conservatives got 47 per cent of the total vote in England in 1979. They got merely 24 per cent of the total in Scotland in 1987. The Labour party on the other hand, got 29.5 per cent of the English vote in 1987, only just ahead of the Alliance with 23.9 per cent. In Wales, Labour got 45.1 per cent in 1987.[10] The north/south divide certainly widened during the whole of the Thatcher period, but this was an inevitable consequence of the Thatcher project which was based on free trade and allowing the market to find a natural balance between supply and demand.

The practical limits to the Thatcher 'revolution' are clearly shown in the work of Geert Hofstede. His cross cultural research came up with some startling conclusions. It was conducted for IBM in 1982 and concerned 53 different countries around the world. An individualism index (IDV) was set up comparing individualism and collectivism according to replies to a written questionnaire. National attitudes were classified and Great Britain came third according to individualism.[11] Another research tried to judge the power distance index (PDI), that is to say a measure of authoritarian relations in civil society. Britain was placed forty-fourth out of a total of fifty-three.[12] Great Britain appears to come in a group of countries that prefer consultation and interdependence between bosses and employees. In other countries such as Malaysia and Guatemala, there was found to exist a great degree of dependence between those in authority and subordinates. Although the research was conducted on large business organisations representing a specific segment of society, this would suggest that Great Britain is a very individualistic, low power distance society. It was thus very difficult for Mrs Thatcher to push the British significantly further down the road of individualism. In terms of attitudes, the people of the United Kingdom could not become much more individualistic.

The environment

One should also mention that the Thatcher 'revolution' sometimes manifested itself more on a symbolic level than on that of political change. The case of the greening of Mrs Thatcher's policies in the late 1980s is a good example of this process. The message was received and yet there was remarkably little action to back up this perceived change of policy. The apparent change in style was due to three main pressures: firstly, increased concern about environmental problems and their electoral significance; secondly, the dramatic rise in environmental pressure group membership at a time when political party membership was falling significantly; thirdly, increased pressure from the European Community and, to a lesser extent, international influences.

The first two terms of office did not produce the expected moves towards deregulation as proposed by the New Right. This was clearly due to electoral reasons. The only piece of legislation that was introduced during the period was the Wildlife and Countryside Act (1981) which was greatly influenced by the National Farmers' Union. Because of this, planning controls on the 'normal' countryside were kept well off the agenda. The Countryside Commission (CC) and the Ramblers Association were not even consulted. This act maintained the voluntarist tradition in environmental matters in Great Britain. In 1987, Mrs Thatcher gave administrative co-ordination to the Department of the Environment (DoE) in the form of Her Majesty's Inspectorate of Pollution. Once again the voluntarist approach was maintained due to underfunding and a lack of inspectors. Fines were kept to a minimum.

An electoral shock came in June 1989 at the European elections where the Green Party won 15 per cent nationally and 20 per cent in parts of the South East. Visibly, green issues could attract the votes of middle-class southerners, and swings of this kind towards the Labour

Party could push the Conservatives out of government. Mrs Thatcher took the threat very seriously and in March 1989 organised a conference on 'Saving the Ozone Layer' in London. At the end of the conference, Britain accepted a 100 per cent ban on CFCs, partly because ICI was well placed in the race to find substitutes. The White Paper This Common Inheritance (Sept 1990) was produced amid a fanfare of publicity but merely provided symbolic protection in an area where Mrs Thatcher wanted to maintain a voluntarist approach.

Thus environmental policy clearly shows us that Mrs Thatcher was very sensitive to electoral reactions. In fact, she preferred to devote Parliamentary time to somewhat ineffective legislation in order to reassure the electorate. Once again she appears to have been more of a pragmatist and a politician than an ideologue. The Thatcher 'revolution' in this case can be seen as superficial and visible rather than structural. The surprising aspect is that this type of communication worked, and by 1992 the Green Party's share of the vote had gone back down to a mere 2 per cent.

The prime minister's attempt at a 'cultural revolution' suffered from the effects of the implementation gap, referred to in previous chapters. This was perhaps inevitable, as a kind of negotiating strategy, since a strong case will often gain moderate results. Mrs Thatcher proposed a revolution and she produced a cultural evolution, that is to say, a significant change in production and economics and administration, and more especially in the minds of the British people.

Notes

1. See Chapter 13 in Anthony Sampson, *The Essential Anatomy of Britain* (London: BCA, 1992) 134.

2. Jean-Claude Sergeant, *La Grande-Bretagne de Margaret Thatcher* (Paris: PUF, 1994) 245.

3. ibid., 93.

4. David Marsh et al (eds) *Implementing Thatcherite Policies* (Buckingham: Open University Press, 1992) 84.

5. See Chapter 3 in Anthony Sampson, *The Essential Anatomy of Britain* 32.

6. Margaret Thatcher, *The Downing Street Years* 662-663.

7. Dennis Kavanagh and Anthony Seldon (eds), *The Thatcher Effect* 246.

8. ibid., 243.

9. Dennis Kavannagh, Anthony Seldon (eds), *The Thatcher Effect* 254.

10. ibid., 259.

11. Geert Hofstede, *Cultures and Organisations* (London: Harper Collins, 1994) 53.

12. ibid., 26.

Chapter 26
The Implications of Commercial Culture

As has been stressed in previous sections, Mrs Thatcher encouraged all forms of commercial culture. By its very nature this category covers most cultural and artistic forms. However, there are two artistic extremes that are excluded. The highbrow elitist end excluded itself by considering the commercial to be inferior, a process that has been well described by the Frankfurt School and its research work. Yet Mrs Thatcher wanted the cultural elite to pay for its lofty superiority. The other extreme was subculture that also excluded itself from mainstream culture because of its anti-commercialism and anti-social behaviour. Consequently, much of subculture was considered to be subversive, although some forms were eventually integrated into mainstream culture. The insistence on commercial culture had many implicit consequences and these need to be highlighted and investigated.

Commercial culture

This is the cultural area that experienced rapid growth during the Thatcher decade and was actively encouraged by the prime minister. The number of jobs that were created in the entertainment and cultural sectors during the Thatcher decade was considerable. A good example to illustrate the process of commercial culture can be studied in the video clip. It appeared in the period under consideration in its by now standardised form (3 to 4 minutes long with images accompanying the music). Most young people would consume them in their homes but they were also to be viewed by them in pubs and bars for youngsters.

In fact the jukebox of the 1950s was replaced by the video clip machine in the 1980s, a new technology superseding an old one.

Video clips were very attractive products for advertisers. Madonna worked for Pepsi and financed some of her touring through a deal with them in the mid- 1980s. Michael Jackson's Thriller clip pushed his worldwide album sales which went well over the 30 million mark. Music of course was a useful way of getting around linguistic and cultural barriers for those interested in global strategies:

> We are looking for customers, trying to build our businesses and looking to reach out and communicate to the youth of the world. The advent of the global marketplace, together with the deregulation of TV, radio privatisation and the introduction of satellite broadcasting in Europe is creating a new game for us all to play. I believe that, over the next decade, corporations, the music industry and broadcasters are going to be working together in ways no one even dreamed of as little as 10 or 20 years ago, probably in ways none of us foresee right now.[...] I'm talking about sponsored TV programming that gives much-needed exposure to the careers of up-and-coming music talent and sponsorship of artists and tours. If privatisation were to progress, to the point the UK is today, advertising revenue in Europe will increase by 55% from $4.5 billion to $7 billion. By the year 2000 I think we'll see the targeting of brand-specific music artists, matched precisely to products. Music will play a major role in this new commercial reality - the emergence of a global market.[1]

The kind of television outlet that used video clips was MTV, an American music channel that started in 1981. It is now present in Europe and is a successful commercial channel:

> Finally advertisers can reach people by television in a way that was only available to them throughout the print media. Now advertisers can hit the 16-34s with MTV's laser sharp targeting - not scattered buckshot. The audience's discretionary income is not in piggy banks or pension funds. MTV reaches its viewers all over Europe with a consistent clarity: it's about the cars they drive, the clothes they wear, the foods they feed themselves with.[2]

One can notice the analogy with hunting in this quotation, and also the association with modern technology in the form of laser beams, as in a very different area during the Gulf War of 1992. If one considers the content side of the video clip, many of the techniques that came to be used are modern and stylish. Dry ice and backlighting are often used to create an atmosphere that is typical of rock concerts. Characters are often seen running up and down stairs, or driving cars in exotic places. Musical climaxes are sometimes punctuated by explosions. War and battles are often depicted. Phallic guitars and women's bodies are given abundant display. These stereotyped images have led to self parody on the part of the actors as the codes of the genre have become increasingly familiar. The video clip's discourse universe is consequently rather limited. Despite the increasing fragmentation of pop music in the 1980s, all the various pop trends used the same basic images and techniques. At one and the same time, Mrs Thatcher approved of the advertising but disapproved of the contents. She promoted commercial culture thus allowing individuals to make their own decisions about their musical tastes. However, she did not approve of the portrayal of women in these video clips and therefore established various organisations such as the Independent Television Commission (ITC) or the Broadcasting Complaints Commission (BCC) to examine the contents.

A trend similar to the pop video clip came along in teenage girls' magazines. These moved away from romance, boyfriends and marriage to consumerism. This aspect was stressed by Angela McRobbie:

> While the [teenage girl] reader is being constructed in these pages as an intelligent and thoughtful being, she is simultaneously being constructed, in a way hitherto unimagined by magazine editors, as a young consumer. The new magazines marketed for 16 year-olds and over, but read by thousands of 12 year-olds up and down the country, carry glossy adverts not just for make-up but also for the Nat West, for the Midland Bank, for Levis, pizzas, films, other magazines, for Barclay's, Benetton and beyond. The 12 year-old might not be able to buy the goods but she is very able to consume the images. She is quite familiar with the world of consumer goods which is now addressing her with greater respect from all sides. Indeed, it celebrates her own independence. It openly welcomes her into the world of emancipated women.[3]

Many of the implications of commercial culture can be seen in these examples. It can have an adverse effect on the development of certain attitudes such as serious love, the encouragement of education, or the value of culture. Video clips are very narrow in their range of expression and can in fact be compared with advertisements. During the 1980s, the values of advertising affected many cultural products. Angela

Mc Robbie's example shows that commercial culture can weaken traditional values, the very ones that Mrs Thatcher also wanted to promote. Yet another paradox in Mrs Thatcher's cultural policy appears. Commercial cultural consumption promoted a private form of cultural practice using new technology. This thereby challenged old forms of communication and traditional loyalties as expressed in civil society. The prime minister wanted to maximise profits and yet also to foster traditional family values when the two were found to be incompatible. This dichotomy was manifest in other examples of commercial culture during the 1980s. In these areas Mrs Thatcher found it difficult to reconcile the tension that exists between commercialism, lowbrow quality with its subversive side, and the moral asceticism she chose as her general target.

The cultural Establishment

What really irritated Mrs Thatcher was the supposed feeling of superiority apparently evinced by people who gathered around metropolitan cultural events. The cultural Establishment in Great Britain goes to certain kinds of events and is formed of professional administrators rather than businessmen. Good examples of this category of people can be seen in Lord Carrington and Lord Gowrie who both went to Eton, both worked in certain areas of government and were also chairmen of Christie's and Sotheby's respectively. Moreover, Lord Gowrie left the chairmanship of the Arts Council because the œ33,000 salary was insufficient for his London lifestyle. Curiously, in 1994, he accepted the job again, but on an unpaid basis. As has been mentioned before in Chapter 7, the prime minister disliked the Civil Service style in general and the Foreign Office manner in particular. Cultural incompatibility was undoubtedly the reason for this antipathy. Mrs Thatcher would have liked to make these mandarins pay the market price for the cultural privileges they received. However, metropolitan culture was also a symbol of national pride and community. The Queen, for example, often goes to gala performances, and certain Royal Albert

Hall concerts represent a national tradition, such as the Last Night at the Proms. Thus despite Mrs Thatcher's initial wishes, she reluctantly decided to maintain the subsidies.

The Foreign Office was not the only example of mandarin superiority that antagonised her. Another section of the cultural Establishment was embodied in the three great British cultural bureaucracies: the Arts Council, the British Council and the BBC. These too had an insatiable appetite for subsidised high art and culture. Mrs Thatcher by contrast assumed that cultural organisations were guilty until proven innocent. State organisations had to convince people of their usefulness in order to have their subsidy maintained. The cultural Establishment on the other hand assumed subsidy to be a right.

Another fact that should be stressed is that with the rapid growth of higher education the cultural Establishment also grew considerably. Previously, during the 19th century, it had been limited to Oxbridge and the Public Schools. During the 1950s and 1960s this had spread to the redbrick universities. The Open University was held up by the Tories as a model of value for money and saw its student numbers rise from 14,000 in 1970 to 47,000 in 1990. At the end of the 1980s period, polytechnics, though offering practical courses, were also included in the university system in order to boost numbers. However, despite this increase, Britain remains one of the countries with the lowest levels of students in Western Europe in terms of international comparisons. Yet, most studies now show that the best way to encourage all types of cultural production and consumption is to educate either in the home environment or at school.[4] Pierre Bourdieu was quite right in this particular domain.[5]

Demand for private cultural goods and services did increase considerably during the Thatcher years and this shows a genuine democratisation of culture during the 1980s. However, by keeping the subsidies of public bodies such as the Arts Council, Mrs Thatcher continued to play in favour of the cultural Establishment. Such a contradiction can only be explained through electoral considerations. Mrs Thatcher was never so radical in her actual actions as in her early pronouncements.

Middlebrow culture

The Frankfurt School had predicted that the cultural industries would produce a mass of passive and mindless consumers. During the 1980s, under the influence of effects research, specialists came to the conclusion that the consumers of the cultural industries were in fact very active in the personal construction of meaning. This ties up with the pluralist thesis and the gradual and general upward movement of cultural levels. The mass commercial market, far from providing an opium for the people, actually empowered the individual in forming a consciousness that had previously been ignored.

Yet the development of commercial culture with its middlebrow content grew at the expense of organic communities which had been in decline for many decades before the 1980s. Sociologists such as Peter Willmott have written about the disappearance of working class communities in London during the 1960s and 1970s.[6] What should be stressed is that these previously organic communities were based on shared values in a centralised local system. At the time, rigid authority structures based on patriarchy, religious authority or trade union power, kept the community together. The prime minister herself weakened these links by limiting the powers of the unions, while at the same time, paradoxically, claiming to encourage traditional values. The situation changed considerably throughout the 1980s. Proto communities came to be the dominant form. These are based on shared lifestyles, empathies and fashions where members consume in similar ways. These empathies are not restricted in any geographical sense and can, for example, bring together people from different social backgrounds for a jazz concert. A good example of the emergence of a proto community would be what happened at the time of the Hillsborough Football disaster in which 95 people died in 1989. Football supporters who survived rushed to the cameras to show viewers that the police had not torn their tickets when spectators entered the stadium. 1.3 million people came to visit the football stadium at Anfield that was covered with flowers. The Press Council was literally inundated with complaints after the Sun and the Daily Mirror published articles claiming that crowd behaviour was responsible for the tragedy. This was the spontaneous reaction of people who refused to be manipulated by the mass media. The proto community which thus came into being was certainly not the passive mass described by the Frankfurt School. It was a unique experience where many people got together in response to a particularly tragic event. In a more general way, one may assert that the encouragement of middlebrow culture empowered many lower and middle class people in Britain during the Thatcher years.

Mrs Thatcher's emphasis on middlebrow and commercial culture led to less centralisation and government control in the cultural sphere. Simultaneously, in all the cultural industries there was a move towards new technology that gave more democratic access to production. In broadcasting, therefore, independent producers flourished while the monolithic corporations were put under financial pressure to become more competitive. The use of subcontracting allowed many more to participate in the process of production. In music, artists were able to record at much cheaper rates than in the 1970s. In fact, now in the 1990s, fashion and cultural production can no longer be imposed or even predicted in the old top-down model. The consumer decides in a bottom-up process. Thus Thatcherism can be seen accompanying as well as fostering a shift in cultural hegemony. While the Thatcher scheme was an attempt to reassert the slipping authority of the state in various areas such as law and order, union power or local government spending, paradoxically, in the cultural domain, Mrs Thatcher in fact intensified the trend towards decentralisation. Paul Willis sums up the situation quite succinctly:

In recent Gramscian analyses of Thatcherism it is far from clear what is supposed to be cause and what effect. Has the Thatcherite hegemony produced post-Fordism and the breakdown of monolithic classes or is it an interpretive and organising response to them? One could mention a much more prosaic, organic, slow moving everyday influence into the debate - common culture has produced increasing numbers of independent and recalcitrant ordinary citizens and voters who are very much more difficult for everybody to handle or understand. Though the evidence is so far very thin concerning actual changes in production, the talk of designer products, shorter lead times etc. (post-Fordism) may be a marketing and displaced political response to these deep cultural changes, not their cause. They demonstrate failed or slipping hegemony - not new forms of it.[7]

What became of the official culture of the cultural Establishment during the 1980s? It fought a rearguard action that was aimed at preserving its symbolic power. However, as the old sender/receiver model had lost its predominance, it had become much more difficult to impose cultural ideas from the top. The development of middlebrow culture meant that the cultural Establishment's role became a residual one, that is was limited to the preservation of highbrow art forms. In the present day world, those that do not open up to the mass market will simply not survive. Once again Paul Willis can help one understand this trend:

> The recent successes of new initiatives and explorations in some museums and art galleries in attracting somewhat higher attendances and the continuing success of many libraries in providing a wider range of symbolic materials rest, not on extending an old idea to new people, but in allowing new people to colonise them, the institutions. Clearer and more focused thinking could reinforce and greatly extend some of these already visible tendencies. The point of 'official' institutions should be not to order or value but simply to preserve - for democratic, unprefigured use - symbolic materials and fine or valuable historical resources which might be lost or otherwise not available.[8]

Mrs Thatcher helped define the limits of middlebrow commercial culture. She found subcultural forms subversive and could not encourage them despite the obvious commercial links. She disliked the vulgarity of certain mass leisure activities. Therefore, not all commercial art forms were to her taste and as time went by, she had increasing reservations about what the market should be free to produce. The example of TV-am is particularly enlightening. The original 1983 idea was to have a serious news programme. The market in fact produced tabloid-style television, and after several years of consideration the licence was finally removed by the ITC in 1992. The official organisation reacted carefully and reflected the opinions of the conservative leaders. Although there was high demand for tabloid quality television, Mrs Thatcher and her successor John Major could not accept this form of low quality broadcasting. From this example one can say that Mrs Thatcher wanted middlebrow culture to move towards the quality end of the market. She defined clear limits to the New Right concept of an unrestricted cultural market. However, the principles behind these choices were never fully explained. Here can be found an example of policy decisions based on reactive, implicit and not deliberately thought out reasoning.

Notes

1. "Lynn looks forward to global market", *Music and Media*, 21 May 1988, 4.
2. MTV Europe Press Release, August 1988.
3. Angela McRobbie, "You should be so lucky", *New Statesman*, 9 September 1988.
4. Consult for example William Morrison and Edwin West, "Child Exposure to the performing arts" *Journal of Cultural Economics*, Vol 10, No 1, June 1986.
5. Consult Pierre Bourdieu, *La Distinction*.
6. See Peter Willmott, *The Evolution of a Community: a Study of Daghenham after Forty Years* (London: Routledge and Keegan, 1963).
7. Paul Willis, Common Culture 156.

8. ibid., 149.

Chapter 27
The 'one of us' Criteria

The highbrow arts and the cultural Establishment were the partial losers in Mrs Thatcher's cultural policies. Such seems to be the unavoidable conclusion of research in this domain. On the other side of the coin, who were the winners of these cultural policies? The prime minister was said to have formulated the alternative in the question: "is he or she one of us?". The question of allegiances is thus of paramount and telling importance. A kind of private club was formed around the prime minister. The problem is what this club, its selection, the nature of its members, can tell us about Mrs Thatcher's actual practices; in particular as concerns the case of the self-made men who were selected, or conversely that of the individuals excluded from the inner circle of influence.

Media moguls

Media magnates were some of the most prominent members of the 'one of us' club. What characterises the media mogul is that he runs or owns major media companies, takes entrepreneurial risks and has personal and sometimes eccentric management styles. Lord Northcliffe was the first of the Press Lords and the first real media mogul in Great Britain. The Canadian, Lord Beaverbrook, was another good example. His eccentricity expressed itself in the form of a pro-Empire stance. In the 1950s another Canadian, Roy Thomson started his career as a media magnate. All these operated in the same fashion, buying up ailing businesses and transforming them into profitable organisations through a change in management and work practices.

A) Rupert Murdoch

In the 1980s, it was Rupert Murdoch who became the symbol of the successful international entrepreneur. Murdoch had a long-term vision and was a solid financier. He used a mixture of short-term opportunism along with a steady long-term strategy. Robert Maxwell, by contrast, took more risks and as a result had to sell companies more often. Murdoch was operative in three geographical areas: Australia, Great Britain and the United States. He also concentrated his efforts on large concerns that had a strong market position. Such a strategy made it necessary for him to have solid banking ties. His typical policy during the 1980s, was buying up loss making media companies and reorganising the management. Usually, profits would reappear after a few years.

In 1983, Rupert Murdoch moved into his second American phase and also became interested in satellite. In 1985, he bought 20th Century Fox for $575 million and this was followed by the purchase of Metromedia and a television station. He then became a United States citizen in order to be able to possess more American companies. In 1986, he engaged in a struggle against the printing unions at Wapping. In many ways, the Wapping dispute was similar to Mrs Thatcher's tussle with the miners in 1984-1985. It was prepared long in advance and measures were taken to dispose of the necessary arms with which to do battle. Mrs Thatcher introduced legislation and coordinated the fragmented police force, while also building up coal reserves. Mr Murdoch, likewise, organised his own private and independent distribution service, thereby reducing the strategic power of the unions. Thus the unions were effectively excluded from the decision processes.

Later, in 1987, he bought Harper and Row, and Collins in 1988 for an estimated $1 billion. In 1988, he acquired $2.85 billion of media companies including TV Guide, Seventeen, Daily Racing Form, once again in the United States. However, the 1989-1991 period was a difficult one because interest rates were high and all three countries where he had concentrated his interests suffered from recession. His News Corporation was therefore on the verge of bankrupcy.

Socially, Murdoch tended to mix with other media moguls and barons. He was well informed and was ready to intervene when a company was to be bought up for a song. He was certainly given legislative favours both in Great Britain and the United States. This is evidence of political influence. Mrs Thatcher protected Rupert Murdoch from the investigations of the Monopolies and Mergers Commission twice: when he acquired the Times group in 1981 and Today in 1987. In the United States, he was allowed to buy up Metromedia, in 1986, the year when technically he needed to be an United States citizen. He was given favourable treatment by the Federal Communications Commission. In Australia most of his business was delegated to individuals such as K. E. Cowley, from 1980 onwards. His ability to delegate day to day policy by maintaining strict financial supervision is borne out in the following statement:

> Every day I receive print outs from each country on each operation item by item. Every newspaper, every magazine, every issue, a profit and loss covering the operation up to, and including, the previous Sunday. On Fridays those sheets are followed by thick books with itemised details of profit and loss figures on every single operation whether it be Perth in Western Australia or in London or San Antonio.
>
> These figures are what keep us up to date. We compare them with previous years and compare it with our budget and take whatever management action is called for.
>
> We do it very simply, (with) very low overheads, (a) very small head office here in New York. What we do it with is management information and for that we spare nothing. We operate the company with weekly information. We can do this because of modern communications which we use not just for our customers but for our internal information.[1]

Encouraged by Mrs Thatcher, Mr Murdoch seems to have been loyal to her in person rather than to the Conservative Party. He in fact intervened in editorials in order to give more positive accounts of Mrs Thatchers politics and policies. He adhered to the tenets of Thatcherism and he wished to help the prime minister. Mr Murdoch is a very good example of the 'one of us' principle. It is his personal commitment that seems to have been decisive in gaining access to the 'one of us' club. In this particular case one can assess concretely the fact that Mrs Thatcher's cultural policy left no one indifferent. Indeed, the prime minister managed to provoke both very positive and very negative reactions.

B) Robert Maxwell

Another media mogul who did extremely well during the Thatcher years was Robert Maxwell. He, by contrast, was not 'one of us', although he benefited from anti-union legislation just as much as his more right-wing competitor Mr Murdoch. He was a fierce British patriot yet gave his support to the Labour Party rather than the individual Labour leaders. His long-term strategy was less clear than Murdoch's and he changed direction more often. In the 1970s, he seemed to be a spent force, after specialising in scientific publishing. In 1980, he bought up the British Printing Company (BPC), laid off many of its staff and transformed it into a profitable company. The same happened with Odhams. In 1984, he bought the Sunday Mirror, the Daily Mirror, the People. In 1987, he miscalculated the launch of a new London evening newspaper, which, due to lack of preparation, was forced to go out of business. In the late 1980s, his interest in newspapers seemed to wane and he moved into cable. In 1988, he specialised in book publishing and data supply. He also transferred a lot of his capital from Great Britain to the United States. Unlike Murdoch, Maxwell found it difficult to delegate. This particular media mogul did very well out of the Thatcher years partly because he was not a member of the 'one of us' club and his ideas and his personality were less in conformity with Mrs Thatcher's line of thought, choices and preferences.

These two major media moguls were backed up by a host of lesser moguls and barons. The difference between the two terms is that moguls actually own and barons merely control as managers. One can name advertisers such as Saatchi and Saatchi and their financier Martin Sorrell, or businessmen such as Richard Branson, Conrad Black or Michael Green. Charles and Maurice Saatchi along with Martin Sorrel were definitely 'one of us' for a certain time. It was Tim Bell of Saatchi and Saatchi who fixed up the deal with the Conservative Party for the 1979 and 1983 general elections. The brothers left the 'club' when they had the audacity to suggest that the problem of the Conservative Party, in 1987, was the prime minister herself.

C) *The Saatchi brothers*

The Saatchi brothers were not obsessed with absolute control in the manner of Murdoch and Maxwell. However, they revolutionised advertising by rejecting the gentlemen's agreement which defined commission at 15 per cent and forbade soliciting work directly. The brothers went and offered their services on the market-place, thus creating new business, and they started buying up other agencies. Their rejection of convention has a certain Thatcher ring to it. However, the financial deals were often based on a buy now, pay later basis. In 1982, they bought the United States agency, Compton. Nineteen takeovers occurred in the 1984-1985 period, including the American company Ted Bates. The Saatchi system rested on the policy of letting others run the various agencies. They did not intervene on a day to day basis. The brothers delegated to others.

In the Saatchi empire, Martin Sorrell played a key role as the financial expert. In 1985, he took over WPP. By 1988, he possessed sixteen agencies including J. Walter Thompson. Sorrell thrived in this atmosphere of confidence, but he was less eccentric than his employers, and when the Saatchis fell out with Mrs Thatcher, he was unaffected by the disgrace. On the other hand, the Saatchis had several problems at the end of the 1980s which combined together, resulted in serious industrial weaknesses, coinciding with their disagreement with Mrs Thatcher. The City was surprised by the amateurish nature of the Saatchi bid for the Midland Bank. The attempt at management consultancy was not an unmitigated success. There were also a series of management problems that were never solved. Moreover, the company was based in London and it was difficult to run a largely American operation from abroad. The denouement came when in 1995, the Saatchi brothers were bought out in a boardroom showdown. The successes of these entrepreneurs, their fall from grace and partial failure, are quite telling of the way the 'one of us' line of action was actually carried out.

D) Richard Branson

Richard Branson was definitely 'one of us'. Like the Saatchis he seemed to represent the spirit of the 1980s. He was the incarnation of the cultural style of the Thatcher decade. This sharp entrepreneur, who had little personal interest in music, started off by signing up pop groups under the Virgin label in 1973. He then went into record sales with the Virgin record shop chain and he built up a reputation of being a tough negotiator. Like Maxwell and Saatchi & Saatchi, he opted for a high risk strategy and failed in the Superchannel satellite project. In 1988, the company went private and shares were issued. However, it is in the world of transport that Virgin Airlines benefited from political connections. Lord King, another friend of Mrs Thatcher's, had made British Airways very competitive during the mid 1980s. Richard Branson moved in on the lucrative transatlantic routes by setting up Virgin Airlines. He gained a great deal of publicity by flying hot air balloons over the Atlantic and the Pacific oceans. Another opportunity for free publicity came in the early 1990s with the revelation that British Airways had deliberately tried to tarnish the reputation of Virgin Airlines. There was a trial and British Airways had to pay for damages. He also used Mrs Thatcher's brand of populism, by wearing baggy pullovers in board room meetings, thus flaunting the fact that he was with the people rather than with the pin-striped directors. Of course this was merely image building. After the Thatcher period, Branson had to weather the financial storm of recession. In 1992, he was forced to sell

Virgin Records to EMI and Virgin Airlines was also ultimately sold off in order to pay for loans.

E) Conrad Black

Conrad Black was another of Mrs Thatcher's loyal supporters. He bought up a share in Telegraph Newspapers in 1985, when the 74-year-old Lord Hartwell came to be short of money due to poor management and old technology. Conrad Black insisted on being given preference in the sale of the rest of Lord Hartwell's options. By 1989, the group was back in profit, having introduced new technology and increased its readership. Conrad Black adopted Mrs Thatcher's style of management, being interventionist with journalists and showing a crusading zeal. Conrad Black was certainly another 'one of us'.

F) Michael Green

The last example of a 'one of us' media baron is Michael Green. He became successful with the rise of video. In the 1980s, he set up various video facilities. This reached a high point in 1988 with the purchase of Technicolor for œ459. Carlton, one of Green's companies, already had many video facilities. Green claimed that the purchase of Technicolor gave him a 40 per cent world market holding in video duplication and film processing. Like Murdoch, Green delegated the actual running of companies but kept a close eye on financial criteria. A significant event occurred in 1985, when Green made a bid for Thames. The IBA proposed a 49 per cent holding, which was not enough for Michael Green. This failure was partly caused by lack of political weight. He was not sufficiently 'one of us' to be supported. This was the price he had to pay for not committing himself fully to the Thatcher camp.[2]

Media moguls were not the only members of the exclusive club. During the 1980s, being 'one of us' was very useful to other kinds of businessmen such as Lord MacAlpine or Lord King. As cultural policy was very fragmented, inside information was of vital importance. No one could form a general picture, which is only now becoming possible with several years of hindsight. On the other hand, belonging to the 'club' was a very personal affair and one might join and later leave it. There was no permanence about the whole business. In fact, it was not just a one-way relationship. This club allowed individuals to exchange influence. Thus, Mrs Thatcher applied private sector work practices to government, and was supported by the Press, and in exchange the media moguls gained information and hidden influence. Being 'one of us' gave strategic advantage to these international moguls who now stand out as symbols of the Thatcher years.

Notes

1. *UK Press Gazette*, 22 August 1988, "The Thoughts of Chairman Murdoch", 20.
2. For more information on this subject see Jeremy Tunstall, *Media Moguls* (London: Routledge 1994).

Chapter 28
Conclusions

Policy aims and realisations

Mrs Thatcher had two overall policy aims that were incompatible. The first was reasserting the authority of the state and was a short-term aim. This she certainly did by carefully legislating, upholding the law, confronting the unions and strengthening the police force. By 1990, the Civil Service and local authorities had adopted some private sector work practices and, in the process, commercial values had permeated most levels of the public sector in general and the administration in particular. The second aim was that of freeing the market, which constituted a long-term aim. The desire existed but the policy realisations, and this applies to all politicians, were far from what had been hoped for. In the particular domain of culture, one can say that at best Mrs Thatcher's policy was fragmented and very uneven despite the rhetoric of radical change. The explanation for this implementation gap is that the short-term won over the long-term, that the practical politician gained the upper hand against the political ideologue.

Throughout the current research, varied cultural policies have been observed. They are all marked by gradualism and voluntarism, which are traditional features of administration in Great Britain. Many are also characterised by their fragmentation and reactivity. Because of their diffuse nature, the people concerned found it very difficult to organise effective opposition against them. This gave considerable strategic advantages to the prime minister. The great variety of policy proposals and their applications can be seen in the following examples, that range from the highly controlled to the wholly free:

> 1.Censorship was set up in response to video nasties. Certain legislation was introduced that restricted individual freedom. This is an example of more and not less 'red tape' and a reactive policy in response to particular circumstances. The increase in subsidy to the British Film Institute is another example of not freeing the market-place;
>
> 2. Certain cultural policies merely tinkered with the existing situation. Broadcasting or the public library service are examples of maintaining a highly regulated system using the social market justification. In the former, the desire for change existed, but because of practical impossibilities, the old system was maintained. In the latter the public library service was not even challenged;
>
> 3. Certain cultural policies aimed at freeing a regulated market. The abolition of the Eady Levy is a good case in point;
>
> 4. Some policies aimed at defining a new and unrestricted market. This applies to the video industry, satellite and cable and all the new cultural industries that expanded in a spectacular form during the 1980s. The vast majority of Mrs Thatcher's cultural policies fall into the category of marginal modifications to the existing system. This hardly qualifies as a 'cultural revolution' which her supporters claimed she would carry out.

All the interventions that were made in the cultural market-place were justified in the name of efficiency. Thus, in the case of television, the publisher model was first introduced with the arrival of Channel 4 in 1982. It was gradually extended to ITV and the BBC in order to reduce costs and union power. This idea of value for money tended to lessen the sense of national identity that had been associated with the BBC. The public service model was replaced by the publisher one. Business practices and efficiency permeated all of Mrs Thatcher's cultural policies. One particular reaction provoked another, producing a boomerang effect. In this series of chain reactions very few people remained neutral. It is in these reactive policies that one can see the conviction politician that Mrs Thatcher always claimed to be. Thus the case of television is a typical example of the effects of Thatcherite cultural policy

One major drawback with the free market justification that Mrs Thatcher used to back up her cultural policies was the problem of market failure. The whole pluralist idea of cultural democracy and improving cultural levels is plagued by its involvement with the market place and its inequalities. Certain individuals are badly placed in the market due to illness, unemployment or very poor 'life chances'. Those who have very limited resources, simply do not have access to certain cultural technology such as personal computers and video production. Herbert Schiller has clearly pointed this out:

> Whatever the unique experiential history of each of the many subgroups in the nation, they are all subject to the rule of market forces and the domination of capital over those market forces. This is the grand common denominator that insures basic inequality in the social order, an inequality that the pluralists and the active audience culturalists most often overlook.[1]

Certain individuals are therefore excluded from the process of cultural consumption. The market also expands and contracts, producing boom periods and recessions. There was rapid expansion in the 1986-1988 period but at the end of the decade there was a sudden decline in the property market, pension funds suffered from decline and the ambitious Docklands project experienced serious difficulties. Thus the market fluctuates and certain investors can lose large sums of money if it is left uncontrolled. The best kind of expansion is progressive and continuous. The free market is therefore a far from perfect tool which structurally disadvantages certain categories of consumers.

Commercial culture

During the 1980s period, national culture was in fact resituated in popular rather than highbrow forms. This represents the biggest change resulting from or accompanying Mrs Thatcher's cultural policies. The prime minister conducted a virulent attack on the dominant cultural forms and proposed the commercial model without realising all the possible consequences, even though she wrote about the 'culture wars of my administration' in her memoirs,[2] this in reference to the clash of opposing ideas that raged during the 1980s. Such a 'war' is graphically defined by Stuart Hall in his analysis of dominant culture:

> The dominant culture represents itself as the culture. It tries to define and contain all other cultures within its inclusive range. Its views of the world, unless challenged, will stand as the most natural, all-embracing, universal culture. Other cultural configurations will not only be subordinate to this order; they will enter into struggle with it, resist or even overthrow its reign - its hegemony.[3]

Mrs Thatcher's 'culture war' against the permissive cultural Establishment was indeed highly successful. Bryan Appleyard describes the climate in the mid 1980s:

> There is a nagging doubt, an air of ennui and irritation. It arises partly from the battles that they fought and are reluctant to fight again and partly from a sense that the tide has turned against them in some indefinable way. They are no longer members of a confident priesthood officiating at the shrine of art with the support of an enthusiastic and aspiring congregation.[4]

Criticism of the Establishment had mass appeal and tapped on the sympathies and frustrations of many people as has been pointed out by David Marquand:

> Like her [David Owen] spoke to and for the raw, down-to earth, thrusting New Men who saw themselves as the harbingers of a new age of realism and enterprise: for the self proclaimed 'achievers', whose ambitious climb up the status hierarchy seemed blocked by a patronising old Establishment which they half-despised and half-envied.[5]

The effect of such a virulent attack on the cultural Establishment was the exclusion of cultural experts and critics. They, along with the intellectuals, had a much reduced role to play in merely advising consumers. By attacking the Establishment, the prime minister excluded a whole class of citizens and thus unwittingly weakened the traditional sense of national identity.

The commercial and popular equivalents that came to replace highbrow national culture as the official one during the Thatcher years had many visible symbols. The walkman, video clips and the video rental shops were all examples of a private form of cultural consumption. They all empowered certain minorities in a pluralist move towards cultural democracy. Video and satellite dishes allowed a new form of communication to develop in the Indian communities and the Turkish community as has already been described earlier.

There were, however, obvious disadvantages in the encouragement of commercial culture. The first is a kind of reductionism due to what may be termed an advertising culture. All cultural objects have to be marketed and target certain categories of consumers within the market-place. This encourages cultural relativism which in most cases is a positive process. However, the 'magic' or 'value' is taken out of art when commercialism is involved. As was argued by the Frankfurt School, the 'aura' disappears and art no longer has a radical role to play. Commercial culture is safe culture. Mrs Thatcher certainly speeded up this process of incorporation that has always been present in oppositional popular culture. During the 1980s, culture somehow became a form of advertising and was affected by the logic of the advertising industry. David Marquand has stressed this particular point: "The range of identities legitimised by the enterprise culture is very limited. It gives increased scope for one's identity as a consumer, but not to other identities. Indeed it is positively hostile to identity-choices that threaten the authority of the entrepreneur and the supremacy of the entrepreneurial values."[6] In this kind of consumption society, art becomes valueless and is just another product within the market. If the modern art movement reflected values of hope and future betterment, then the post-modern art movement has lost these values and moved very much closer to the surface. Mrs Thatcher, despite her supposedly Victorian values, was closer to the post-modern than to the modern.

The prime minister encouraged commercial culture and yet she did not understand popular culture. She even admitted as much in her memoirs when describing rock 'n' roll: "I cannot pretend to have liked, or even understood, all the expressions of this new popular freedom. When rock 'n' roll was imported from America, along with names such as Bill Haley and Elvis Presley, I assumed it would be a nine days' journalistic wonder."[7] One can also cite her description of the 1960s:

Indeed, this was a period of obsessive and naive interest in 'youth'. Parents worried so much about the 'generation gap' that even teenagers began to take it seriously. A whole 'youth culture' of misunderstood mysticism, bizarre clothing and indulgence in hallucinatory drugs emerged. I found Chelsea a very different place when we moved back to London in 1970. I had mixed feelings about what was happening. There was a vibrancy and talent, but this was also in large degree a world of make-believe. A perverse pride was taken in Britain about our contribution to these trends. Carnaby Street, the Beatles, the mini-skirt and the maxiskirt, were the new symbols of 'Swinging Britain'. And they did indeed prove good export earners. Harold Wilson was adept at taking maximum political credit for them. The trouble was that they concealed the real economic weaknesses which even a talented fashion industry and entrepreneurial record companies could not counter-balance.[8]

These extracts clearly show that Mrs Thatcher realised something important was happening although she had neither understanding nor sympathy for popular culture in its lowbrow forms. Paradoxically she somehow felt that popular culture leads to evolutionary rather then revolutionary change. By encouraging commercial culture Mrs Thatcher at one and the same time promoted gradual progressive change and inevitably deradicalised content. This is due to a continuous process of excorporation and incorporation. As a result the cultural mainstream is in a constant process of flux. This sense of movement contributed to a feeling of destabilisation during the 1980s. Those who looked for a timeless national identity took refuge in heritage and nostalgia.

Mrs Thatcher's cultural policy and politics

Where exactly do Mrs Thatcher's cultural policies stand with regard to political philosophy? Various British political positions can be outlined: the 'one nation' Tory, traditional Labour, the New Left, and the New Right. (Refer to Table 2.1 on page 406 concerning the effects of politics on cultural policy.)

The traditional conservative stance with regard to cultural affairs was that of 'one nation' conservatism. This proposed the preservation of highbrow art forms as symbols of national unity and cohesion. Conservatives, such as Sir Ian Gilmour or Lord St John Stevas, rightly considered the Thatcherite project as a challenge to the cultural Establishment. Their right to self-subsidy, using national cohesion as an all-purpose justification, was questioned by Mrs Thatcher. On the content side, the arts were reduced to just another product within the market. Tthe cultural Establishment found this unacceptable, and therefore offered fierce resistance.

Like the 'one nation' conservatives, the traditional Labour position up until the 1980s was one of democratising highbrow culture. This had been the justification for Harold Wilson's considerable increase in arts spending and the setting up of the Open University. The Labour project was more ambitious than the conservative one in that it was to touch all minorities through a system of positive discrimination. Education was to improve the cultural level of the whole population and not be reserved for the social elite. Thatcherite cultural policies were considered by traditional Labourites as a disempowerment of minority cultures.

In marked contrast with these two traditional positions, both the New Left and the New Right believed in cultural democracy but through very different means. The New Left believed that the supposedly free market was inegalitarian and did not benefit all the citizens of a country. In order to balance the market and remove structural inequalities, governments had a duty to prevent over-concentrations in the ownership of cultural industries. The state also had a duty to provide cultural facilities to the lower sections of the community. Mrs Thatcher considered such state assistance to be a waste of money, especially as many of the cultural 'animateurs' were supposed by her to have left-wing sympathies. The prime minister sided with the New Right's idea that cultural democracy would come through the freeing of the market-place. The removal of subsidies was to allow the market to find its own 'natural' level. New and cheaper technology was to allow cultural levels to rise in a genuinely democratic process. The implementation gap that has been observed in so many of Mrs Thatcher's cultural policies can be explained by a theoretical position that was firmly in the New Right camp and the fact that many of her cultural policy realisations were often in the traditional conservative sphere. The prime minister oscillated between theory and practice, between New Right and 'one nation'

Toryism. She announced a revolution and at best fostered an evolution on the line of traditional Tory policies.

The nature of the Thatcherite plan and the implementation gap

The Thatcherite plan was not so much a clear ideological plan, but more a question of gathering people who agreed to act together. The club system was based on a personal network that developed in an unprecedented fashion. The result was that government was freed from a certain amount of red tape and this was achieved by means of unelected boards that were appointed by the prime minister. Thus in 1979, there were 2410 quangos. By 1983 the number had dropped to 1900. By 1994, that is just after the end of the time period under study, there were 5,521 appointed boards.[9] These figures, of course, were used by the opposition parties to show that Mrs Thatcher had not come from the 19th century, but from the 18th century with its system of patronage. She had replaced the 'old boy network' (the Public School and Oxbridge system of preference for jobs in the City and government) with a 'new boy network'. Those who, like Sir William Rees-Mogg, found themselves in the Thatcher network and were 'one of us', discovered there were considerable advantages in belonging. Businessmen could start by contributing to Conservative Party funds. If Mrs Thatcher found them acceptable, they might get non-governmental appointment to a government body. After many years of loyal and often lucrative services, the person concerned might hope for a knighthood or a Lordship. Mrs Thatcher also encouraged business practices in the Civil Service, thus making it easier for Civil Servants to work in the City after retirement; their political power could thereby be transformed into economic dividends.

Such policies also help to explain a certain aspect of the implementation gap. Applying commercial methods to politics, Mrs Thatcher considered that she had to gain room for manoeuvring in the negotiating process. New Right ideas allowed her to gain this room. By demanding a large amount she was sure to gain at least a little change.

This is what happened in cultural affairs as well as in other domains. Mrs Thatcher proposed radical new directions, asking for subsidy cuts and tax reductions. In so doing, she challenged the whole logic of the cultural Establishment and thereby gave herself enough leeway with which to negotiate. This is where the system based on networks of personal committment proved beneficial. Her methods made it possible for her to attract personalities from areas that were not directly connected with the political circuits, and thus were fraught with new energy.

The changing nature of culture in the 1980s

The very nature of culture and its implications changed during the 1980s. The class based separation of culture into antagonistic highbrow and lowbrow extremes remained true up to the beginning of the study period. By 1990, this distinction, for the most part, had disappeared. Cynthia Ozick, an American academic pointed this out: "High art is dead. The passion for inheritance is dead. Tradition is equated with obscurantism. The wall that divided serious high art from the popular is breached; anything can count as 'text'."[10] During the Thatcher decade, cultural products of whatever styles came more and more to be consumed on an equal basis. National culture was partly redefined in non-artistic terms. In the meantime, as the highbrow arts became increasingly pressurised by the international commercial market, Mrs Thatcher started to worry about standards and also a defence of national values.

The prime minister paradoxically supported popular and commercial culture and yet did not appreciate many of its aspects. One explanation may be that culture was not one of her policy priorities. If one counts the number of artists and musicians mentioned in her autobiography, one arrives at a figure of a dozen entertainers such as the Beatles and Dame Kiri Te Kanawa. Arts and music were simply not priorities in Mrs Thatcher's life. However, she also admits that common culture had a great influence in her formative years. She mentions the sense of escape and liberation involved in watching Hollywood films and listening to the radio.[11] Although she had little leisure time in her personal life, she chose common culture in preference to highbrow culture.

There is also a practical reason behind the 'implementation gap'. The whole cultural sector expanded considerably and governments found it difficult to supervise complex cultural phenomena. It may explain why it was mostly reactive and fragmented policies that were promoted by the prime minister. The government acted when necessary, without having to devise a set of administrative processes. The diffuse nature of the policies is further evidence of short-term rather than long-term planning and also a sign of the post-modern with its image obsession, its commercial consumption, its insistence on individual responsibility, pragmatism and short-term objectives. By contrast, modernity often represented a long-term project based on coherent plans, a sense of national community and culture. By encouraging modern technology Mrs Thatcher strengthened individualism over collectivism. Television, walkmen, video clips do not encourage a sense of community: they do not foster a group of like-minded people. Such new technology often isolates and individualises. Many American Republicans are now realising that maximising profits through technologically advanced cultural consumption has its price.[12] It is a weakened sense of both local and national community. The contrary aspects of this promotion of technology reflect the Thatcher paradox: a desire for change that immediately and necessarily triggers off a certain nostalgia for the past, and particularly for imaginary Victorian values and stable communities.

Thus the theoretical free play of market forces and the rather limited policy realisations unleashed forces that challenged tradition. In this way Mrs Thatcher was a destabilising influence. She weakened the traditional British symbols of the Monarchy, the Civil Service, the professions, the universities and the teaching profession in general. Mrs Thatcher did not replace the traditional system with any coherent alternative. Her 'one of us' club could in no way represent the nation. Robert Hewison agrees with this negative interpretation in no uncertain terms: "Cultural policy in the eighties destroyed the culture of community, replacing it with a sterile public culture whose lack of connection with reality was demonstrated by the follies of the Arts Council of Great Britain in its final years."[13] This weakened public culture was further watered down by globalisation. Transnational companies have global strategies. Global and not national issues became more and more those that are in the minds of the young: pollution, the effects of CFCs on the ozone layer, nuclear testing and proliferation, the destruction of the Amazonian rain forest. At the end of the period, and at present, what your international neighbour does may concern you directly. All these trends have weakened a national sense of identity. Mrs Thatcher did not compensate for this reduced sense of community. By keeping to the safe side and by avoiding general choices, she was unable to fight those centrifugal tendencies as she might have.

Perhaps the most important criticism of the Thatcher cultural project was that the swing to individualism could not go much further. As Geert Hofstede has shown, Britain is an extremely individualistic nation. Mrs Thatcher's 'culture wars' were doomed from the start. What now seems to be missing in Great Britain is the sense of belonging to a small, local community that is often represented in the English village myth.[14] There seems to have existed a moral vacuum in the consumer society of the eighties that is apparently widening in the nineties. In 1973, Daniel Bell had already predicted these changes in the United States:

In Western society we are in the midst of a vast historical change in which old social relations (which were property-bound), existing power structures (centred on narrow elites), and bourgeois culture (based on notions of restraint and delayed gratification) are being rapidly eroded. The sources of the upheaval are scientific and technological. But they are also cultural, since culture, I believe, has achieved autonomy in Western society. What these new social forms will be like is not completely clear. Nor is it likely that they will achieve the unity of the economic system and social structure which was characteristic of capitalist civilisation from the mid-eighteenth century to the mid-twentieth. The use of the hyphenated prefix post- indicates, thus, that sense of living in interstitial time.[15]

Daniel Bell remarkably predicted the arrival of the information society and the importance of technology. Mrs Thatcher warmly encouraged this technological change. At the same time her fragmentary and sometimes contradictory cultural policy failed to produce the new values that were to replace the older traditional ones. It was at a Royal Academy dinner in May 1980, that Mrs Thatcher was to say: "We should see to it that our people are steeped in a real knowledge and understanding of our national culture".[16] In 1990, when she had to resign, the work still needed to be done. However, in all fairness, should a prime ministre be expected to do it? Are we not asking too much of her, to lead the country and at the same time to come out with a new version of culture? The premier did not achieve all that she had promised to do, but then, should a cultural transformation be expected from any single individual?

Notes

1. H. Schiller, Culture Inc., *The Corporate Takeover of Public Expression* (Oxford: OUP, 1989) 153.
2. Margaret Thatcher, *The Path to Power* 78.
3. Robert Hewison, *Culture and Consensus* 116.
4. Bryan Appleyard, *Culture Club: Crisis in the Arts* (London: Faber and Faber, 1984) 10.
5. David Marquand, *The Progressive Dilemna* (London: Heinemann,1991)187.
6. P. Heelas, P. Morris (eds), *The Values of the Enterprise Culture* (London: Routledge, 1992) 65.
7. Margaret Thatcher, *The Path to Power* 77.
8. ibid., 153.
9. Robert Hewison, *Culture and Consensus* 230.
10. Cynthia Ozick, "A Critic at Large: T. S. Eliot at 101" *New Yorker*, 20 November 1989, 152.
11. Margaret Thatcher, *The Path to Power* 14, 22.
12. see "The Evolution of Despair" in *Time* 28 August 1995, 32-38.
13. Robert Hewison, *Culture and Consensus* 307.
14. "The Archers" series on BBC Radio 4 is the expression of the village myth.
15. Daniel Bell, *The Coming of the Post-Industrial Society* (New York: Heinemann, 1974) 37.
16. *ACGB Annual Accounts* 1982/3 10.